C# and Game Programming

C# and Game Programming:
A Beginner's Guide
Second Edition

Salvatore A. Buono

A K Peters
Wellesley, Massachusetts

Editorial, Sales, and Customer Service Office

A K Peters, Ltd.
888 Worcester Street, Suite 230
Wellesley, MA 02482
www.akpeters.com

Copyright © 2005 by A K Peters, Ltd.

All rights reserved. No part of the material protected by this copyright notice may be reproduced or utilized in any form, electronic or mechanical, including photocopying, recording, or by any information storage and retrieval system, without written permission from the copyright owner.

Library of Congress Cataloging-in-Publication Data

Buono, Salvatore A., 1968-
    C# and game programming : a beginner's guide / Salvatore A. Buono. – 2nd ed.
      p. cm.
   ISBN 1-56881-236-1
    1. C# (Computer program language) 2. Computer games—Programming. I. Title.

QA76.73.C154.B85 2004
005.13'3—dc22

2004053412

Printed in the United States of America
09 08 07 06 05   10 9 8 7 6 5 4 3 2 1

To my unborn son

Though I have already felt your spirit, though I already love your soul, I still wait in anticipation, for your presence to make me whole.

Matthew Salvatore Buono, Born 9/28/03

Table of Contents

Preface xvii

PART ONE: Programming Basics 1

Chapter One: C# from the Beginning 3

An Overview of the C# Language 3
A Little History on the Cs 4
What is the .Net Framework? 5
Managed Code and Assemblies 6
Algorithms 7
The .Net Compiler 8
Compiling and Executing 10
Comments 15
Screen Output 16
The Newline Character 18
The WriteLine Command 20
The Semicolon 22

Whitespaces 22
Preprocessor Directives 22
Indenting 23
Naming Variables 23
Declaring Variables and the Integer Data Types 26
The Data Types float and double 28
The Data Type decimal 30
The Data Types character and string 31
Keywords sizeof and unsafe 33
Enabling unsafe mode in C# 33
The Data Type void 35
Assignment Statements 36
Type Compatibility: Implicit Conversions 36
Formatting Strings 37
Arithmetic 38
Keyboard Input 44
Uninitialized Variables 45
Access Modifiers: constant, Readonly, and volatile 46
Incrementing and Decrementing Operators 48
Type Safety versus Metonym Data Types 49
Keyword Defaults 50
Using, System, and Namespace 51
Hungarian Notation 52
Things to Remember 53
Troubleshooting 53
Questions 57

Chapter Two: Branches, Loops, and Functions   59

The if Statement 59
The else Statement 63
The else-if Statement 64

Program Walkthrough	65
Compound if Statements	66
and, or, and not	68
Nested if Statements	69
Mathematical Abbreviations	71
The while Loop	73
Battle Bit	77
The do-while Loop	81
The for Loop	83
The switch Statement	85
Converting from C++ to C#	88
Boolean Expressions	90
Short Circuit Evaluation	91
The Conditional Operator	92
Predefined Functions	93
Type Casting: Explicit Conversions	99
References, Values, and the Boxing Technique	100
Introduction to User-Defined Functions	101
Writing Our First User-Defined Function	102
Variable Scope	103
Functions that Return Values	105
Passing Variables: Calls-By-Value	108
Writing Functions as Black Boxes	110
Passing Variables: Calls-By-Reference	112
The Keyword out	114
An Introduction to Polymorphism	115
Introducing Recursion	118
Inline Functions	119
Troubleshooting	119
Things to Remember	121
Questions	123

PART TWO: Game Programming Basics — 127

Chapter Three: Introducing DirectX — 129

- Writing Games 131
- Game 1—Paddle Tennis 132
- Brainstorming 132
- Drawing Characters 133
- Plotting Motions 138
- Writing an Algorithm 139
- Displaying Graphics Using Native C++ 143
- Displaying Graphics Using C# 143
- Displaying Graphics Using DirectDraw 144
- Introducing Object-Oriented Programming 146
- Adding Files to Our Projects 146
- Programming a Character 148
- DirectInput: the Keyboard 149
- Erasing Residual Images 150
- Collision Detection: The Players' Boundaries 151
- Collision Detection: The Ball in Motion 152
- Collision Detection: Deflecting the Ball 154
- A Few Minor Details: Scores, Speed Settings, and Additional Graphics 156
- Adding Colors 160
- Adding Sounds Using Windows Multimedia 161
- Adding Sounds Using DirectSound 162
- Adding in the Mouse 164
- DirectInput: The Mouse 168
- DirectInput: The Joystick 169
- Introducing Menus 171
- Introduction to Artificial Intelligence 176
- Paddle Tennis: Putting It All Together 179
- Bonus Games 179
- Game 2—Space Fighters 179

Brainstorming 180
Selecting Characters & Plotting Motions 181
Writing the Algorithm 183
Animating Characters: Animating Spaceships 185
Animating Characters: Projectiles and Explosions 187
Adding DirectInput: The Keyboard and Joystick 188
OnPaint 189
Defining Hyperspace 190
Boundaries & Projectile Limits 191
Drawing with DirectDraw 194
Artificial Intelligence: Evasion 196
Including Obstacles: The Sun 199
Gaining Momentum 200
Including More Obstacles: Asteroids as Extra Credit 201
Menus 202
Space Fighters: Putting It All Together 204
Game 3—Asteroid Miner 204
Brainstorming 204
Asteroid Miner: Putting it All Together 208
Troubleshooting 209
Things to Remember 212
Questions 212

Chapter Four: Arrays, Pointers and Strings   215

Arrays 215
Declaring and Referencing Arrays 217
Assigning Values to Arrays 220
Passing Arrays to Functions 222
Multidimensional Arrays 225
Three-Dimensional Arrays 228
Searching Arrays 232
Dynamic Arrays in C# 235

The foreach loop	237
Enumerating Constant Integers	238
Pointers	239
Enabling unsafe Mode	240
Pointer Variables	242
Call-By-Reference Values with Pointer Arguments	244
Pointer Arithmetic	246
String and Address Arithmetic	248
The void Pointer	252
Finding the Mean, Median, Mode, and Range	254
Pointers as Arrays: The Keyword stackalloc	256
Double Asterisk Pointers	258
Functions Returning Pointers	259
Storage Class Specifiers: extern and static	260
Manipulating String Data	262
Converting and Safeguarding Data	264
From Strings to Streams: System.IO	265
Exampling Object Types	266
The Keywords checked and unchecked	266
The goto Statement	268
Game 4—Battle Wave	269
Brainstorming	270
Brainstorming	270
Drawing Characters and Defining Motions	271
Drawing Characters	273
Alternative Rendered Designs	277
Animating Characters: Displaying Characters	279
Animating Our Characters: Patterns of Movement	280
Defining Character Limitation	282
Keyboard Controls	283
Force Feedback Controls	284
Artificial Intelligence	286
Resetting Levels	287

Saving and Retrieving Data	287
Expanding Our Arsenal	288
Brainstorming	288
Battle Wave: The Heart of the Game	289
Game 5—Battle Tennis	289
Adding Graphics	290
Input Devices: Keyboard, Joystick, and Mouse	295
The Properties of Sound	297
Three-Dimensional Sound	299
Using Sound Effects	300
Changing Levels	303
Completing the Game	304
Troubleshooting	304
Things to Remember	305
Questions	306

Chapter Five: Object-Oriented Design   309

Structures	309
Declaring and Assigning Fields	310
Multiple Structures	313
Complex Structures	315
Structures as Function Arguments: Calls-by-Value	316
Structures as Function Arguments: Calls-by-Reference	318
Passing Entire Structures	319
Storing and Retrieving Data	321
Introducing Classes	324
Replacing Structures with Classes	325
private and protected Fields	328
The Internal Access Modifier	333
Arrays as Member Fields	335
Overloading Member Functions	336
private and protected Member Functions	338

Constructors 340
Overloading Constructors 342
Assigning Instances 343
Reading and Writing to Private Members 344
The Keyword this 344
Destructors 349
Introducing Operator Overloading 350
Overloading Comparison Operators 354
Nesting Overloaded Operators 356
Overloading Unary Operators 358
Introducing Inheritance 359
Inheritance versus Composition 361
Inheriting Constructors and Destructors 362
private versus protected Inheritance 362
Using Multiply Linked Single-Inheritance 364
Overriding and Virtual Methods 366
Abstract 371
The Keyword base 375
Exception Handling 376
Nested try Blocks 378
The Keyword throw 379
User-Defined Exception Classes 380
Nested Exceptions 382
The Binary Operator as 384
Delegates 385
Preprocessor Directives 387
The external Modifier 388
The explicit Operator 389
The implicit Operator 390
Fixed Pointers 390
The get and set Accessors 391
Linking Interfaces 393
The is Operator 396

The Keyword lock	397
The Keyword params	398
The Keyword sealed	399
The Keyword stackalloc	400
Metafiles Defined	400
Building Game Classes	401
Game Classes—AnimatedImage.cs	401
Animation	403
Displaying	404
Adding Substance to Characters	405
Creating Infinite Space	409
Other Types of Deflection	409
Inheriting from AnimatedImage.cs—Player.cs	410
Inheriting from Player.cs—PlayerImageArray.cs	411
Inheriting from PlayerImageArray.cs—MultiImagePlayer.cs	413
Inheriting from PlayerImageArray.cs—Shapes.cs	414
Inheriting from Shapes.cs—Patterns.cs	418
GameState.cs	420
GameTimer.cs	422
TimedEvent.cs	424
Utils.cs	425
Wall.cs	427
Introducing Direct3D	429
Brainstorming	430
Game 6—Ground Assault	431
Brainstorming	431
Graphics	432
Game 7—Rat Racer	432
Adding Animation	432
Brainstorming	432
Troubleshooting	435
Assignments	435
Conclusion	435
Questions	435

Appendix A: Keywords/Reserved Identifiers	437
Appendix B: Reserved Identifiers Defined	439
Appendix C: Accessors	473
Appendix D: Order of Precedence	475
Appendix E: Displaying Message Boxes	477
Appendix F: Graphics	483
Appendix G: Colors	489
Appendix H: Algorithms	491
Appendix I: Adding DirectX References	499
Index	501

Preface

This is an introductory textbook that covers Microsoft's C# and game programming at the same time with a unique combination of traditional source coding and game programming techniques. Written in accordance with ECMA (European Computer Manufacturers' Association) certification standards, its purpose is to bring to the student everything taught in a traditional first semester classroom without the traditional first semester boredom. This book would also serve well as a second semester tutorial on object-oriented programming and the .Net Base Class Library. Whether you're a beginner just trying to learn the C# language or an experienced programmer trying to find your way into the .Net programming environment (not to mention the Microsoft Visual Studio series), *C# and Game Programming* is the book for you.

How to Use this Book

When I designed this book, I knew it had to serve two purposes: The first being to teach the C# language in a fun, yet practical, context, and the second to introduce the novice programmer to the more advanced concepts of object-oriented programming and .Net design. I accomplished both of these tasks by first designing a traditional programming text and then adding in several programming examples that simulate the old arcade style games of the late 1970s and early 1980s. While the games are enjoyable and do motivate study, their true purpose is found in their collective relationship to object-oriented principles. As with the game programming portions, the order of the traditional source coding is designed to emphasize an easy flow and a simple approach to programming. Nevertheless, do not interpret that to mean that this text won't be a handful. The material should take several months to complete with its Base Class Libraries serving as an invaluable source for further study.

C# and Game Programming

What You'll Need

The graphics and sound portions of this text are based on the Windows XP (Home or Professional) and 2000/ME operating systems. C# as a whole will potentially be available on any number of operating systems, including UNIX, Linux, IBM's O/S2, BeX OS, Apple-Macintosh X, and Alpha's OpenVMS.[1] The basic requirements for learning the C# language include a computer and a .Net level compiler. However, due to current restrictions, you'll also need to run your compiler under either Windows XP, 2000/NT, or ME. The hardware requirements listed to run Microsoft's .Net 1.1/2.0 beta include a Pentium II Class PC with a minimum of 233 MHz, 64 megabytes of RAM, 1.5 gigabytes of free hard drive space, 4x Speed CD-ROM, and a SVGA monitor. Additional components required and/or referred to in this book include a mouse, sound card (with speakers), and (optional) modem—see your compiler's manual for additional restrictions and/or requirements.

What I Used

The programs written for this text are developed with the understanding that not everyone can afford the very best in technologies. The compilers referenced include a list of student, beta, and trial editions, with the more advanced coding progressing into the standard and professional versions. Again, the compilers were installed under several Windows environments including Window's XP through NT. I also used a host of hardware configurations ranging from AMD & Intel's latest to a few much older AMD and Cyrix type machines.

About the CD-ROM

The companion CD-ROM included with this book covers the source code (programming text) and several previously compiled programs, all labeled and listed in the order discussed in the text. Each set of programs is placed in a folder titled after its chapter (as in Chapter 1, Chapter 2, etc.). In addition, I have included an assortment of games, all meant to aid in your learning and productivity. To load the source codes off the CD-ROM just follow the instructions listed on the next page.

---

[1] Please check with those vendors for the appropriate compiler(s).

Preface

To load and use the source code that accompanies this book:

1. Create a new directory and/or subdirectory. This will be used to store the programs from the CD-ROM and the programs you create on your own. Name your folder and note where you place it (in the C drive, D drive, etc,), including which subdirectory and/or subdirectories you chose to place it under. If you use the default, you'll more than likely find your lost files under: C:\\Documents and settings*YourUserName* \My Documents\Visual Studio Projects*ProjectsNameHere*.
2. Make sure your compiler is installed and working properly.
3. Load and make active the C# compiler. Close any and all nonessential windows (this includes the C# tour box). Closing unnecessary background programs will also help to speed up your system.
4. Insert the CD-ROM into the appropriate drive.
5. Select "Open" from the C# compiler's file menu (see Screen Shot 1).

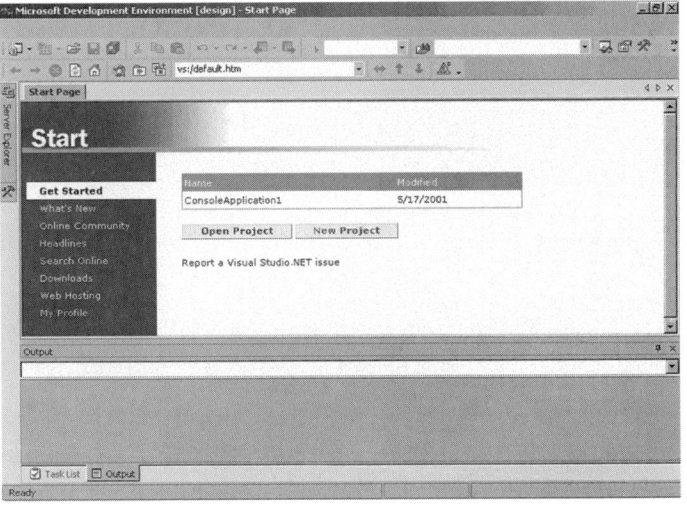

Screen Shot 1.

6. From the "Open" Windows menu, select the folder titled "Source" and then the appropriate subfolder(s). The subfolder titled "MSNET" contains all of the source code for the Microsoft .Net compiler(s)[2] (see Screen Shots 2 and 3).

. . . .
[2] The programs depicted in this text were intended for use with Microsoft's .Net compiler.

C# and Game Programming

Screen
Shot 2.

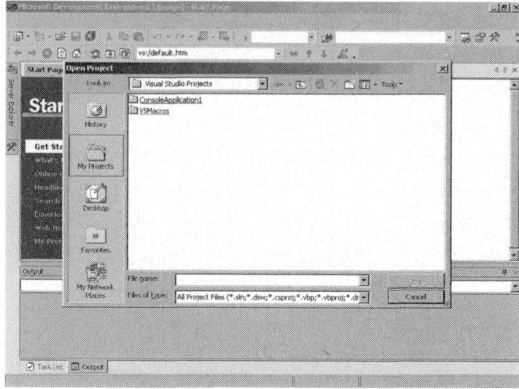

Screen
Shot 3.

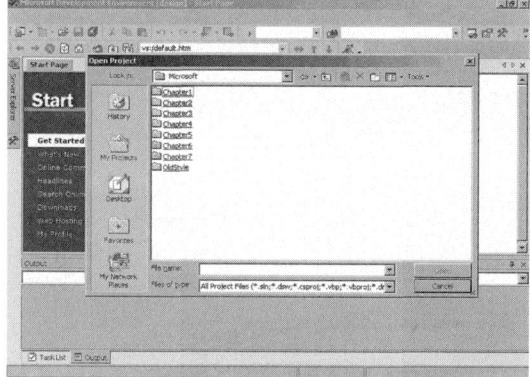

7. Select "Save As" from that file's menu and save it to the directory you created in Step 1 (see Screen Shot 4).

Screen
Shot 4

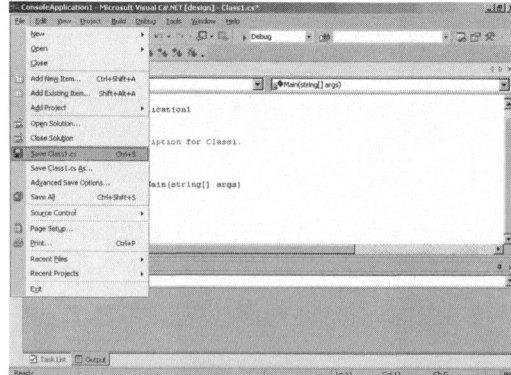

Your program is now linked to that directory. You can remove the CD-ROM from its drive (remember to repeat these steps for each program as needed). To edit the source code and/or to proceed with compiling, see the instructions listed in Chapter 1.

How to Read this Book

This book is written for everyone wanting to learn the C# language in a fun yet practical context. The book is broken up to accommodate three skill levels.

Part 1: Programming Basics covers the most fundamental portions, including programming history, how to setup your compiler, and algorithms. It also introduces critical material on the .Net framework, data types, input and output commands, legacy coding, the Base Class Library, comparisons and loops, switch statements, type casting, boxing and unboxing, and method manipulations (arguments, polymorphism, and recursion).

Part 2: Game Programming Basics also covers very basic concepts—namely single and multidimensional arrays, pointers (under unsafe mode), string functions, and streams—but eventually leads the reader out of the novice stage. Other key topics include an introduction to object-oriented programming, using Window's applications for graphics and sounds, and realtime game programming techniques. Seasoned C/C++ programmers can usually jump in at this level, using the earlier portions as a convenient point of reference.

Part 3: Object-Oriented Programming begins with structures, but quickly migrates into classes and the principles behind object-oriented programming. Fields, methods, and operator overloading are discussed early on, with inheritance, virtual functions, delegates, and exception handling expanding our capabilities. Here, we'll also expand upon the principles of the .Net environment, including reflection, threads, synchronization, CLS (Common Language Specifications) complaints, language specifications, and a further study of the Base Class Library.

This book can also be used by anyone taking C# in a standard college course. Thus, the text covers topics such as bubble sorting, search algorithms, and most teachers' favorite, default settings (although I personally prefer using parenthetical expressions).

In addition to following the book from chapter to chapter, you could also reroute your studies to include alternate paths or approaches. One such example would be to proceed from Chapter 2 straight to Chapter 4, since the gaming portions might not interest you. Alternatively, you could skip some of the more difficult gaming concepts listed in Chapters 3–5 and then return to that material after finishing the traditional studies. It is, however, recommended that you do eventually work through those games in order to apply some of the more advanced concepts on object-oriented programming and .Net design.

Getting Help from the Author

Since this book is meant to teach one of the vast and often expanding C languages, I felt that it was necessary to include a continuously updated e-mail forum and internet newsletter, that is, a forum that will include any new or improved features, including programming errors and ways to fix problems. I'd also like to encourage all beginner programmers by generating a list of web sites, source coding (including arcade style clones), and any other new developments. To register for your FREE internet newsletter, or to write in with a problem or request, please address your email to Plague@iwon.com.

The Student Perspective

This book was written from the perspective of the student. Every attempt was made to move the reader along in a logical and progressive manner. Nearly every keyword and command has a working (live code) example, and when necessary, the reader is presented with a list of background information and troubleshooting sections that are usually covered by an instructor or gained in some previous programming language.

There are several sections that cover the secondary steps of programming such as C# to Windows setups, compiler setups, and topics on game coding. The game coding, while considered trivial by many instructors, is one of the most effective ways of demonstrating C#'s object-oriented potential. Each new game is constructed with the intent of maximizing the use of the coding studied in that chapter. The games, while entertaining, also force the reader to press beyond simple logic and answer questions that are not staged or limited to simple text based outputs.

The chapters follow an almost evolutionary pattern that begins with the basics of C# and progresses through the techniques of structured, modular, and Object-Oriented Programming (OOP), with the last section obviously concluding with the latest advances in Microsoft's .Net architecture. Both our text concepts and the games developed are part of that evolution, which primarily defines which games can and will be developed with the keywords and commands available.

Preface

Remember: for the best results, I suggest using the same compiler and operating system(s) I use; Microsoft's Visual C# .Net 2003/2005 beta, under Windows XP Home or Professional.

Book Reviews: *The Washington Post* said, "I don't know what to say about it." *The New York Times* raved, "It came in the mail." And Ebert & Roeper said "We don't review books, please stop calling!"

About the Author

When I was a boy, I had a "TRS Color Computer." It was hooked up to a TV set and had a cassette drive. I used it to write simple text style games and AI driven chess programs. A few years later, my mother bought me an Amiga 500 (a highpowered gaming computer). I used it to write simple games like Tennis, Space Fighter, and Rat Racer (all in the name of education, I swear). Shortly after receiving that computer, I entered college. From there, I earned two degrees, the first in Math and the second in Engineering. Eventually I had to sell that old Amiga and buy/build myself a newer IBM/Intel compatible computer. Upgrading that computer actually turned into a career of sorts, leading first to online technical support and eventually to game programming. After graduating, I turned my talents toward writing, or more specifically, toward technical writing, but you should have guessed that. I also managed to get married, buy a little house, win a few Jiu-jitsu tournaments, and well, there is that whole gaining superpowers thing. As for my TRS Color Computer, I removed its plug and gave it to my nephew as a toy typewriter—just imagine the day when the Pentium IV becomes that outdated.

There's a mouse on the desk, there's a mouse on the desk...
I'm sure there's been a mistake here, does anyone know why there's a mouse on my desk?

Programming Basics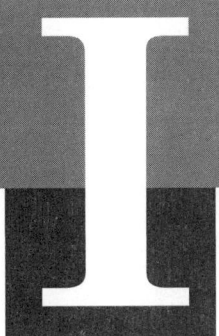

C# from the Beginning

Chapter One

"Everything should be made as simple as possible, but not simpler."
—Albert Einstein

his chapter covers the basic aspects of the C# language including its history, compilers, algorithms, variables, and the use of the Base Class Library. Each section is designed to facilitate a quick and easy introduction and to ensure a strong foundation in programming and problem solving. Special attention was placed on what a new programmer needs to know and/or might be confused about; the sections can, however, be covered quickly. There are a few sections set aside to cover history and theory, but the core of this chapter is about programming. Two sections promote good programming habits and there is a section on runtime, programming, and compiler errors (recommended reading even if you don't get into trouble). If you've skimmed the lessons, you know that this first chapter doesn't include any games, but don't let that fool you. All of the concepts covered here are just as important for games as they are for business and/or math related topics.

An Overview of the C# Language

C# is a high- or mid-level programming language (and just in case you didn't know, a programming language is the collection of words, phrases, and syntax rules used to communicate with the computer). Although there are many high-level programming languages (BASIC, JAVA, FORTRAN, Pascal, Lisp, ADA, Modula-2 and Logo), few have reached the popularity of the original C and C++ languages. C and C++ have been used to create everything from operating systems and word processing packages to compilers for other high-level languages. C and C++ have been the programming languages of choice for more than 50 percent of all programming applications, and with their advances in object-oriented programming and Internet applications, both Managed C++ and C# are sure to fuel the popularity of C languages well into this new millennium.

A Little History on the Cs

C was developed in the 1970s by Dennis Ritchie while he worked at AT&T Bell Laboratories. Before C, there was a language called B developed by Ken Thompson. While there was an A language, B was actually developed from Basic Combined Programming Language (BCPL), which was developed from a combination of two other languages, namely CPL and Algol60. C++'s object-oriented portions are attributed to still another language known as Simula67. CPL begot BCPL; BCPL begot B; B begot C; C begot C++; and C++ begot C#. In 1979, Bjarne Stroustrup (also at AT&T Bell Laboratories) developed the first version of C++ to be an enhanced version of the C language (initially referred to as C with classes). C++ was significantly enhanced with the addition of the Standard Template Library (STL) developed by Alexander Stepanov and Meng Lee at Hewlett-Packard. The STL was based heavily on previous work done by both Stepanov and Musser, from Rensselaer Polytechnic Institute.

Both C and C++ spread quickly in power and use, but eventually all the added features and expansions lead to incompatibilities and frustrations. Two standards were created, first with the American National Standards Institute (ANSI) C standard of 1983, and then the American National Standards for Systems Information and International Standards Organization (ISO) C/C++ standards of 1998 (Note: C was also updated in this second standard). The 1998 ANSI/ISO standard is generally referred to as Native C++, while Microsoft's .Net Extensions are known as Managed C++. C# was also standardized with its first release under what is known as the 2001/2002 ECMA certified standard.

C# was developed by a team of Microsoft programmers led by chief architect Anders Hejlsberg. It is intended to supplement the development of applications required for both stream users and intranet/internet programmers alike. C# is definitely one of the most sophisticated languages ever developed, and similar to the entire .Net architecture, it will alter the way programmers think about programming for many years to come.

Hejlsberg was also responsible for the development of Microsoft's Visual J++, Turbo Pascal, and Delphi, for which he finally received the Dr. Dobb's Journal Award for Excellence in Programming early in 2001. For further information on the history of Turbo Pascal, Visual J++, and the Dr. Dobb's Journal Award, you should consult your local library... now let's get back to business.

As you can see, C# evolved from the simpler languages.
Hey, I thought it was created by a programmer.

What is the .Net Framework?

The .Net framework is a multitasking, class-based programming library and interface that allows for both the interoperable exchange and execution of data. As a library, the .Net base classes are as powerful as the traditional Windows API function set, but have the added advantage of being completely object-oriented. Object-oriented programming (as explained throughout this book) is a practical method used to develop programs that promotes both the reusability and reliability of code. The .Net runtime (also known as the Common Language Runtime or CLR) serves as a shell or intermediate environment that assists the operating system with program execution(s).

The .Net framework also allows for program interoperability, requiring a Common Type System (CTS) governed through the *Intermediate Language* commonly known as *Microsoft's Intermediate Language* (MSIL) and/or the *Common Intermediate Language* (CIL). Intermediate Language should not be confused with Java's interpreted byte-type coding, which does not have the ability to be compiled. Microsoft has also developed a secondary type of compilation known as JIT (just in time) compilations. Under JIT, programs are not only installed into our systems, but the code is optimized for the processor. In addition, JIT compilation shortcuts the basic startup time by limiting compilation to only the required portions, which also improves overall performance.

The .Net architecture also offers some interesting advantages, including memory management (also known as garbage collection) and zero-impact installation. Garbage collection (stemming from Java) is a systematic approach to eliminating previously allocated memory that is no longer being referenced. While garbage collection diminishes the programmer's power to control memory deallocation, it does help to prevent dangerous memory leaks, and saves the programmer additional time that would normally be spent implementing destructors. Likewise, zero-impact installation has been developed to save the programmer and consumer many hours of frustration by eliminating the errors caused by faulty reversioning. Under normal Windows operation, a typical .*dll* type file would be included as part of a centralized reference, which in turn would make it subject to deletion whenever a new version is installed. If that new version is not entirely backward compatible, then the replacement file can cause the program to fail. With zero-impact installation, alternate versions of otherwise identical files can exist side by side, thereby eliminating this problem.

In addition, .Net offers increased code security, application domain restrictions, strong typing, and namespacing. The increase in security allows the consumer to control the level of access granted to any single program, with MSIL also determining the level of access requested by a program before its execution (This may help to prevent some unscrupulous programmers from damaging our files.). *Application domain restrictions* prevent memory conflicts between interrelated applications through the use of *virtual memory barriers,* which are barriers that restrict access, but do not impose processor delays. (This process is controlled through MSIL). *Strong typing*, also governed by MSIL, requires that we specifically state data types, thus preventing ambiguous runtime errors; unfortunately, this also prevents us from using templates (excluded from the C# programming language). Finally, *namespacing*, originally designed to prevent Native C++ naming conflicts, is now a requirement of the .Net architecture, wherein all types must be defined with either an explicit or a global namespace.

Managed Code and Assemblies

Managed code is the term used to define the coding implemented under the .Net framework, while the terms *native* and *unmanaged code* are used to indicate coding that bypasses this new architecture and is implemented directly through the Windows API. *Assemblies* are units in which managed coding is stored. Assemblies also contain information packets referred to as *metadata*: metadata packets keep track of an assembly's contents including its objects, methods, and types. Shared assemblies are stored in a central area referred to as the assembly's *cache*. Metadata packets are stored in an area inside these assemblies known as the *manifest*.

Algorithms

Before we can jump into writing programs, we'll have to learn a little bit about designing them. The first step in designing a program is writing its *algorithm*. Writing an algorithm is not the same as writing a program; it doesn't require the use of a computer language, or even a computer. An algorithm can be applied to any task or set of tasks. Writing down directions is probably one of the most common examples of an algorithm; recipes, diets, and math solutions are others. Some beginner programmers don't understand the need for algorithms, believing instead that they can plan their programs as they go, or after completing the introductory part of their coding. However, such programming styles often lead to hazards such as additional time spent problem solving and/or more time spent rewriting code to incorporate each new idea or feature. Thus, it is always best to start with an algorithm. Therefore, I've included an outline of the algorithm used to write a C++ version of the first arcade style game taught in Chapter 3—Paddle Tennis (see Example 3.5).

> **Example 1.1. Abbreviated Algorithm for Paddle Tennis.**
>
> 1. Create a viable Windows handle accessible through the Windows console settings.
> 2. Write a function to draw the player's characters.
> 3. Include a function that paints/clears the screen.
> 4. Define most of the variables as a member of a single class, with the most notable exception being the color settings.
> 5. Set the variables/member, setting the ball to a random direction.
> 6. *Create a while-loop that ends when the game ends.*
>
> Inside the while loop
> 7. Write a function that removes our residual images using a combination of calls to blank characters and/or a full-blown clear screen function.
> 8. Set the colors: Since these colors never change, this can be done from either the do-while or internal while loop.
> 9. Display the players, ball, and the scores (0 to 0 as we start).

10. Write a function that reads the players input from the keyboard.
11. Write a function to propel the ball.
12. Write a function to limit the area in which the players can traverse.
13. Include sounds when the ball bounces
14. Check to see if the ball and player have collided (see Collision Detection: The Ball in Motion). The ball should bounce off the player.
15. If the ball gets to the end of the screen and the player is not there, give the other player a point. Now, reset the ball.
16. Repeat the loop until either player scores a specified number.
17. Ask player(s) if they want to play again. Remember a good game loop should always allow the player(s) the option of playing again.
18. End or repeat game.

If this seems a bit long, keep in mind that the actual Paddle Tennis subroutines are part of a program that is more than 100 pages long, and even the simplest professionally designed program will tend to run over a 1000 pages. Algorithms do not have to include complete sentences, have correct grammar, or even need to be entirely in English. Yet, having something that you can actually read and that lists the steps to the solution is important. Further, when writing an algorithm shared by others, never assume that they can read something written in C#; after all, they might be planning to write the program in another language such as VISUAL BASIC, managed C++, or just plain old-fashioned C.

The .Net Compiler

A traditional compiler translates higher-level languages into the machine's own language, appropriately named *Machine Language*. Programmers developed higher-level languages such as C and C++ to bridge the gap between human languages and the computer's binary code of ones and zeroes. As difficult as C# and other high-level languages seem, their difficulty doesn't compare to the complexity of trying to

Chapter 1: C# from the Beginning

understand the endless rolls of ones and zeroes, such as 01010011 00010100 00011101, found in machine language. In addition to machine language, there is also a low-level language known as *Assembly Language*, which serves as an intermediary between C and that binary code. However, the advent of C# and the .Net framework replaced this concept.

The new way of thinking about compilation is to break it into two steps: The first step is, a conversion to MSIL, which allows for both the construction and testing of our products from within the compiler's simulated environment. The second step, JIT compilation, isn't implemented until the moment of execution, hence the name just in time. With this new form of compiling, Microsoft has been able to implement several new features, including role-type and code-type based security, memory type safety, and interoperability. *Role-type and code-type based security* relate to a program's base of identity and the level of access granted to that code. If an unauthorized program attempts to access/alter any other application without MSIL's express permission, the execution of that program is not allowed. The same is true for *type safety;* if the MSIL environment detected that any newly executed program will cause a memory address conflict, that program is also denied system access. In addition, this new method opens up our coding to an entirely new level of code *interoperability*; with it, we can intermix between objects written in different languages, step between references, and even use those objects as inheriting classes. There is also the potential for reflective comparisons with respect to both interoperable and internal files (See later chapters for details.).

Common Language Specifications: While the .Net framework is designed to promote language interoperability, the use of the C# language does not guarantee that level of interaction. We can, however, make C# CLS compliant with what are generally only minor adjustments to our overall method of programming. For example, we must adjust our programs to avoid the use of unsafe coding (specifically, pointer notation). In addition, we must avoid the use of some data types, namely `sbyte`, `ushort`, `uint`, and `ulong`. Finally, we'll have to restrict our naming practices to avoid conflicts with Visual Basic's inability to distinguish between upper and lower case settings (e.g., `Class1` and `class1`).

Compiling and Executing

While the theories of proper compilation and execution were outlined in the previous sections, we still haven't established a practical method for the implementation of our applications. Before our programs can be executed either with or without an external .Net environment, they must first go through a process known as *compilation*. Hence, to start, you'll need a computer program known as a *compiler*. I recommend Microsoft's C# .Net in any of its packaged standards (trial, standard, professional, or enterprise). I've also included simple step-by-step instructions on how to set up those compilers.

Quick Setup for Microsoft Visual C# .NET:

1. Make sure your compiler is installed and working properly.
2. Load and activate the C# compiler. Close any nonessential windows.
3. From the "File" menu, select "New" and then "Project" (see Screen Shot 1.1).

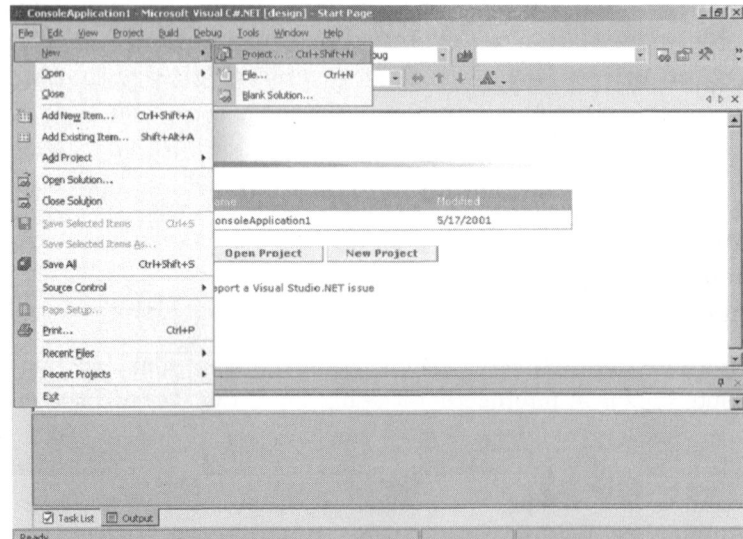

Screen Shot 1.1.

4. At this point, a second window should open. Select the icon labeled "Console Application" (see Screen Shot 1.2).

Chapter 1: C# from the Beginning

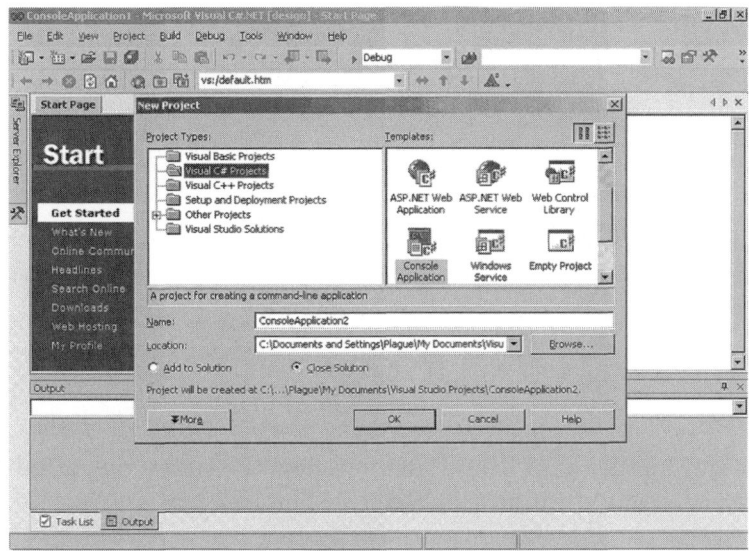

Screen Shot 1.2.

You will need to enter a name in the box titled "Name." I called this first example "Chapter1," but you can use any name you like. Once you have entered a name, the "OK" button is enabled; click it to continue. Your compiler is now set up and ready for input. For further details on how to setup the C# compiler, see the Troubleshooting section at the end of this chapter, check your compiler's help files, or check out Microsoft's online guide at: http://msdn.microsoft.com/vcsharp/.

Now, without regard for any particular compiler or series, we'll want to test to make sure that everything is set up and running correctly. We'll do this by inputting what is known as a "do-nothing" program, that is, a program that creates no significant output, yet by compiling, conveys the message that our compilers are ready. The actual commands used in this program are unimportant at this time.

5. Typing in your C# source coding is as simple as entering text into a word processor. Just make sure that the larger window to the right is active. Note that an active window is usually marked by a blinking cursor.

C# and Game Programming

Example 1.2. Our first program.

```
using System;

namespace Chapter1 {
    class Class1 {
        static void Main () {
            /* "executable statements go here" */
        }
    }
}
```

6. Now, from the main "Build" menu, select the submenu option also labeled as "Build" (see Screen Shot 1.3).

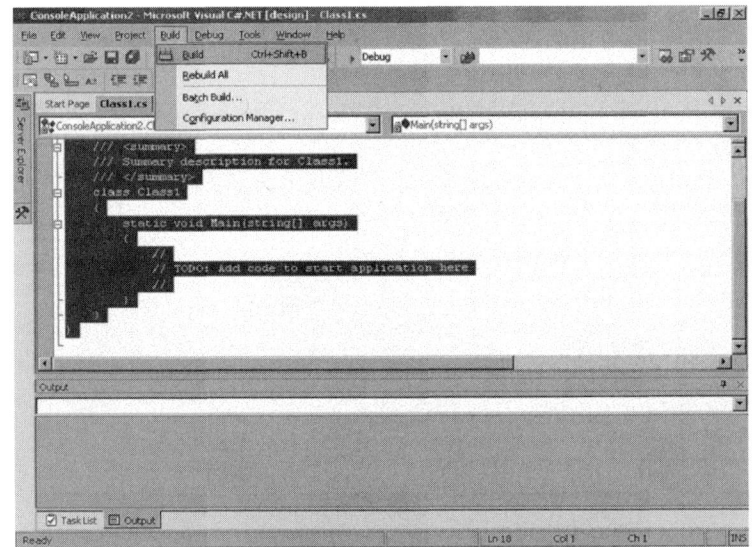

Screen Shot 1.3

You should notice a stream of information appearing in the lower compiler window, normally located at the bottom of the screen. Make sure you get a message saying zero errors and zero warnings (see Screen Shot 1.4).

Chapter 1: C# from the Beginning

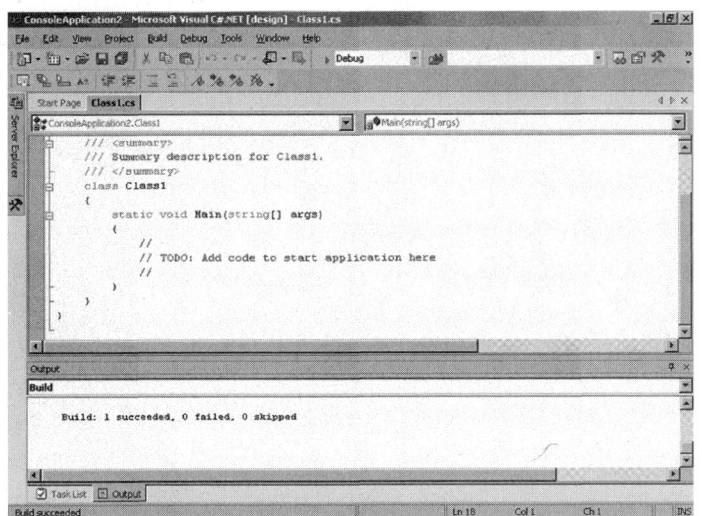

Screen Shot 1.4.

If you got an error at this step, it means the project was not set up correctly. Repeat all the steps again or see the Troubleshooting section at the end of the chapter.

7. Finally, to execute the program, simply click on the "Debug" menu and select "Start Without Debugging." Your do-nothing program will now produce a large window asking you to "Press any key to continue." Doing so will end the program (see Screen Shots 1.5 and 1.6).

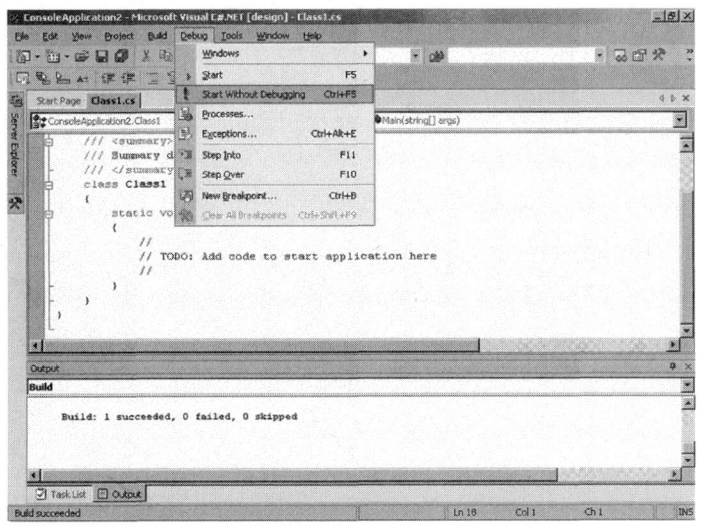

Screen Shot 1.5.

Screen Shot 1.6

Example 1.2 Explained

C# uses several data types, including integers, real numbers, characters, and void. *Void,* for all practical purposes, means without a type. Moreover, since the main function doesn't usually require a data type, `void` is the simplest to use. Data types such as int, `float`, `double`, `char`, and `void` are explained in detail later in this chapter.

    The commands `static void Main (string [] args)` and `static void Main ( )` are most commonly referred to when indicating the main method. The main method serves as the controller to the rest of the program. In these beginning stages, we'll write all commands inside of the main method, but later, as our programs advance, we'll migrate to other subprograms that will do specific tasks. The main method will then serve as a controller to these subprograms. Writing programs in this manner is akin to an older method of programming known as *structured programming*, which is a very important part of both C and Native C++ that the object-oriented approach will eventually surpass.

    The *opening* and *closing braces* (also known as a *block*) simply mark the beginning and ending of the program's environment. The computer recognizes these symbols as markers telling it where to start and where to end. Without such markers, programs would not know which coding belonged to which method. Each block, then, indicates a subenvironment, whereas the namespace's exterior block represents the global environment (Note: Comments are explained in the next section).

Comments

Comments are nothing more than system notes, usually written by a programmer, to mark or explain a certain passage that may not seem as obvious to us at a later date. For example, we might mention that the main method ends with a particular brace or that we need to alter or repair a line or two to increase system performance. Examples 1.3 and 1.4 demonstrate the general use of single and multiple line comments, while Example 1.5 demonstrates a third type of pseudo-comment that is part of C#'s ability to manipulate internet resources.

Example 1.3. Single line comments.

```
using System;

namespace Chapter1 {
    class Class1 {
        static void Main ( ) { // Main method
            // Begin executable statements
        }   // End main method
    }
}
```

Example 1.4. Multiple line comments.

```
/* Longer comments (comments spanning two lines or more) are
 * often set aside with these special markers.
 * Comments are ignored by the compiler and thus
 * do not affect the program's speed. */
using System;

namespace Chapter1 {
    class Class1 {
        static void Main ( ) { /* Main method */
                    /* Put something here please! */
        } /* End main method */
    }
}
```

C# and Game Programming

Adding additional forward slashes will not invalidate our comments, but they will open our C# coding to accept the *Extended Markup Language* (XML) commands. XML commands are included as part of the collective .Net framework to make Webpage design faster and more convenient (see Example 1.5).

Example 1.5. XML commands.

```
using System;

namespace Chapter1 {
    /// Place your XML tags here
    /// ...
    class Class1 {
        static void Main () {
            /* this is still a do nothing program */
        }
    }
}
```

Screen Output

Now that we have the basics of writing a do-nothing program, let's see if we can add something other than comments to it. Traditionally, a first program will display the message "Hello, world!" However, since this book emphasizes game programming, what could be more appropriate then "Game Over?" (see Example 1.6).

Example 1.6. Screen output 1.

```
using System;

namespace Chapter1 {
    class Class1 {
        static void Main () {
            Console.Write ("Game Over! \n");
        }
    }
}
```

Now there are two commands added to our do-nothing program that, in fact, make it do something. The actual commands that make the words "Game Over" appear can be simplified to:

```
Console.Write ("Game Over!");
```

The command that moves the cursor to the next line is:

```
Console.Write ("\n");
```

We have combined these two commands in Example 1.6. Replacing `Console.Write` ("Game Over!"); with `Console.Write` (""); would result in a program that seems to do nothing, since there was nothing written between the inner and outer quotes (changing "Game Over!" to "Hello, World!" produces the classic result—see Example 1.7).

Example 1.7. Screen output 2.

```
using System;

namespace Chapter1 {
    // Purpose: Displays the words "Hello, world!"

    class Class1 {
        static void Main () {
            Console.WriteLine ("Hello World!");
        }
    }
}
```

You can replace the words "Hello, World" with virtually any other sentence, or you could add additional sentences to the program by repeating the Write command. Example 1.8 displays a program with two lines of output. Feel free to input a few lines of your own.

Example 1.8. Screen output 3.

```
using System;

namespace Chapter1 {
    class Class1 {
```

C# and Game Programming

```
static void Main () {
    Console.Write ("Hello, Programmer.\n");
    Console.WriteLine ("How are you today?");
}
}
}
```

Symbols	Purpose
\a	Alert (bell)
\b	Backspace
\f	Formfeed
\n	Newline
\r	Carriage return
\t	Horizontal tab
\v	Vertical tab
\?	Literal quotation mark
\'	Single quotation mark
\"	Double quotation mark
\\	Backslash

Table 1.1. Escape sequences.

The Newline Character

The symbols backslash and n (\n) were used in the previous section inside a pair of quotes, but they were not displayed to the screen with the words "Game Over" or "Hello, World!" This combination, known as the *newline* character, serves as a marker telling the program when to move to the next line. The newline character is one of many specialized characters referred to as *escape sequences* (see Example 1.9). For a complete list of escape sequences, see Table 1.1.

Example 1.9. The newline character.

```
using System;

namespace Chapter1 {
    class Class1 {
        static void Main ( ) {
            Console.Write ("Hello, Programmer. ");
            Console.Write ("How are you today? \n");
        }
    }
}
```

> In this program, the newline character was not placed after the phrase "Hello, Programmer." As a result, the program did not move to a new line, and thus "How are you today" did not transfer to the second line, producing, instead, the single line "Hello, programmer. How are you today?" A similar result is shown in Example 1.10.

Example 1.10. More practice with the newline character.

```
/* more practice with the newline character */
using System;

namespace Chapter1 {
    class Class1 {
        static void Main() { //Begin main
            Console.Write ("This is line 1\n");

            Console.Write ("This is line 2\n");
            Console.Write ("This is line 3");
            Console.Write ("This is still line 3\n");
            Console.Write ("This is line 4\n");
        }
    }
}
```

 We can also disable the automatic formatting of the newline character (or any other escape sequence), thus reproducing the codes as actual text. This is done using the @ symbol as shown in Example 1.11.

Example 1.11. Disabling the escape sequences using the @ symbol.

```
using System;

namespace Chapter1 {
    class Class1 {
        static void Main() {
            Console.Write(@"\n This is line 1");
            Console.Write("\n This is line 2");
            Console.Write("\n This is line 3");
            Console.Write(@"\n This is still line 3");
            Console.Write("\n This is line 4\n");
            Console.Write(@"\n This is line 5\n");
        }
    }
}
```

The `WriteLine` Command

An alternative to returning one's cursor position with the newline character is to replace it with the `WriteLine` command.

```
Console.WriteLine ("");
```

The `WriteLine` command is written in a manner similar to the `Console.Write` command, but it does not require the newline character. It can also be used as an output stream or statement, and (as shown above) it can be referenced without any other comments or information. To demonstrate, we'll revise our last example, replacing its Write command with a `WriteLine` statement (see Example 1.12).

Example 1.12. The `WriteLine` command.

```
using System;

namespace Chapter1 {
```

```
    class Class1 {
        static void Main() { // Begin main
            Console.WriteLine("This is line 1");
            Console.Write("This is line 2\n");
            Console.Write("This is line 3");
            Console.Write(" This is still line 3\n");
            Console.Write("This is line 4\n");
        }
    }
}
```

We can also combine separate sentences inside a single command by linking their statements and dividing them up with newline commands, which can be done with either the Write or WriteLine commands (see Example 1.13).

Example 1.13. The `WriteLine` command continued.

```
using System;

namespace Chapter1 {
    class Class1 {
        static void Main() { // Begin main
            Console.WriteLine("This is line 1\nThis is line 2");
            Console.Write("This is line 3" + " This is still line 3\n"
                + "This is line 4\n");
        }
    }
}
```

From the user's perspective there will be no difference, yet to the programmer there is quite a change in coding. Example 1.14 ends this section by replacing every newline character with a `WriteLine` command; reexecution of these last few programs should provide identical results.

Example 1.14. Replacing newline characters with `WriteLine`.

```
using System;

namespace Chapter1 {
    class Class1 {
        static void Main() { // Begin main
```

```
            Console.WriteLine("This is line 1");
            Console.WriteLine("This is line 2");
            Console.Write("This is line 3");
            Console.WriteLine(" This is still line 3");
            Console.WriteLine("This is line 4");
        }
    }
}
```

The Semicolon

When the compiler detects a semicolon (;), it knows that the command line has ended and that it should move to the next set of instructions. This is especially important when dealing with commands that are often written in varying sizes or those that extend over more than one line. Having such a requirement also limits or restricts the potential for overlapping errors found during compilation. The semicolon is always placed at the end of a complete statement and is always used to signal the end of that statement. Commands that do not require a semicolon often do not terminate until the end of a particular section or set of commands. Some programming commands do not terminate until the program itself ends, and hence, do not require a semicolon.

Whitespaces

Whitespaces are simply blank spaces used to separate coding terms. Variable names as well as keywords require these separations, but in many other cases, these whitespaces are just ignored. It is, however, important to remember that these spaces do not indicate the end of a line, terminations of any coding, or any other such control. You should be careful not to abuse this ability to separate command lines (abuse would be any instance where such spacing causes visual confusion on the part of the programmer).

Preprocessor Directives

If you have ever worked with either C or C++, you're probably wondering when we'll talk about preprocessor directives, since it was through the use of those directives that we were given access to the bulk of what was known as the runtime libraries. If you've never heard of preprocessor directives or the terms included and/or header files, then here's a quick bit of history.

Included files (listed as `#include <filename>`) were simple communiqués that allowed the addition of specialized files to programs. In effect, they mean "include this," with "this" being whichever header file followed. The pound symbol was always placed in front of the included statement, which allowed the compiler to identify it. The files accessed were essentially little side programs that usually did something useful like print words to the screen, or even to the printer. Included statements and the functions that they linked to our programs were essential to programming in C and C++. However, this is no longer the case, since C# has eliminated the need for such references and instead uses an object-oriented approach. This approach is actually what defines the .Net architecture and is what is meant by the Base Class Libraries (not to worry, all of these topics will be explained in greater detail later in this text).

Note: For C++ Programmers:
While it may appear that the *using* and #include statements are of similar design, that assumption is incorrect. In fact, the key purpose of the using feature is merely to allow for abbreviated class name references.

Indenting

Indenting is a simple way to keep your programs looking neat and organized. Indenting has been shown in all of the examples, and simply means to set commands several spaces inward from the first line of a segment, which is done to indicate that they are part of that segment. When a line is not indented, it can mean that it is not part of the segment. Indenting, while easier on the eyes, has only a cosmetic effect on source coding and will not affect the computer's/compiler's view of the material.

Naming Variables

Regardless of the language, the simplest method of storing and/or manipulating generalized data has always been the use of variables. A *variable* is used by programs to store and retrieve both character and numeric data. While we'll save the technical/coding portions for the next few sections, we'll want to at least understand the naming procedures before moving forward. There are three basic rules when naming variables:

1. Variables consist of only letters, numbers, and the underscore symbol.
2. Variables must always start with a letter or the underscore symbol. (Note: Underscores and coded prefixes are usually reserved by large projects and companies).
3. Variables cannot have the same name as a reserved word or keyword (see Table 1.2 for a complete list of keywords). It is possible to use the special @ symbol to override this limitation as in @char, but this is usually unnecessary.

In addition to these variable rules, there are also some good naming practices that should be followed.

Naming suggestions

1. Give the variable a descriptive name such as player_1, ball, or joystick2; descriptive names reduce the likelihood of confusion.
2. Use a consistent style when writing variables, such as alien_1 and alien_2 or Alien_1 and Alien_2. Do not randomly mix upper and lower case letters as in AliEN_1, AliEn_1. C#, like both C and C++, is a case sensitive language—it reads uppercase and lowercase letters as different symbols, and thus, these randomly named variables will not be read as the same value.
3. To remain consistent, you can adopt one of two styles: *Humpback*, which capitalizes the first letter of each word (PlayerOne); and *Camel* (also known as Pascal), which capitalizes the first letter of interior words, but not the initial letter (playerOne). These notations are the standard for most companies, including Microsoft.
4. C and C++ also follow a special naming procedure known as *Hungarian Notation*. This notation involves giving data types beginning letters that identify their declared types. Since C# uses an object based method, the practicality of using Hungarian Notation is limited. However, for backward compatibility and historical purposes, it is helpful to have a knowledge of this notation (see the Hungarian Section later in this Chapter).

abstract	decimal	float	namespace	return	try
as	default	for	new	sbtye	typeof
base	delegate	foreach	null	sealed	uint
bool	do	goto	object	short	ulong
break	double	if	operator	sizeof	unchecked
byte	else	implicit	out	stackalloc	unsafe
case	enum	in	override	static	ushort
catch	event	int	params	string	using
char	explicit	interface	private	struct	virtual
checked	extern	internal	protected	switch	void
class	false	is	public	this	volatile
const	finally	lock	readonly	throw	while
continue	fixed	long	ref	true	

Table 1.2. Keywords.

Example 1.15 demonstrates how to use a variable named OurVariable, and uses several commands not yet completely explained in this section. Therefore, we'll only need to focus on the highlighted lines. You should edit and recompile this program several times, testing different variable names. Remember, you can use any name you want as long as it follows the rules stated above.

C# and Game Programming

Example 1.15. Naming variables.

```
using System;

namespace Chapter1 {
    class Class1 {
        static void Main() {
            int OurVariable; // an integer data type.
            OurVariable = 1; // we can assign the value 1 to the variable
            Console.WriteLine("The number is " + OurVariable);
        }
    }
}
```

Remember that if you change the name in the declaring line, you'll also have to change it in the assigning and referencing lines.

Other possible variable names include:
- Number   integer   whole_number   computer_data
- Lives   game_lives   deaths   bombs_on_ship

Declaring Variables and the Integer Data Types

There are five basic data types: `integer (int)`, `float`, `double`, `character (char)`, and `void`. Each of these has a specific purpose, but to apply these variables properly we must first learn how to declare them. An integer is any positive or negative whole number (see Example 1.16). To declare an integer, use the keyword `int`, followed by the variable name and a semicolon (Remember the semicolon ends the command line.). We can declare data types using either the common method or by expressly stating their CTS type. We can also declare multiple variables in any one program by either repeating the `int` keyword or adding additional variables to the line as is implied by the use of the comma operator (see Examples 1.17 and 1.18).

Example 1.16. A number line of integers.

-10, -9, -8, -7, -6, -5, -4, -3, -2, -1, 0, 1, 2, 3, 4, 5, 6, 7, 8, 9, 10...

Example 1.17. Declaring variables using common method.

```
using System;

namespace Chapter1 {
    class Class1 {
        static void Main() {
            // these variable were declared using the data type integer
            int Number1, Number2;

            Number1 = 1; // Their assignment values both equal one.
            Number2 = 1;

            // And, they're both displayed using the WriteLine function.
            Console.WriteLine("The first number is " + Number1
                + "\nThe second number is " + Number2 + "\n");
        }
    }
}
```

Example 1.18. Declaring variables using the CTS type.

```
using System;

namespace Chapter1 {
    class Class1 {
        static void Main() {
            System.Int32 Number1, Number2;

            Number1 = 1;
            Number2 = 1;

            Console.WriteLine("The first number is " + Number1
                + "\nThe second number is " + Number2 + "\n");
        }
    }
}
```

The integer data type uses less memory than the other basic numerical data types; thus, it is the format of choice for programming tasks that do not require a floating point (real number) variable. You can also increase or reduce an integer's storage size by replacing

C# and Game Programming

that keyword with any of the other seven predefined integer data types: byte, sbyte, ushort, short, uint, ulong, and long. Byte and sbyte require the least amount of systems RAM, with 8 bits of unsigned and signed allocated space and a range of 0 to 255 and -128 to 127, respectively. Ushort/short also reduces the amount of storage space needed by a variable while ulong/long increases that amount. Increasing the size allows you to input larger integers, while decreasing it saves system memory (see Example 1.19).

Example 1.19. Using data types `ulong/long` and `ushort/short`.

```
using System;

namespace Chapter1 {
    class Class1 {
        static void Main() {
            ushort Number1;  // unsigned short
            long Number2;    // long integer

            Number1 = 1;
            Number2 = 1;
            Console.WriteLine("The first number is " + Number1
                + "\nThe second number is " + Number2 + "\n");
        }
    }
}
```

The unsigned data types, *byte, ushort, uint,* and *ulong* (all other variables are signed by default) do not actually modify a variable's memory capacity, rather, they merely alter the range of those variables. An unsigned *short (ushort)*, for example, gives us twice the upper limit by shifting the total range from -32,768, -32,767 to 0, 65,535 (for a complete list of ranges, see Table 1.3).

The Data Types `float` and `double`

The data types `float` and `double` are both floating point data types, and thus can be explained together. Floating point arithmetic allows higher precision in calculations. Some floating point values are shown in Example 1.20.

Example 1.20. Floating point values.

1.0	2.5	5.15
7.146	18.001	178.01

C# uses the keywords float and double in nearly the same way, but doubles have twice the precision. Doubles are twice as accurate as floats and do not suffer the same risk of data loss when assigned to constants. The precision range of a float is seven digits ($\pm 1.5 \times 10^{-45}$ to $\pm 3.4 \times 10^{38}$), while the range for doubles is 15–16 digits ($\pm 5.0 \times 10^{-324}$ to $\pm 1.7 \times 10^{308}$). Examples 1.21 and 1.22 demonstrate these keywords.

Example 1.21. Using data type `float`.

```csharp
using System;

namespace Chapter1 {
    class Class1 {
        static void Main() {
            float Number1, Number2; // float is short for floating point
            Number1 = 1.0f; // using the f converter
            Number2 = 1.1f; // to convert to float

            Console.WriteLine("The first number is " + Number1
                + "\nThe second number is " + Number2 + "\n");
        }
    }
}
```

Example 1.22. Using data type `double`.

```csharp
using System;

namespace Chapter1 {
    class Class1 {
        static void Main() {
            double Number1, Number2;
```

```
            Number1 = 1.0;
            Number2 = 1.1;

            Console.WriteLine("The first number is " + Number1
                + "\nThe second number is " + Number2 + "\n");
        }
    }
}
```

The Data Type `decimal`

In addition to the basic data types, there are also several expanded data types (including the predefined integer types listed earlier and several advanced types that we'll hold off on until later). This section introduces probably the most obvious of the floating point values, the `decimal`.

The decimal is, of course, used to calculate monetary equations that bring the highest level of accuracy to the dollar amount (see Example 1.23). Note: Conversion from literal constants to the decimal data type require the M symbol to indicate a decimal amount = 1.50M.

Example 1.23. Using data type `decimal`.

```
using System;

namespace Chapter1 {
    class Class1 {
        static void Main() {
            decimal Number1, Number2;
            Number1 = 1.0M;
            Number2 = 1.1m;

            Console.WriteLine("The first number is " + Number1
                + "\nThe second number is " + Number2 + "\n");
        }
    }
}
```

The Data Types `character` and `string`

The `character` (`char`) and `string` data types are declared and assigned in the same manner as the numeric variables, the main difference being that they allow for the storage of characters rather than numeric information. Technically, numbers are also included in this list of characters, but their values are not equivalent to their numeric counterparts. Character variables are declared using the keyword `char`, and can be assigned through user input and/or as a part of a declaration/assignment. They are only capable of holding a single character value, and are assigned using single quotation marks.

Strings, in contrast, allow for multiple character storage. A host of words, or sentences, can be placed inside of a single string variable. Strings can also take input from outside sources, including direct input, stored files, etc. They are assigned using double quotation marks (see Example 1.24). Traditionally, the character data type consumed the smallest amount of system RAM (8 bits); however, this changed with the introduction of the new Unicode standard (16 bits). The change represents a move to a universal character base that includes most of the world's languages, which is, of course, an important part of international commerce (Unicode is explained in more detail in Chapter 3).

Example 1.24. The `character` and `string` data types.

```
using System;

namespace Chapter1 {
    class Class1 {
        static void Main() {
            char Symbol;
            string Sentence;
            Symbol = 'A';
            Sentence = "This is a string.";

            Console.WriteLine("The first letter in the alphabet is "
                + Symbol + ".");
            Console.WriteLine(Sentence);
        }
    }
}
```

 Note: We can also use the "@" symbol to create a literal string, for example: Console.Writeline(@ "The \n character is neat.") This example is slightly obvious – the string will print out "The \n character is neat." Without the @, it would print out "The
Character is neat."

Names	CTS Type	Description	Approximate Range
Sbyte	System.SByte	8-bit signed integer	-128 to 127
Short	System.Int16	16-bit signed integer	-32768 to 32767
Int	System.Int32	32-bit signed integer	-2,147,483,648 to 2,147,483,647
Long	System.Int64	64-bit signed integer	-9223372036854775808 to 9223372036854775807
Byte	System.Byte	8-bit unsigned integer	0 to 255
Ushort	System.UInt16	16-bit unsigned integer	0 to 65,535
Uint	System.UInt32	32-bit unsigned integer	0 to 4,294,967,295
Ulong	System.UInt64	64-bit unsigned integer	0 to 18,446,744,073,709,551,615
Float	System.Single	32-bit single precision floating-point	$\pm 1.5 \times 10^{-45}$ to $\pm 3.4 \times 10^{38}$
Double	System.Double	64-bit double precision floating-point	$\pm 5.0 \times 10^{-324}$ to $\pm 1.7 \times 10^{308}$
decimal	System.Decimal	128-bit high precision decimal notation	$\pm 1.0 \times 10^{-28}$ to $\pm 7.9 \times 10^{28}$
Char	System.Char	16-bit Unicode character	N/A
String	System.String	Unicode character string	N/A
Bool	System.Boolean	true & false values	N/A
Object	System.Object	Type root	N/A

Table 1.3. Approximate storage capacities.

Keywords `sizeof` and `unsafe`

As with C++, C# can use the `sizeof` keyword to gather information pertaining to the size of data types. Unfortunately, this also requires the use of a secondary command, `unsafe`, which is used to mark the unsafe nature of that code. The practicality of using such coding is limited, considering that it takes us out of the .Net environment and puts us back in the anarchical world of Windows API. There are, however, legitimate reasons for reverting to that standard; one example is backward compatibility, and another is performance issues. The steps to enable `unsafe` mode, as well as a simple `sizeof` program, are shown in Example 1.25).

Example 1.25. Sizeof and unsafe mode.

```
using System;

namespace Chapter1 {
    class Class1 {
        static unsafe void Main() {
            Console.WriteLine("Byte = " + sizeof(byte));
            Console.WriteLine("Sbyte = " + sizeof(sbyte));
            Console.WriteLine("Ushort = " + sizeof(ushort));
            Console.WriteLine("Short = " + sizeof(short));
            Console.WriteLine("Uint = " + sizeof(uint));
            Console.WriteLine("Int = " + sizeof(int));
            Console.WriteLine("Ulong = " + sizeof(ulong));
            Console.WriteLine("Long = " + sizeof(long));
            Console.WriteLine("Float = " + sizeof(float));
            Console.WriteLine("Double = " + sizeof(double));
            Console.WriteLine("Decimal = " + sizeof(decimal));
        }
    }
}
```

Enabling unsafe mode in C#

Once a project is loaded into the .Net compiler, it becomes a simple matter of altering that project's build configuration to enable `unsafe` mode.

1. From the folder labeled "View," select the file titled "Solution Explorer" (see Screen Shot 1.7).

C# and Game Programming

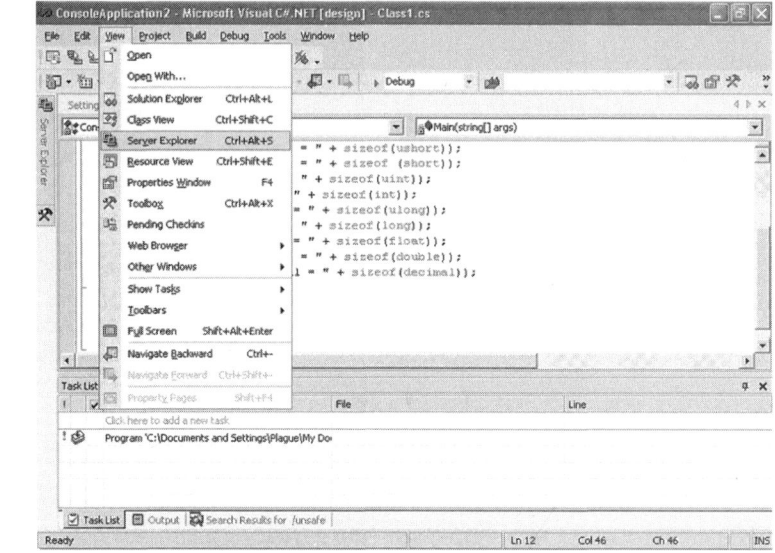

Screen Shot 1.7

2. A second side window will open—make sure to highlight the project rather than the file name. Select "Properties," the third icon depicted in that smaller window (see Screen Shot 1.8).

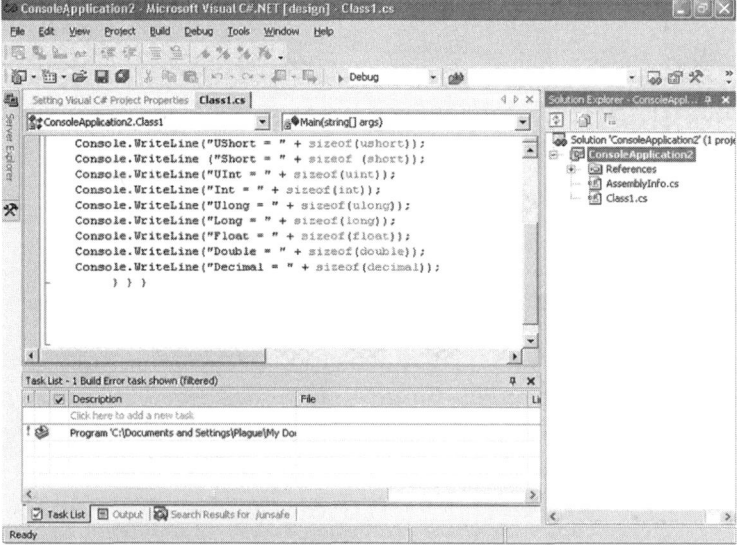

Screen Shot 1.8

Chapter 1: C# from the Beginning

3. Now go to the listing labeled "Configuration Properties." Select "Build" from that sublist and click on the "False" value under "Allow Unsafe Code Blocks." From there, an arrow will appear—use it to select the "True" setting, press "Apply," and then "OK" to finish (see Screen Shot 1.9).

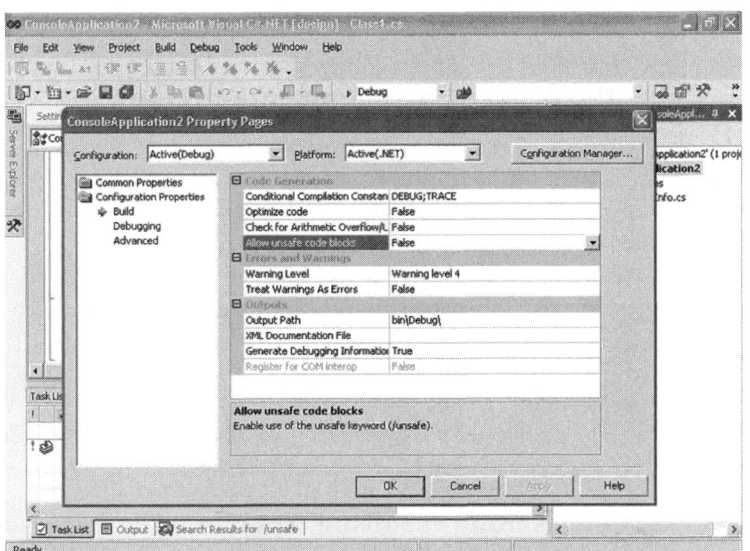

Screen Shot 1.9

The Data Type `void`

As previously mentioned, `void` is a data type that holds no data. It thus serves the purpose of telling the compiler that a variable or returning function requires no data, which is logical since the ending of the main function is also the ending of the program, and there would be no program to receive information. The data type `void` is also most commonly associated with user-defined functions that use reference variables (explained in Chapter 2) and generalized pointer-variables (explained in Chapter 4). Unlike the other data types, `void` does not take a position in memory. Therefore, we don't need to measure its size in bytes.

Assignment Statements

One other aspect of the above examples remains to be explained, namely, the equal sign (also known as the *assignment operator*). Quite obviously, using an equal sign means to make the variable equal to whatever number we assign, and is therefore known as an *assignment statement*. This works equally well for assigning a variable to a literal constant or a referenced variable (as demonstrated in Example 1.26).

Example 1.26. Using the equal sign assignment operator.

```
number_shown = x + 1;
    // Arithmetic will be explained later in this chapter
```

Unlike mathematical expressions, assignment statements are always formulated with the receiving variable positioned to the left. Example 1.26, although similar to an algebraic expression, does not involve any inference of data. In fact, an unreferenced or undefined variable used to assign such a value would result in the minimum of a compiler warning (see Example 1.27).

Example 1.27. Compiler warning resulting from an undefined variable.

```
- int n, x = 2, y;
// Any variable assigned to another
// variable must by requirement be
- n = x + 1;
// assigned a value itself, before
// that secondary assignment can occur.
n = y + 1;
// variable referenced without being assigned a value.
```

Type Compatibility: Implicit Conversions

Before we begin to combine numbers in the form of equations, we have to make sure that their data types are compatible. Numeric data types, as you remember, were `byte`, `short`, `int`, `long`, `float`, `double`, and `decimal`. The best way to calculate and assign these data types is to use their matching data types (for example; *short* to *short*, *float* to *float*, and *double* to *double*), but when this is not possible, converting between data types is an option. The safest data conversions always involve converting from smaller to larger data types, e.g., `short` to `int`, `int` to `long`, `long` to `float`, and `float` to `double`, or any of the smaller to larger types (see Table 1.3 for data type sizes). Any other type of conversion may result in the loss of data and/or a calculation error. Since `float`, `double`, and `decimal` are all floating point values, you may not notice a problem when preparing your algorithm (that's not to say there wouldn't be a problem, just that you might not notice it). The worst type of intermixing would be from floating point to integer, which would be allowed under native C/C++, but C# demands that any integration between our data types is strictly regulated. That said, many programmers still write programs that involve the intermixing of these larger to smaller data types relying on compiler defaults to calculate them in their favor.

Dear IRS, in regards to my last SEVEN tax returns: There was a slight error in my program's ability to convert data types and although it was quite an amusing error...

Formatting Strings

In addition to being able to display simple text layouts using the `Write` and `WriteLine` commands, we can also format text to give our programs a more controlled output. This works especially well when dealing with variables. A single numeric value indicates a reference to the appropriate variable: {0}, {1}, and {2} reference the first, second, and third variables, respectively. Moreover, we can also apply right and left justifications by inserting a secondary control sequence for example, inserting a positive number, as in {0, 6}, denotes a shift to the right, in this case 6 spaces, whereas the insertion of a negative control sequence results in a left-handed shift: {0, -3} would move the cursor three spaces to the left.

We can also exert a third level of control, which involves string formatting, for example {0, -3:C2}, where C stands of our local currency and 2 represents the number of decimal places to be displayed (See Table 1.4 for a complete list of formatting strings). Finally, we can use the

C# and Game Programming

numeric symbol (#) as a placeholder, as in Console.WriteLine ("{0.#.00}", variable); (for further examples, see the Arithmetic section).

String Format	Description
C	Currency (local)
D	Decimal (decimal point)
E	Exponential (Scientific Notation)
F	Fixed point
G	General (E or F, to reduce space)
N	Number (inserts commas, e.g., 1,313.02)
P	Percent
X	Hexadecimal

Table 1.4. Commands for formatting strings.

Arithmetic

Using arithmetic operators in C# is much like using a handheld calculator or doing arithmetic on paper. There aren't any formulas or fancy codes to remember, it's just adding, subtracting, multiplying, dividing, and finding remainders (yes, remainders, like the ones you use to find before learning long division). Since we've already seen an example of adding that's where we'll start. To add two or more numbers together we'll have to use the plus sign (+). Nevertheless, you can't just write "1 + 1 =" and expect the computer to do the rest—you'll have to write it out into a program as shown in Example 1.28.

Example 1.28. Integer addition.

```
using System;

namespace Chapter1 {
    class Class1 {
        static void Main() {
```

```
            int number1, number2, total; // these are my variables
            number1 = 5;
            number2 = 2; // did you notice they're both integers?
            total = number1 + number2;

            Console.WriteLine("{0} + {1} = {2} ",
                number1, number2, total);
        }
    }
}
```

> **Program Walkthrough**
>
> This program starts with the normal introductory comments—the using and namespace references (remember, these references are required when working with our Base Class Library). Next, there's the void data type linked to Main. Then as we start the main method, we declare three variables, all of type integer. We assign the first two variables values of 5 and 2 using the assignment operator (=). Then, something new: We tell the computer to make the third variable equal to the sum of the other two. Finally, we displayed the equation "5 + 2 = 7."

Try compiling and running this program and you'll see that the WriteLine command displays our equation. You can also change the variables to any positive or negative whole number. Recompile and watch the display change.

Not surprisingly, subtraction, multiplication, and division are used in exactly the same manner (see Examples 1.29–1.31). You can retype each example or just reedit the first one to match the changes; you might also want to experiment with alternate data types, comments, and the variables names.

Example 1.29. Integer subtraction.

```
using System;

namespace Chapter1 {
    class Class1 {
        static void Main() {
            int number1, number2, total;
            number1 = 5;
            number2 = 2;
            total = number1 - number2;  /* 5 - 2 */
```

```
            Console.WriteLine(" {0,3}\n-{1,3}\n ---\n {2,3}",
                number1, number2, total);
            Console.WriteLine("\n {0,3:D}\n-{1,3:D}\n ---\n {2,3:D}",
                number1, number2, total);
            Console.WriteLine("\n {0,3:X}\n-{1,3:X}\n ---\n {2,3:X}",
                number1, number2, total);
        }
    }
}
```

To multiply and divide, use the asterisk (*) and the forward slash (/), respectively.

Example 1.30. Multiplication with data type `float`.

```
using System;

namespace Chapter1 {
    class Class1 {
        static void Main() {
            float number1, number2, total;
            number1 = 5.0F;     // When using float include an F
            number2 = 2.0f;
            total = number1 * number2;   /* 5 Multiplied by 2 */

            Console.WriteLine(" {0,3:C2}\nx  {1,3:F}\n ---\n {2,3:C2}",
                number1, number2, total);
        }
    }
}
```

Example 1.31. Division with data type `double`.

```
using System;

namespace Chapter1 {
    class Class1 {
```

```
static void Main() {
    double number1, number2, total;
    number1 = 5.0;
    number2 = 2.0;
    total = number1 / number2; /* 5 divided by 2 */

    Console.WriteLine (" {0,3:E}\n/ {1,3:E}\n ---\n  {2,3:E}",
        number1, number2, total);
    Console.WriteLine ("\n {0,3:F}\n/ {1,3:F}\n ---\n  {2,3:F}",
        number1, number2, total);
    Console.WriteLine ("\n {0,3:G}\n/ {1,3:G}\n ---\n  {2,3:G}",
        number1, number2, total);
  }
 }
}
```

We can also use combinations of symbols, as shown in Example 1.32. This example maintains the values for number1 and number2 as previously introduced; it multiplies them together (5 x 2 equals 10) and then adds the value of number1 to that product (10 + 5= 15).

Example 1.32. Order of operations 1.

```
Total = number1 * number2 + number1;
       15 = 5 * 2 + 5
```

To change the order of the calculation, use parentheses as shown in Example 1.33. This equation now adds the last two numbers first and then multiples their sum by the first value working left to right(in the default), multiplication and division take precedence over addition and subtraction, making the total 35, showing the importance of defining the order of operations.

Example 1.33. Order of operations 2.

```
Total = number1 * (number2 + number1);
       35 = 5 * (2 + 5)
```

In some cases, the order of calculations can be left to the default settings, but most of the time we'll want to guarantee the order of execution through the enlistment of parenthetical expressions. Example 1.34 shows how confusing an undistinguished expression can be, while Example 1.35 clears up much of the confusion with a minor bit of effort.

Example 1.34. Order of operations 3.

```
Total = number1 * number2 / number1 + number2 - number1;
    By order of operations: 5 * 2 / 5 + 2 - 5 = -1
```

Example 1.35. Order of operations 4.

```
Total = ((number1 * number2)/number1) + number2 - number1;
    By order of parentheses: ((5 * 2) /5) + 2 - 5 = -1
```

There is one last arithmetic symbol, but its meaning isn't as obvious. It is the remainder, as in, to find the remainder of a number divided by a second number. Example 1.36 gives a sample of how to write this in a program.

Example 1.36. The remainder symbol.

```
Total = number1 % number2;
// the remainder of 5 divided by 2 is 1.
```

Since we have been using the data type `integer`, 5 divided by 2 is not 2.5, but 2, because, the result is the truncated integers(by definition are whole numbers) and therefore a whole number; thus, we use the remainder symbol (%) to find the remainder (see Example 1.37).

Example 1.37. The remainder symbol with data type `integer`.

```
using System;
namespace Chapter1 {
```

```
class Class1 {
    static void Main() {
        int number1, number2, total, remainder;
        number1 = 5;
        number2 = 2;

        total = number1 / number2;
        remainder = number1 % number2;
        Console.WriteLine("\n   {0,7:N}\n/ {1,7:N}\n ---\n   {2,7:N}",
            number1, number2, total);
        Console.WriteLine("And the remainder is {0,7:N}", remainder);
        Console.WriteLine("\nAnd the remainder is {0:#.00}",
remainder);

        double percent, num1 = 5.0, num2 = 2.0;
        percent = num2 / num1;
        Console.WriteLine("\n{0} is {1,0:P} of {2}",
            num2, percent, num1);
    }
}
}
```

If you find any of the equations confusing, try rewriting them out on paper, choose some new numbers, and see if you can predict their outcome; then when you're ready move on to the next section, which, by the way, finally explains how to input data from the keyboard.

Function	Symbol	Written as
1. Addition	+	total = number1 + number2;
2. Subtraction	-	total = number1 − number2;
3. Multiplication	*	total = number1 * number2;
4. Division	/	total = number1 / number2;
5. Remainder	%	total = number1 % number2;

Table 1.5. Arithmetic Operators.

Keyboard Input

The Read and ReadLine commands, as their names imply, allow us to input information from the keyboard. Both statements are written as console methods, similar to the Write commands, the difference being that they are used to extract information rather than project it. The basic Read command is only capable of storing single character inputs (see Example 1.38). The ReadLine method, in contrast, can input virtually all data types. Doing so, however, requires a *parse* conversion reference that is linked to the appropriate data type, with *string* as the default setting. Parse, like the ReadLine and WriteLine, is not actually a keyword, but rather a referencing method available through the .Net architecture via the "system" reference.

Example 1.38. The Read command.

```
using System;

namespace Chapter1 {
    class Class1 {
        static void Main() {
            char character;
            int integer;

            Console.WriteLine("Enter a number here: ");
            integer = Console.Read();
            character = (char) integer;
            Console.WriteLine("And the number you entered is "
                + character);
        }
    }
}
```

Program Walkthrough

Like all of the previous programs, this one begins with a comment describing its purpose. The .Net system is referenced, and the void data type declares the main function. The first statement prints the text line "Enter a number here." Now the ReadLine function waits for the user to input a number. When a number is entered, the program will store this information into the variable my_number. The program will then reprint its value after the words "The number you entered is:" This process can be repeated for any of the real number data types, as well as the character data type—see Example 1.39.

Example 1.39. The ReadLine command with various data types.

```
using System;

namespace Chapter1 {
    class Class1 {
        static void Main() {
            string Name, convert;
            float RealNumber;

            Console.WriteLine("Enter a number here: ");
            convert = Console.ReadLine();

            Console.WriteLine("Enter your name here: ");
            Name = Console.ReadLine();

            RealNumber = float.Parse(convert);
            Console.WriteLine("Your name is " + Name);
            Console.WriteLine("And the number you entered is "
                + RealNumber);
        }
    }
}
```

Uninitialized Variables

Another key component of the C# language and .Net 2003 compiler is the inaccessibility of undeclared variables. This new standard produces an error rather than a warning upon any attempt to access that unassigned memory location. The decision to change was based primarily on the need to offset the abundance of minor errors found when those unassigned values were represented by random data access. Understandably, if we do not filter out those random value, our results become unpredictable and subsequently useless in any matter of importance. Keep in mind that we have been properly declaring and initializing variables throughout this text. Moreover, in our last few examples, we even expanded upon the methods used to assign those variables. However, the most practical of all the methods is to include an assignment statement at the moment of declaration, thereby removing any chance of error (see Example 1.40).

Example 1.40. Declaring and initializing variables.

```
using System;

namespace Chapter1 {
    class Class1 {
        static void Main(string[] args) {
            int OurVariable = 1;
            Console.WriteLine("Our variable was assigned as "
                + OurVariable);
        }
    }
}
```

Access Modifiers: `constant`, `Readonly`, and `volatile`

We can also simultaneously declare and initialize variables using the variable type `constant`. A constant variable cannot change its value after it has been specified (this is also true for the `readonly` modifier). Declaring a constant variable is similar to our last example, but with the added keyword `const`, which, of course, stands for constant. Adding the keyword `const` notifies the compiler of its unchanging nature and allows it to optimize strange space for that value (see Example 1.41).

Example 1.41. Declaring constant variables.

```
using System;

namespace Chapter1 {
    class Class1 {
        static void Main() {
            const int OurVariable = 1;
            Console.WriteLine("Our variable was assigned as "
                + OurVariable);
        }
    }
}
```

Adding the keyword `const` to a variable of data type `float`, `double`, or `char` would make them constants as well. Keep in mind that their values also have to be assigned as they are declared (see Example 1.42).

Example 1.42. Constant variables of various data types.

```
using System;

namespace ConsoleApplication1 {
    class Class1 {
        static void Main() {
            const int number1 = 1;
            const float number2 = 2.5F;
            const double number3 = 3.14159; // PI
            const char symbol1 = 'A';
            const string sentence = "This is a constant string!";

            Console.WriteLine("This is a constant of type integer "
                + number1);
            Console.WriteLine("This is a constant of type float "
                + number2);
            Console.WriteLine("This is a constant of type double "
                + number3);
            Console.WriteLine("This is a constant of type char "
                + symbol1);
            Console.WriteLine(sentence);
        }
    }
}
```

Readonly is also a constant data type used as part of a class reference (declared as a field—see the Methods section in Chapter 5); it is assignable at only one point in the program and then acts as a constant. In contrast, the keyword volatile (also addressed in Chapter 5) expresses that the variable it precedes will change dramatically. For example, that value may be altered by the system's clock, or used to pass data to a component in hardware. In either case, foregoing the volatile command will result in the compiler automatically limiting that variable (this is done to optimize the program's performance). Thus, in order to keep a variable's access open to many possibilities, we'll need to insert the volatile command before such variables (see Example 1.43).

Example 1.43. Readonly and volatile.

```
namespace Chapter1 {
    class Class1 {
        public readonly double variable2 = 3.14159;
```

```
        public volatile char variable3 = 'A';

        static void Main() {
            /* This is a do nothing program */
        }
    }
}
```

> **#define:** Unlike C and C++, C# cannot use the preprocessor directive `#define` to declare constant variables. It does, however, allow for a Boolean type assignment, which signals to the compiler that a certain definition has either been defined (interpreted as true) or not defined (interpreted as false)—see preprocessor directives in Chapter 5 for details.

Incrementing and Decrementing Operators

The incrementing (++) and decrementing (– –) operators increase and decrease their variables by one numeric value, respectively. This holds true for all numeric data types, including the standard integer, floating point, or decimal references (character information is handled differently). The operators can be used in either *postfix mode* (*x*++) or *prefix mode* (++*x*). Prefix mode refers to a calculation that must occur before a variable is accessed by a secondary equation, whereas postfix mode allows for that variable to be read, equated, and then altered after the completion of the equation. There are, of course, advantages to each type, and the latter explains the pun C++. Use Example 1.44 to test these operators. You should revise the example using several of the other numeric data types, as well as both postfix and prefix modes.

Example 1.44. Incrementing operators I.

```
using System;

namespace Chapter1 {
    class Class1 {
        static void Main(string[] args) {
            int number = 1;
```

```
            number++;

            Console.WriteLine("The number is " + number++); // 2
            Console.WriteLine("The number is " + number); // 3
        }
    }
}
```

Example 1.45. Incrementing operators II.

```
using System;

namespace Chapter1 {
    class Class1 {
        static void Main(string [] args) {
            int number = 1;
            number++;

            Console.WriteLine("The number is " + ++number); // 3
            Console.WriteLine("The number is " + number); // 3
        }
    }
}
```

Type Safety versus Metonym Data Types

A metonymic expression is a name or phrase used to identify an object or person that goes beyond their basic description or that of their official designation. This could mean giving a pet name to a car or referring to a friend by their screen name. In either case, you are just identifying the person, place, or thing with an alternate name. C and C++ use the keyword *typedef* (which literally means to define what's entered) to add additional names for data types, but this is not permitted in C#. As stated from the beginning, C# is a strong typed language; it cannot use access modifiers to create unsigned or extended data types, and it does not allow for the ambiguity permitted by user-defined data types. Thus, if a C/C++ command is encountered, remember that it can be quickly replaced with the appropriate explicit definition (see Examples 1.46 and 1.47).

Example 1.46. C++.

```
#include <iostream>
using namespace std;

void main (void) {
    typedef int cat; // cat becomes a metonym for int
    cat number = 1;
}
```

Example 1.47. C#.

```
using System;

namespace Chapter1 {
    class Class1 {
        static void Main() {
            int number = 1;
        }
    }
} // no ambiguity here
```

Keyword Defaults

The C/C++ language includes a few keywords, namely `auto` and `signed`, used to declare actions that are equivalent to the system's default settings. These keywords are not of the C# language, but they are still important when dealing with upgrading. The first of these, `auto`, a storage class specifier, is used to express the need for each variable declared under that title to be localized as a single function, where localized means created when the block is opened and destroyed as the block is closed. This action is part of the definition used to describe local variables and hence `auto` is not needed when declaring C# variables. The keyword *auto* goes back to the days of the B language, and only exists now to keep a backward compatibility with some older C programs.

`Signed`, allows variables to hold both positive and negative values; again, something we assume when declaring variables. Using the reverse, `unsigned`, is very common in C++ and is usually an attempt to save memory while increasing an integer's positive range, but alas, it too has no real practical value, i.e., you won't see it much, but when you do, you'll need to understand the concept behind it.

Using, System, and Namespace

One very noticeable change from C++ to C# is the altered use of the *iostream* classes, and hence, the keywords `using` and `namespace`. These redefined commands are a result of the larger object-oriented changes found in the Base Class Libraries. The most notable alterations include the reference to the namespace `System` (as in `using System`), and the external user-defined `namespaces` (as in `Chapter1`, etc.). `System` is one of the larger namespaces developed for the Base Class Library, with our own `Chapter1` representing a much smaller grouping. We can also nest and/or expand[1] those namespaces to include a hierarchical structure. While we've already worked with many of the abbreviated examples, it is also important to become familiar with the extended form (as in Example 1.48).

> When we place our coding inside a `namespace`, we are actually declaring a scope or globally unique partition. The types contained in that `namespace` are then accessible through both direct access (from within that body) and through the `using` namespace-directive, which allows us to use its values without qualification.

Example 1.48. Not using using.

```
namespace Chapter1 {
    class Class1 {
        static void Main() {
            System.Console.WriteLine("Hello, World!");
        }
    }
}
```

Additionally, if we were to encounter a secondary `namespace` that offered an identical, thus conflicting reference, then there would be few options that didn't include writing out an alias to the formal definition or the formal definition (see Example 1.49).

. . . .
[1] That is, to include within a secondary or multiple set of files.

Example 1.49. **Using and namespace.**

```
using sys = System;

namespace Chapter1 {
    class Class1 {
        static void Main() {
            sys.Console.WriteLine("Hello, world!");
        }
    }
}
```

Hungarian Notation

Hungarian notation, named for the ethnicity of its developer Charles Simonyi, is Microsoft's formal way of identifying variables based on their data types. This notation is used by many programmers, especially those who work for Microsoft, and it is not limited to the C++ language. The notation uses prefixes attached to variables that are always written in lowercase. For example, the prefix that identifies a character is simply the letter c, thus, a declaration of a character can be as simple as (`char cVariable;`). The integer data type is identified with the letter i, the letter n identifies a short integer, and l indicates a long integer (e.g., `int ipassword; short nID;` and `lAccount`). (Note: While there is less of a need for such notation, we still use Pascal/Camel Notation as part of our C# references—see Table 1.6).

> Hungarian notation does not include prefixes for the data types `float`, `double`, or `decimal`. This makes sense, since they're all floating point variables and the lack of notation is in essence a form of notation.

We might also consider the reasoning that floating point variables should always reflect their data requirements, and should only be converted or declared using higher precision data types in order to avoid data loss.

Data Types:	Prefixes
Boolean	b
BYTE (unsigned char)	by
Character (for types char, WCHAR, and TCHAR)	c
Integer used as x, y lengths (c stands for count).	cx, cy
Double WORD (unsigned long integer)	dw
Function	Fn
Handle	H
Integers	i
Integer used as x, y coordinates	x, y
f stands for "flags"	f
Long Integers	l
String	S
String terminated by 0 character	Sz
Pointer	p
Short Integers	n
WORD (unsigned short integer)	w

Table 1.6. Prefixes for various data types.

Troubleshooting

Before going through the steps involved in the process of troubleshooting, let's make sure that we understand the four basic types of errors. The first type, known as a *syntax error*, is what might be described as a grammatical error. The compiler, acting as a spell-checker, looks through our programs trying to find any and all misspelled commands and/or forgotten punctuation marks. If it finds any errors, the compiler immediately sends notification and directs us to the problem. Programs with this type of error cannot be "built", and thus no linkable objects are produced.

The second type of error is known as a *runtime error*. Runtime errors usually involve asking the computer to do something it can't, such as dividing by zero or storing a character as a number. This type of error will not be detected by the compiler and will almost always produce a program prone to problems and crashes, or one which will just not run.

The third type of error is a *logic error*, which could also be called the poor planning error. Examples of this type include telling the computer to subtract when you meant for it to add, or telling it to skip a line when you wanted it to print. Not thinking out the problem and/or not writing out an algorithm usually causes this type of error. Logic errors, like runtime errors, won't usually show up when you're compiling, but they're sure to show up at some point. The best way to detect a problem of this nature is to rerun the program for several situations and, if possible, to recheck the results against a secondary source.

The fourth type of error, described as a *linking error*, occurs when data is missing, faulty, or just unavailable at the time of compilation. If your program compiles without errors, but there are errors when you build/rebuild it, then you've more then likely made a mistake setting up your program. If your compiler is not mentioned in this chapter, you must consult your user manual to find the problem. If you're using Microsoft Visual Studio .Net 2004 or any of the earlier versions, repeating the aforementioned procedures should solve your problem.

Common Errors, Problems, and Pitfalls

1. Like C and C++, C# is a case-sensitive language; thus, any discrepancy in case settings will result in an error. For example, incorrectly writing void as either VOID or Void would result in a syntax error. (Hint: Most compilers identify keywords with a change in color).
2. The main method should have the word Main followed by both opening and closing parentheses.
3. The program should begin with an opening brace, e.g., {and end with a closing brace}.
4. Comments require two forward slashes, as in //, not back slashes \\. In addition, comments spanning two or more lines require

both an opening forward slash and an asterisk, and a closing asterisk and forward slash, as in /* comments here */.
5. If you can't find the error, try removing all the comments and any other unnecessary coding, saving the file under a different name so that you can revert back to the original after you've isolated the error
6. Braces placed after a comment (as in // this is a note}) are included as part of the comment and will not be read by the compiler.
7. The newline character must be written as forward slash n (/n); using the back slash will result in a syntax error.
8. Both the Write and WriteLine commands require encapsulating parentheses.
9. If you're using an older C++ compiler, you'll need to use #include <iostream> and the namespace std or <iostream.h> header without using the namespace commands.
10. Did you follow the rules given in this chapter on naming variables? Breaking these rules usually causes syntax errors.
11. One error can cause your compiler to spit out several compiling errors; thus you should always attempt to recompile your program if no other errors seem likely.
12. Did you misspell the variable's name? Undefined statement errors are usually caused by such misspellings.
13. Did you forget the comma when adding several variables to a single line?
14. Did you forget a semicolon or did you put one were it wasn't suppose to be?
15. Did you forget the single quote or use double quotes when assigning a character variable?
16. You must use an integer value when calculating a remainder.
17. Listing any keywords or variables with a space between the letters is always an error.

If your program compiles without errors, but there are errors when you build/rebuild them, then you've more then likely made a mistake setting up your program. If your compiler is not mentioned in this chapter, you must consult your user manual to find the problem. If you are using Microsoft Visual Studio .Net 7.0 or any of the earlier versions, you more than likely selected "Win32 Application" without the word "Console," or one of the other choices. In any event, you should carefully repeat the steps given for setup.

> **Things to Remember**
>
> 1. When creating a new compiler project always set it to "Console."
> 2. Most compilers change keywords to blue, green, or red (Microsoft uses blue); if a keyword doesn't change color it just might be misspelled.
> 3. After a program is compiled and linked, it can then be executed from either the Windows MS-DOS prompt or its executable Windows icon (XP, ME, and Windows 2000 all have MS-DOS prompts, they've just been relocated to a spot under the "Accessories" submenu).
> 4. Comments should be used to explain source coding and to mark important points.
> 5. Using integers or bytes reduces the amount of RAM (Random Access Memory) that your program will need. Games that use less RAM can be played on more computers (also, the extra RAM can be used to improve graphics and sounds or just plain speed things up).
> 6. When using floating point variables, you can save memory by choosing *float* over *double*.
> 7. The character data type can only hold one letter or symbol and uses the single quote (don't worry, there are ways to store whole words, and even sentences, but they're several chapters away).
> 8. Variables should not be read without first being initialized.
> 9. The user cannot change variables declared as constants; using the keyword `volatile` prevents unwanted optimization.
> 10. Indenting makes things easier to read but does not affect the way the computer reads the material.
> 11. Although your compiler doesn't care about good grammar, you should make sure to use proper spacing, including adding one space after each comma and spaces between arithmetic operators.

12. You should take the time to study your operating system and compiler; feel free to experiment with keywords and commands—try to get a feel for what they do and where on the screen they do it.
13. Avoid variable names that start with single or double underscores, as these may cause conflicts with advanced assignment statements.
14. Use parentheses rather than relying on the order of operations when using arithmetic operators. Using excess parentheses won't harm your program, but excluding necessary ones will. The key is to make things clear through the use of spacing and a comfortable amount of parentheses.
15. Finally, don't worry about rushing to the end or trying to jump right into the advanced code. Everything you'll need is in this book; you'll just have to be patient.

Questions

1. Define the terms .Net and C#.
2. Who was the chief architect of C#?
3. Who is the author of this book?
4. What is ECMA certification?
5. Define managed code.
6. Write an algorithm that explains how to play the card game fifty-two pickup.
7. Write and compile a "do-nothing" program.
8. Define the types of comments used in C#.
9. Write a "do-nothing" program that includes an initial comment describing the programs purpose and then two other comments marking the beginning and the ending of the main method.
10. Write a program that displays the words "Hey, look at me! I've written a program!"
11. Continuing from Question 10, use the newline character to separate "Hey, look at me!" from "I've written a program!"
12. Continuing from Question 10, use the `WriteLine` command, replace the newline character without altering the programs output.

13. Write a program that declares four separate variables using the data types `int, float, double,` and `char`.
14. Continuing from Question 13, add four additional lines of coding that assign appropriate values to each of the listed variables.
15. Continuing from Question 13, using only the declared statements, assign appropriate values to each variable.
16. Using only integers, write a program that adds and then subtracts two numbers.
17. Using either single or double precision values, write a program that first multiplies and then divides two numbers.
18. Write a program that finds the digits after the decimal point for any irrational number.
19. Write a program that reads in a character and echoes it back using both `Write` and `WriteLine`.
20. Write a program that uses both incrementing and decrementing operators.

Branches, Loops, and Functions

*I long to accomplish a great and noble task,
but it is my chief duty to accomplish small
tasks as if they were great and noble.*
—**Helen Keller**

This chapter covers the basic control sequences, including comparisons and iterations. It also covers an introduction to methods, basic polymorphism (overloading), and recursion. Mathematical abbreviations are also discussed in this chapter, as well as Boolean expressions, short circuit evaluations, and type casting.

The `if` Statement

Before we can begin to write even the simplest of games, we'll have to first offer our players some choices. These choices will enable players to choose correctly or incorrectly, which consequently will allow them to either win or lose. Luckily, C# offers an abundance of ways to accomplish this task; the simplest of these is the `if` statement, thus, this is where we'll begin.

All of our programs have followed a single path. That is, they do one step and then the next without regard for our input. Example 2.1 demonstrates this nonresponsive, linear form of programming. To test this program, try inputting something other then the requested data.

C# and Game Programming

Example 2.1. A nonresponsive program.

```
using System;

namespace Chapter2 {
    class Class1 {
        static void Main() {
            // Begin main
            int cResponse;

            // Step 1 - try typing N for NO
            Console.WriteLine ("Input <Y> for YES: ");

            // Step 2
            cResponse = Console.Read ();

            // Step 3
            Console.WriteLine ("\n You typed Y\n");
        }
    }
}
```

Now, in order to make this program respond correctly (i.e., responding where the proper key is depressed), we'll have to give our program the ability to compare data. This is done with the keyword `if` and the comparison operator (e.g., = =, see Table 2.1). The first step, then, is to rewrite the last program using the `if` statement (see Example 2.2).

Remember the C# language is case sensitive, thus the letters Y and y are not considered equivalent inputs. For the correct response, the uppercase Y is required.

Example 2.2. Using the `if` statement.

```
using System;
namespace Chapter2 {
    class Class1 {
```

```
        static void Main() {
            int cResponse;

            // Step 1
            Console.Write("Input <Y> for YES:   ");

            // Step 2
            cResponse = Console.Read();

            // Step 3 - if response equals 'Y'
            if ((char) cResponse == 'Y')
                Console.WriteLine("\n You typed Y\n");
        }
    }
}
```

This program still displays the message "You typed Y," but now only if the letter Y is actually entered. If any other character is entered, the program simply ends and nothing is written to the screen. This is true for any letter or character data as long as it equals the variable. Try reediting this program so that it responds to both upper and lowercase letters ('Y' || 'y'). If you alter the required input, remember to alter the accompanying inquiry. For our next task, we'll modify the program so that it uses numerical data (see Example 2.3).

Example 2.3. Using the `if` statement with numerical data.

```
using System;

namespace Chapter2 {
    class Class1 {
        static void Main() {
            int iAnswer;

            // Step 1
            Console.Write("1 + 1 =  ");

            // Step 2
            iAnswer = int.Parse(Console.ReadLine());

            // Step 3 - numbers do not require quotes
            if (iAnswer == 2)
                Console.WriteLine("\n That is correct!\n");
```

C# and Game Programming

```
            // Step 4
            if (iAnswer != 2)
                Console.WriteLine("\n Wrong!!!\n");
        }
    }
}
```

Floats and doubles will work equally well in these comparisons. You might also want to try a varied list of operators such as byte, ushort, and ulong, (keeping in mind that u stands for unsigned). The next section actually continues with the *if* statement, combining *if* with the keyword else. Everything that we've studied here still applies, but else gives if some added control.

1.	Two equal signs "= =" meaning "equal to," e.g., – if (variable1 = = variable2) – // 5 is equal to 5
2.	Less than symbol "<" meaning "less than," e.g., – if (variable1 < variable2) – // 5 is less than 10
3.	Less than or equal to "<=" meaning "less than or equal to," e.g., – if (variable1 <= variable2) – // 5 is less than or equal to 10
4.	Greater than ">" meaning "greater than," e.g., – if (variable1 > variable2) – // 20 is greater than 10
5.	Greater than or equal to ">=" meaning "greater than or equal to," e.g., – if (variable1 >= variable2) – // 20 is greater than or equal to 10
6.	Not equal "!=" meaning "Not equal," e.g., – if (variable1 != variable2) – // 20 does not equal 10

Table 2.1. Comparison Operators.

> Your programming abilities should now enable you to alter the program's data type, add comments, rename variables, and edit the output message without further mention. However, I will still mention any opportunities to use the data types byte, ushort, and ulong, should they arise.

The else Statement

Else is the first logical extension to the if statement. It adds an additional line of reasoning and an additional path for programs to follow. Else cannot be used by itself; it links easily to the tail end of the if structure. Example 2.4 uses the if-Else statement to redefine the previous program. The addition of else negates the need for the second if statement, and its simplicity adds a more elegant feel to our coding.

Example 2.4. The *if-else* statement.

```
using System;

namespace Chapter2 {
    class Class1 {
        static void Main() {
            string input;
            double Answer;

            Console.Write("1 + 1.5 =  ");
            input = Console.ReadLine();
            Answer = double.Parse(input);

            if (Answer == 2.5)
                Console.WriteLine("\n That is correct!\n");
            else
                Console.WriteLine("\n Wrong!!!\n");
        }
    }
}
```

The if-else statement works in basically the same manner as the if statement. The term else implies "in all other cases," or an "everything else here" type situation. This ability to alter the direction of our programs is what defines it as a programming technique. if-else, however, is still limited to two directions, of which the second is nonspecific. To specify the second direction or multiple paths, we would have to use the third type of if statement known as the else-if statement.

The else-if Statement

Else-if, like else is a dependent or secondary extension to the original if statement. Yet else-if definitely adds something new to the table. Since else-if must be added after an if statement, we'll alter the previous program once again, this time giving the user a little more to go by than just the word wrong—see Example 2.5.

Example 2.5. The else-if statement.

```
using System;

namespace Chapter2 {
    class Class1 {
        static void Main() {
            string input;
            double Answer;

            Console.Write("1 + 1.5 =  ");
            input = Console.ReadLine();
            Answer = double.Parse(input);

            if (Answer == 2.5)
                Console.WriteLine("\n That is correct!");
            else if (Answer > 2.5)
                Console.WriteLine("\n Wrong, too high!!!");
            else if (Answer < 2.5)
                Console.WriteLine("\n Wrong, too low!!!");
        }
    }
}
```

Else-if includes a second conditional response with respect to if. Because else-if statements are dependent, they are only read by the computer if the first if statement is false (see Example 2.6).

Example 2.6. The else-if statement as a dependent statement.

```
using System;

namespace Chapter2 {
    class Class1 {
        static void Main() {
            string input;
            double Answer;

            Console.Write ("1 + 1.5 =  ");
            input = Console.ReadLine ();
            Answer = double.Parse (input);

            if (Answer == 2.5)
                Console.WriteLine ("\n That is correct!");
            else if (Answer > 2.5)
                Console.WriteLine ("\n Wrong, too high!!!");
            else
                Console.WriteLine ("\n Wrong, too low!!!");

            Console.WriteLine ("I hate the if statement!");
        }
    }
}
```

Program Walkthroug

The last two programs are essentially identical, with the minor exception of the altered else statement, which concludes Example 2.6. This emphasizes the key points on how the if, else-if and *else* statements are linked. Following the logic of the if statement, we find that if our number is not 2.5, the program proceeds to the next else-if. If we then find that the number is not greater than the 2.5, we again move to the next else. In order to get to the *else* statement, our number would have to be smaller then 2.5. Therefore, we do not need to test to see if that value is actually smaller.

Compound `if` Statements

A *compound statement* is a group of statements combined into a bundle enclosed by a pair of braces. A compound `if` statement is an `if` statement that executes this bundle as if it were a single action. The proper way to write a compound statement is demonstrated in Example 2.7. (Note: Either `else` or `else-if` could still be used simply by placing those keywords at the end of the compound statement.)

Example 2.7. A compound `if` statement.

```
using System;

namespace Chapter2 {
    class Class1 {
        static void Main() {
            string input;
            float MyNumber;

            Console.WriteLine("How old are you? ");
            input = Console.ReadLine();
            MyNumber = float.Parse(input);

            if (MyNumber >= 18) {   // compound statement
                Console.WriteLine("\n You're an adult");
                Console.WriteLine("You can vote\n");
            } else
                Console.WriteLine("\n Your turn will come");
        }
    }
}
```

The rules guiding the execution of compound if statements are simple. When the `if` statement is true, all the statements inside the compound statement are executed, and when the `if` statement is false, all the statements are ignored. This may not seem like much when discussing a compound statement made up of only two lines, but imagine dealing with compound statements of over two hundred lines. Many C# commands can be placed inside of these compound statements including other *if* statements, but we'll leave such matters to the sections ahead. The `else` and `else-if` statements can also use compound statements, as demonstrated in Example 2.8. Notice how important it becomes to comments when programs become longer and more complicated.

Example 2.8. Compound *if* and *else-if* statements.

```
using System;

namespace Chapter2 {
    class Class1 {
        static void Main() {
            string input;
            float MyNumber;

            Console.Write("How old are you? ");
            input = Console.ReadLine();
            MyNumber = float.Parse(input);

            if (MyNumber >= 18)
                Console.WriteLine("You're an adult\n" + "You can vote\n");
            else if (MyNumber == 17)
                Console.WriteLine("Your turn will come \n");
            else if (MyNumber == 16) { // compound statement
                Console.Write("\n Don't rush it boy you'll only be young
                    once\n"
                    + "How old are you again? ");
                input = Console.ReadLine();
                MyNumber = float.Parse(input);
            } else
                Console.WriteLine("\n You're just too young!!!\n");
        }
    }
}
```

This is the last example for this section, but `if` statements are explained further in the next two sections. As for compound statements, they'll be used repeatedly in several types of loops including the `while` and `for` loops coming up shortly. These new commands also follow the same rules (i.e., run when true; ignore when false); after a while this type of behavior should seem natural. The next section discusses three new decision operators: `and`, `or`, and `not`. These, like the comparison operators, can be combined with `if` statements and programming loops to define program paths.

and, or, and not

There are three decision operators: and (written as &&), or (written as ||), and not (written as !). Of these, and (&&) and or (||) are used to combine if and else-if statements while the third operator not (!), is used to reverse our comparison's outcomes, the operators && and || inside the parenthetical structure of if statements (see Table 2.2). By adding an && or a || we can reduce wasteful and repetitive if statements. Example 2.9 shows how the || operator can turn two *ifs* and six commands into one if and three commands.

1. - -	and (&&) meaning "both must be true for the statement to be true" if (variable1 > variable2 && variable2 == variable3) // 20 > 10 and 10 = 10
2. - -	or (||) meaning "only one needs to be true for the statement to be true" if (variable1 == variable2 || variable2 < variable3) // 20 = 20 or 20 < 10

3.
-
-
	not (!) meaning "makes true statements false and false statements true"
	if !(1 == 1) // 1 = 1 then not (true) or false
	if !(1 == 2) // 1 = 2 then not (false) or true

Table 2.2. The and, or, and not operators

Example 2.9. Reducing if statements by using the *or* operator.

```
using System;

namespace Chapter2 {
    class Class1 {
        static void Main() {
            string input;
            double Age, Weight;
            int cQuickAnswer;
            Console.Write("How old are you? ");
            input = Console.ReadLine();
            Age = double.Parse(input);
```

```
            Console.Write("How much do you weigh?");
            input = Console.ReadLine();
            Weight = double.Parse (input);

            if (Age < 3) {
               Console.Write("\nThe law requires you to "
                   + "sit in a car seat\n"
                   + "\n Do you have a car seat? ");
               cQuickAnswer = Console.Read();
            }

            if (Weight < 35) {
               Console.Write("\nThe law requires you to "
                   + "sit in a car seat\n"
                   + "\n Do you have a car seat? ");
               cQuickAnswer = Console.Read();
            }

            if (Age < 3 || Weight < 35) {
               Console.Write("\nThe law requires you to "
                   + "sit in a car seat\n"
                   + "\n Do you have a car seat? ");
               cQuickAnswer = Console.Read();
            }
         }
      }
}
```

The not operator is placed directly in front of an expression (as show in Table 2.2). Although the not operator can be useful, it can also be confusing. I suggest reediting Example 2.9 so that it uses the not operator. [Hint: the *if* statement would be written like this as (age > 3 || weight > 35)].

Nested `if` Statements

Just as it is possible to write a program using more than one `if` statement, it is also possible to place one or more `if` statements inside a compound `if` statement. These internal or *nested* `if` statements have nothing to do with the controlling `if` statement, but since we're using the same keyword, it can become confusing. Nested `if` statements work just as independently as any other if statement placed anywhere in the program, including inside a compound `else` or `else-if` statement. Example 2.10 demonstrates a complex blend of nested `if` and `else-if` statements.

C# and Game Programming

Example 2.10. Nested `if` and `else-if` statements.

```csharp
using System;

namespace Chapter2 {
    class Class1 {
        static void Main() {
            string Input;
            float Age, Weight;
            int iQuickAnswer;

            // Note: you'll want to hit return before entering the second
            //    answer
            Console.Write("How old are you and how much do you weigh? ");
            Input = Console.ReadLine();
            Age = float.Parse(Input);
            Input = Console.ReadLine();
            Weight = float.Parse(Input);

            if (Age < 3 || Weight < 35) { // start compound if statement
                Console.Write("\nThe law requires you to sit in a car
                    seat\n"
                    + "\n Do you have a car seat? ");
                iQuickAnswer = Console.Read();

                if (iQuickAnswer == 'y') // nested if statement
                    Console.Write("\n Good, but using it would be
                        better.\n");
                else { // nested else compounded
                    Console.Write("\n No, do you care about your
                        baby?\n");
                    if (iQuickAnswer == 'y') // nested if in nested else
                        Console.Write("\n Well then get a car seat!\n");
                    else if (iQuickAnswer == 'n') // nested else-if in
                                                  // nested else
                        Console.Write("\n You sicken me!\n"
                            + "\n Your baby is worth it!\n");
                    else // nested else in nested else
                        Console.Write("\n Your baby is worth it!\n");
                }
            } // end compound if statement
            else if (Age > 85 || Weight > 500)
                Console.WriteLine("\n Sorry I asked!\n");
        }
    }
}
```

Mathematical Abbreviations

Sometimes, as programs become larger and more complex, they also become wordy and drawn out. To alleviate this problem, programmers often use abbreviations. Our coverage here mimics what we've already studied under the section on arithmetic. Table 2.3 defines these shortcuts, and Example 2.11 demonstrates how they're written. I've included arithmetic statements in both longhand and shorthand forms to make them easier to compare. I've also thrown in several if-*statements*, which were already covered in this chapter. You'll need to rerun this program a minimum of five times, entering the proper characters once for each shortcut. You might also want to try removing the longhand statements or rewriting it using the `while` loop (explained in the next section).

Example 2.11. Shorthand notation.

```
using System;

namespace Chapter2 {
    class Class1 {
        static void Main() {
            string Input;
            int iVariable1, iVariable2, iVariable3, iCharacter;
            // Note: later we'll learn techniques that will allow us
            // to read partial bits of info, but until then we'll still
            // want to enter each number with a return statement
            Console.Write("\n Enter two numbers: ");
            Input = Console.ReadLine();
            iVariable1 = int.Parse(Input);
            Input = Console.ReadLine();
            iVariable2 = int.Parse(Input);
            iVariable3 = iVariable1;

            Console.WriteLine("\n Enter one symbol: \n addition (+) "
                + "\n subtraction (-) \n multiplication (*)"
                + "\n division (/), or \n remainder (%): ");
            iCharacter = Console.Read();

            if (iCharacter == '+') {
                iVariable1 = iVariable1 + iVariable2;
                Console.WriteLine("\n Your longhand sum is "
                    + iVariable1);
```

```csharp
            iVariable3 += iVariable2;
            Console.WriteLine("\n Your shorthand sum is also "
                + iVariable3);
        }

        if (iCharacter == '-') {
            iVariable1 = iVariable1 - iVariable2;
            Console.WriteLine("\n Your longhand difference is  "
                + iVariable1);
            iVariable3 -= iVariable2;
            Console.WriteLine("\n Your shorthand difference is  "
                + iVariable3);
        }

        if (iCharacter == '*') {
            iVariable1 = iVariable1 * iVariable2;
            Console.WriteLine("\n Your longhand product is  "
                + iVariable1);
            iVariable3 *= iVariable2;
            Console.WriteLine("\n Your shorthand product is  "
                + iVariable3);
        }

        if (iCharacter == '/') {
            iVariable1 = iVariable1 / iVariable2;
            Console.WriteLine ("\n Your longhand quotient is  "
                + iVariable1);
            iVariable3 /= iVariable2;
            Console.WriteLine ("\n Your shorthand quotient is  "
                + iVariable3);
        }

        if (iCharacter == '%') {
            iVariable1 = iVariable1 % iVariable2;
            Console.WriteLine("\n Your longhand remainder is  "
                + iVariable1);
            iVariable3 %= iVariable2;
            Console.WriteLine("\n Your shorthand remainder is  "
                + iVariable3);
        }
      }
   }
}
```

Arithmetic	(int iNumber = 5;)	Abbreviates to	Returns
Addition:	iNumber = iNumber + 1;	iNumber += 1;	6
Subtraction:	iNumber = iNumber − 1;	iNumber -= 1;	4
Multiplication:	iNumber = iNumber * 2;	iNumber *= 2;	10
Division:	iNumber = iNumber / 2;	iNumber /= 2;	2
Remainders:	iNumber = iNumber % 2;	iNumber %= 2;	1

```
// Assume Variable1 = 5 and Variable2 = 2 and that they're a
numeric data type.
1. Addition:
Variable1 = Variable1 + Variable2
Variable1 += Variable2
// variable1 now equals 7 since -    7 = 5 + 2
2. Subtraction:
Variable1 = Variable1 - Variable2
Variable1 -= Variable2
// variable1 now equals 3 since -    3 = 5 - 2
3. Multiplication:
Variable1 = Variable1 * Variable2
Variable1 *= Variable2
// Variable1 now equals 10 since -   10 = 5 * 2
4. Division
Variable1 = Variable1 / Variable2
Variable1 /= Variable2
// Variable1 now equals 2.5 since -   2.5 = 5 / 2 (When
Variable1 is either float or double)
// Variable1 now equals 2 since -    2 = 5 / 2 (When variable1
is of type integer)
5. Remainders:
Variable1 = Variable1 % Variable2
Variable1 %= Variable2
// Variable1 now equals 1 since -    1 = 5 % 2 (Variable1 should
only be used with integers)
// Remember % stands for the remainder of 1 as in 5 / 2
```

Table 2.3. Numeric Abbreviations

The `while` Loop

In the last section, we were forced to restart our program five times in order to test the results of five characters. Although this might be acceptable in a book which teaches programming, it would not be acceptable for a real program. This section therefore shows us how to repeat a program, or portions of a program, in a repeating cycle or loop. The first type of loop we'll examine uses the keyword `while`; thus, it is called the `while` loop. The `while` loop can be set up to repeat and/or terminate in several different ways: the most common include using a predetermined count (as in to repeat an iteration five times then end); using the user's input (end by request); and a termination command (a command that short-steps or breaks the loop—we'll learn about these shortly).

A `while` loop compares most directly to a compound `if` statement. `while`, like `if`, is written first, followed by a comparison operator and then a set of compound statements. When `while` is true, all the statements between its brackets will be executed, and when it is false, all of its statements will be skipped. `while`, unlike `if`, will not terminate when the last statement is executed. Rather, and if it remains true, it will then execute the compound statement again. This process repeats indefinitely, ending only when something is altered to cause the comparison to become false or other special steps are taken to reroute the computer's line of execution. The techniques for terminating a `while` loop are thus just as important conceptually as the keyword `while` Example 2.12 demonstrates a limited or predetermined type of `while` loop; this example terminates when the variable tests at a value greater then four.

Example 2.12. A while loop limited to five passes.

```
using System;

namespace Chapter2 {
    class Class1 {
        static void Main()  {
            int iCounter_1 = 0;

            while (iCounter_1 < 5) {   // while loop
                Console.WriteLine(iCounter_1++);
            }

            Console.WriteLine("Program complete!\n");
        }
    }
}
```

> When the `while` loop is first executed, the value of the counter is compared to 5. Since zero is less than five, the loop is executed and the variable "iCounter_1" is incremented by one. The loop retests itself, finding the variable at one, which is still less than five. The loop continues to run until the counter variable is incremented to 5, at which point, the loop ends. The program moves to the next line—Console.WriteLine ("Program complete!"); and the program ends. This would hold true if we had made the value 15 or even 50 million, although that would take a bit longer to execute.

Program Walkthrough

We could have used an arithmetic statement or shortcut to alter our indexing variable's value, e.g., counter = counter + 1 and counter += 1. We could have even rewritten five as negative 5 instead of 5 and counted backwards using the decrementing operator or shortcut -= 1. Any such combination would work as long as we made sure the variable would eventually reach a value that terminates the loop. Otherwise we have written a program with a *nonterminating* or *infinite* loop; which usually locks up programs, making them unusable. The second type of termination is by user input; this can be done either with the user's knowledge, as in asking the user "Would you like to continue?" or without the user's knowledge, as in when his ship is destroyed, the loop automatically ends. Example 2.13 demonstrates a simple user-terminated loop.

Example 2.13. This `while` loop ends when I say it ends, got it?

```
using System;

namespace Chapter2 {
    class Class1 {
        static void Main() {
            string Quit = "no";

            while (Quit != "yes") {
                Console.Write("\n Would you like to end this loop? ");
                Quit = Console.ReadLine();
            }

            Console.WriteLine ("Program complete!\n");
        }
    }
}
```

Program Walkthrough

> The first thing we do is declare the variable Quit and initialize it. We'll use "no" as its initial value (note: "no" has no real meaning to the program). Next, we'll set up a *while* loop that compares the value of Quit to "yes" and makes the loop comparison true only when Quit's value does not equal "yes." We then ask the user from inside the compound statement whether he or she wishes to end the loop. The user's input is then stored in the variable Quit; the loop will continue to repeat until the user enters "yes." Then, the last statement "Program complete!" will be executed and the program will terminate.

As with counting loops, user input loops can be made nearly infinite if you forget to tell the user how to end them (which, of course, should be avoided). For the third type of termination, we'll have to introduce the keyword `break`. `break`, as its name implies, terminates any enclosed loop or conditional statement. Example 2.14 demonstrates this final *while* termination technique.

Example 2.14. Hey, you broke my `while` loop!

```
using System;

namespace Chapter2 {
    class Class1 {
        static void Main() {
            string Quit = "no";

            while (Quit != "yes") {
                break;                    // breaks loop
                Console.Write ("\n Would you like to end this loop? ");
                Quit = Console.ReadLine ();
            }

            Console.WriteLine ("Program complete!\n");
        }
    }
}
```

When `break` is executed, it simply breaks the loop and moves down to the next statement, skipping the remaining loop statements, and the while loop is considered complete.

The program executes the last command "Program complete! \n" and then terminates. `break` works as an instant end to an otherwise structured loop.

Another interesting keyword in `continue`, which, like `break`, shortcuts its iterations; but rather than ending the loop, it merrily brings the loop back up to the top. The loop continues from the top with a new iteration and everything else continues accordingly (see Example 2.15).

Example 2.15. The keyword `continue`.

```
using System;

namespace Chapter2 {
    class Class1 {
        static void Main() {
            int iVariable1 = 10, iVariable2 = 0;

            while (iVariable1 == 10) {    // while loop
                iVariable2 = iVariable2 + 1;
                if (iVariable2/iVariable1 < 1)
                    continue;
                iVariable1 = iVariable1 - 1;
            }

            Console.WriteLine (iVariable2);
        }
    }
}
```

Battle Bit

Finally, after many painful hours of lost sleep, burning eyes, screams of madness, and dogged determination, you have reached the pinnacle of gaming knowledge and can now create dynamically animated, graphically breathtaking, and hardware accelerated three-dimensional video adventures capable of running on all platforms and computer systems. Hey, wake up! This is Chapter 2. Real game programming doesn't even start until Chapter 3, and there's nothing in that chapter about hardware acceleration or three-dimensional programming. As for your abilities up until this point, well maybe, just maybe, you might be ready to try out a little text style program that, at least partially, will ease you

C# and Game Programming

into the whole gaming concept. The game is called Battle Bit and the player's objective is to destroy the aliens before they land. To play, you simply guess the aliens' location, which is represented by numbers typed into your computer's keyboard. To win you must guess the correct answer before you use up your shots. Oh, and if you fail, I've set up a bug that will automatically erase your hard drive—but don't fret, it shouldn't take too long to reinstall everything!

Example 2.16. Battle Bit: The Text Adventure.

```
/* You're a lieutenant in earth's toughest military fleet. Your
 * current mission is to guard earth's intergalactic conference hall. */
using System;

namespace Chapter2 {
    class Class1 {
        static void Main() {
            string input;
            int iAmmo = 12, // player has 12 guesses
                iAlienShip = 49, // the alien ship starts here
                iTarget = 50;   // This variable stores your input

            /* Game introduction - explains to the player what he needs to
             * do, why he is doing it.  The introduction should also, be
             * used to set the games mood and excite the player. */

            Console.WriteLine("\n Captain, aliens are attempting "
                + "to land peacefully!\n"
                + "What? How dare they and on the day we're suppose "
                + "to start peace talks.\n"
                + "It just goes to show you, you just can't trust "
                + "those alien scum.\n"
                + "Lieutenant, lock target, I don't want to see one "
                + "alien left alive.\n"
                + "But captain, isn't that the ambassadors ship!\n"
                + "And wasn't he suppose to be coming today?\n"
                + "Lieutenant, are you going to target the alien "
                + "ship or not?\n"
                + "But sir. \n Type in the ships location and fire
                    soldier!\n"
                + "But sir!\n"
                + "Lieutenant, you'll take out that alien scum or I'll "
                + "take you out!\n"
```

```
            + "(The captains gun points oddly at your head.) "
            + "Got it? Yes sir!\n");

    // location of ship - this just makes it harder to find the
    // ship
    iAlienShip = ((iAlienShip * iAmmo) / (iTarget + 1)) + 3;

    while (iAmmo > 0) {  // when ammo runs out the loop ends
        Console.WriteLine("\n\n Enter targeting information?");
        input = Console.ReadLine();
        iTarget = int.Parse(input);

        if (iTarget == iAlienShip) {
            // if your input equals the ships location
            Console.WriteLine("Alien ship hit, the ships been
                destroyed sir.");
            break; // break ends loop
        } else if (iTarget > iAlienShip) {
            // when input is too high
            Console.WriteLine("You missed, try aiming a little
                lower");
            iAmmo--; // ammo-reduces the total ammo by 1
        } else {
            // when input is to low
            Console.WriteLine("You missed, try aiming higher");
            iAmmo--; // also reduces ammo by 1
        }

        // The location of the ship moves with each shot
        if (iTarget == 0) {
           iTarget = 1;
        }
        iAlienShip = (iAlienShip * iAmmo) / iTarget;
    }

    if (iAmmo > 0) // if you have ammo you must have hit the alien
        Console.WriteLine("\n Good work soldier, remind me to
            promote you.");
    else // if your out of ammo you can't protect the hall
        Console.WriteLine("\n BOOM!!! You're dead.\n");

    Console.WriteLine ("\n Game Over\n");
      }
    }
  }
```

```csharp
            + "(The captains gun points oddly at your head.) "
            + "Got it? Yes sir!\n");

        // location of ship - this just makes it harder to find the
        // ship
        iAlienShip = ((iAlienShip * iAmmo) / (iTarget + 1)) + 3;

        while (iAmmo > 0) {   // when ammo runs out the loop ends
            Console.WriteLine("\n\n Enter targeting information?");
            input = Console.ReadLine();
            iTarget = int.Parse(input);

            if (iTarget == iAlienShip) {
                // if your input equals the ships location
                Console.WriteLine("Alien ship hit, the ships been
                    destroyed sir.");
                break; // break ends loop
            } else if (iTarget > iAlienShip) {
                // when input is too high
                Console.WriteLine("You missed, try aiming a little
                    lower");
                iAmmo--; // ammo—reduces the total ammo by 1
            } else {
                // when input is to low
                Console.WriteLine("You missed, try aiming higher");
                iAmmo--; // also reduces ammo by 1
            }

            // The location of the ship moves with each shot
            iAlienShip = (iAlienShip * iAmmo) / iTarget;
        }

        if (iAmmo > 0) // if you have ammo you must have hit the alien
            Console.WriteLine("\n Good work soldier, remind me to promote you.");
        else // if your out of ammo you can't protect the hall
            Console.WriteLine("\n BOOM!!! You're dead.\n");

        Console.WriteLine ("\n Game Over\n");
        }
    }
}
```

Chapter 2: Branches, Loops, and Functions

The do-while Loop

The second type of `while` loop, which is known as the `do-while` loop, is essentially the `while` loop turned up-side down. Here we insert the `while` loop comparison at the end of the loop, which also allows for one complete execution before the 1st comparison takes place.

Example 2.17. A do-while loop I.

```
using System;

namespace Chapter2 {
    class Class1 {
        static void Main() {
            string Quit = "no";
            do {
                // this is an endless loop
            } while (Quit != "yes"); // notice the semicolon?
        }
    }
}
```

The keyword *do* is placed at the top of the loop and the keyword `while` is placed at the end. The compound statement is written directly after the keyword *do*, just as it was with `while` and `if`. One obvious difference between the `while` loop and the `do-while` loop is that the comparisons are not made until the loop is already running. Again, this guarantees us at least one execution before the coding is tested. Example 2.18 demonstrates the do-while loop in action.

Example 2.18. A do-while loop II.

```
using System;

namespace Chapter2 {
    class Class1 {
        static void Main() {
            string Quit;

            do { // do-while loop
                Console.WriteLine("\n Would you like to end this loop? ");
```

```
            Quit = Console.ReadLine(); // users input
        } while (Quit != "yes");

        Console.WriteLine("Program complete!\n");
        }
    }
}
```

Needles to say, the `while` and `do-while` loops can also take advantage of the *and* (&&), *or* (||), and *not* (!) operators. They can be rewritten without compound statements as single-line `while` and `do-while` statements (although that would be considered poor programming style). Moreover, you can nest `while`/`do-while` loops inside of each other. Example 2.19 gives an example of both the nesting technique and the && operator. You may also want to test this program using either the || or ! operators, but I'll leave the exact phrasing of those two operators up to you.

Example 2.19. Nested `while` and `do-while` loops.

```
using System;

namespace Chapter2 {
    class Class1 {
        static void Main() {
            // Begin main
            int iNumber = 0;
            string Quit;

            do { // begin do-while loop
                Console.Write("\n Would you like to end this loop? ");
                Quit = Console.ReadLine(); // users input

                while (Quit == "yes" && iNumber < 10) { // nested while
                                                        //loop
                    Console.WriteLine("We're sorry the exit you have
                        chosen "
                        + "is not available "
                        + "at this time\n please try again");
                    Quit = Console.ReadLine();
                    iNumber++;
                }

            } while (Quit != "yes");      // end do-while
```

Chapter 2: Branches, Loops, and Functions

```
            Console.WriteLine("Program complete!\n");
        }
    }
}
```

Program Walkthrough

If you're trapped, the secret to escaping is in understanding the comparisons. First, if you enter anything other then "yes" you can't exit the do/while-loop. If you do enter "yes," the program goes into the nested while loop. After entering the while loop, if you enter anything other than "yes," you're forced to repeat the do-while loop and the process starts all over. However, if you enter "yes" the nested *while*-loop keeps repeating itself.

The solution requires you to enter "yes" eleven times. Once to get into the *while* loop and ten times to get out. The incrementing variable iNumber will cause the nested while loop, to become false, and since the character's string "Quit" is still equal to "yes," the do-while loop will also false and the loop will end.

You don't have to use the same variable in both loops; in fact, the use of the same variable is what made this example so confusing. In addition, for preset numbers such as zero to ten you might be better off using the for loop, which just happens to be the subject of the next section.

The for Loop

The for loop, also known as the for statement, is a repetitive process that is set up under certain conditions to run a particular number of times. This terminating factor will also help us to separate it from the other two looping processes, because it's not dependent on an unknown variable. The for-loop thus predefines its variable as part of its initial statement. The comparison operators are still used to determine whether to continue or terminate, but this will always happen at a predetermined point in the loop, as when our variable equals 10, 100, or *x* number of cycles. The for statement is constructed much like the while loop, but with its initializing variable and its incrementing operator both becoming one with its declaration (see Example 2.20).

C# and Game Programming

Example 2.20. The `for` loop.

```
using System;

namespace Chapter2 {
    class Class1 {
        static void Main() {
            int iCounter_1;

            for (iCounter_1 = 0; iCounter_1 < 5; iCounter_1++) {
                Console.WriteLine(iCounter_1);
            }

            Console.WriteLine("Program complete!\n");
        }
    }
}
```

Program Walkthrough

> The `for` statement begins by assigning our variable the value zero. This value is then compared to 5 and found true since zero is less than five. The incrementing operator then adds one to the value of our variable making its value one. The loop is then executed and our variable iCounter_1 is displayed. The loop then finds the variable is still less than five, and the variable is then incremented a second time. The third time the loop runs, our value increases to three, which is still less than five, so the loop runs again. The fourth iteration increases our value to four and the loop runs again. Finally, our variable equals five and the loop terminates. The program moves to the next line "Program complete!" and the program ends.

Nesting is just as legal and useful in `for` loops as it is in the other loops introduced earlier, but it is also just as dangerous (or as trying) when you are caught in an infinite loop. Thus, you should avoid using the `for` loop's tracking variable for anything other than keeping track of that `for` loop. If you think you're up to it, you can go back and rewrite the `while` and `do-while` programs using only `for` loops.

The `for` loop can become an infinite loop or mindless hole with even the most subtle of errors. For example:

```
for (iCounter_1 = 0; iCounter_1 < 5; iCounter_1++) {
    iCounter_1 = 1;
    Console.WriteLine (iCounter_1);
}
```

That's it for the looping processes, but there are still two additional comparison processes—the `switch` statement and the `foreach` statement. Both are very similar to the `if` and `else-if` statements, but they can handle much longer lists of comparisons without repeating themselves or becoming cluttered. With respect to game programming techniques, these comparisons also makes long lists of comparisons smoother and simpler to modify.

The `switch` Statement

The `switch` statement, like the `if` and `else-if` statements, is used to execute a statement, or set of statements, depending on a value. However, unlike the `if` and `else-if` statements, the `switch` statement doesn't use comparison operators; instead, it simply reads the value of the variable and attempts to direct the program to the proper channel. A second keyword, `case`, is also used in this process. The keyword `case` is written and used multiple times from within the `switch` statement,; each `switch` statement holds a numeric or character value for comparison. If the value held by a `case` statement matches the value read by the `switch` statement, then everything following that `case` statement is executed.

Another useful keyword used with the `switch` statement is `default`, meaning when no other case matches. `default` is usually placed at the end of a *switch* statement, thus allowing us to execute selected statements based on the fact that they do not match any of the previous values (see Example 2.21).

Example 2.21. `switch` **statement.**

```
using System;

namespace Chapter2 {
    class Class1 {
        static void Main() {
            int Grades;
```

```
// Begin main
        Console.Write ("How would you grade yourself so far A, B, or
            C? ");
        Grades = Console.Read ();

        switch (Grades) { // switch statement
            case 'A':
            case 'a':
               Console.WriteLine ("You'll make a great programmer");
                break;

            case 'B':
            case 'b':
               Console.WriteLine ("You're sure of yourself");
                break;

            case 'C':
            case 'c':
               Console.WriteLine ("You don't let hard work keep you
                    down");
                break;

            default:
               Console.WriteLine ("A, B, and C inputs only!");
                break;
        } // end switch statement
    }
  }
}
```

Note that this termination sequence is actually only the keyword break, which does nothing more than move us out of a block and onto the next segment. break, like case, is repeated for each comparison.

C# also requires a break statement, which prevents the falling through of case values. You can, however, include multiple case statements, just as long as they do not contain executable statements. This new method, while only a minor change in syntax, should flag several of the older C/C++ conversions. To those programmers that don't like to write their *switch* statements using only individually controlled *case* statements, I apologize (see Example 2.22).

Example 2.22. Switch statement continued.

```
using System;

namespace Chapter2 {
    class Class1 {
        static void Main() {
            string input;
            int byNumber;

            Console.Write("Enter a number greater than one: ");
            input = Console.ReadLine();
            byNumber = int.Parse(input);

            switch (byNumber) {
                default:
                    Console.WriteLine("\n Good job now take a lap!");
                    break;

                case 0:
                    Console.WriteLine("\n Zero is not greater than
                        one!\n");
                    break;

                case 1:
                    Console.WriteLine("\n I said a number greater than
                        one!");
                    break;
            }

            Console.WriteLine("\n Program complete\n");
        }
    }
}
```

It is possible to have switch statements using either character or integer data types, but the set case types must be literal or variable constants. You cannot set two cases to the same value even if it's written as a variable, and you cannot have more than one default in any single switch statement. switch statements can have if statements in their *cases*, and if statements can have switch in their compound statements. In addition, you can place switch statements in while and do-while loops or write those loops into *case* statements, but switch statements inside of other switch statements should be used sparingly to avoid confusion.

> **Defining a Block:**
> A block (opening and closing brackets { }), although technically identical to a compound statement, can in fact refer to any set of brackets placed anywhere in a program. For example, the main program is enclosed by opening and closing brackets but is not considered as a compound statement. Blocks allow programmers to separate special sections of code, opening up new ways to use local variables, or enclose certain code including confining subroutines (discussed later in this chapter). When a block is nested within another block, the outsider block is considered global to the inner block, just as code written outside of the main program is considered global to the program. Global and local concepts are very important when working with C# and will be discussed in greater detail throughout this text.

Converting from C++ to C#

While many of us may remember the older C and C++ I/O notations, it is safe to assume that not everyone reading this text can do so without some type of reference. This section defines the C/C++ commands that were replaced by our Write and WriteLine extensions. When the older commands are encountered, the trick is to replace them with the appropriate combination of extensions and formatting strings.

The `printf` and `cout` functions are alternatives to the Write and WriteLine commands, and the `scanf` and `cin` function are alternatives to the Read and ReadLine commands. Like our Reads and Writes, these functions are not keywords, but instead they are added commands linked by the older included file structure (see Chapter 1). The included file that controlled these commands were <cstdio> (written as #include <cstdio> and #include <stdio.h>) and iostream (written as #include <iostream> and #include <iostream.h>); <stdio.h> actually reaches back to the original C language. `Printf`, and for that matter scanf, have the most in common with C#'s notation, which becomes obvious when comparing them directly. For an extended list of `printf` / `scanf` notation, see Table 2.4.

	Specifier	Definition	Example
1.	%d	Holds positive or negative whole numbers -int variable1 (signed int variable1)	scanf("%d", &variable1); printf("Your number is %d", variable1);
2.	%u	Holds only positive whole numbers -unsigned int variable1	scanf("%u", &variable1); printf("Your number is %u", variabe1);
3.	%f	Holds floating point (real) numbers -float variable1	scanf("%f", &variable1); printf("Your number is %f", variable1);
4.	%c	Holds a single character data type -char variable1	scanf("%c", &variable1); printf("Your symbol is %c", variable1);
5.	%s	Holds a string or array of characters -char variable1[7] (or any positive number)	scanf("%s", &variable1); printf("Your word is %s", variable1);

Table 2.4. Using Conversion specifiers with printf () and scanf ().

Two interesting command functions that continue to evolve through the C languages are the old style and member functions `puts` and `gets`. The original `puts` was accessed in essentially the same manner as `printf`, but with the restriction that it could only display character data (as in `puts`("this is a test 1, 2, 3.");. `Gets`, like `scanf`, was also used to read data, but everything read is interpreted as a character string. This can also be thought of as an array (which we'll discuss in Chapter 4). The extended member function versions of these two types are unfortunately limited to only single character references as in `cout.puts ('A')` and `cin.get (character)`, so their practicality is limited. Two alternative replacements for these older style functions are `cin.getline (characters, sizeofline)` and `cout.write (characters, sizeofline)` These will also be explained in Chapter 4 (see Example 2.23). Note that while the `puts` function automatically moves data to the next line, `cout.write` does not.

Example 2.23. C/C++ versus C#.

```
using System;

namespace Chapter2 {
    class Class1 {
        static void Main() {
            int Number;    // char name [10];
            string Answer; // char Answer; or char Answer [];
```

```csharp
            Console.Write ("\n Hello, please enter a number: ");
            // printf ("\n Hello, please enter a number: ");
            // cout << "\n Hello, please enter a number: ";
            // std::cout.write("Please enter a name: ", 24);
            // puts("Please enter your name:");

            Number = int.Parse(Answer = Console.ReadLine ());
            // scanf("%d", &Number);
            // cin >> Number;
            // std::cin.getline(name, sizeof(name));
            // gets(Number);

            Console.WriteLine("You entered {0} is that correct?", Number);
            // printf ("\n You entered %d is that correct?", Number);
            // cout << "\n You entered " << Number << " is that correct?";

            Answer = Console.ReadLine();
            // scanf ("%s", &Answer);
            // cin >> Answer;
        }
    }
}
```

We could also convert multiple references, including formatting strings, to represent the change in notation (see Example 2.24).

Example 2.24. Converting multiple references.

```
Console.WriteLine("\n You entered the number {0, D} and also the letter {1}", iNumber, cAnswer);
printf("\n You entered the number %d and also the letter %c\n", iNumber, cAnswer);
```

Boolean Expressions

Boolean expressions are mathematical representations for the concepts of true and false. That is, while their actual evaluations are based on mathematical data, their outcomes are in fact determined by a conceptual understanding. This type of determination is represented in C# as the data type *bool*, with its variables assigned to the Boolean constants *true* or *false*. In the past, as with C and C++, this process could also include a numeric substitute, namely the numeric constants one and zero with zero equaling false and the value one or any nonzero positive or negative number equaling true. In C#, however, this numeric substitution is not allowed. Example 2.25 demonstrates this sequence for a `while` loop, but you should attempt to rewrite the program as a `do-while` loop before proceeding to the next section.

Example 2.25. Boolean expressions—true or false.

```
using System;

namespace Chapter2 {
    class Class1 {
        static void Main() {
            bool Variable1 = true;
            string Test;

            while (Variable1) {
                Console.Write("\n Would you like to end this loop? ");
                Test = Console.ReadLine();    // yes will break the loop

                if (Test == "yes" || Test == "YES")
                    Variable1 = false;
            } // end while loop

            Console.WriteLine ("Program complete!");
        }
    }
}
```

Short Circuit Evaluation

Short circuit or *partial comparisons* are comparisons that can be deduced without testing the entire statement. This deduction can be made for logical types && or ||, but with opposite results, as shown in Table 2.5.

Non-specific Equations	Evaluation Process	Reasoning
1. (True && True)	Complete evaluation	True + True = True
2. (True && False)	Complete evaluation	True + False = False
3. (False && True)	Short circuit evaluation	False + Test Skipped = False
4. (False && False)	Short circuit evaluation	False + Test Skipped = False
5. (True || True)	Short circuit evaluation	True + Test Skipped = True
6. (True || False)	Short circuit evaluation	True + Test Skipped = True
7. (False || True)	Complete evaluation	False + True = True
8. (False || False)	Complete evaluation	False + False = False

Table 2.5. True and false determinations.

As you can see, Tests 1 and 2 required complete evaluation because neither outcome could be determined without the second evaluation. This is not the case when using short circuit or partial comparison reasoning (as shown in Tests 3-8). In such cases, the decision to label the comparison as true or false would be done without the second test, and would thus save us the time and trouble of the second comparison. In addition, we can use this partial comparison to safeguard against runtime errors such as dividing by zero—see Example 2.26.

Example 2.26. A partial comparison used to safeguard runtime errors.

```
Console.WriteLine("Enter any number other than zero: ");
variable1 = Console.Read();

// Some smart user enters zero, the system crashes.
while (5/variable1 < 1);
// Later that day... you're fired!

// Alternatively, you could have used short
// circuit evaluation. And later that same day,
while (variable1 != 0 && 5/variable1);
// you could have been surfing the web as RedHotPartyPants.
```

The Conditional Operator

The *conditional operator*, which is also described as a *ternary operator* (because of its three operands), is essentially an abbreviated `if-else` expression that uses two symbols: a

Chapter 2: Branches, Loops, and Functions

question mark (?) and a colon (:). The statement requires three expressions: an `if-else` comparison, a true calculation, and a false calculation as shown below.

First, the comparison is made:
```
x = y ? 41 : 72

if(x == y)
// followed by an assignment
    x = 41;
else
// and then an else
// statement
    x = 72;
```

Where *x* equals *y*, the comparison is true and *x* is reassigned as 41. When *x* does not equal *y*, *x* is reassigned as 72.

```
Comparison ? Equation1 : Equation2:
```

> The conditional operator can also be placed inside of other commands and statements (including the `while`, `do-while`, and `Write` commands).

Predefined Functions

There are two types of functions (also known as methods) used in C#: those that are written by us and used like little subprograms, and those that were written for us and used to save us the time of writing them ourselves. The first type, referred to as user-defined functions, are a bit more complicated and aren't completely explained until the end of this chapter. The second type are most commonly referred to as predefined functions, which I actually began back in Chapter 1. This section takes a moment to introduce formally the concept of the predefined function.

The good news is that with the advent of the .Net architecture we no longer have to memorize dozens upon dozens of included file references in order to use a few simple commands. The bad news is that most of us have already memorized so many of them that it just might feel a little bit unfair, to which I say not to worry—the basics of the new structure aren't that different from the old one and everyone, including the newbies, should pick it up pretty quickly. Again, all predefined functions referenced under this new architecture involve an object (class); thus, the procedures for referencing those functions are very similar to what you might expect when referencing a standard C/C++ method (or member function). Now, not all of our user-defined functions are accessed in the same way (this should become apparent with time). Moreover, not even the best of us can truly claim to know them all, but they're now much easier to access, especially when you're using a visual compiler. The next few paragraphs explain some of the most common extensions.

Characters

The first function we'll define is Char.ToUpper, which literally means to make a letter that is lowercase into one that is uppercase. This function also has an antonym named Char.ToLower, which changes uppercase letters into their lowercase counterparts. The ToUpper function is useful when you cannot control the user's input, as we couldn't in Example 2.2. In that example, I had to ask that you limit your responses to uppercase Y. This was necessary at the time, but is no longer the case, since we can easily rewrite this program to use the ToUpper function (see Example 2.27).

Example 2.27. Using ToUpper.

```
using System;

namespace Chapter2 {
    class Class1 {
        static void Main() {
            int Response;

            Console.Write("Input <Y> for YES:  ");
            Response = Console.Read();
            Response = char.ToUpper((char) Response);

            if (Response == 'Y')
                Console.WriteLine ("\n You typed {0}\n", (char) Response);
        }
    }
}
```

Math

The next few functions we'll cover are from the predefined method Math. These function can be extremely useful when calculations are required. Our first function is `Math.Sqrt( )`, which stands for the square root of a number. This function returns the square root of any value placed within its parentheses (see Example 2.28).

A second function linked to Math is the `Math.Pow( )`, which stands for an exponential power of a number (remember we can always substitute variables for literal constants). This could be used to reverse the square root, or with other powers such as cubes.

Our third and fourth functions are `Math.Ceiling` and `Math.Floor`, which are used to round real numbers to their highest or lowest whole value, respectively. The most important point to remember when working with these functions is that Ceiling always rounds up and Floor always rounds down, regardless of the size of the decimal value they're reading. That is, Math.Ceiling would round 3.2 to 4 and Math.Floor would round 3.9 to 3.0. Therefore, you'll have to decide which way you want to go before using either one.

Trigonometric Functions (where x is a double/floating point value read in radians):

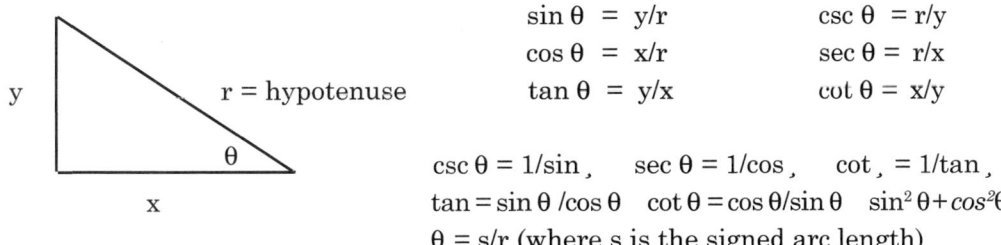

$\sin \theta = y/r$ $\csc \theta = r/y$
$\cos \theta = x/r$ $\sec \theta = r/x$
$\tan \theta = y/x$ $\cot \theta = x/y$

$\csc \theta = 1/\sin$, $\sec \theta = 1/\cos$, $\cot = 1/\tan$,
$\tan = \sin \theta / \cos \theta$ $\cot \theta = \cos \theta / \sin \theta$ $\sin^2 \theta + \cos^2 \theta$
$\theta = s/r$ (where s is the signed arc length)

Example 2.28. A few common math functions.

```
using System;

namespace Chapter2 {
    class Class1 {
        static void Main() {
            string input;
            double number1, number2, number3 = 2.0;
```

C# and Game Programming

```csharp
            Console.Write("Enter a number and I'll give you its square
                root: ");
            input = Console.ReadLine();
            number1 = double.Parse(input);

            number2 = Math.Sqrt(number1);
            Console.WriteLine("\nThe square root of {0} is {1}",
                number1, number2);

            number2 = Math.Pow(number2, number3);
            Console.WriteLine("Do these number match {0} and {1}?",
                number1, number2);

            number1 = Math.Ceiling(3.2);
            number2 = Math.Floor(3.9);

            Console.WriteLine("Math.Ceiling(3.2) = {0}", number1);
            Console.WriteLine("Math.Floor(3.9) = {0}", number2);
        }
    }
}
```

Additional extensions include some useful functions that determine absolute values and references that convert from character data to integer and double, but the most important extension relating to game programming is the random number generator. Pseudo-randomly generated numbers, based on the internal clock, are especially important to us in game programming because they help guide what the user sees as spontaneous events and an unpredictable opponent. This is also the groundwork for simple artificial intelligence, but I won't get into that until the next chapter. For now, let's just see how far we can push these functions and everything else we've studied in the last two chapters with a sequel to our Battle Bit game Battle Bit II—This is War! (See Example 2.29).

Example 2.29. Battle Bit II: This is War!

```csharp
/* Battle Bit II - THIS IS WAR! Some mad dog soldier shot down the
 * alien Ambassador's convoy and it sparked an intergalactic war.
 * Earth's defenses was weak form warring with several hundred other
 * worlds. So now, it's all up to you. */
using System;

namespace Chapter2 {
    class Class1 {
        static void Main() {
```

Chapter 2: Branches, Loops, and Functions

```csharp
    string input;
    char cYesNo;

    Random rnd = new Random();

    do { // do-while loop
        double iAlienShip1 = Math.Round (rnd.NextDouble() * 100) + 1,
            iAlienShip2 = Math.Round (rnd.NextDouble() * 100) + 1,
            iTarget = 0,
            iAliensMissiles = 0;
        const double iYourLocation = 50;

        Console.WriteLine("Captain, are you in there? Captain?\n"
            + "(Crying is herd form his quarters)\n"
            + "This is ground control to lieutenant Bob.\n"
            + "Your brother Major Tom has been shot down,\n"
            + "Repeat he has been shot down.\n"
            + "The aliens have destroyed our space outpost and \n"
            + "are now on route to Earth.\n"
            + "I know it's a long shot Lieutenant,\n"
            + "but I promised my wife and kids you'd  stop them.\n"
            + "I'll do my best...\n");

        while ((iAlienShip1 > 0) || (iAlienShip2 > 0)) {
            Console.Write("\n\n Enter targeting information: ");
            input = Console.ReadLine();
            iTarget = byte.Parse(input);

            Console.WriteLine("{0},{1}", iAlienShip1, iAlienShip2);

            if (Math.Ceiling(iTarget) == Math.Ceiling(iAlienShip1)
                    || Math.Ceiling(iTarget) == Math.Floor(iAlienShip1)
                    || Math.Floor(iTarget) == Math.Ceiling(iAlienShip1)
                    || Math.Floor(iTarget) == Math.Floor(iAlienShip1)) {
                Console.WriteLine("Alien ship hit, you got him!");
                iAlienShip1 = -1;
            }

            if (Math.Ceiling(iTarget) == Math.Ceiling(iAlienShip2)
                    || Math.Ceiling(iTarget) == Math.Floor(iAlienShip2)
                    || Math.Floor(iTarget) == Math.Ceiling(iAlienShip2)
                    || Math.Floor(iTarget) == Math.Floor(iAlienShip2)) {
                Console.WriteLine("\nAlien ship hit, you took him
                    down!!\n");
                iAlienShip2 = -1;
            }
```

```csharp
                if ((Math.Round (iTarget) > Math.Round (iAlienShip1))
                    && (Math.Round (iTarget) > Math.Round (iAlienShip2)))
                    Console.WriteLine("\n You missed, try aiming a
                        little lower\n");
                else if ((iTarget < iAlienShip1) && (iTarget <
                    iAlienShip2))
                    Console.WriteLine("\n You missed, try aiming
                        higher\n");
                 else
                    Console.WriteLine("\n I can't get a lock on
                        them\n");

                if (Math.Ceiling(iAliensMissiles) ==
                    Math.Ceiling(iYourLocation)
                        || Math.Ceiling(iAliensMissiles) ==
                            Math.Floor(iYourLocation)
                        || Math.Floor(iAliensMissiles) ==
                            Math.Ceiling(iYourLocation)
                        || Math.Floor(iAliensMissiles) ==
                            Math.Ceiling(iYourLocation))
                    break;
                else
                    iAliensMissiles = rnd.NextDouble();
            } // end loop

            if ((iAlienShip1 + iAlienShip2) < 0)
                Console.WriteLine("\n Good work lieutenant, "
                    + "or should I say captain.\n");
             else
                Console.WriteLine("\n BOOM!!! You're dead.\n");

            Console.WriteLine("\n Game Over\n"
                + "\n Would you like to play again? (Y/N)");
            input = Console.ReadLine();
            cYesNo = char.Parse(input);
            cYesNo = char.ToUpper(cYesNo);
        } while (cYesNo == 'Y');
    }
  }
}
```

Type Casting: Explicit Conversions

Before we jump into user-defined functions, let's cover one additional topic that actually allows the conversion of numeric data into other various sized data types without those annoying warnings about truncation and undue data loss. Remember that in Chapter 1 we covered implicit conversions, which generally fell under the category of smaller to larger transfers of data. *Type casting* is an explicit conversion and is used for conversion from smaller to larger to protect against calculating errors, or lager to smaller to redefine those parameters when a value's precision overshadows its requirement (see Text Examples 1 and 2). In either case, the action of declaring an explicit conversion notifies the compiler of our intention and automatically reassigns those variables.

Text Example 1:

When a value is larger than is required for practical purposes, that value can be truncated to save space or to refine the final displayed statement, e.g.,$10.012 becoming $10.01, the amount owed.

Text Example 2:

When an irrational number is the result doing integer mathematics, the value is always truncated to an integer value. This will happen regardless of the assigned variables data type and without regard for the truncating variables true value. For example, in the equation 9 divided by 2, the real quotient should be 4.5, but after truncating, using rules of integer division, we are left with the value of 4. Although incorrect, this is the value passed to the variable, even if that variable is of a floating-point data type. The simplest way to correct this is to make at least one of the values a real number, for example 9.0/2 equals 4.5. However, the problem here is that this type of change only works for literal constants and not for variables that hold integer data (as in $x = 9$, $y = 2$, x/y yielding 4). A more creative solution would be to use type casting. Type casting, as explained above, allows us to convert both literal constants and variables by using data type conversions, e.g., (*double*)9 or *double*(9) (see Example 2.30).

Example 2.30. Type casting.

```
using System;
namespace Chapter2 {
```

```
class Class1 {
    static void Main() {
        double number1 = 9/2; // Warning - returning 4
        Console.WriteLine(number1);

        double number2 = (double)9 / (double)2; // returning 4.5
        Console.WriteLine(number2);

        int integer1 = (int)(4.7); // 4
        Console.WriteLine(integer1);

        if ( 9/2 >= (double)9 / 2 ) // always false
            Console.WriteLine("4 >= 4.5"); //Unreachable code detected

        int integer2 = 9;
        double number3 = (double)integer2 / 2; // 4.5
        Console.WriteLine(number3);

        int integer3 = (int)((double)9 / (double)2 + .5);  // 5.0
        Console.WriteLine(integer3);
    }
}
```

Unsigned values by definition have twice the range of signed values, thus the potential of data loss increases when attempting to convert to a restricted data type.

References, Values, and the Boxing Technique

In addition to being able to convert between the standard types, we can also apply these techniques to include both value to reference and reference to value conversions. This process is most commonly referred to as *boxing*, with the term *unboxing* denoting the return of those values to their original state. The process follows the same steps used for basic type casting, but with an added note of caution when attempting to return or unbox our values: They can return to new variables, but those variables must be of the same type as the original boxed data. The conversions are made using the keyword object, as shown in Example 2.31.

Example 2.31. Boxing and unboxing.

```
using System;

namespace Chapter2 {
    class Class1 {
        static void Main() {
            double Happy = 4.0;

            object MrBox = Happy;

            // This line should work well
            double StillHappy = (double)MrBox;

            // This line may compile, but it will surely fail on execution
            int NotHappy = (int)MrBox;
        }
    }
}
```

Introduction to User-Defined Functions

What are *user-defined functions*? Simply put, they are subprograms (subroutines or secondary methods) linked to a main or secondary method and subsequently used to carry out a list of tasks when that method requests it. They can receive information from other functions (including the main method) and they can send information back to their referencing function. They are both commands (like the predefined functions) and lines code used to implement those commands, which we create as programmers. Technically, everything placed inside a user-defined function could just as well have been left inside its main method, but in professional programs, this would lead to confusion and a very large and cluttered main method. In addition, there are many techniques that can be applied to user-defined functions (including *calls-by-references*, *overloading*, and *recursion*), all of which can be applied repeatedly rather than asking the programmer to repeat that coding over and over again in a single linear method. To start, we'll begin with the simpler functions and then expand on these topics one section at a time.

Writing Our First User-Defined Function

Writing a user-defined function isn't that different from writing a main function. In fact, if you compared the two, you'd find that the underlying rules are basically the same. One key advantage when declaring user-defined functions is their flexibility in descriptive naming, which gives the programmer an instant, if not complete, description of what the function will do. Microsoft's Hungarian notation and Camel notation, along with the simple rules of variable naming (all discussed in Chapter 1) are what we'll use when declaring our user-defined functions. Our first example demonstrates how a simple function is written. You should use this example to compare the two types of functions, e.g., Main ( ) versus OurFunction ( ) (see Example 2.32).

Example 2.32. Our first function call.

```
using System;

namespace Chapter2 {
    class Class1 {
        static void OurFunction() {
            /* This is a do nothing function */
        }

        static void Main () {
            OurFunction();
        }
    }
}
```

Referencing a user-defined function is not unlike referencing a predefined function.

Although this program is similar to the do-nothing programs of Chapter 1, it still represents a true user-defined function. From here, we could have inserted a slue of information including declared variables, predefined functions, loops, and switch statement. Still, it's best if we hold off on some of these at least until we've completely defined user-defined function. The next few sections include descriptions of prototypes, global and local variables, data structures, and *return* statements all of which are crucial to that definition, so try to be patient.

A second way to write a simple do-nothing function is to place it under the main function as in Example 2.33. If you take a moment to examine this example, you'll find that it is relatively unchanged in regard to its contents and purpose (this being to do nothing). The minor revision simply moves the completed function out of the way while we return to work on the main method.

Example 2.33. Our second function call.

```
using System;

namespace Chapter2 {
    class Class1 {
        static void Main() {
            OurFunction();
        }

        static void OurFunction() {
            /* This is a do nothing function */
        }
    }
}
```

Variable Scope

Local variables are variables declared inside the main or subsequent methods. Their values are not known beyond the limitations of their block. Programmers who wish to transfer data from one block to another must do so using a referencing function. There are generally two types of passing variables: *calls-by-mechanism*, where information is merely passed to new variables, and *calls-by-reference*, which allow the programmer to alter the original memory locations. Local variables, as well as their secondary counterparts, can be passed and repassed endlessly, so limitations are minimized. In addition, user-defined functions have the ability to return data to the main or other calling functions.

C# doesn't actually allow for truly global variables, but the word global can be used to distinguish between localized and inclusive variables within a single method or class. *Global variables* allow for the exchange of data, but do not require a passing variable (see Example 2.34).

Example 2.34. Local and global variables.

```
using System;

namespace Chapter2 {
    class Class1 {
        static int NumberOne, NumberTwo, GlobalTotal = 0;

        static void Main() {
            string input;

            int LocalTotal = 0;
            Console.Write("\n How many apples did Johnny shoplift? ");
            input = Console.ReadLine();
            NumberOne = int.Parse(input);

            Console.Write("\n How many apples did Bobby shoplift? ");
            input = Console.ReadLine();
            NumberTwo = int.Parse(input);

            LocalTotal = NumberOne + NumberTwo;
            OurFunction(LocalTotal);
        }

        static void OurFunction(int Total) {
            GlobalTotal = NumberOne + NumberTwo;
            Console.WriteLine("\n Good news, Johnny and Bobby were "
                + "arrested for shoplifting.\n"
                + "By the way would you like an apple? "
                + "I have {0} of them, {1} apples is a lot.", Total,
                    GlobalTotal);
        }
    }
}
```

All global references that conflict with local variables are generally hidden by the compiler when those blocks are accessed, thus a local reference will always be chosen over a global value. When working with local and global variables that require dual references, two important distinctions must be made. First, a new function reference must be declared and second, the global variables must be completely defined using the class'definition (see Examples 2.35).

Chapter 2: Branches, Loops, and Functions

Example 2.35. Variable scope.

```
using System;

namespace Chapter2 {
    class Class1 {
        // global variable (also the value of a gold bar on earth).
        const double GoldBar = 1000.00;

        static void Main() {
            // local variable (also the value of a gold bar in hell).
            double GoldBar = 0;

            Class1 GlobalCA2 = new Class1();
            Console.WriteLine("The value of gold on earth is "
                + "${0} per ounce", Class1.GoldBar);
            Console.WriteLine("The value of gold in hell is "
                + "${0} per pound", GoldBar);
        }
    }
}
```

Functions that Return Values

Our next step will be to re-equip our user-defined functions with nonvoid data types that require some type of returning calculation. The keyword *return* passes back a single value to the calling function. The value in question must be of the qualified type, and in cases where the returning type is void it can be omitted. *Return* statements are required with all nonvoid user-defined functions and methods. We'll begin by developing a simple, but effective function that finds the sum of two values and returns that value to the main method (we could also revise this example to compute their difference, product, quotient—see Example 2.36).

Example 2.36. Returning values.

```
using System;

namespace Chapter2 {
```

```csharp
class Class1 {
    static void Main() {
        string input;
        int iNumberOne = 0, iNumberTwo = 0; // Local variables

        iNumberTwo = RandomNumber();

        while (iNumberOne != 99) { // 99 ends loop
            Console.Write ("\n Guess the number, hint: "
                + "it's between ten and three.\n"
                + "Can you guess it he, he, he? ");
            input = Console.ReadLine();
            iNumberOne = int.Parse(input);

            if (iNumberOne == iNumberTwo) {
                Console.WriteLine("\n Hey you win, with a smile "
                    + "with a grin!!!");
                iNumberTwo = RandomNumber();
            } else if (iNumberOne > iNumberTwo) {
                Console.WriteLine("\n Too high smart guy!");
                iNumberTwo++;
            } else {
                Console.WriteLine("\n Too low slow Joe");
                iNumberTwo--;
            }
        }
    }

    static int RandomNumber() {
        Random rnd = new Random();
        int n2 = (int)Math.Round(rnd.NextDouble() * 9) + 1;

        return (n2);
    }
}
```

Our next comparison opens the field a bit by making our random function capable of returning character data. Here we also included a `while` loop that protects our function from returning anything other than a letter (see Example 2.37).

Example 2.37. Letter generator.

```csharp
using System;

namespace Chapter2 {
    class Class1 {
        static void Main() {
            char Letter = ' ', Response;
            string input;

            Console.WriteLine ("This program attempts to guess "
                + "the first letter\n"
                + "of your first name by randomly generated letters.\n"
                + "All you have to do is reply with a \"y\"\n"
                + "or a \"n\" after each guess\n"
                + "You can also enter \"q\" to quit "
                + "the game at any time.\n"
                + "My first guess is...\n");

            do {
                Letter = LetterGenerator(Letter);
                Console.WriteLine("{0} is this correct?\n", Letter);
                input = Console.ReadLine();
                Response = char.Parse(input);

                if (char.ToUpper(Response) == 'Y')
                    Console.WriteLine("Great let's play again");
                else
                    Console.WriteLine("How about...");
            } while (char.ToUpper(Response) != 'Q');
        }

        static char LetterGenerator(int Letter) {
            Random rnd = new Random();
            Letter = ((int)Math.Round(rnd.NextDouble() * 100));
            while (!(Letter >= 65 && Letter <= 90)) {
                Letter = ((int)Math.Round(rnd.NextDouble() * 100));
            }

            return ((char)Letter);
        }
    }
}
```

The main method is also easily adaptable to include both storage data types and the return statement (see Examples 2.38 and 2.39). Note that referencing a return statement from within the main method causes the immediate termination of that program.

Example 2.38. Main function with data types.

```
using System;

namespace Chapter2 {
    class Class1 {
        static int Main() {
            return 0;
        }
    }
}
```

Example 2.39. Empty return statements.

```
using System;

namespace Chapter2 {
    class Class1 {
        static void Main() {
            return;
        }
    }
}
```

Passing Variables: Calls-By-Value

The *call-by-value type mechanism* is a mechanism used to transfer data between methods that does not allow for continued access to the original fields. The data is then considered to be a value type, which is appropriately stored on the "stack"—the computer's temporary memory—and will be removed, or "popped off," when that method is terminated. Again, the changes in these secondary variables will not affect the original fields, nor will there be deletions. The call-by-value formal parameters refer to the variables referenced from inside user-defined functions as demonstrated in Example 2.40 (a simple example that finds the square root of a number).

Example 2.40. Passing our first variable.

```
using System;

namespace Chapter2 {
    class Class1 {
        static void Main() {
            string input;
            float number = 0, root = 0;

            Console.WriteLine("This program will find the "
                + "square root of any number\n"
                + "To continue just enter a number when prompted\n"
                + "Your results will appear after you press enter\n"
                + "To quit just enter the number \"1\"\n"
                + "Enter your first value now: ");
            input = Console.ReadLine();
            number = float.Parse(input);

            while (number > 1) {
                root = SquareRoot(number);
                Console.WriteLine(root);

                Console.WriteLine("Enter your next value now: ");
                input = Console.ReadLine();
                number = float.Parse(input);
            }
        }

        // This function generates square roots using Newton's method

        static float SquareRoot(float n) {
            float test1, test2;
            test1 = n - (float).01 - ((n - (float).01) * (n - (float).01) - n)
                / (n * (n - (float).01));
            test2 = test1 - ((test1 * test1) - n) / ((n) * test1);

            while (test1 != test2) {
                test1 = test2;
                test2 = test1 - (test1 * test1 - n) / ((n) * test1);
            }
            return (test2);
        }
    }
}
```

> We could also have replaced that user-defined function with the predefined function Math.Sqrt ( ).

Writing Functions as Black Boxes

The *black box theory* is simply a concept that stresses the idea that most, if not all, functions should be thought of as independent or self-containing subprograms. It also reasons that the coding used to construct such a function does not need to be studied or known by a programmer who only wants to invoke that function. Thus, the only information needed to access a function is the proper passing variables and the knowledge of what would be returned by the function. This is analogous to being able to drive a car, but not knowing how to repair the engine. This is actually the norm in C#, since all predefined functions are black boxes to most programmers and the idea of enhancing them would literally force us to open them up and redesign them to some new standard (which unfortunately is usually necessary in game programming). Of course, if you were to write your own user-defined functions, you'd certainly know how each one of them worked.

Creating a black box style function requires or restricts us to the use of encapsulated controls. This, of course, means that you must avoid using global variables and that you must include comments with every prototype to alert any other programmer to the variable settings and to their results. In addition, you should keep in mind that in later chapters, we'll be both reading and writing to user-defined functions from separate files, thus creating a real need for detailed comments explaining what these different function calls do.

> **Applying the black box approach to Example 2.40**
> Let's assume that you didn't really understand the second portion of the last example, but you used the square root function anyway. While it is a bit disheartening to the mathematician in me, this will not affect the way the program executes that data, and in fact, actually makes my point. If however, that coding piqued your interest then here's a quick overview of the mathematics (see Example 2.41).

Example 2.41. The square root function explained.

```
static float SquareRoot (float n){    // Newton's Method (Basic Calculus)
float test1, test2;                   // X_{n+1} = X_n - f(X_n)/f'(X_n)  n = 1, 2, 3,
    . . .
   test1 = n-(float).01 -             // X_0 = Guess-Estimate
      ((n-(float).01)*(n-(float).01) - n)/(n*(n-(float).01));
   test2 = test1 - ((test1*test1)-n)/((n)*test1);

   while (test1 != test2){            // X_1 = X_0 - (X_0^2 - Number)/(Number*X_0)
      test1 = test2;                  // X_2 = X_1 - (X_1^2 - Number)/(Number*X_1)
      test2 = test1 -                 // X_3 = X_2 - (X_2^2 - Number)/(Number*X_2)
         (test1*test1 - n) /          // X4  = X_3 - (X_3^2 - Number)/ (Number*X_3)
             ((n)*test1);             // X_5 = X_4 - (X_4^2 - Number)/(Number*X_4)
   }
   return (test2);                    // until X_{n...} = X_{n...+1}
}
```

Again, we can also reconstruct the last program using the predefined function Math.Sqrt() (see Example 2.42).

Example 2.42. User-defined versus predefined functions.

```
using System;

namespace Chapter2 {
    class Class1 {
        static void Main() {
            string input;
            float number = 0, root = 0;

            Console.WriteLine("This program will find the "
                + "square root of any number\n"
                + "To continue just enter a number when prompted\n"
                + "Your results will appear after you press enter\n"
                + "To quit just enter the number \"1\"\n"
                + "Enter your first value now: ");
            input = Console.ReadLine();
            number = float.Parse(input);
```

C# and Game Programming

```
            while (number > 1) {
                root = (float)Math.Sqrt(number);
                Console.WriteLine(root);

                Console.WriteLine("Enter your next value now: ");
                input = Console.ReadLine();
                number = float.Parse(input);
            }
        }
    }
}
```

> We'll want to take the black box approach to most, if not all, of the predefined functions listed in this text.

Passing Variables: Calls-By-Reference

The *call-by-reference mechanism* is an assignable mechanism, where the variables that are passed to a function are not just passed as values, but include actual memory references. Thus, by altering those values, we are also altering the values accessed by the main program. These variables, then, are not created and destroyed as part of a temporary stack; rather, they are created and stored by the heap, which is a memory location that exists for the entire life of the program's execution. This has the minor disadvantage of not allowing us to send numeric or literal constants as we could with the call-by-value mechanism, but it does expand our options when dealing with otherwise globally restricted data. The correct way to define a call-by-reference variable includes the use of the keyword `ref` preceding both the call and the function's signature. The subprograms can then be made to carry out anything from a single, or subsequently large list of black box type actions (see Example 2.43 for a basic example of such referencing). Note that without such referencing, all of the changes would have to be made from within the main program.

Example 2.43. A day at the races.

```
using System;

namespace Chapter2 {
```

```csharp
class Class1 {
    static void Main() {
        string input = "Y", Horse;
        int iNumber1 = 0, iNumber2 = 0, iNumber3 = 0;

        Console.WriteLine("Let's have a horse race.\n"
            + "To play select one of the horses below");

        while (char.ToUpper(char.Parse(input)) != 'N') {
            Console.WriteLine("(1) for Whitefire\n"
                + "(2) for The Train and, \n"
                + "(3) for Noisy Glue\n");
            Horse = Console.ReadLine ();

            TheRace(ref iNumber1);
            TheRace(ref iNumber2);
            TheRace(ref iNumber3);

            TieBreaker(iNumber1, ref iNumber2);
            TieBreaker(iNumber2, ref iNumber3);
            TieBreaker(iNumber1, ref iNumber3);

            Console.Write("And the winner is ");
            if (iNumber1 > iNumber2 && iNumber1 > iNumber3)
                Console.WriteLine("Noisy Glue"); // 3
            else if (iNumber2 > iNumber1 && iNumber2 > iNumber3)
                Console.WriteLine("The Train"); // 2
            else
                Console.WriteLine("Whitefire"); // 1

            Console.WriteLine("Would you like to play again (Y/N)?");
            input = Console.ReadLine();
        }
    }

    static void TheRace(ref int Num) {
        Random rnd = new Random();

        Num = (int)Math.Round(rnd.NextDouble() * 1000);
    }

    static void TieBreaker(int Num1, ref int Num2) {
        if (Num1 == Num2) {
```

C# and Game Programming

```
            TheRace(ref Num2);
            TieBreaker(Num1, ref Num2);
        }
    }
  }
}
```

The Keyword out

The keyword out is a special exception marker that notifies the compiler that the variable under scrutiny does not need to be assigned before it can be passed as a referenced variable. This is usually the case when dealing with variables that wouldn't otherwise have a meaningful value before the appropriate functions can be executed. Since an out value is also a referenced value, this keyword negates the need for the second reference (ref) (see Example 2.44).

Example 2.44. The keyword out.

```
using System;

namespace Chapter2 {
    class Class1 {
        static void Main() {
            string input = "Y", Horse;
            int iNumber1, iNumber2, iNumber3;

            Console.WriteLine("Let's have a horse race.\n"
                + "To play select one of the horses below");

            while (char.ToUpper(char.Parse(input)) != 'N') {
                Console.WriteLine("(1) for Whitefire\n"
                    + "(2) for The Train and, \n"
                    + "(3) for Noisy Glue\n");
                Horse = Console.ReadLine ();

                TheRace (out iNumber1);
                TheRace (out iNumber2);
                TheRace (out iNumber3);

                TieBreaker (iNumber1, ref iNumber2);
                TieBreaker (iNumber2, ref iNumber3);
                TieBreaker (iNumber1, ref iNumber3);
```

```
            Console.Write ("And the winner is ");

            if (iNumber1 > iNumber2 && iNumber1 > iNumber3)
                Console.WriteLine("Noisy Glue"); // 3
            else if (iNumber2 > iNumber1 && iNumber2 > iNumber3)
                Console.WriteLine("The Train"); // 2
             else
                Console.WriteLine("Whitefire"); // 1

            Console.WriteLine("Would you like to play again (Y/N)?");
            input = Console.ReadLine();    }
        }

        static void TheRace(out int Num) {
            Random rnd = new Random();
            Num = (int)Math.Round(rnd.NextDouble() * 1000);
        }

        static void TieBreaker(int Num1, ref int Num2) {
            if (Num1 == Num2) {
                TheRace(out Num2);
                TieBreaker(Num1, ref Num2);
            }
        }
    }
}
```

An Introduction to Polymorphism

Polymorphism (also known as *overloading*) occurs when any reference has a closely matching, but not identical definition. These secondary, or substitute functions, while not technically required, generally tend to stay within the confines of the first function's purpose. If an overloading function were to be altered to a degree that promoted a completely new definition, then overloading would not be necessary. While overloading functions do share the same referencing title, their definitions must differ in arrangement by at least one transferring data type. The use of these differing access points guides the compiler to the correct (overloading) function. Since more than one possible referencing point exists, there is also an increased chance of miscalling that function, thus creating a runtime error. Examples 2.45 and 2.46 give alternate functions that can produce the same results, but only one is actually performing correctly.

Example 2.45. Overloading a function.

```csharp
using System;

namespace Chapter2 {
    class Class1 {
        static void Main() {
            string input;
            int iNumber1 = 0, iNumber2 = 0, iNumber3 = 0, iTotal;

            Console.WriteLine("Please enter two to three "
                + "numbers to be added\n"
                + "If you only have two numbers make "
                + "the third number equal to zero:\n");

            input = Console.ReadLine();
            iNumber1 = int.Parse(input);
            input = Console.ReadLine();
            iNumber2 = int.Parse(input);
            input = Console.ReadLine();
            iNumber3 = int.Parse(input);

            if (iNumber3 == 0)
                iTotal = Sum(iNumber1, iNumber2);
            else
                iTotal = Sum(iNumber1, iNumber2, iNumber3);

            Console.WriteLine("The Sum of these numbers was {0}", iTotal);
        }
        static int Sum(int iNumber1, int iNumber2) {
            int iSum;
            iSum = iNumber1 + iNumber2;
            return (iSum);
        }

        static int Sum(int iNumber1, int iNumber2, int iNumber3) {
            int iSum;
            iSum = iNumber1 + iNumber2 + iNumber3;
            return (iSum);
        }
    }
}
```

Chapter 2: Branches, Loops, and Functions

> If you're not sure if this program is working correctly, try retesting the three variables using two zeros and a negative one.

Example 2.46. This program does not overload the function.

```
using System;

namespace Chapter2 {
    class Class1 {
        static void Main() {
            string input;
            int iNumber1 = 0, iNumber2 = 0,
                iNumber3 = 0, iTotal;

            Console.WriteLine("Please enter two to three numbers"
                + "to be added\n"
                + "If you only have two numbers "
                + "make the third number equal to zero: \n");

            input = Console.ReadLine();
            iNumber1 = int.Parse(input);
            input = Console.ReadLine();
            iNumber2 = int.Parse(input);
            input = Console.ReadLine();
            iNumber3 = int.Parse(input);

            iTotal = Sum(iNumber1, iNumber2, iNumber3);

            Console.WriteLine("The Sum of these numbers was {0}", iTotal);
        }

        static int Sum(int iNumber1, int iNumber2, int iNumber3) {
            int iSum;
            iSum = iNumber1 + iNumber2 + iNumber3;
            return (iSum);
        }
    }
}
```

Introducing Recursion

A *recursive function* is a user-defined function that contains one or more odd iterations caused by the unusual placement of a secondary call to that function. The position or placement of this secondary function call is considered unusual or at least a special topic because it invokes a function from within that function. That is to say, when the programmers created the function, they included it in a call to itself that causes that function to loop repeatedly, or at least multiple times. (Note: This would also mean that it would have to return to itself multiple times before returning to the main or calling function). The reasons for manipulating a function in this manner are diverse and at times confusing, but ultimately, the coding for such examples is quite simple, as shown in Example 2.47. Note the recursive function used to test our horseracing program earlier in this chapter.

Example 2.47. Recursion.

```csharp
using System;

namespace Chapter2 {
    class Class1 {
        static void Main() {
            Password();
        }

        static void Password() {
            string input;
            int password;

            Console.WriteLine("\n Enter Your Access Code Now: ");
            input = Console.ReadLine();
            password = int.Parse(input);
            if (password == 1024) {
                Console.WriteLine("\n Access Granted");
                return;
            } else
                Password();
        }
    }
}
```

Inline Functions

Another interesting thing about C# is its automatic use of `inline` *functions*, which are functions that are inserted into every line that requires its reference. That is, rather than having the function reference search out the function at runtime, the function is compiled into that line of coding. This speeds up the program, but it also increases the code size. The biggest problem with "inlining" in C/C++ was that it was only a request and not an order, so the compiler could refuse to do it. The majority of compilers (and this includes the Microsoft's Visual C++ series) won't inline a recursive function, nor will they allow functions that are referred to through pointers (see Chapter 4 for information on pointers). The C/C++ keyword `inline` is not required in C#, and thus falls under the list of antiquated coding. Note: Microsoft versions of both C and C++ also included two variations on the inline command, (__inline and __forceinline); these keywords also have no place in C#.

Troubleshooting

It's time for another deep breath and a bit of problem solving. Remember that if you don't find the answers here they might have been explained in the last troubleshooting section (see Chapter 1). First, let's look at the problem from a logical standpoint; let's assume that you've worked, successfully, with all of the programs listed in the last chapter. If so, then any problems would have to relate to syntax. Question: do errors occur at compilation? Try resetting the warning level to a lower setting; did those errors become warnings? Perhaps you had a syntax error; look for errors caused by using the wrong symbols in your comparisons. If there are no compiling errors, but the program's data is still producing incorrect output, try looking for reversed symbols, typographical errors, or incomplete coding errors.

Common Errors, Problems, and Pitfalls

1. Symbol combinations such as ==, !=, and >= cannot be written with spaces between them (= =, ! =). incorrect and should always be avoided even if the program seems to work.
2. Do not confuse = with = =. Remember = is used to assign a value and = = is used to compare two values.
3. Attempting to use a single equal sign inside an `if` statement will result in an error.

4. `While` loops do not require a semicolon, but `do-while` loops do (as in do…while (something);).
5. Most compilers don't recognize names beyond the first thirty characters so be careful with long names that are too similar.
6. Leaving off a closing bracket usually causes several errors. In addition, forgetting to delete an excess bracket usually causes an unexpected error.
7. Forgetting to terminate a `While` loop is a prime example of a logical/runtime error. The program does everything it's told to do, but that causes it to become stuck. The solution is simply to cancel the program either with a Ctrl-<C> or by closing the executable window with the mouse and then rewriting the loop to include an event that will end it at the right time. This type of error is most commonly called an *infinite loop error*.
8. All values should be initialized before any information is taken from them, not doing so will result in a *corrupted data* error.
9. Of course, you still can't divide by zero, so don't even try it. However, if you fear that occasionally your data might total zero, you'll need to test for that result and work around it. This can be done in many ways, but the easiest is with the `if` statement (think about short-circuiting).
10. You cannot increment or decrement a complex variable. For example, you wouldn't be able to increment the sum of two numbers, e.g., [(x+5)++].
11. One of the most common errors is to mistakenly reverse a less than or greater than symbol from inside a loop's termination sequence, causing the comparison to never find its match: this is a typographical error that creates a runtime error (an infinite loop).
12. Did you place a semicolon at the end of the first line of an `if` statement, `for` statement, or `switch` statement? Doing so would indicate to the compiler that these lines are blank or null and your block or single statement would not be viewed as part of that sequence.
13. Remember, from inside a function's definition, you must declare each data type individually as in int one, int two; attempting to include them just with a comma results in a compiling error.

14. Remember C# requires that all case statements conclude with a break reference.
15. Remember the `out` statement replaces the `ref` statement when defining calls-by-reference.

> **Things to Remember**
>
> 1. *If* statements are used with limited comparisons, while *switch* statements are used in multiple cases.
> 2. A compound statement is a set of statements that are contained between to braces.
> 3. Mathematical shortcuts should only be used if they make things simpler to read. (Note: Some compilers will convert these shortcuts into faster running code.)
> 4. System.Console.Write, and using System; with Console.Write do exactly the same thing.
> 5. The *while* loop test and then runs its first cycle, whereas the *do-while* loop runs first and tests after running its first cycle.
> 6. You'll have to remember everything about predefined and user-defined functions. The best way to remember them is through practice, so I'll include as many as I can—the rest you'll have to practice on your own.
> 7. Remember C# doesn't require function prototypes or included files.
> 8. Calls-by-reference can completely replace global variables.
> 9. Overloaded functions must not contain the same arrangement of passing variables.
> 10. Recursion means nothing more than repeating the same function from within that function.
> 11. When writing a statement that stretches over a single line try to break it up. Break at a comma or other marking to make the split easier to read.

12. Always use a standard predefined function when possible; they speed up programming tasks and increase program portability.
13. The goal of any good programmer is to write code that can be reused in several projects. Don't waste time rewriting the same code.
14. When using `if-else` statements try to place the most common occurrence first; this will speed up your program by moving you to the right info faster.
15. Converting several `if` statements into fewer `if-else` statements also speeds up programs, since more comparisons can be skipped and time is saved.
16. Some programmers use brackets to enclose every `if-else` statement. I'll do this on occasion, but I usually leave single statements as is.
17. It should be noted that not every `switch` statement requires a concluding default statement, and that these defaults could be listed at the top or anywhere inside the switch statement. However, there are some things to be said about sticking with the standard— in this case, it will make your programs easier to read.
18. You should also note that loops based on counters such as the `for` and `while` loops will become infinite if their marks are counting the wrong way or start after the mark. These are also considered infinite loops, but can be much harder to find.
19. Always remember when asking the user for inputs such as name, social security number... You can echo that information to allow for changes.
20. Be careful when comparing real numbers: Remember, 4.001 does not equal 4.00005, and neither equal the integer value 4.
21. Avoid using floating point variables (float and double) to count loops.
22. C#, like C/C++, always attempts to shortcut a comparison when it is written using an && symbol; this will save time... Thus to speed up your programs you should try to place the more commonly false tests first.
23. Some programmers feel that keywords such as `break` and `continue` violate the structured programmer's ideals. These

keywords, however, speed up programming tasks and are considered valuable by many programmers.
24. When it comes to value versus reference use, remember that reference values are faster, but value types are safer.
25. Remember, the inline qualifier is automatic in C#.
26. Try to limit each function to a single task. If one function requires a large list of variables, or if it does the job of many functions, then it's probably too big. Remember, the ultimate goal of the programmer is to write for both reusability and portability.

Questions

1. Using three `if` statements, write a program that tests two variables such that if it finds that the first variable is equal to, less than, or greater than the second, a corresponding message is displayed.
2. Using the keyword `else-if`, simplify the previous program (Hint: Use one `if` statement and two `else-if`s).
3. Using the keyword `else`, simplify the first program to use one *if* statement, one `else-if` statement, and one `else` statement.
4. From Question 3, revise each comparison to include the compound *if,* `else-if,` and `else` statements.
5. Write a program that uses a nested *if* statement that first asks the user if he/she has two numbers to compare and then repeats Question 4.
6. Revise the program from Question 5 using the `or` operator as is ('Y' || 'y').
7. Revise the program from Question 5 using the "and" and the "not" operators.
8. Find the sum of two numbers using the abbreviated form +=.
9. Repeat Question 8 for subtraction, multiplication, division, and remainders.

10. Write a program that allows the user to choose from any one of the five basic math types. Use a `while` loop to repeat the choices after each calculation.
11. Revise the program from Question 10 using a *continue* statement that forces the `while` loop to skip the actual calculation.
12. Revise the program from Question 10 using the `do-while` loop.
13. Revise the program from Question 10 using the `for` loop.
14. Alter the program from Question 10, replacing all the *if* statements with `switch` statements.
15. Revise the program from Question 14, replacing `cout` with `printf` and `cin` with `scanf`.
16. Revise the program from Question 14, replacing `cout` with `puts` and `cin` with `gets`.
17. Write a program that tests an `if` statement using the Boolean data type (`bool` test).
18. Write a program that uses short circuit evaluation to safeguard against division by zero.
19. Write a program that uses type casting to convert a double constant (as in 1.3) to the float data type.
20. Revise the program from Question 5 by replacing (Y || y) with the ToUpper function.
21. Write a do-nothing program that calls the user-defined function Hello ( ). Hello should display the words "Hello world!"
22. Revise the program from Question 21 to use a prototype to Hello ( ).
23. Using global variables, write a program that compares two variables inside a user-defined function.
24. Revise the last program using local variables; use Hello (*int* iVal1, int iVal2).
25. Revise the last program so that the two variables are declared and assigned inside the user-defined function and only the final value is sent back to the main function (Hint: Use *static int* Hello( )).
26. Write a program that uses two user-defined functions, one to add the sum of two numbers, the other to add the sum of three numbers, using an overloaded user-defined function.
27. Write a user-defined function that uses recursion to count from zero to ten.

Game Programming Basics II

Chapter Three
Introducing DirectX

*The marble not yet carved can hold the form
of every thought the greatest artist has.*
    –**Michelangelo**

Managed DirectX is an alternative Application Programming Interface (API), developed by Microsoft, to handle the higher demands of graphic and sound programming found in today's applications. Managed DirectX allows for direct access to video, sound, and input devices to include video cards, sounds cards, keyboards, mice, and joysticks. There are several components that make up Managed DirectX, including Direct3D, Draw, Input, Play, Sound, AudioVideoPlayback, Diagnostics, and Security, but for this introductory chapter, we'll limit ourselves to the concepts and techniques relating to DirectDraw, Sound, and Input. We'll also use this chapter to introduce several game algorithms and the concepts of character development, animation, collision detection, and artificial intelligence, as well as techniques to display both hand-drawn and rendered graphic. The benefits to using Managed DirectX include the elimination of the Component Object Model (COM) interoperability layer, which decreases code size while improving performance.

> Inside DirectX:
> DirectX gains its speed by bypassing the standard Window's API; there are two underlying layers that interface with DirectX: the HAL (Hardware Abstract Layer), which interfaces directly with our hardware, and the HEL (Hardware

C# and Game Programming

> Emulation Layer), which serves as a secondary interface. When our hardware does not support a certain feature or function, specific device support is given as a product of a Globally Unique Identifier or GUID. The advantages of using manufacture-composed device drivers include hardware-independence, increased performance, and complete access to special features and functions (see Diagram 3.1).

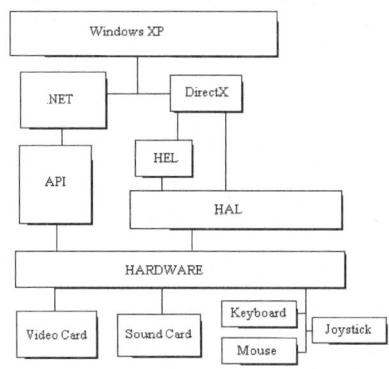

Diagram 3.1. DirectX

Referencing DirectX

To install DirectX simply download Microsoft's SDK (Software Development Kit), available free from Microsoft. You can find detailed instructions on the CD included with this book. You'll be prompted with two choices, Debug and Release; both are adequate for our purposes. DirectX is linked to our files using one of two methods; the first is to create a standard Windows Application, loading the DirectX-components from the "Add Reference" menu (see Appendix I). Second, we can create our projects using the DirectX 9 Visual C# Wizard, selecting "DirectDraw," "Audio," and "DirectInput." Note that Windows inserts a certain level of base coding; while this coding can be a useful starting point, for study purposes, we'll delete all pre-generated code and begin from scratch (See Screen Shot 3.0).

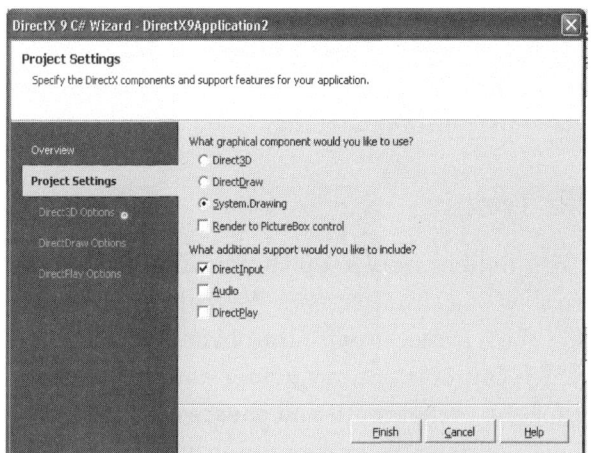

Screen Shot 3.0

If you were left on a deserted island and you could only bring one thing, what would that be? I'd bring scratch, because everything is made from it.

Writing Games

Before we can write a program, game, or otherwise, we must first have an idea of what our program is going to be about. Next, we'll have to develop our idea using a list of thoughts usually expanding in phases and always increasing in detail. As we progress, we'll also want to turn this list into a formal document, or algorithm. This algorithm could then be enhanced both logically and pictorially through the use of mathematical and graphical designs. For the beginner, this usually means peeking into the C# language, but for the moment we won't really begin to write code. In gaming terms, this also often requires the ability to draw or the enlistment of a graphic artist, but for these examples, we'll rely primarily on simple mouse and hand-drawn graphics. In addition, when we do begin to convert to code, we'll also want to develop our tasks using the simplest coding possible, but with the added criteria that it is generic in nature. Remember, the higher the level of abstraction, the greater the level of reusability.

Game 1—Paddle Tennis

For our first game, we'll deliberately keep things simple with three objects, one background image, and an area of a single screen. We'll also restrict our motion and keep the physics to a minimum, which leaves us with the obvious choices of twin tennis players and a simple tennis ball. We can create a net using simple graphics, and of course, we'll include basic sounds for the racket, ball, and cheers of the crowd, but again, all of these steps should be done in the proper order, beginning with the creation of an outline…

Brainstorming

Brainstorming is the first creative step. It's nothing more than throwing out ideas, but it's also the foundation for everything that follows. Example 3.1 shows what we might write if we were planning to create a sports game like Paddle Tennis.

 Brainstorming

Example 3.1. Brainstorming Paddle Tennis.

1. The game should have two players. One placed on the right, the other on the left.
2. There should be a net that divides the screen vertically.
3. The players should move freely, up, down, left, and right, but they should not be allowed to leave the screen or cross over to the other player's side.
4. There is a ball that bounces around, which the players can hit back and forth, with the upper and lower limits used to simulate the ground.

5. The ball can increase in size when it's moving closer to the net, thus simulating a 3D environment.
6. When one player misses the ball, the other player should get a point and/or win the serve.
7. The game should start with a simple menu that allows players to select the type of game, e.g., two players, one player, or demo mode. (Note: One player and demo modes mean that we'll have to write some simple artificial intelligence coding).
8. The game should also allow our players to quit at any time via the ESC key. Asking the players if they're sure they want to quit before actually ending the program could also be an option.
9. The game should be colorful with a blue background, yellow net and two brightly dressed characters (it would be best if the tennis ball actually looked like a tennis ball).
10. The game should also have sounds when the ball hits the ground (edges of the screen) and/or the players. There should also be a cheer from the unseen viewers when a player scores.
11. You may also want to put in a timer that automatically starts the demo mode if nothing happens for, say, two minutes. Finally, the game should reset itself to allow for repeated play.

Drawing Characters

Now that we have a general idea of what we'll need pictorially, we'll have to convert those ideas into actual illustrations, and then we'll have the fun task of figuring out how those images are going to be manipulated. The actual designs aren't really that important, but the steps used to access and complete those designs are. The first step then is to familiarize ourselves with how the graphic tools work in this new environment. Note: If you're not an artist not to worry, the CD-ROM includes a complete list of predrawn images relating to all of the games listed.

To begin, I'll assume you're sitting in front of your computer with your .Net compiler fully loaded and that you have already selected both the "New Project" listing and the "Windows Application" icon Note: do not confuse this application with the console version used in the pervious chapters). Now change the name of the project to "Chapter3" and press "OK" (see Screen Shots 3.1–3.3).

C# and Game Programming

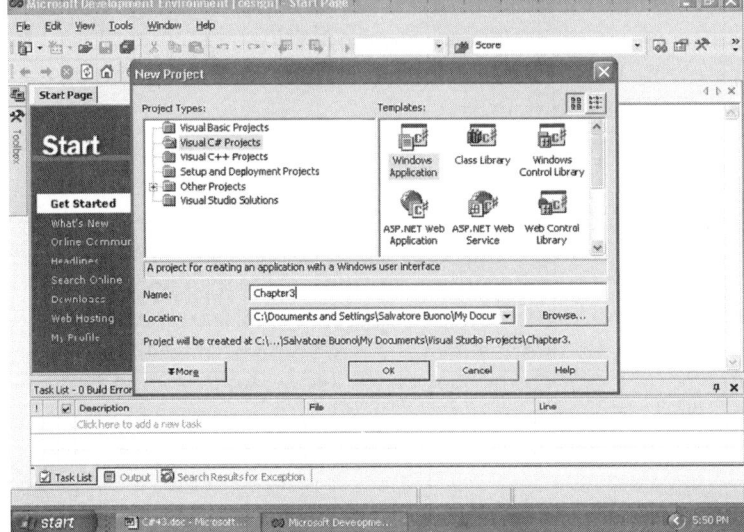

Screen Shot 3.1.

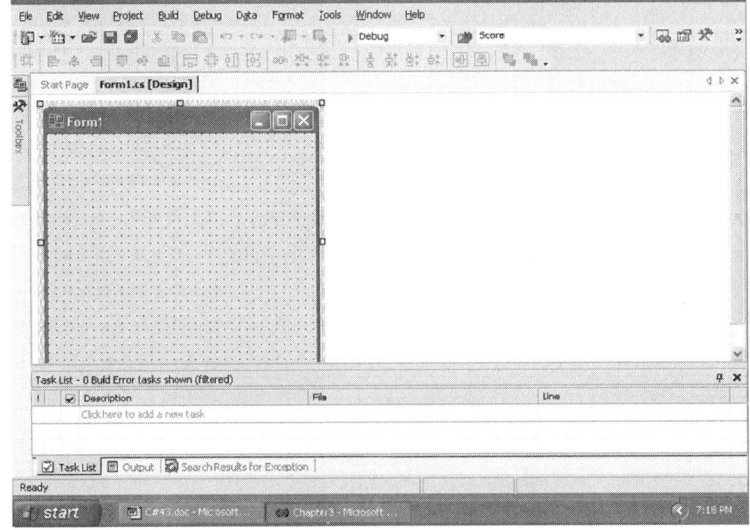

Screen Shot 3.2.

Chapter 3: Writing Games

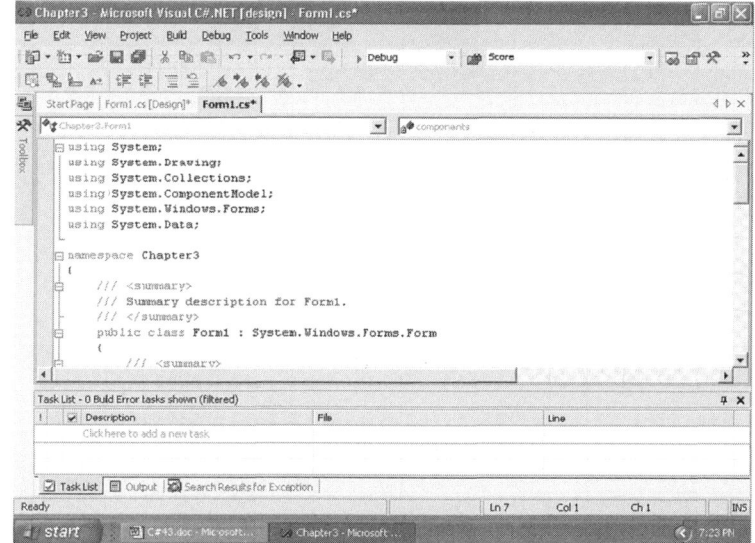

Screen Shot 3.3.

> The first screen you'll see is only the visual portion of our program; to open the text portion, simply double click on that grid (see Example 3.2 on the CD-ROM).

Next, we'll want to open a new graphics file. To create such a file, simply click the "File" menu and select "New," and then the secondary "File" listing. A second window labeled "New File" should appear with a host of options; select the icon titled "Bitmap File" and then press "Open" (see Screen Shots 3.4 and 3.5).

C# and Game Programming

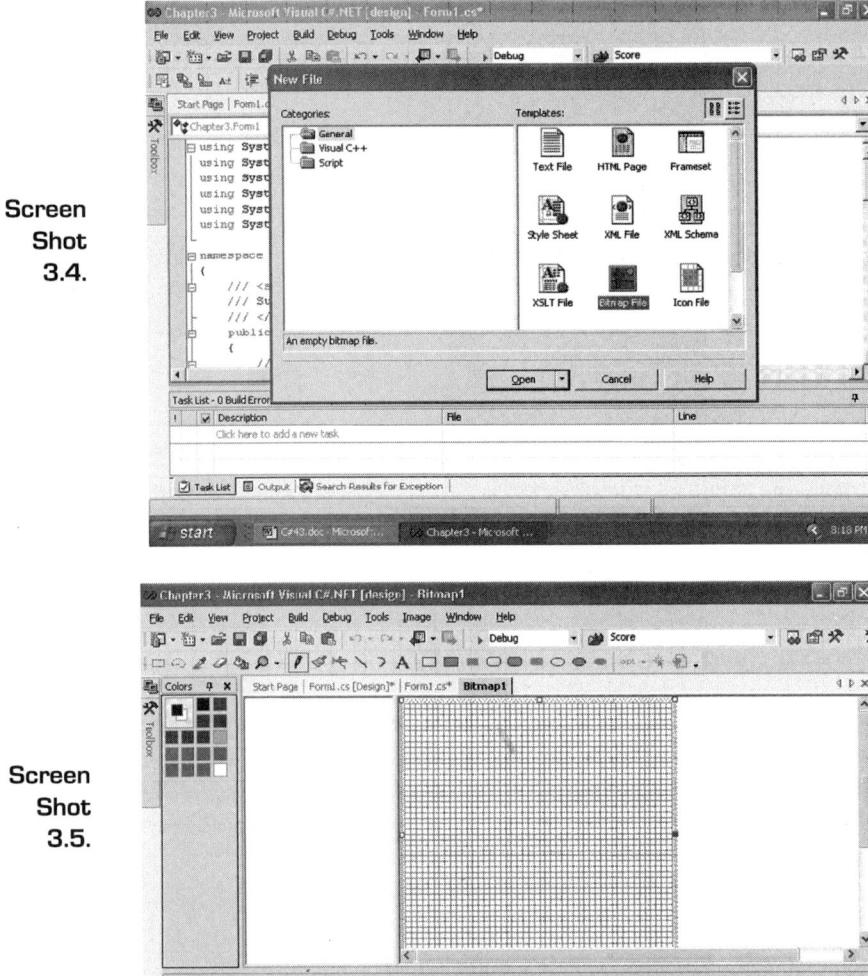

Screen Shot 3.4.

Screen Shot 3.5.

From this point, we'll use these tools in basically the same manner as any other graphics program; in fact, if you prefer, you can run all your designs through an alternative program, just as long as you make those files available to your project(s).

Chapter 3: Writing Games

The three characters we'll concern ourselves with are the two players and their tennis ball. To shortcut this further, we'll assume that the two players will just be the reverse of each other (see Screen Shots 3.6–3.8).

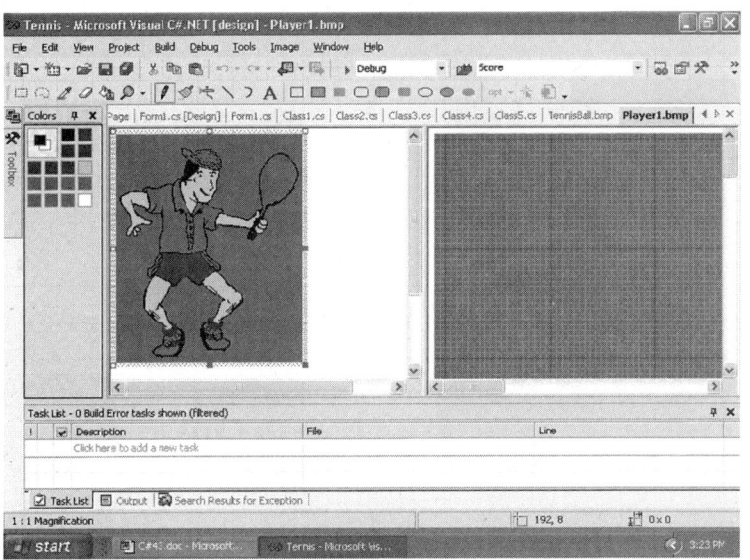

Screen Shot 3.6.

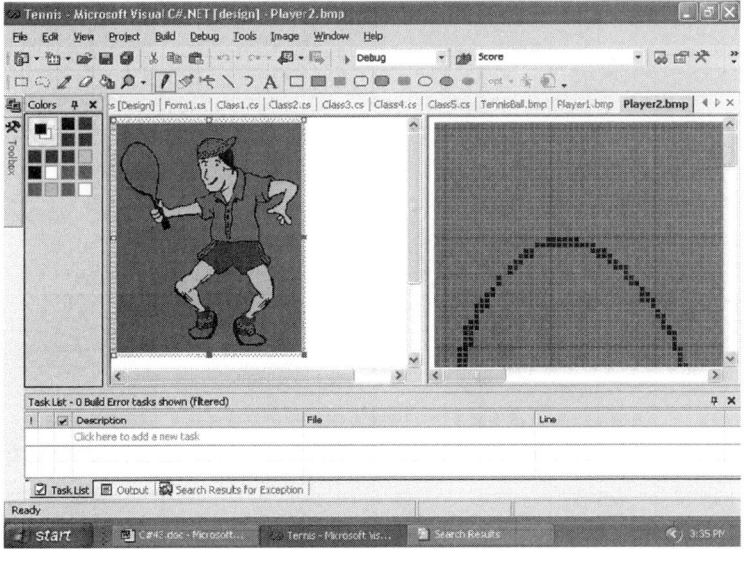

Screen Shot 3.7.

C# and Game Programming

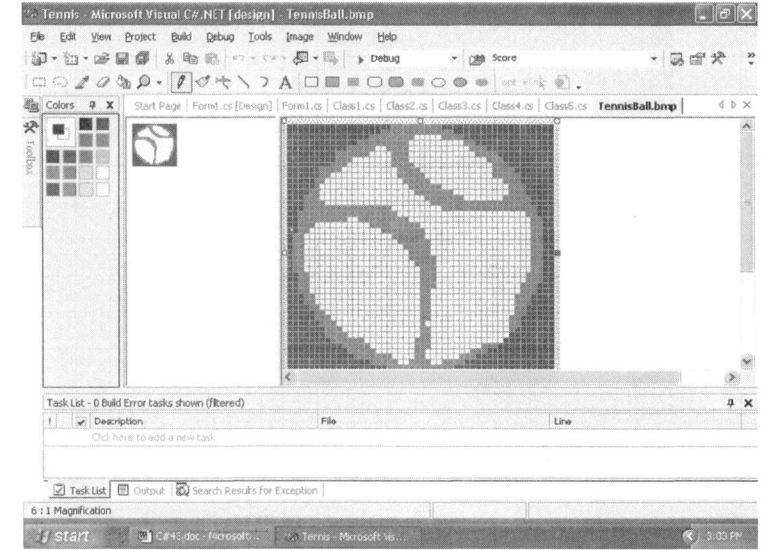

Screen Shot 3.8.

Plotting Motions

The next step is to plot the motions of our players and their ball. The player's movements are a bit easier to define so we'll discuss those first. The players have free and easy two-dimensional movement. Their playing field is limited to the screen size and they are not allowed to cross into the other player's area (see Example 3.3).

Example 3.3. Two-dimensional movement.

One-dimensional movement   Two-dimensional movement

The ball, unlike the players, requires us to include diagonal movements, which technically are still only two-dimensional movements; the added visual effect is important when conveying the feel of free motion. This, however, still only totals six directions, since we won't allow the ball to travel directly up or directly down (see Example 3.4).

Example 3.4. Movement of the ball.

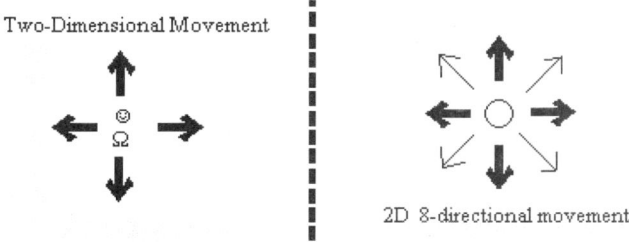

Again, the ball is not allowed to move outside the viewable screen, and it should bounce off our characters. When a player misses the ball, it should automatically reset to the scorer's side and position. Finally, the ball's initial motion will be decided by a random motion function, e.g., *Random () rnd = new Random ()*. We'll also want to add a random change of motion as the players interact with the ball, and potentially, we may allow the players to alter the ball's path by striking it from different angles.

Writing an Algorithm

After brainstorming, choosing characters, and plotting their motions, the next logical step is to weave those images into a program document or algorithm. An algorithm, as introduced in Chapter 1, is an abstract, yet detailed, list of everything that needs to occur inside of a program. Since this is only a quick look at algorithms, and since there are still several programming aspects that haven't been explained, once again we won't worry too much about completely defining all the details that make up this program. Eventually, however, when our programs actually necessitate an algorithmic breakdown, we'll include all such details (see Example 3.5).

> **Example 3.5. Algorithm for Paddle Tennis.**
>
> 1. Create a new Windows Application Project (Note: do not confuse the Windows Application setting with that of the Console Windows Application setting). Here we'll also want to use "using System.Drawing;" and "using System.Windows.Forms;" The Drawing namespace will allow us to access Graphics and Bitmaps, while the Forms namespace will allow us to use keyboard, mouse, and paint functions. We'll also want to give our project a notable name as in "Tennis."

2. At the top, we'll include constants for changeable references such as size, counts, and media.
3. We'll want to include graphic buffers (buffers are used to flip-pages, which is a very simple way of reducing flickering), menus, and links to classes namely the game classes listed on the CD-ROM. (Note: classes will be defined in chapter five).
4. As we build, we'll want to place all of our code into regions – each region relating to a particular aspect of the game.

Game loops are real-time loops that <u>are not</u> dependent on the users action, thus there's no grantee that the loop will ever end. However, at the same time when the loop does end, it should end in a structured manner and it should give the player the option of playing again or quitting.

5. Setup & Initialization
   a. Load images: Here we'll want to use jpegs (also written as jpg). Jpegs use only a faction of the memory required by bitmaps (bmp) with only a minor loss in quality (Note: The DirectX versions of these games require the bitmap format, using .jpg or any other format will cause an error.) As far a GDI+ is concerned, you can switch between data types just by changing the extension, provided you have a file stored in that format.
   b. Set players/characters position: We'll have to choose starting positions for the players. The players, as well as the ball will be reassigned throughout the game. The Net has a fixed position.
   c. Define player restrictions: The Ball deactivates as it leaves the screen, but the players do not, thus we'll have to prevent them from leaving the screen. We'll also want to stop the players from passing through the net.
   d. Define Menu: There will be three game choices, two-player, single-player, and demo; the menu should reflect those choices.
6. Paint Methods: Write two functions with the first being used to setup the buffer and the second being used to display. We'll also want to include an introduction for when the game is inactive, the characters to be displayed being Players, Ball, Scoreboard, and Net.

7. Player Input
   a. Key Controls: Assign player keyboard controls, escape keys
   b. On Mouse: Assign player mouse controls
8. Player Controls: Setting the ball to a random direction: When converting directions to coding I often use the numeric keypads layout as my foundation (4 equals left, 6 is right, 8 is up, 2 is down and so on). If we apply this technique to a function such as rnd () and a random number count form 1 to 9 our game ball will then seem to have random motion. Write a function to propel the ball. As explained in an earlier section the ball will move in one of six directions. This function then modifies the balls location continually in one of those direction based on the selected path. (Note: The function's call should be subject to that balls activation).
9. We should include sounds when the ball bounces: Sound effects are simple, but important –an enhancement that really makes a big difference in game programming. All the games have there own pre-recorded sounds, but you're welcome to replace them with your own.
10. Check to see if the ball and players have collided (collision detection II). The ball will bounce off the player: The actions of the ball on the playing characters would be identical to that of the ball and the wall if not for the additional patterns and added randomness of srand. We've also considered allowing the playing characters to alter the balls course by hitting it form an angle, but we won't discuss how to implement such details until we're in the programming stage.
11. If the ball gets to the end of the screen and the player is not there give the other player a point. Now, reset the ball: To add a scoring point we simply increment the players score, but before restarting or redrawing the ball, we'll have to reset/reassign its location to the other player's side. To make things simple we'll just use the scoring player's last position and the spacebar as the shared serving key.
12. Repeat the loop until either player scores five points: We'll terminate either the loop on request or when a certain score is

reached. Here, we'll also use the two-point rule (explained in coding).

13. Ask the player(s) if they want to play again. Remember a good game loop should always allow the player(s) the option of playing again.
14. Tennis AI: Player Left: Limited to vertical movement (one-dimensional), Player Right: Complete two-dimensional movement. (Note: Remember to make the computers choices somewhat faulty).
15. Event Processors: Timed Events, Single Player, Two Player and Demo, these should all be tied to the start menu, and should not be made changeable except when starting a new game.
16. Write a function to limit the area in which the players can traverse. This is our first case of collision detection and as such, we'll make it simple. The characters our placed on the screen based on preset location. When the player inputs a movement, the program processes that movement by adding or subtracting one unit of distance from that player's location. This distance is based on a general understanding that the first space of the first line is coordinate (0, 0). Since the player is now confined to a mathematical grid, we can "lock him down" by not allowing those values to increase or decrease beyond a certain point. The ball works in a similar manner with its deflection being based on a change in path rather than resetting its location.
17. Game Over: Ending the gaming loop in our case means ending the game and returning to the menu portion, this then allows the users to either quit the program or continue into another game.

When thinking of how we might implement those functions using a C# model it becomes obvious that the most direct solution would be to convert those tools into methods (methods are functions that are called from the vantage point of a class). Expanding our classes to include multiple tasks also gives them a greater level of control, as well as a more practical sense of reusability.(See Diagram 3.2)

Chapter 3: Writing Games

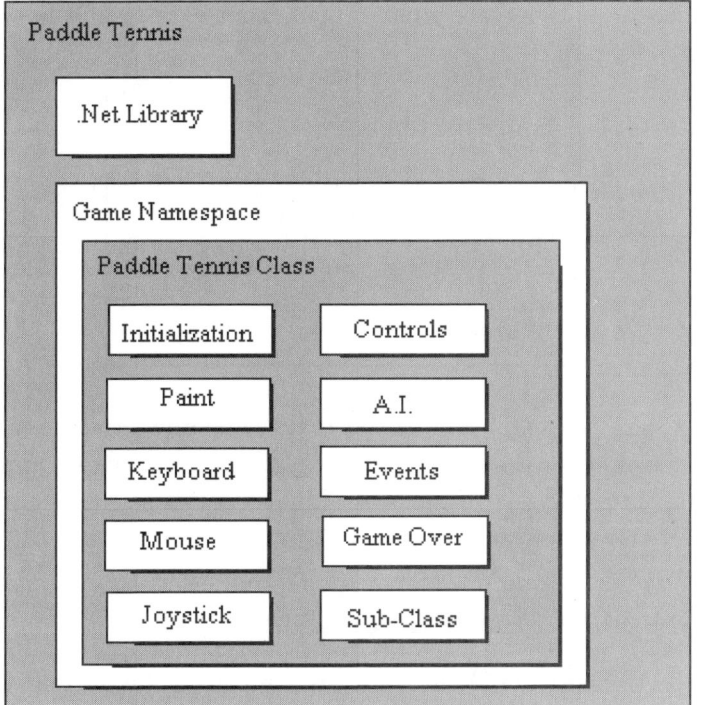

Diagram 3.2

Displaying Graphics Using Native C++

Once we've completed our drawings and have a basic sense of motion, we'll want to include the appropriate coding such as the visual parameters, setups, system calls, etc. The original coding for these games was written in the good old console version of C++, where animation meant repositioning block characters using a COORD command (which stood for coordinates as in the *x,y*, or Cartesian, coordinate system) and then setting our window to that position using the "SetConsoleCursorPosition" function. That also meant that we had to repeatedly remove the previous image and redisplay the new characters to actually see the animation, but that was then and this is now.

Displaying Graphics Using C#

Despite the advances, we'll still need to understand the basic Cartesian coordinate system, at least as it pertains to our screen. Here the *x* and *y* coordinate values start as zeros at the

C# and Game Programming

upper left-hand corner and increase when moving both to the right, respectively, downward as is shown in Example 3.6.

Example 3.6. Cartesian coordinates.

```
(0, 0)  >>  (40, 0)  >>  (80, 0)
              O (40, 12)
(0, 25)
```

The value of x increases as the ball travels to the right and decreases as it travels back to the left. The value of y behaves similarly, only its value increases as it travels down, and decreases as it travels up. Thus, through a combination of these points our characters can travel anywhere on the screen (see Example 3.7 on the CD-ROM).

Displaying Graphics Using DirectDraw

The Hardware Acceleration Layer (HAL) is comprised of a host of sub-HAL components, these components reflect the different aspects of DirectX e.g., DDHAL (DirectDraw Hardware Acceleration Layer), DIHAL (DirectInput Acceleration Layer), DSHAL (DirectSound Acceleration Layer), etc. DirectDraw as its name implies allows for direct or near direct access to our video hardware. The DDHAL can be built into the display driver or included as a Dynamic Link Library (DLL). We as programmers do not interface directly with the DDHAL; rather our requests are delegated through the DirectDraw component (see Diagram 3.3).

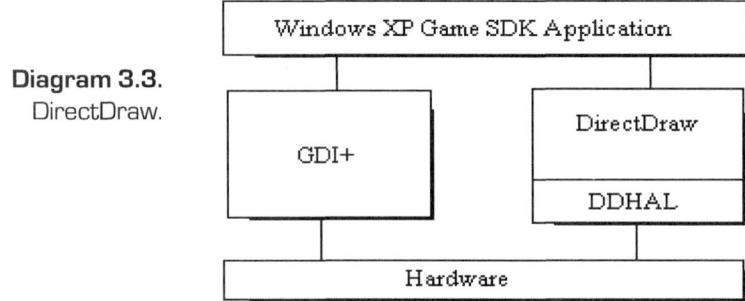

Diagram 3.3. DirectDraw.

Managed DirectDraw is the simpler of two graphical components used in Managed DirectX; the other Direct3D also includes two-dimensional application, offering support for textures, increases speed, and alpha blending, etc. (see Chapter 5 for details).

To include DirectDraw we'll need to follow several steps. The first is to add the declaration private Microsoft.DirectX.DirectDraw.Device draw = null;. Here, the word draw could be replaced with any variable name; examples include Draw, ScreenDisplay, device, the variable begins with a null value, but is later assigned as draw = new Microsoft.DirectX.DirectDraw.Device ();. Next, we'll declare the primary and secondary surfaces; the primary surface is the screen area used by the program, the secondary surface is a buffered surface, which is switched with the primary surface after all character surfaces are included. The variable name primary is commonly used to represent the primary surface e.g., private Surface primary = null; The secondary surface is common dubbed offscreen or backbuffer, character surfaces often include descriptive names as in private Surface PlayerLDraw = null;. Another essential part to creating our primary and secondary surfaces is the concept of clipping. Clipping simply means to delete any graphics that go beyond the defined area. For example, through clipping, our little tennis player would not be allowed to sneak off the screen and find his way into Atari's pong. Using the variable name clip is very common as in private Clipper clip = null; Here, we'll also define our area as in a simple rectangle, again the name destination is common among DirectX programmers e.g., private Rectangle destination = new Rectangle ();. Now that we have our preliminaries in order, we'll want to build a CreateSurface function. This function is the setting for our description, primary, and clipper values as well as a crux for our bitmap references. Once all the components are in place, it becomes a simple mater of setting the coordinates of the surface and referencing the bitmap (see CD-ROM's Example 3.8).

> Example 3.8 implements a simple try-block exception handler (Exception Handling is explained in Chapter 5), this is done to avoid the WasStillDrawException, which can occur when flipping between buffered and primary graphics, as well as the InvalidRectangleException, which can occur when a character moves off screen. Both exceptions are considered insignificant and do not exist in Direct3D. Alternatively, we could have used a Microsoft.DirectX.DirectXException.IgnoreExceptions ();.

Introducing Object-Oriented Programming

In order to understand the concepts behind the development of object-oriented programming, we must first discuss the principles behind its predecessors, such as top-down design, structured programming, and modular programming. Top-down design is a linear approach to programming where you start at the top and work your way down, whereas structured programming is more of a systematic approach to problem solving based primarily on the idea of *divido et vinco* (divide and conquer). This process allowed the programmer to develop larger and more complex programs, but it did not initially allow for reuse without modification. Structured programming complements top-down design and lead to a concept known as generic coding. The combined power of structured programming and generic coding also allowed for the restringing of functions to solve additional problems. Modular programming developed as an expansion to structured programming, allows for the linkage of files and generically coded subprograms, but this too fell short of meeting the demands placed on today's programmers.

Object-oriented programming is both a collection of the above techniques and a progression from object-based programs to object-driven programs. Generically written structure, and then classes, became the emphasis, and objects became the guiding tool used by most programmers. Classes took on a new approach that included friend and member functions (and now what is referred to as methods) to create a generic framework that can be applied to a multitude of tasks. Inheritance was developed along with a slue of new methodologies and concepts. In this new framework, variables are often replaced by class members and functions by methods. While the coding that defines these objects won't actually be discussed until Chapter 5, the practical applications that allow for their use will be implemented here. This is possible though the use of the black box method applied to both members and methods (again, see Chapter 5 for details).

Adding Files to Our Projects

To properly implement the previous program, we must first transfer its supplemental files to the appropriate main or subdirectory. This can be done through a simple copy and paste procedure as explained below.

Chapter 3: Writing Games

Adding Files to our Projects:

1. Locate the files required by our project (this book's CD-ROM's source code files referenced in the previous sections). (Note: The necessary files are bundled as part of Chapter 3's "AnimationTest1").
2. Select and copy the required files as shown in Screen Shot 3.9 (this will include AnimatedImage.cs through Walls.cs, Player1.bmp, Player2.bmp, TennisBall.bmp...).
3. Open the appropriate directory and paste those files to that directory (this is the directory usually created by the compiler as part of your current project – see Screen Shot 3.10).

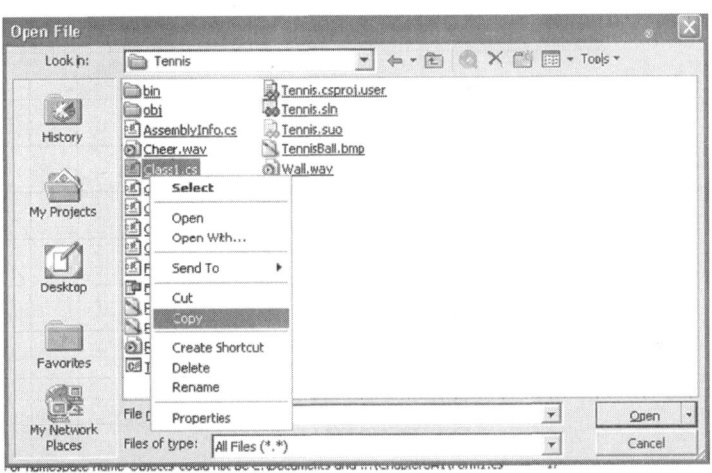

Screen Shot 3.9.

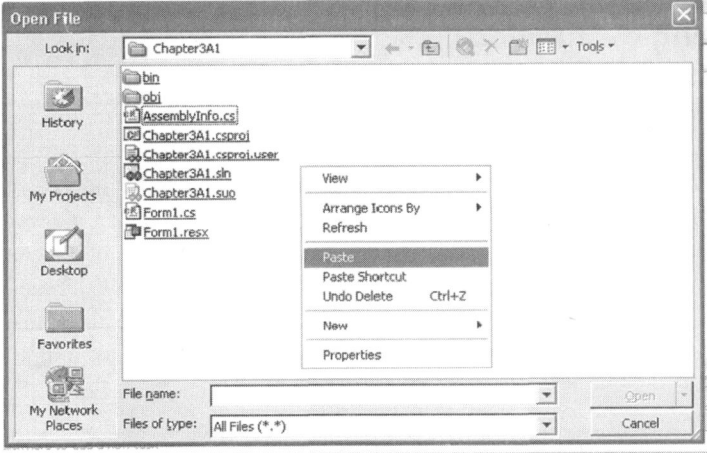

Screen Shot 3.10.

C# and Game Programming

Next, we'll need to link these files to our current project. Note that included files such as "headers" do not exist in C#.

4. From the C#'s compiler menu, select "File" and then the attribute labeled "Add existing item(s)" Choosing that attribute will bring up the corresponding menu, namely "Add existing item—*YourProjectsNameHere*." Again, make sure to repeat these steps for each item added (see Screen Shot 3.11).

Screen Shot 3.11

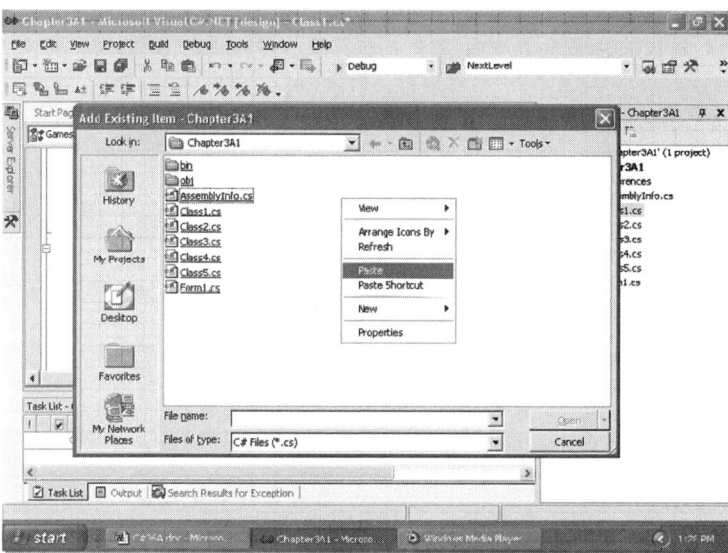

Programming a Character

Real-Time Game Programming Basics
In the older C++ model, we used simple commands like Kbhit() and getch(), which were the real-time equivalents to both cin >> and scanf(). Since C# also allows for quick and easy access to both console and windows-type applications, we can progress quite easily into OnKeyDown and OnKeyPress type examples. These Windows commands allow for multitasking, or what beginner game programmers might call basic real-time programming. The term real-time refers to the continuation of actions within a particular time frame without regard for the users' response.

Our second step is to animate our first character. This is done through a combination of the OnPaint and OnKeyDown commands. Once again, we'll use the incrementing operator to change the characters' position, but this time we'll also need to include the decrementing operator for reversing that motion (remember both of those examples are bundled within our first class, AnimatedImage.cs—see Chapter 5 for details). We'll use the arrow keys to control our characters (see Example 3.9 on the CD-ROM).

> **Note**
>
> The player's input is the data gathered by the OnKeyDown command. This is translated into movements by the computer and allows us to change the direction of the character. The player's x and y components indicate the player's current position. The initial settings place our first character at about eye level, but to the right of the screen (as in the accompanying sketch).
>
> |
> | (577, 220) : ☺

DirectInput: the Keyboard

In the last section, we introduced the concept of data input through the keyboard. Our first gamming model (Example 3.8 on the CD-ROM) included the GDI+ function OnKeyDown (KeyEventArgs e), which Windows periodically references as users' input is detected. Our OnKeyDown function also included a reference to e.KeyCode, the Key Event Argument Key Code, which allowed us to read and respond to the input provided by our users. The GDI+ model thus offers us the simplest way to derive our users' intentions while still confining us to a single function. DirectInput, in contrast, forces us to take a more global approach.

As part of creating a DirectInput keyboard reference, we'll need to include a device assignment. Device assignments are generally listed as private class members. We'll also want to include a timer reference, for example:

```
using Microsoft.DirectX.DirectInput;

    private Microsoft.DirectX.DirectInput.Device keyboard = null;
    private System.Windows.Forms.Timer Keyboard;
```

Next we will need to include a reference to that timer, as well as an event handler:

```
    this.Keyboard = new System.Windows.Forms.Timer (this.components);
    this.Keyboard.Tick += new System.EventHandler (this.Keyboard_Tick);
```

Remembering to include our actually Keyboard_Tick function and the reference, we use:

```
    Keyboard.Start ();
```

Finally, we'll need to test this sequence (see Example 3.10 on the CD-ROM).

> While the background color used to create the tennis ball bitmap is blue, the `ColorKey colorkey = new ColorKey ();` and `BallDraw.SetColorKey (ColorKeyFlags.SourceDraw, colorkey);` commands along with the `buffer.ColorFill (Color.Blue);` actually allow us to reuse that drawing with alternate background colors.

Erasing Residual Images

Erasing residual images is an important step in the creation of the illusion of animations; each character must be erased before its temporal counterpart can be displayed. This process is usually handled through the *invalidation* of a rectangle or defined area. The actual work or process is handled by Windows, but the referencing of that system is done from within our programs. Surprisingly enough, we've already included an invalidating reference, which is almost plugged in without thought. Yet there should also be a set of cautions that come with this reference, since the overuse of invalidating commands will cause undue flickering and possibly make our games unplayable. For an intermediate reference, we'll also want to *localize* our rectangles, which will reduce overall flickering (this will become especially important when working with more complex games).

Our third step, although slightly out of phase with our algorithm, will be to demonstrate these techniques. This task could be accomplished in a number of ways, but to get the best results (as little flickering as possible), we'll have to use our invalidation command sparingly, and thus we'll only call that command when a change in imagery is absolutely necessary. For example, if the ball is active we'll have to call it, and if a player moves to a new position we'll have to call it, but if the ball is in motion and the player moves, only the predominating ball movement needs to invalidate the screen, since the entire screen will still be updated.

Remember, the source code is included on the CD-ROM.

Collision Detection: The Players' Boundaries

Now that we have a player who can roam around our screen, we'll want to give him some limitation. After all, we cannot have him wandering off now, can we? The code used to stop our character's excess motion is actually quite simple, just a *switch* statement, and some incrementing and decrementing operators. These statements will probably seem a bit complex and possibly confusing, but that's because we're also using them as part of both our user-defined and class-based methods (just remember that the principles are basically the same). If you feel you need a little bit more of an explanation, just have a look at the next example. Here, we're looking at a method that is included as part of our first character-based class. When we declare an object such as Player1, Player2, or even the ball, we'll gain access to that method. Now, when we want to test for those parameters, we'll simply call that method by writing it out as: OurObject.DeflectPlayers (), OurObject.DeflectBall. Alternatively, we may want to read a value such as OurObject.Vector.ReadValue (), or with the keyword *this*, as in this.OurObject.Vector.ReadValue (), depending upon the type of reference (see Example 3.11).

Example 3.11. Player boundaries from Player.cs : AnimatedImage.cs

```
using System;
using System.Drawing;
using System.Windows.Forms;

using GameClasses; // Our common utility classes
namespace Games {
   public class PaddleTennis : System.Windows.Forms.Form {
   Player playerL; // Object representing the left player
   Player playerR; // Object representing the right player

   // Default Constructor
   public PaddleTennis() {
      // Initialize the players
      playerL = new Player(5, 225);
      playerR = new Player(580, 225);

      playerL.isActive = true;
      playerR.isActive = true;
      // Draw a box (x, y, width, height) that constrains each player
      playerL.constraintBox = new Rectangle(0, 0,
         (this.ClientSize.Width >> 1) - 10, this.ClientSize.Height);
      playerR.constraintBox = new Rectangle(
         (this.ClientSize.Width >> 1) + 10, 0,
         this.ClientSize.Width - ((this.ClientSize.Width >> 1) + 10),
         this.ClientSize.Height);
      }
   }
}
```

Collision Detection: The Ball in Motion

The next few steps momentarily abandon the player and put our focus on the ball. The ball uses the same character-based class and methods as the players, but with a few minor changes. The ball should also be deflected by the walls, but this time we'll want to use those walls to implement changes in that object's direction, which, of course,

Chapter 3: Writing Games

should resemble at least a rough physical model (not to worry, it should all be common sense stuff). The model we'll use is based on the numeric keypad/10-key system with the numbers in their default positions (4 is left, 6 is right, 7 is upper left, 9 is upper right, 1 is lower left, and 3 is lower right—8, 5, and 2 are not used). If the order of our numbers doesn't seem to make sense, try looking at them again from the point of view of the keypad as shown in Example 3.12.

Example 3.12. Numeric keypad directions..

```
Upper Left   7 8 9    Upper Right
Left         4 5 6          Right
Lower Left   1 2 3    Lower Right
```

This is also easily converted to code using a *switch* statement with the cases set to those values (e.g., *case* 1:, *case* 2:, *case* 3:, etc.), but we'll save that coding for later. Our next step will be to redefine or change the paths as the ball collides with the walls. Remember that the ball is guided by an inherent force and when the ball is deflected, its path will not be reversed or made random. Instead, we'll use a simple conversion form upper right to lower right and lower left to upper left. This can be expressed numerically as 9 to 3, 3 to 9, 7 to 1, and 1 to 7 (see Example 3.13).

Example 3.13. Numeric representation of the ball's deflection.

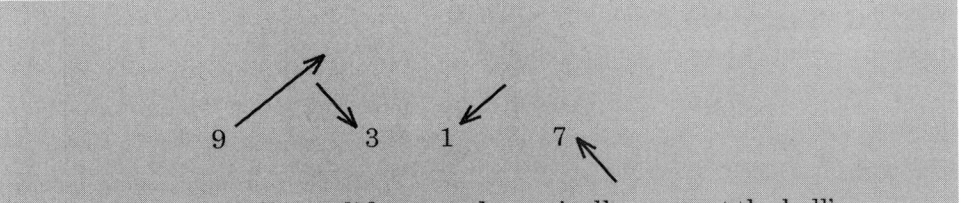

Although technically we <u>did not</u> mathematically map out the ball's path, we did manage to give the ball a close representation of what would have happened in an actual two-dimensional elastic collision (an elastic collision being one that does not alter the shape of the objects impacted).

Still words and pictorials don't teach coding, so here's a stand-alone example of a bouncing ball (see Example 3.14 on the CD-ROM). My suggestion is that you study it, alter the ball's speed, size, and boundaries, then try to add the player back into the game. If you can't figure out the last part, don't worry about it, I'll definitely do it for you. Next up, we'll go back to our players and give them the ability to deflect the ball.

> When multi-rendered scenes exist simultaneously, the adverse effect is a display error referred to as tearing. To avoid such an effect, graphical output is often buffered and flipped in a single reference.

Collision Detection: Deflecting the Ball

The next thing we'll want to do with our players is give them the ability to deflect the ball. This will become ever more useful once we've covered how to combine the two. In the first method, we'll discuss changing the ball's direction using the same principles covered in the previous section, but with a different order of deflection. A new order of deflection is necessary to keep the players' interest by providing a wider variety of patterns to perceive. In addition, as was mentioned, we'll also want to plug in some random paths, which will allow for other less conditional patterns, but we'll get to those in a moment.

Our first step will be to plot our players' patterns of deflection. These, as you should remember, are the patterns that the ball takes after it collides with an object. Once again, we'll use the numeric keypad/10-key system as our point of reference (see Example 3.15).

Example 3.15. Numerically plotting players' patterns of deflection.

```
Incoming:   1              3
          ■ 4            6 ■
            7              9
Outgoing:   9              7
          ■ 6            4 ■
            3              1
```

The number scheme for this example splits the numbers up horizontally rather than vertically with 7 to 9, 9 to 7, 1 to 3, and 3 to 1. In addition, two alternate paths are introduced, namely path 4 (left) and path 6 (right). These will have to be handled with random functions since they simply do not fall into our basic patterns of change. Reclaiming them as diagonal paths will also be handled by randomization (see Example 3.16).

Example 3.16. Players deflecting the ball.

```
public void HitTheBall() {
   if (!theBall.isActive)
       return;

   // There are three possible directions, so pick a random number
   // from 0-2.
   Random rnd = new Random();
   int seed = rnd.Next(3);

   // If the player serving is on the right the possible directions
   // are 1, 4, and 7 (seed * 3 + 1)
   if (theBall.imagePosX > this.ClientSize.Width >> 1) {
      if (theBall.direction == AnimatedImage.WEST ||
          theBall.direction == AnimatedImage.NORTHWEST ||
          theBall.direction == AnimatedImage.SOUTHWEST) {
         return; // We've already hit it! Can't hit it again
      }
      theBall.direction = seed * 3 + 1;
   } else {
      if (theBall.direction == AnimatedImage.EAST ||
          theBall.direction == AnimatedImage.NORTHEAST ||
          theBall.direction == AnimatedImage.SOUTHEAST) {
         return; // We've already hit it! Can't hit it again
      }

      // possible directions are 3, 6, 9 (seed * 3 + 3)
      theBall.direction = seed * 3 + 3;
   }
   theBall.Animate();
   Utils.PlaySound(Utils.Config["Sound.Racket"]);
}
```

A Few Minor Details:
Scores, Speed Settings, and Additional Graphics

Now that we've plotted the characters' motions, including our boundaries and patterns of deflection, and since we've already put together a working example of both the players and their ball, it would seem that there would be little else to do but to put all these pieces together and call it a game. This, unfortunately, is not the case, since there are still several issues that need to be addressed. For example, we'll need a way to implement our players' scores and a way to terminate the game when a player reaches a certain score. In addition, we'll also need to discuss adjusting the ball's speed, adding in the net, and controlling the serve. Not to worry, these are all relatively simple issues and we'll get back to the fun stuff momentarily.

Keeping score

Optimally, in order to maximize the reuse of our program's coding, we'll have to declare most of our variables as members of a class. These members will normally be stored as private members, thus, we'll also have to create member functions (also known as methods) to access these values. Methods are usually referenced in pairs: one to store the data and another to retrieve it. At this level, however, we won't worry too much about the details used to create these classes, and instead we'll focus on how to use them. The two key references that control the players' scores are assignments and increments (see Example 3.17).

Example 3.17. Keeping score—step one.

```
playerL.score = 0;
playerR.score = 0;
int score1 = playerL.score;
int score2 = playerR.score;
```

We also want to create overloaded versions of our incrementing and decrementing operators, which, of course, will be used to alter the players' scores (see Example 3.18).

Example 3.18. Keeping score—step two.

```
playerL.score++;
playerL.score--;
playerR.score++;
playerR.score--;
```

Chapter 3: Writing Games

Displaying scores is just a matter of referencing our data in the correct manner. This time, in addition to retrieving that data, we'll also need to convert it into a string value before attempting to display it (see Example 3.19).

Example 3.19. Keeping score—step three.

```
public void DoPaint(Graphics g) {
   ...
   // Draw the scores
   Font Normal = new Font("Time New Roman", 14, FontStyle.Bold);
   g.DrawString((playerL.score).ToString(), Normal, myBrush,
      new Rectangle(new Point(4 * SCALE, SCALE),
      new Size(24 * SCALE, 12 * SCALE)));

   g.DrawString((playerR.score).ToString(), Normal, myBrush,
      new Rectangle(new Point(16 * SCALE, SCALE),
      new Size(24 * SCALE, 12 * SCALE)));
   ...
}
```

To learn more about drawing tools, shapes, and colors see appendices F–H.

Game Controls

The next step is to create a real-time loop not unlike a console *while* loop, but this time we'll let Windows handle most of the work. Here, we'll rely on our second class GameControls (listed under GameState.cs), which we will continually test to see if our value GameActive is true. If the value is not true, then the playable portion of the game will terminate. We'll also use this class to define the game's speed, i.e., the speed of the ball (see Examples 3.20–3.23).

Example 3.20.

```
GameState gameState = new GameState();
```

Example 3.21.

```
// Start the game
gameState.currentState = GameState.State.Started
// Stop the game
gameState.currentState = GameState.State.Stopped
```

Example 3.22:

```
// End the game if either side has scored MAX_POINTS.
if (gameState.currentState == GameState.State.Started &&
    (playerR.score == MAX_POINTS || playerL.score == MAX_POINTS)) {
        gameState.currentState = GameState.State.Stopped;
}
```

We can also increase or decrease the playable speed with a simple call to the game's speed reference, `gameState.currentSpeed;`. Remember, increasing the value increases the looping process, which subsequently increases the ball's speed. The larger the value, the faster the ball will move (this may seem odd to programmers familiar with the older C++ sleep function, since increasing that value had the opposite affect).

Example 3.23. Setting the game's speed.

```
GameState gameState = new GameState();

gameState.currentSpeed = SPEED_DEFAULT;
int speed = gameState.currentSpeed;
```

The Net

We can draw a net and load it using a few simple commands such as `Image DisplayNet; DisplayNet = Image.FromFile (@"c:\Games.Net\Tennis\Net.bmp"); this.AutoScrollMinSize = DisplayNet.Size;`, followed by a graphic reference such as `dc.DrawImage (DisplayNet, 350, 0, 10, 550)`. Or, we can use a function from the list presented in the next section (see Example 3.24).

Example 3.24. Drawing the net.

```
// Draw the "net". 5x5 square spaced 15 apart
Brush myBrush = Brushes.Yellow;
for (int Y = 0; Y <= this.ClientSize.Height; Y += 15) {
    g.FillRectangle(myBrush, 12 * SCALE, Y, 5, 5);
}
```

See the adding colors section on the next page for details.

Controlling the Serve

First, we'll need to develop a random number generator that sets the initial path of our projectile (the ball). Second, we'll need to keep track of the projectile's location and set up scenarios that allow for the ball to switch sides. For convenience, we'll also want to bundle these procedures into a simple function (see Example 3.25).

Example 3.25. Controlling the serve.

```
public void Serve() {
    if (!theBall.isActive) {
        theBall.isActive = true;
        HitTheBall();

        if (theBall.direction == AnimatedImage.EAST ||
            theBall.direction == AnimatedImage.NORTHEAST ||
            theBall.direction == AnimatedImage.SOUTHEAST) {
            theBall.imagePosX = playerL.imagePosX + playerL.imageWidth + 1;
            theBall.imagePosY = playerL.imagePosY;
        } else {
            theBall.imagePosX = playerR.imagePosX - theBall.imageWidth;
            theBall.imagePosY = playerR.imagePosY;
        }
    }
}
```

C# and Game Programming

Adding Colors

There are two very basic color references—background and foreground. We've already referenced the background colors this.BackColor = Color.Blue;, which, of course, can be changed to a whole range of references (140), not including any user-defined references (as shown in Screen Shot 3.12). The foreground colors are equally obnoxious, I mean beautiful, and again, the same plethora of choices is available. We can also set colors using the brush option, Brush YellowBrush = Brushes.Yellow;, and/or with the pen option, Pen YellowPen = new Pen(Color.Yellow, 3);, where the "3" represents the thickness of the pen. Once we have declared a color, we might also think about using that color to specify a basic shape—a square, rectangle, circle and/or ellipse (see Example 3.26).

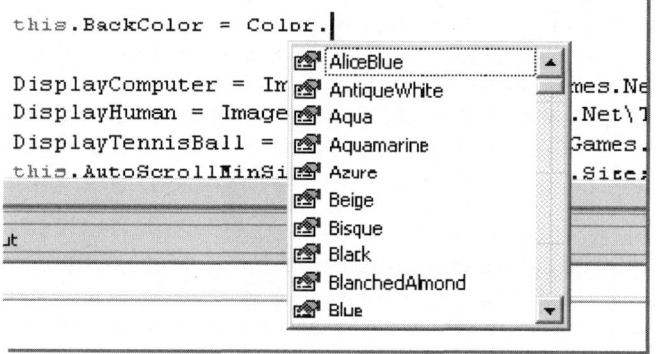

Screen Shot 3.12.

Example 3.26. Using color to specify shape.

```
protected override void OnPaint(PaintEventArgs e) {
    Graphics g = e.Graphics;

    Brush yellowBrush = Brushes.Yellow;
    g.FillRectangle(yellowBrush, 390, 100, 25, 25);

    Pen yellowPen = Pens.Yellow;
    g.DrawEllipse(yellowPen, 390, 200, 25, 25);
}
```

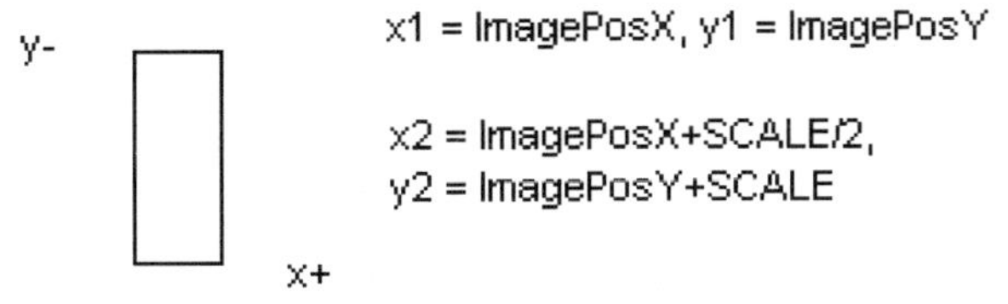

```
              x1 = ImagePosX, y1 = ImagePosY
    y-
              x2 = ImagePosX+SCALE/2,
              y2 = ImagePosY+SCALE

        x+
```

Diagram 3.4 The Paddle

Paddle Tennis GDI+: The GDI+ version of Paddle Tennis uses two basic shapes, the `FillRectangle` and the `FillEllipse`. The rectangle is used to create both the net and the players (the coding for the net is identical to the Windows Forms version). The players are constructed using a simple format, brush color, *x*-coordinate, *y*-coordinate, width, and height. All colors need to be declared before being referenced, as in `Brush WhiteBrush = new (Color.White);`, etc. The *x*- and *y*-coordinates are governed by the object references, as in `this.X` and `this.Y`, for whichever instance to which they are declared. The `Scale` component is a constant that is used to control the size; in this case, the value is 25, so the width is 12 and the height 25, giving the paddle a rectangle shape.

The ellipse, used to represent the ball, is written in the same manner, as was the rectangle; the color is entered first, followed by the *x*- and *y*-coordinates, the width, and then the height.

Adding Sounds Using Windows Multimedia

Another important aspect to game programming is the use of sounds. Sounds can be used to enhance the overall quality of our games, and for other minor tasks such as system notifications, popup ads, and virus alerts. While the recording of our sounds won't be handled through the .Net compiler, the storage for such sounds should be made part of any current project or at least as part of a central media base. There are two factors involved in declaring sounds: the Windows reference, and the executing statements (see Examples 3.27).

C# and Game Programming

Example 3.27. Windows multimedia sound.

```
public class AnyClass : System.Windows.Forms.Form {
   [DllImport ("winmm.dll")]

   public static extern long PlaySound(String lpszName, long hModule, long dwFlags);

   public void AnyMethod () {
      PlaySound(@"C:\SourceCode\Wall.wav", 0, 0);
```

> Sounds may also be copied from the CD-ROM to local directories. Sounds are listed according to their project reference (see Chapter3\project1, project2...).

In addition to inserting coding for sound, we may also need to modify our compiler's settings to include the ability to access these sounds. Here you may need to add an additional library reference or change some other settings within your project (see your compiler's documentation for details).

> Remember, you can reposition these commands to create sounds anywhere in your programs, but be careful not to over use them. Multiple sound references can disrupt the game flow and cause other minor errors.

Adding Sounds Using DirectSound

DirectSound is the DirectX alternative to using Windows Multimedia to produce sound. Here we'll mimic the initial steps used to include DirectDraw and Input e.g., adding a namespace, including variables, setting a cooperation level, etc. However, rather than creating a single DirectSound function (as compared to `OnPaint`, `Keyboard_Tick`, etc.), we'll apply our techniques as part of our gaming model. DirectSound has two types of buffers used to hold audio data; the stock *Buffer* object and its derivative the *SecondaryBuffer* object (see Example 3.28/Complete code listed on CD-ROM Example 3.28).

Example 3.28. Sound Test I.

```
using Microsoft.DirectX.DirectSound;
using Buffer = Microsoft.DirectX.DirectSound.SecondaryBuffer;
using Microsoft.DirectX.DirectInput;
```

We'll begin by including the DirectSound namespace; we'll also have to remember to add the appropriate DLL. Sound also requires a secondary buffer, as well as a device variable, we'll use sound = null;

```
private Microsoft.DirectX.DirectInput.Device keyboard = null;
private Microsoft.DirectX.DirectSound.Device sound = null;
private SecondaryBuffer SoundBuffer = null;
```

It is important to qualify device references, as the combination of DirectX namespaces will cause conflicts. The cooperation level can be set to Normal, Priority, or Write Primary (I've set this example to priority to include the highest level of performance).

```
// DirectSound
 sound = new Microsoft.DirectX.DirectSound.Device();
 sound.SetCooperativeLevel (this, CooperativeLevel.Priority);}
```

Finally, we'll want to reference the sound. Note that the file reference can be either an audio data stream or a file name type. Setting the cooperative level to default (default offering the highest level of multitasking) its priority set to zero (for a complete list of settings see Table 3.0).

```
for (Key k = Key.Escape; k <= Key.MediaSelect; k++){
    if (state[k] && k == Key.Space){
        try {
            SoundBuffer = new SecondaryBuffer ("..\\..\\Racket.wav", sound);
            SoundBuffer.Play (0, BufferPlayFlags.Default);
            }
        }
    }
```

Methods.Properties:	Description:
`BufferPlayFlags.Default`	Default, the first property of the method `public enum BufferPlayFlags` allocates to hardware and software.
`BufferPlayFlags.LocateinHardware`	Boolean type; sound supported through hardware.
`BufferPlayFlags.LocateinSoftware`	Boolean type; sound supported though software.
`BufferPlayFlags.Looping`	Looping, Repeats sound indefinitely.
`BufferPlayFlags.TerminatebyDistance`	Selects buffer by 3D distance (farthest).
`BufferPlayFlags.TerminatebyPriority`	Selects buffers by priority (lowest priority).
`BufferPlayFlags.TerminatebyTime`	Selects buffer by time (longest running).

Table 3.0. Sound Methods and Properties.

Adding in the Mouse

Another interesting feature to add to our games is the little object sitting to the side of our keyboards (yes, I mean the mouse). The mouse was invented in the 1960s by a man named Douglas C. Engelbart of Stanford Research Institute (SRI), and later put to use at the Xerox Palo Alto Research Center (known as PARC) as part of the first Graphical User Interface (or GUI). The mouse was also made popular by Steven Jobs with the release of a primitive type of computer known historically as the Macintosh... The basic controls we want to work with include the OnMouseUp, OnMouseDown, OnMouseMove, and the OnMouseWheel (Note: the OnMouseWheel also requires an IntelliMouse, a specially designed three button mouse manufactured by Microsoft). The two key functions we'll work with are OnMouseMove and OnMouseDown events, but the other two can be applied in basically the same manner.

Note: We'll also want to use the x, y coordinates to mark the graphical positioning. The constant 341 is used to restrict a character's movements horizontally; no vertical restrictions are required, since they would not affect the limitation implied by the rules of the game. One should also note that these movements would not be updated unless the ball is also found to be in motion; this is done to reduce screen static, or flickering that is caused by excessive updates (see Example 3.29).

Chapter 3: Writing Games

Example 3.29. Adding in the Mouse

Step 1. Marking the mouse's position.

```
// The player on the right "follows" the mouse
protected override void OnMouseMove(MouseEventArgs e) {
    Cursor.Current = Cursors.UpArrow;
    // Demo mode can't allow interaction from user
    if (gameState.currentMode == GameState.Mode.Demo)
        return;

    if (gameState.currentState == GameState.State.Started) {
        playerR.imagePosX = e.X;
        playerR.imagePosY = e.Y;
    }
}
```

Next, we'll want to add some button controls, like our players' ability to serve the ball. Again, this can be done with either an OnMouseDown or an OnMouseUp command (see Example 3.30).

Step 2. Giving a player the ability to serve the ball.

```
protected override void OnMouseDown(MouseEventArgs e) {
// Demo mode can't allow interaction from user
    if (gameState.currentMode == GameState.Mode.Demo)
        return;

    if (gameState.currentState == GameState.State.Started) {
        Serve ();
    }
}
```

In addition, we'll want to reference our cursors with the *show* and/or *hide* functions. It is important to keep a balance between these two features by calling only one hide and one show per cycle. If a programmer fails to keep track of these procedures, the hides and/or the shows will end up overlapping and the cursor will be lost indefinitely.

165

C# and Game Programming

Step 3. Showing and hiding the cursor.

```
Cursor.Hide ();
Cursor.Show ();
```

Finally, you may wish to alter the icon used to represent your mouse as in the arrow/hand, which can be done through a simple reassignment, e.g., Cursor.Current = Cursors.Hand; (see Table 3.1).

Chapter 3: Writing Games

Code	Cursor file
`Cursor.Current = Cursors.NoMoveHoriz;`	Im_panh.cur
`Cursor.Current = Cursors.NoMoveVert;`	Im_orgv.cur
`Cursor.Current = Cursors.PanEast;`	Im_pane.cur
`Cursor.Current = Cursors.PanNE;`	Im_panne.cur
`Cursor.Current = Cursors.PanNorth;`	Im_pann.cur
`Cursor.Current = Cursors.PanNW;`	Im_pannw.cur
`Cursor.Current = Cursors.PanSE;`	Im_panse.cur
`Cursor.Current = Cursors.PanSouth;`	Im_pans.cur
`Cursor.Current = Cursors.PanSW;`	Im_pansw.cur
`Cursor.Current = Cursors.PanWest;`	Im_panw.cur
`Cursor.Current = Cursors.SizeAll;`	Trck4way.cur
`Cursor.Current = Cursors.SizeNESW;`	Trcknesw.cur
`Cursor.Current = Cursors.SizeNS;`	Trckns.cur
`Cursor.Current = Cursors.SizeNWSE;`	Trcknwse.cur
`Cursor.Current = Cursors.SizeWE;`	Trckwe.cur
`Cursor.Current = Cursors.UpArrow;`	Up_m.cur
`Cursor.Current = Cursors.VSplit;`	Splith.cur
`Cursor.Current = Cursors.WaitCursor;`	Wait01.cur

DirectInput: The Mouse

Here, we'll want to replace the GDI+ mouse model with the DirectInput version. As with the DirectX Keyboard, the DirectX Mouse requires several initializing steps before the actual mouse function can be accessed. Set up includes a device assignment and timer reference, as well as two Boolean references, namely MouseInquire and MouseOverride.

```
// DirectInput
private Microsoft.DirectX.DirectInput.Device mouse = null;
...
private System.Windows.Forms.Timer Mouse;
bool MouseOverride = false;
bool MouseInquire = false;
```

MouseInquire and MouseOverride are user-defined variables; their purpose is to test for mouse accessibility on the part of the user, the user's options being to disable the mouse when joystick or even keyboard play is desired. We use MouseInquire to make our inquirer and MouseOverride to retain the choice made by the player, e.g.:

```
   if (!MouseInquire) {
      DialogResult result = MessageBox.Show (this,
      "Do you want to enable the mouse?",
      "Mouse Detected", MessageBoxButtons.YesNo,
    MessageBoxIcon.Question, MessageBoxDefaultButton.Button1,
    MessageBoxOptions.RightAlign);

      MouseInquire = true;
      if (result == DialogResult.Yes) {
         MouseOverride = true;
      }
   }
```

The mouse also requires a timer and event-handling references, as well as a start up call:

```
         this.Mouse = new System.Windows.Forms.Timer (this.components);
         this.Mouse.Tick += new System.EventHandler (this.Mouse_Tick);

         Mouse.Start ();
```

Example 3.30 replaces Example 3.29 for our DirectX version of the game.

Example 3.30. DirectInput: the Mouse.

```
private void Mouse_Tick(object sender, System.EventArgs e) {
mouse = new Microsoft.DirectX.DirectInput.Device(SystemGuid.Mouse);
MouseState mouseData = new MouseState ();

mouse.SetDataFormat (DeviceDataFormat.Mouse);
mouse.Acquire ();
mouse.Poll ();

// Get the current state of the mouse device.
mouseData = mouse.CurrentMouseState;

if (MouseOverride) {
   ...

   byte [] buttons = mouseData.GetMouseButtons();
   if (0 != buttons[0] && !theBall.isActive) {
       Serve ();
   }
}
}
```

DirectInput: The Joystick

Stephen D. Bristow and Steven T. Mayer invented the joystick in 1975 (Patented 1977) while working at Atari Gaming Systems; little did they know then that their invention would change not only the way games were played, but also the way they were perceived. The ability to step away from the table—to shift the body and lean from left to right as our characters stroll, jump, and even fall—is simply implacable to the concept of game play. Today joysticks include features like programmable functions, rotating handles, on-board processors, force feedback, and downloadable game-specific controller profiles. Designs include throttles, game pads, gloves, and flight yokes; yet the basic concept remains the same. Here we'll want to include a very simple joystick design: basic two-dimensional movement with a single button reference. The steps then mimic the steps used to set up the keyboard. Device assignments are generally listed as private class members, including a timer reference, e.g.:

C# and Game Programming

```
public class AnimationTest : System.Windows.Forms.Form {
// DirectInput
private Microsoft.DirectX.DirectInput.Device joystick = null;
   ...
public JoystickState JState = new JoystickState();
private System.Windows.Forms.Timer Joystick;
```

Next we will need to reference the timer, as well as an event handler:

```
this.Joystick = new System.Windows.Forms.Timer (this.components);
this.Joystick.Tick += new System.EventHandler (this.Joystick_Tick);

   Joystick.Start ();
```

Finally, we'll need to include a call to start our joystick and the function used by our game (see Example 3.31).

Example 3.31. DirectInput: the Joystick.

```
private void Joystick_Tick(object sender, System.EventArgs e) {
   foreach (DeviceInstance instance in Manager.GetDevices(DeviceClass.GameControl,
            EnumDevicesFlags.AttachedOnly)){
      joystick = new Microsoft.DirectX.DirectInput.Device(instance.InstanceGuid);
        break;
   }

   if (joystick == null) {
       return;
   }

   joystick.SetDataFormat (DeviceDataFormat.Joystick);
      foreach (DeviceObjectInstance d in joystick.Objects) {
         if ((0 != (d.ObjectId & (int)DeviceObjectTypeFlags.Axis))) {
            joystick.Properties.SetRange (ParameterHow.ById,
               d.ObjectId, new InputRange (-1000, 1000));
            . . .

            joystick.Acquire ();
            joystick.Poll ();
            JState = joystick.CurrentJoystickState;
            playerR.direction = 0;
            bool Joystick = false;
```

```
        if(-400 < JState.X) {
           playerR.direction = AnimatedImage.WEST;
           Joystick = true;
        }
        else if(-500 > JState.X) {
           playerR.direction = AnimatedImage.EAST;
           Joystick = true;
        }

        if(-600 > JState.Y) {
           playerR.direction = AnimatedImage.SOUTH;
           Joystick = true;
        }
        else if(-500 < JState.Y) {
           playerR.direction = AnimatedImage.NORTH;
           Joystick = true;

    . . .

        if(theBall.isActive == false && gameState.currentState !=
           GameState.State.Stopped) {
           byte[] buttons = JState.GetButtons();
           foreach (byte b in buttons) {
              if (0 != (b & 0x80)) {
                 Serve ();
    . . .
```

Introducing Menus

Another interesting feature available to us as Visual C# programmers is the ability to create a host of menus both visually and through basic text references. The visual method, while straightforward, is not always as complete as the text-based method, hence the need to understand both techniques. Our first look will be at how to create a basic visual menu (this technique also applies to labels, buttons, boxes, pictures, etc.). First, we'll need to reference our design window (Forms.cs [Design]). Next, we'll need to reference the toolbox menu (located to the left side of our screen) and choose the appropriate interface (in this case, the Main Menu). From there we'll simply drag and drop that selection onto our grid. (See Screen Shots 3.13 and 3.14).

C# and Game Programming

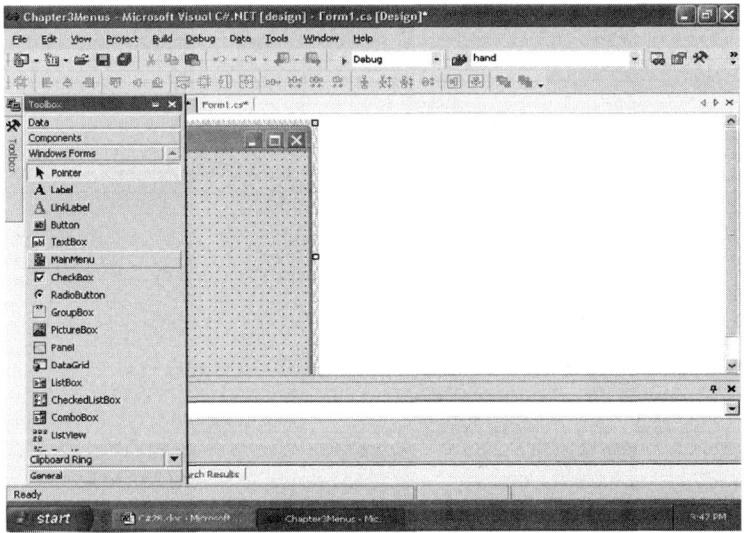

Screen Shot 3.13.

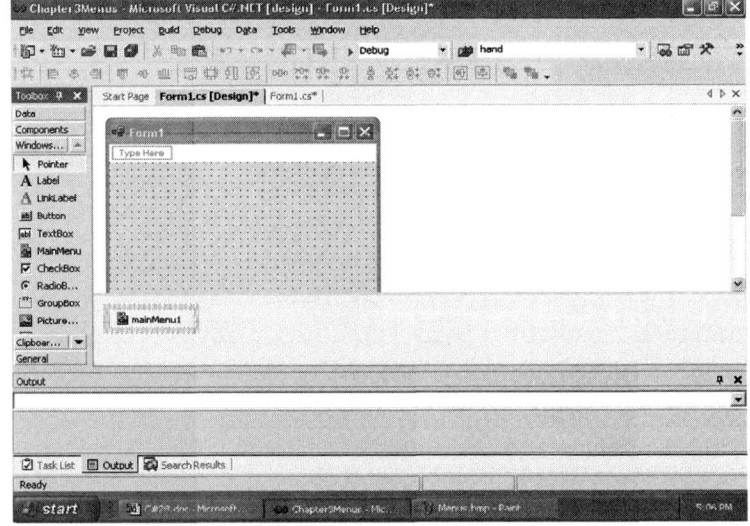

Screen Shot 3.14.

Chapter 3: Writing Games

To add the appropriate menu items, simply double click onto that menu (or submenu) and type in the appropriate heading(s) (see Screen Shot 3.15). For reference, I've labeled those items 1, 2, and 3. You should also notice the secondary listing available to the right; clicking this option allows us to create additional submenus (see Screen Shot 3.16).

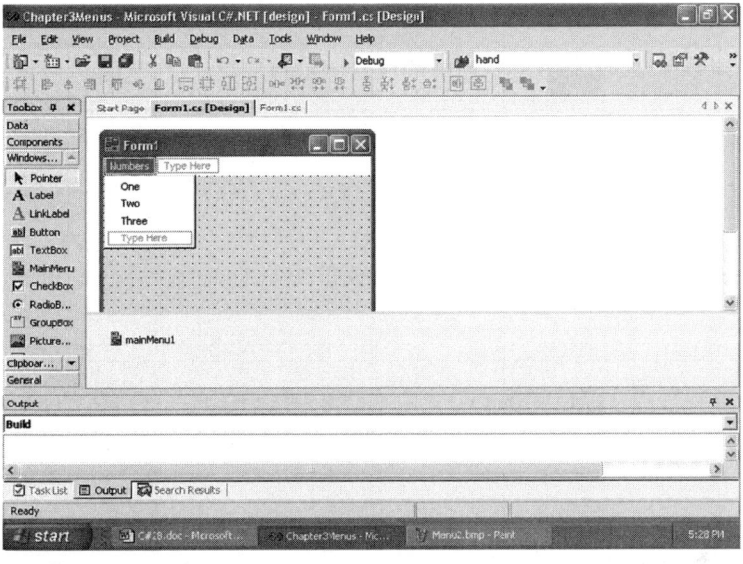

Screen Shot 3.15.

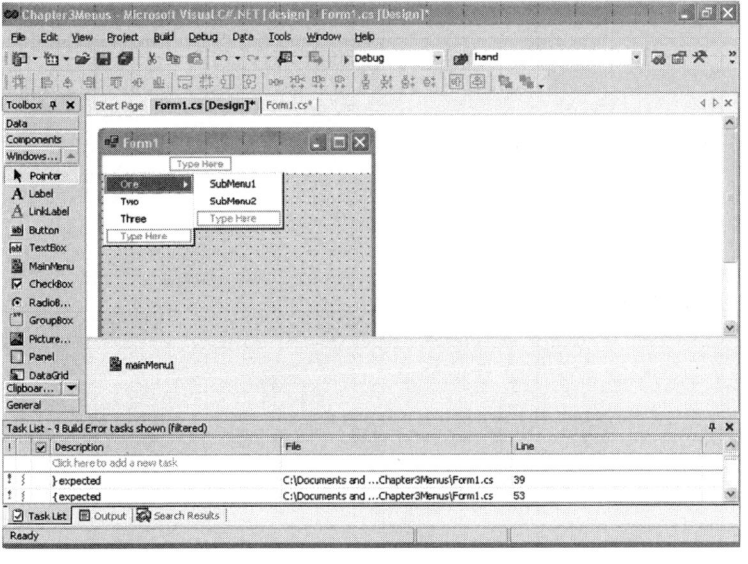

Screen Shot 3.16.

C# and Game Programming

Now, simply switch back to the text portion of our project (Forms.cs) and note the changes. Here we'll find everything from the basic references to the names we inserted as menu items (see example 3.32). Of course, if we wanted to create these files by hand, it would just be a question of inputting those references manually. It is important to remember to list each item, as well as their accompanying index points.

Example 3.32. Creating a text menu.

```
using System;
using System.Windows.Forms;

namespace Example32 {
    public class Form1 : System.Windows.Forms.Form {
        private System.Windows.Forms.MainMenu mainMenu1;
        private System.Windows.Forms.MenuItem menuItem1;
        private System.Windows.Forms.MenuItem menuItem2;
        private System.Windows.Forms.MenuItem menuItem3;
        private System.Windows.Forms.MenuItem menuItem4;

        public Form1() {
            InitializeComponent ();
        }

        #region Windows Form Designer generated code
        private void InitializeComponent() {
            this.mainMenu1 = new System.Windows.Forms.MainMenu ();
            this.menuItem1 = new System.Windows.Forms.MenuItem ();
            this.menuItem2 = new System.Windows.Forms.MenuItem ();
            this.menuItem3 = new System.Windows.Forms.MenuItem ();
            this.menuItem4 = new System.Windows.Forms.MenuItem ();

            this.mainMenu1.MenuItems.AddRange (
                new System.Windows.Forms.MenuItem [] {this.menuItem1});
            this.menuItem1.Index = 0;

            this.menuItem1.MenuItems.AddRange (
                new System.Windows.Forms.MenuItem [] {
                    this.menuItem2,
                    this.menuItem3,
                    this.menuItem4});
            this.menuItem1.Text = "Menu";
```

```
            this.menuItem2.Index = 0;
            this.menuItem2.Text = "One";
            this.menuItem3.Index = 1;
            this.menuItem3.Text = "Two";
            this.menuItem4.Index = 2;
            this.menuItem4.Text = "Three";

            this.ClientSize = new System.Drawing.Size (292, 266);
            this.Menu = this.mainMenu1;
            this.Name = "Form1";
            this.Text = "Form1";
        }
        #endregion

        [STAThread] static void Main() {
            Application.Run (new Form1());
        }
    }
}
```

From here, we'll want to link those items to a specific function and or a set of functions, depending upon what we're using those items to reference. In our key example, the Paddle Tennis game, we'll use these points to reference the game's starting points, the two-player, single-player, and demo version options (see Examples 3.33–3.36).

Example 3.33. Two-player menu option.

```
// Menu event handler
private void TwoPlayer_Click(object sender, System.EventArgs e) {
   gameState.currentMode = GameState.Mode.TwoPlayer;
    Setup();
}
```

Example 3.34. Single-player menu option.

```
// Menu event handler
private void SinglePlayer_Click(object sender, System.EventArgs e) {
   gameState.currentMode = GameState.Mode.SinglePlayer;
    Setup();
}
```

Example 3.35. Demo version menu option.

```
// Menu event handler
private void DemoVersion_Click(object sender, System.EventArgs e) {
   gameState.currentMode = GameState.Mode.DemoMode;
    Setup();
}
```

Example 3.36. Subfunction called by the menu option.

```
public void Setup() {
   // (Re) set member variables.
   gameState.currentState = GameState.State.Started;
   gameState.currentSpeed = GameState.SPEED_DEFAULT;

   playerR.imagePosX = 595;
   playerR.imagePosY = 200;
   playerR.score = 0;
   playerL.imagePosX = 5;
   playerL.imagePosY = 200;
   playerL.score = 0;
   theBall.isActive = false;
   theBall.imagePosX = playerR.imagePosX;
   theBall.imagePosY = playerR.imagePosY;

   Cursor.Hide();

   Invalidate();
}
```

Introduction to Artificial Intelligence

Artificial Intelligence (AI), in its simplest form, is essentially the modeling or simulation of human responses that pertain to a certain situation or set of conditions. These responses might be based on patterns or mathematical equations such as tracking or evasion, but the initial reactions are usually random base movements. Artificially driven programs must include both a realistic representation of human limitation, like the ability to make errors and/or the occasional lucky shot, but it must also represent an impersonal, consistent opponent in its ability to repeat the same level of skill over and over (at least until we tire and shut it off). Of course, the AI we'll discuss here is only a minor introduction to that

Chapter 3: Writing Games

subject, but don't let the simplicity of these references fool you—programming for artificial intelligence can be surprisingly thought provoking, tactically tricky, and well worth the time it will take to master. To begin, we'll focus on the key points needed to complete this game; a model of tracking and random motion.

Tracking

Tracking, as its name implies, is the ability to keep track of, or follow, a moving character as it travels across a predefined area. This is accomplished by an independent portion of programming, a subroutine, that can either implement position changes or send that information to a secondary subroutine. The coding used to track an object resembles the coding used to implement our characters' movements. The only difference is that it is implemented by the computer's judgment, for example, when a comparison "says" that the tracked object is higher or lower, allowing it to adjust its position. Unfortunately, this technique has one fault, which is that the computer cannot make mistakes, and that breaks the primary rule of humanistic realism. Luckily, we can overcome this need for perfection by adding in random events, hence the necessity of applying these techniques in unison.

Random Motion

In the last two chapters, we've used random numbers several times to create new information and to dynamically change the results of otherwise predictable behaviors. This process is also very useful when attempting to break the monotony of projected movements and is the primary source of new input used by our artificial characters. The one key twist that makes this procedure a bit different is that we'll use that random input to reduce the artificial players' ability to seek the projectile. The idea behind this maneuver is to increase the level of error, and hence, the playability of the game (see Examples 3.37 and 3.38).

Example 3.37. Tennis AI left player.

```
// Left player artificial intelligence
public void TennisAIplayerL() {
   // if ball active move left player
   if(theBall.isActive  == true) {
      switch(theBall.direction) {
```

```
        case 1:  // if ball is moving SW move south to meet
            if(theBall.imagePosY > playerL.imagePosY) {
                playerL.direction = AnimatedImage.SOUTH;
            }
            break;

        case 4: // if ball is moving W playerL will line up to meet
        case 8:
            if(theBall.imagePosY < playerL.imagePosY) {
                playerL.direction = AnimatedImage.NORTH; // move north
            } else if(theBall.imagePosY > playerL.imagePosY) {
                playerL.direction = AnimatedImage.SOUTH; // move south
            }
            break;

        case 7: // if all is moving NW move north to meet
            if(theBall.imagePosY < playerL.imagePosY) {
                playerL.direction = AnimatedImage.NORTH;
            }
```

Example 3.38. Tennis AI right player.

```
// Right player artificial intelligence
public void TennisAIplayerR() {
    // stops playerR from trying to hit the ball after it passes
    if(theBall.imagePosX > playerR.imagePosX+25){
        return;
    }

    switch(theBall.direction) {
        case 3: // ball moving southwest
            if(theBall.imagePosY > playerR.imagePosY) {
                if(theBall.imagePosY < this.Width/2)
                    // move SW to spike
                    playerR.direction = AnimatedImage.SOUTHWEST;
                else
                    // move south to line up with ball
                    playerR.direction = AnimatedImage.SOUTH;

            } else
                // move back to give playerR more time
                playerR.direction = AnimatedImage.EAST;
            break;
```

Paddle Tennis: Putting It All Together

Our final construct is built using the namespace Games and will include references to classes and techniques taught throughout this text. This version of Paddle Tennis requires DirectX 9 or higher; Chapter 3 includes four versions of this game (Forms, GDI+, DirectX, and DirectX with GDI+). (See the CD-ROM for details). GameClasses is a common utility used to define all aspects of our characters movement, including boundaries, sounds, and life span (see Example 3.39/Tennis.C# on the CD-ROM).

MEDIA_ROOT is an abbreviated reference used to find the location of our graphic and sound files; .\media\ refers to a subfolder listed with each game. The hardwired version reads as `@"C:\C# and Game Programming DirectXEdition\Chapter3\Tennis.C#\ TennisDX9.C#\Media\";`.

Bonus Games

Before jumping back into the thick of C#, I thought you might enjoy crunching out a few more games. This will provide an opportunity to introduce a few more topics and some time to improve upon our initial techniques. For this second game, I'll assume that you've already mastered the techniques presented earlier and that you'd prefer a shorter review. I will, however, still take the time to mimic the creation of the game and to give a realistic view of how one might go about developing it (keeping everything in real time, of course).

Game 2—Space Fighters

Our second game, Space Fighters, although simple, does include several techniques that you should find useful. We'll begin by jotting down a quick list of thoughts, a.k.a. brainstorming, and we'll take a few moments to develop our characters.

 **Brainstorming**

Example 3.40. Brainstorming Space Fighters.

1. The game should have two players that will appear as spaceships.
2. Again, one player will be placed on the right and the other on the left. The game starts the moment it's loaded.
3. The players' movements should be two-dimensional with respect to the screen, but they should also include diagonal movements.
4. The ships should have a thrust, but not a brake or reverse, allowing momentum to carry them forward.
5. The two ships will have weapons, or at least one weapon, namely a missile that can be fired at its opponent. But to keep things simple, the missiles won't be able to injure their own ship.
6. Again, we'll set up a menu option for one or two players, and we'll add in some AI for a one-player option.
7. We'll use a black background with stars randomly placed across it. The stars will be smaller versions of our sun.
8. The ships should have contrasting colors—those colors will also represent the color of their weapons.
9. The ships should make sounds including a thrust, weapon's fire, and an explosion when hit.
10. The ships should not be able to fire when dead, nor should they be able to get hit.
11. Set the game to end once a player gets, say, five kills. Also, if a player is killed by crashing into the sun, he will lose a point.
12. Players will have to restart after they die.
13. We'll include a command that allows players to revive their damaged ships; these controls can double as hyperspace mode, allowing active ships to randomly travel through unseen dimensions, reappearing on some other portion of the screen (including appearing inside the sun and/or on top of the other ship).

Chapter 3: Writing Games

> 14. We'll also place a sun in the middle of the screen, and use a set number of cycles to simulate the force of gravity pulling the ships into the sun. Gravity will also make a sound as it pulls in the ships.

Selecting Characters & Plotting Motions

Our second step is to draw out some basic images, like spaceships, their exhaust trails, and a large sun that will be conspicuously placed in the center of our screen. The ships will be basically identical, but with contrasting colors, and the exhaust trail will be superimposed onto those ships when their engines are active (see Screen Shots 3.17–3.19).

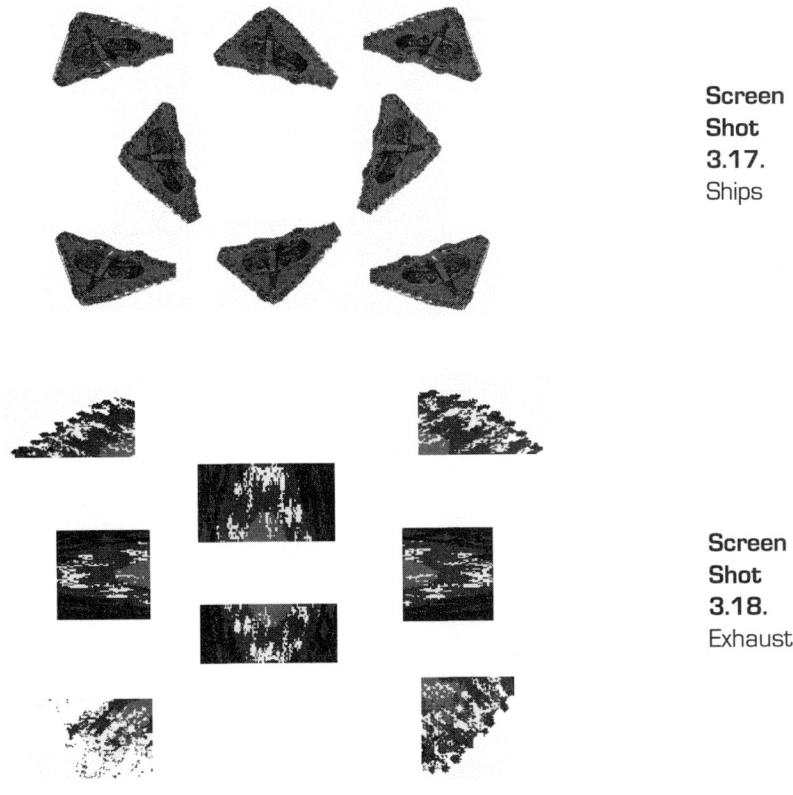

Screen Shot 3.17. Ships

Screen Shot 3.18. Exhaust.

181

Screen Shot 3.20. The sun.

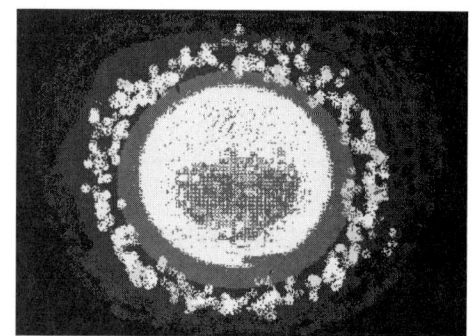

The movements for these characters will be simple, with one key set aside as a thrust and two others set to turn the crafts to alternate sides (see Example 3.41). We'll continue to use the arrow keys and the numeric keypad for movements. The left and right arrows will adjust the direction of the vessel, and the upward arrow key will be the thrust. The downward arrow key will revive the characters and send the ships into hyperspace, and the zero key will fire weapons. For Player Two, <Q> turns left; <A> turns right; <X> thrusts; <S> sends the ship to hyperspace, and the spacebar fires weapons. The angles of motions are shown in Example 3.41.

Example 3.41. Angles of motions.

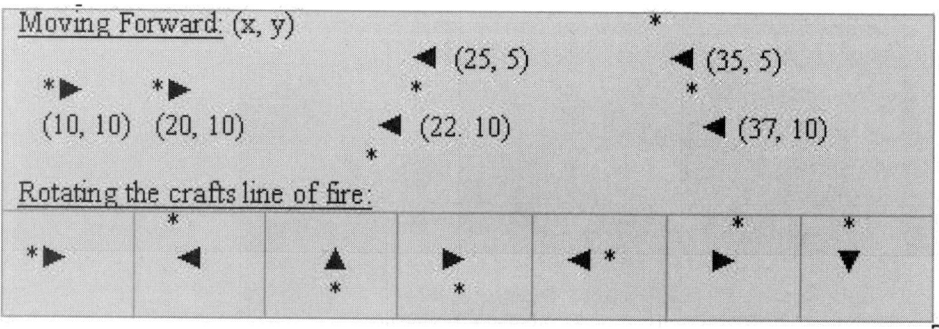

We'll also need two characters to represent their missiles and another image to represent explosions (see Screen Shot 3.21).

Chapter 3: Writing Games

 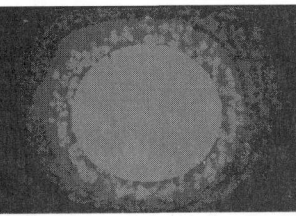 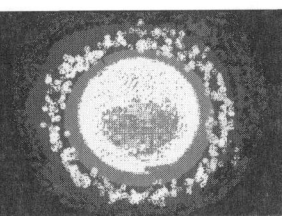

Screen Shot 3.21.

Finally, we'll want to give our crafts some momentum (momentum being the force that keeps ships gliding in one direction even after we've turned it to another). Momentum will fade within a few program cycles, but the effects will combine when the thrust key is applied at more frequent intervals (see Example 3.42).

Example 3.42. The Ship's Momentum.

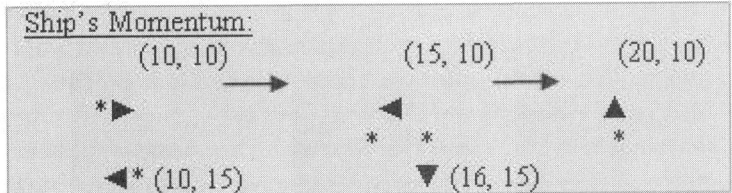

Writing the Algorithm

The comments listed here are supplemental to the Paddle Tennis algorithm. Here, we'll expand the descriptions to include the details of these secondary subprograms. Again, these instructions are in reference to the older version of this program, but there are still many similarities between the two languages.

> **Example 3.43. Algorithm for Space Fighters.**
> 1. Link our program to the previous game, using menu.cpp, games.cpp, etc.
> 2. Reference our main function screen size and access the proper subprograms.

3. Write a function to handle the unique turning motions required by this game (see Example 3.37).
4. Include a function that paints the stars and the screen black.
5. Again, we'll want to access our variables as class members listed in an additional subprogram.
6. Set the variables/members including paths.

Inside the while loop:

7. Write a function that removes all residual images using a combination of calls to blank characters and the paint star function.
8. Set the colors remembering to change the color for each vessel. Each change in color will require its own declaration.
9. Display all characters.
10. We'll still need to animate our weapon—this time we'll use all eight directions (see Example 3.44).
11. Our limits will no longer stop the characters; instead we'll wrap their movements around the screen. Projecting our characters to the opposite side means that we won't have to alter their paths.
12. There are four sounds associated with this game—Hit.wav (used when a player dies), Fire.wav (used to represent weapons fire), Gravity.wav (used to emphasis the pull of gravity), and thrust.wav (used to represent the ship's engine).
13. Collision detection (usually ends up in the destruction of a ship). Activate the collision detection routine whenever a weapon is active.
14. Set the weapon's movement. Make it equal to the path each ship is facing at the moment the weapons are fired. If the missiles reach the end of the screen, they'll also be rerouted (traveling a total of 100 cycles before termination).
15. Add a force of momentum that keeps the ship moving in one direction even if the ship turns.
16. Only display the characters when they're active. If they're not active, display the exploding ship in their place.
17. Repeat the loop until either player scores five kills; either the loop will terminate on request or when that goal is reached.

Chapter 3: Writing Games

> 18. Ask player(s) if they want to play again: Remember a good game loop should always allow the player(s) the option of playing again.
> 19. End or repeat game: Ending the gaming loop in our case means ending the game and returning to the menu portion. This allows the users to either quit the program or continue on to another game.

Example 3.44. Eight directions of movement.

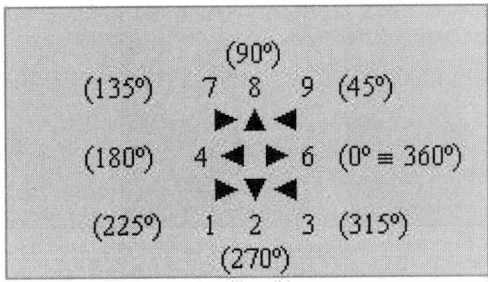

Setting up the Compiler

At this point, we need to get the compiler up and running; repeat the steps used to link the class base and all of its counterparts. If you'd prefer to use `chapter3\project2`, you can just load it up, but if you're building from scratch you'll have to remember to add each file to the project, and in some cases, you'll have to remember to load the Windows Multimedia Library. Again, we'll need to build several user-defined functions with a final main function that controls this game (refer to the previous sections as needed).

Animating Characters: Animating Spaceships

The key to animating the spaceship is keeping track of the direction the spaceship is facing and then drawing the corresponding image for that direction. Since each player can turn the spaceship, we need to update the direction of the spaceship (see Example 3,45). Now that we can keep track of the direction, we need a function that will display the appropriate image for that direction (see Example 3.46). In Example 3.47, you can see how this function is called for Player 1. The code is similar for Player 2. Note that this function makes use of arrays which are covered in Chapter 4.

C# and Game Programming

Example 3.45. Spaceship character direction (AnimatedImage.cs).

```
// Rotate the direction by the specified amount
// increment is in 45 degree steps
virtual public void RotateDirection(int increment) {
    int result = increment + direction;

    if (result > 8) {
        result %= 8;
        if (result == 0)
            result = 8;
    } else if (result < 1) {
        result = (result % 8) + 8;
    }
    direction = result;
```

Example 3.46. Displaying graphics (PlayerImageArray.cs).

```
// overridden member which displays the image with an index ==
// to the heading associated with the image.
override public void Display(Graphics g) {
    if (direction >= 0 && direction <= aImages.GetLength(0))
        g.DrawImage(aImages[direction], imagePosX, imagePosY,
            imageWidth, imageHeight);
}
```

Example 3.47. Code to draw Player 1's Ship and Exhaust

```
player1.Display(g);
if (p1Event.isActive) {
    exhaustImages[player1.direction].imagePosX =
player1.imagePosX;
    exhaustImages[player1.direction].imagePosY =
player1.imagePosY;
    exhaustImages[player1.direction].Display(g);
}
```

> As with a ship's image, displaying the exhaust trail is simply a matter of reading in the ship's coordinates and displaying the appropriate image.

Animating Characters: Projectiles and Explosions

As with their character counterparts, our projectiles must rely on a combination of functions and events including activation, animation, collision detection, and deactivation. While most of these attributes are integrated within other functions we can still define a projectile's behavior based on a few lines of coding (see Example 3.48).

Example 3.48. Collision detection.

```
public bool CheckShipCollision(Player player) {
    Player opponent = (player == player1) ? player2 : player1;

    // Collided with another ship?
    if (player.Intersects(opponent)) {
        // Successful ramming action!!
        ShipCollided (opponent, player);
        return true;
    }

    // Collided with the sun?
    if (player.Intersects(theSun)) {
        ShipCollided (player, null);
        return true;
    }

    // Asteroid collision?
    if (useAsteroids) {
        for (int i = 0; i < MAX_ASTEROIDS; i++) {
            if (asteroids[i].isActive) {
                if (asteroids[i].Intersects(player)) {
                    ShipCollided (player, null);
                    return true;
                }
            }
        }
    }
}
```

Adding DirectInput: The Keyboard and Joystick

A ship in space moves quite differently than a man on a tennis court. Thus, it is logical to assume that our constructs for the keyboard and joystick would be quite different. It is also important to note that Space Fighter does not require the use of a mouse; hence, no mouse applications will be included. Space Fighter does require a thrust and two angles of movement, 45 degrees positive and 45 degrees negative, effectively turning the vessels both left and right. Keeping in mind that the two vessels begin in different position and that our algorithm requires a generic solution, we conclude that an abstract model of rotation is required (see Example 3.49).

Example 3.49. Keyboard and Joystick controls.

```
private void Keyboard_Tick(object sender, System.EventArgs e) {

    keyboard = new Microsoft.DirectX.DirectInput.Device(SystemGuid.Keyboard);
    keyboard.Properties.BufferSize = 8;
    keyboard.Acquire();

    KeyboardState state = keyboard.GetCurrentKeyboardState();

    for (Key k = Key.Escape; k <= Key.MediaSelect; k++) {
        if (state[k] && k == Key.W) {
        . . .

private void Joystick_Tick(object sender, System.EventArgs e) {
    foreach (DeviceInstance instance in
        Manager.GetDevices(DeviceClass.GameControl,
        EnumDevicesFlags.AttachedOnly)) {
        joystick = new Microsoft.DirectX.DirectInput.Device(instance.InstanceGuid);
         break;
    }

    if (joystick == null) {
        return;
    }
```

```
joystick.SetDataFormat (DeviceDataFormat.Joystick);
foreach (DeviceObjectInstance d in joystick.Objects) {
    if ((0 != (d.ObjectId & (int)DeviceObjectTypeFlags.Axis))) {
        joystick.Properties.SetRange (ParameterHow.ById,
            d.ObjectId, new InputRange(-1000, 1000));
        . . .
    joystick.Acquire();
    joystick.Poll();
    State = joystick.CurrentJoystickState;

    if (-600 > State.Y) {
        if (!player2.isActive)
        player2.isActive = true;
        player2.RandomizePosition();
    }

    if (player2.isActive == true) {
        if (-400 < State.X && -600 > State.Y) {
            player2.RotateDirection(1);
            . . .

    byte[] buttons = State.GetButtons();
    foreach (byte b in buttons) {
        if (0 != (b & 0x80)) {
            for (int i = 0; i < MAX_MISSILES; i++) {
                if (player2Missiles[i].isActive == false) {
                    FireMissile (player2, player2Missiles);
                    break;
                    . . .
```

Of course, we can also use a smaller version of the sun to represent the ships as they burst into flames (Remember: A ship that has been destroyed is not effected by additional weapons fire, nor should it be effected by the sun's gravity). Again, a combination of both `if` and `switch` statements are used to reduce clutter.

OnPaint

We will override the Windows OnPaint method to create a simple, yet collective list of display commands that generate the visual portion of our game. It is important to include conditional commands that restrict/control the direction of the ships and the exhaust (which will be inde-

C# and Game Programming

pendent entities), and display and/or hide the asteroids, as necessary. We will use the OnPaint method to display introductory statements as well as some background stars and the sun. (see Example 3.50.) Asteroids are defined later in this chapter.

Example 3.50. Space Fighter graphics.

```
// Draw the scores
buffer.ColorFill(Color.Black);
buffer.ForeColor = Color.Red;
buffer.DrawText(4 * SCALE, 2 * SCALE, player1.score.ToString(), false);
buffer.ForeColor = Color.Blue;
buffer.DrawText(16 * SCALE, 2 * SCALE, player2.score.ToString(), false);

// Draw player 1 & its appropriate exhaust
try {
   destination = new Rectangle(player1.imagePosX, player1.imagePosY,
      SCALE, SCALE);
   buffer.Draw(destination, PlayerLDraw [player1.direction],
      DrawFlags.Wait);
} catch (SurfaceLostException) {
   CreateSurfaces ();
   . . .
if (p1Event.isActive) {
   try {
      int X = player1.imagePosX
         + exhaustImages[player1.direction].imageOffsetX;
      int Y = player1.imagePosY
         + exhaustImages[player1.direction].imageOffsetY;
      destination = new Rectangle(X, Y, SCALE / 2, SCALE / 2);
      buffer.Draw(destination, ExhaustDraw [player1.direction],
         DrawFlags.Wait);
   } catch (SurfaceLostException) {
      CreateSurfaces();
      . . .
```

Defining Hyperspace

Most of us see the world as a 4-dimensional platform, i.e., *x*, *y*, *z*, and time, and this severs us well in our daily lives. Yet, when working with the concept of space travel, we have to consider the possibility of moving through a fifth dimension, a.k.a. hyperspace. In hyperspace, time, distance, and matter are irrelevant, given that they do not intersect with us. To visualize hyperspace just imagine yourself watching television; see the box in front of you as having all four dimensions. The actors move through their world the same as we do, they age and live and die, but their dimensions (including time) do not effect us. Thus, if we could reach into the box and take an item, if only to immediately put it back, the item would appear to travel instantaneously in the actors' world. Thus if we are inside the Space Fighter game and our spaceship is moving through hyperspace, then we'd see our spaceship moving instantly from position to position. Of course, we as programmers, which would place us in a sixth dimension, can easily build a function that can simulate such movement, as in a function to randomize that ships position (see Example 3.51).

Example 3.51. Randomized position (AnimatedImage.cs).

```
// reposition the object in a random place within its constraintBox
public void RandomizePosition() {
    Random rnd = new Random ();
    imagePosX = rnd.Next(constraintBox.Width - imageWidth);
    imagePosY = rnd.Next(constraintBox.Height - imageHeight);
    direction = rnd.Next(1, 8);
}
```

Boundaries & Projectile Limits

The next two key components are the ship's boundaries and the limits of the ships' projectiles. Since this game wasn't based on a set field of screen limits, our previous limitations should not apply. Instead, we'll use those boundaries to indicate a chance to loop or reposition using x, y-zero to x, y-max as our coordinates. Our players' paths will not change, nor will the ships' vectors (see Example 3.52).

Example 3.52. Looping the screen boundaries (AnimatedImage.cs).

```
virtual public bool WrapInBox() {
    bool retVal = false;

    if (!isActive)
        return false;
```

```
      if (imagePosX < constraintBox.X) {
         imagePosX = constraintBox.X + constraintBox.Width - imageWidth;
         retVal = true;
      } else if ((imagePosX + imageWidth) >
         (constraintBox.X + constraintBox.Width)) {
         imagePosX = constraintBox.X;
         retVal = true;
      }

      if (imagePosY < constraintBox.Y) {
         imagePosY = constraintBox.Y + constraintBox.Height -
         imageHeight;
         retVal = true;
      } else if ((imagePosY + imageHeight) >
         (constraintBox.Y + constraintBox.Height)) {
         imagePosY = constraintBox.Y;
         retVal = true;
      }

      return retVal;
}
```

Additionally, the WeaponLimits function will be used to access that rerouting subroutine. The secondary purpose of this function, however, will be to terminate a weapon's fire if it fails to make contact with an object after a set limit of 100 cycles. This combination will aid in creating the illusion of a truly open environment (see Examples 3.53–3.54).

Example 3.53. Initiating weapons.

```
// Fire a missile (if any available) from the given player
public void FireMissile(Player player, AnimatedImage[] missiles) {
   if (!player.isActive)
      return;

   for (int i = 0; i < MAX_MISSILES; i++) {
      // shoot the first missile that's not already out there!
      if (!missiles[i].isActive) {
         // set missiles properties so that it will get
         // properly animated
         missiles[i].isActive = true;
         missiles[i].direction = player.direction;
         missiles[i].imagePosX = player.imagePosX;
```

```
            missiles[i].imagePosY = player.imagePosY;

            TimedEvent missileEvent = timer.getEvent("playerMissile" + i);
            missileEvent.Reset();

            try {
               SoundBuffer = new SecondaryBuffer(MEDIA_ROOT + "Fire.wav",
                   sound);
               SoundBuffer.Play(0, BufferPlayFlags.Default);
            } catch {
               Utils.PlaySound(MEDIA_ROOT + "Fire.WAV");
            }
            break;
      }
   }
}
```

Example 3.54. Animating weapons.

```
public void MoveMissile(TimedEvent e, Object obj) {
   if (gameState.currentState == GameState.State.Stopped) {
       e.isActive = false;
       return;
   }

   AnimatedImage missile = (AnimatedImage) obj;
   if (!missile.isActive) {
       e.isActive = false;
   }

   for (int i = 0; i < gameState.currentSpeed; i++) {
       missile.Animate ();
       missile.WrapInBox ();

       CheckMissileCollision (missile);
   }

   if (e.tickCounter <= 1)
       missile.isActive = false;
```

Drawing with DirectDraw

> **Note**: In Chapters 5, we take an extended look at the properties associated with the Direct3D and GDI+ drawing tools. This section is meant to introduce a limited set of DirectDraw methods used to create fonts, lines, curves, and shapes, which will aid in creating rendered versions of our first set of games.

DirectDraw provides us with several methods used to produce everything from basic shapes to some intricate designs. Here, I'll introduce some of the alternative drawing tools and many of the techniques associated with rendered graphics. (For information on rendered graphics using Direct3D, see Chapter 5.)

DirectDraw: Text

Before we begin to draw, first we'll want to learn to write. This is done using three simple references, namely ColorFill, ForeColor, and DrawText. ColorFill is used to paint the background, while ForeColor and DrawText are used to paint and display text, respectively. Failing to assign a ForeColor or assigning a single color to both ForeColor and ColorFill will result in undetectable text. The DrawText method includes four parameters: int X, int Y, String, and, draw at last position (a Boolean type), where X and Y are Cartesian coordinates, String is the content to be display, and the last parameter, draw at last position, is set to false, as it is superfluous (see Example 3.55 and Example 3.56 on the CD-ROM).

Example 3.55. Text display.

DirectDraw: Lines

The simplest image to draw is undoubtedly the straight line. Here, only two points are required, P_1 (x_1, y_1) and P_2 (x_2, y_2) (as defined by the Cartesian coordinate system). A straight line is created when these two points are connected. Straight lines can be both horizontal and vertical; they require ColorFill and ForeColor references, as well as a call to `DrawLine (int x`$_1$`, int y`$_1$`, int x`$_2$`, int y`$_2$`);`. Diagonal lines can also be created using `DrawLine`, but if the line is asymmetrical it will appear coarse or jagged. In such a case, a solution known as anti-aliasing is used. Anti-aliasing is a smoothing technique, based on shading, which is used to reduce sharpness. To the artist this would mean applying softer shades, shadows that follow the line; to the programmer this includes implementing new techniques (GDI+ offers `SmoothingMode` and `PixelOffSetMode`). As for DirectDraw, a more hands-on approach is required (see Example 3.57 and Example 3.58 on the CD-ROM).

Example 3.57. Lines display.

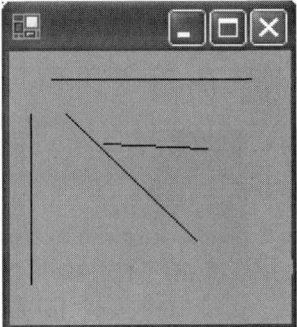

DirectDraw: Shapes

DirectDraw has only two basic shapes, the rectangle, and the ellipse. The rectangle is referred to as a `DrawBox`, while the ellipse has three references `DrawCircle`, `DrawEllipse`, and `DrawRoundedBox`. Here, `ColorFill` can be used with `DrawBox` to create solid rectangles (see Example 3.59 and Example 3.60 on the CD-ROM).

C# and Game Programming

Example 3.59. Rectangles and ellipses display.

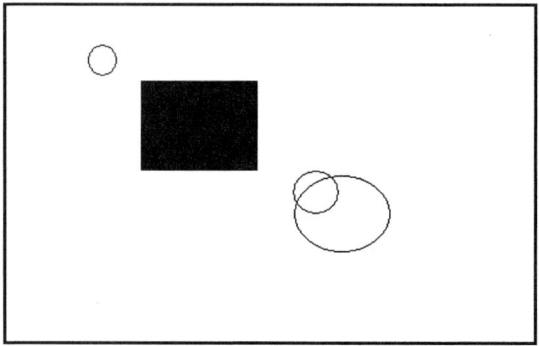

In addition to DrawBox, we can also create rectangles using the DrawFast option. While DrawFast does not increase hardware draw time, it can increase software draw time by approximately 10%. DrawFast is written using the *x*- and *y*-coordinates, source surface, source rectangle, and a flag setting).

```
// DrawBox
destination = new Rectangle(100, 100, 150, 150);
buffer.ColorFill (destination, Color.Green);
buffer.DrawBox (100, 100, 150, 150);
```

Artificial Intelligence: Evasion

The previous section on artificial intelligence explained the basic concepts of tracking and random motions, but we left out another concept commonly known as *evasion*. Evasion, in coding terms, is simply the reverse of tracking. Here, rather than moving closer to an object, our opponent's characters are told to avoid it, thus creating the illusion of intelligently driven tactics. We'll need to include a fourth function that allows for weapons fire; these functions are listed as Examples 3.61–3.64.

Example 3.61. AI managing subprogram.

```
public void SpaceFighterAI() {
    if (!player1.isActive) {
        player1.isActive = true;
        player1.RandomizePosition();
    }
    Random rnd = new Random();
    int rndNum = rnd.Next(10);

    if (rndNum < 5) // 50% of the time do nothing
        return;

    if (rndNum < 8) { // 80% of the time check for imminent crash
        if (player1.imagePosX < theSun.imagePosX + 70 &&
            player1.imagePosX > theSun.imagePosX - 70 &&
            player1.imagePosY > theSun.imagePosY - 70 &&
            player1.imagePosY > theSun.imagePosY - 70)
            player1.RandomizePosition();
    }

    if (rndNum < 8) { // 20% (only if 6 & 7)
        for (int i = 0; i < MAX_MISSILES; i++) {
            if (player2Missiles[i].isActive) {
                Evade(player2Missiles[i]);
                p1LastDirection = player1.direction;
                EngageThrusters(player1);
                return;
                . . .
    if (!player2.isActive)
        return;

    // Seek him out!
    Track();
    p1LastDirection = player1.direction;
    if (rndNum >= 9) // 1/10 of the time
        EngageThrusters(player1);
    else if (player1.imagePosX > player2.imageOffsetX &&
        player1.imagePosY < player2.imagePosY &&
        player2.imagePosX - player1.imagePosY ==
        -1 * (player2.imagePosY - player1.imagePosY)) {
        FireMissile (player1, player1Missiles);
    }

    (int)Math.Round(rnd.NextDouble() * 10))
```

Example 3.62. Tracking.

```
public void Track() {
    int tempDir = 0;

    if (player1.imagePosX > player2.imagePosX &&
        player1.imagePosY > player2.imagePosY)
        tempDir = AnimatedImage.NORTHWEST;
    else if (player1.imagePosX  > player2.imagePosX &&
        player1.imagePosY < player2.imagePosY)
        tempDir = AnimatedImage.SOUTHWEST;
        . . .
    Random rnd = new Random ();
    if (rnd.Next(10) > 5) {
        player1.direction = tempDir;
        player1.Animate();
    }
}
```

Example 3.63. Evasion.

```
public void Evade(AnimatedImage inbound) {
    int tempDir = 0;

    switch(inbound.direction) {
        case AnimatedImage.SOUTH:
            if (player1.imagePosY > inbound.imagePosY) {
                if (player1.imagePosX > inbound.imagePosX)
                    tempDir = AnimatedImage.EAST;
                else
                    tempDir = AnimatedImage.WEST;
            }
            break;
        case AnimatedImage.WEST:
            if (player1.imagePosX < inbound.imagePosX) {
                if (player1.imagePosY <= inbound.imagePosY)
                    tempDir = AnimatedImage.NORTH;
                else
                    tempDir = AnimatedImage.SOUTH;
            }
            break;
            . . .
```

```
    if (tempDir > 0) {
        Random rnd = new Random();
        if (rnd.Next(10) > 5) {
            player1.direction = tempDir;
            player1.Animate();
        }
    }
}
```

Example 3.64. AI managing Timer.

```
public void AlienAI_Timer_Click(object sender, System.EventArgs e) {
    if (gameState.currentMode == GameState.Mode.SinglePlayer)
        SpaceFighterAI();
}
```

Including Obstacles: The Sun

Another excellent way to increase the enjoyment of a game is in the insertion of field obstacles. The first obstacle we'll create is a small sun in the middle of our screen, which is like a little gravity well, slowly pulling in its prey until Bang! The ships make contact with its center. We'll set up the force of gravity to pull once every 20 cycles, displacing the ships with increasing increments (see Examples 3.65 and 3.66).

Example 3.65. The sun.

```
    // Initialize the sun
    theSun = new Shapes(this.ClientSize.Width/2,this.ClientSize.Height/2);
    theSun.RescaleImage(2 * SCALE, 2 * SCALE);
    theSun.isActive = true;
    theSun.imagePosX = this.ClientSize.Width/2;
    theSun.imagePosY = this.ClientSize.Height/2;

    newEvent = new TimedEvent(new TickHandler(Gravity));
    newEvent.isActive = true;
    timer.addEvent(newEvent, GRAVITY_SPEED, "");
```

Example 3.66. The sun's gravitational pull.

```
public void ExertGravitationalPull(Player player) {
    if (player.imagePosX != ClientSize.Width >> 1)
        player.imagePosX += (player.imagePosX >
            (ClientSize.Width >> 1)) ? -GRAVITY_EFFECT : GRAVITY_EFFECT;
    if (player.imagePosY != ClientSize.Height >> 1)
        player.imagePosY += (player.imagePosY >
            (ClientSize.Height >> 1)) ? -GRAVITY_EFFECT : GRAVITY_EFFECT;
}
```

Gaining Momentum

Unlike our tennis game, we'll also want to think about how the ships experience motion. For example, how far should the thrusters push our characters, and what happens if players change course after they apply thrusts? This question can be answered quite simply through a solid function dedicated to the concept of momentum. We don't really have to stress over any of the physical details; rather, we focus only on the appearance of the movement. This can be accomplished through the use of some simple timers and animation calls as shown in Examples 3.67.

Example 3.67. Adding momentum to the game.

```
// Start up the player's thrusters
public void EngageThrusters(Player player) {
    if (player.isActive) {
        if (player == player1)
            p1Event.Reset(); // reset the timer from now
        else
            p2Event.Reset(); // reset the timer from now
        try {
            SoundBuffer = new SecondaryBuffer(MEDIA_ROOT + "Thrust.wav", sound);
            SoundBuffer.Play(0, BufferPlayFlags.Default);
        } catch {
            Utils.PlaySound(MEDIA_ROOT + "Thrust.WAV");
        }
    }
    . . .
```

Chapter 3: Writing Games

Including More Obstacles: Asteroids as Extra Credit

Here we will develop a secondary set of characters that can be used to increase the difficulty of our second game; these characters will have a list of attributes that allows for independent interaction. The attributes should include character positioning, object animation, and partial to full destruction with multiple strikes. The asteroids' bodies should be developed using the ASCII code characters 219 (as a block) and 32 (as a blank). Combinations of these characters, including varying sizes, are shown Example 3.68.

Example 3.68. Developing an asteroid.

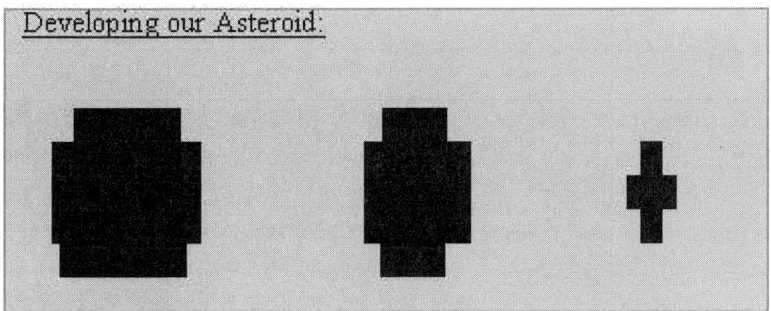

As with the previous characters, the asteroids should have unique patterns of movement. Here, the asteroids will both travel across the screen and change direction as they are struck by players' fire. The asteroids need to be rerouted to the opposite side of the screen whenever those screen limits are reached. Since we'll be writing for four asteroids, we'll conveniently use the four basic directions (upper right (9); lower right (3); upper left (7); and lower left (1)—see Example 3.69).

Example 3.69. Adding asteroids to the game.

```
// Initialize the asteroids
Random rnd = new Random();
asteroids = new Shapes[MAX_ASTEROIDS];
for (int i = 0; i < MAX_ASTEROIDS; i++) {
    // Note, there are only 4 image positions so strange
    // things happen when MAX_ASTEROIDS > 4
```

C# and Game Programming

```
    asteroids[i] = new Shapes((i % 2 == 1) ? 3 * SCALE :
        20 * SCALE, (i < 2 ? 3 * SCALE : 12 * SCALE));
    asteroids[i].direction = rnd.Next(1, 8);
    if (asteroids[i].direction == 0) {
        asteroids[i].direction = i; // default
     }
    asteroids[i].constraintBox = this.ClientRectangle;
    asteroids[i].RescaleImage(2 * SCALE, 2 * SCALE);

    newEvent = new TimedEvent(new TickHandler(MoveAsteroids));
    newEvent.payload = asteroids[i];
    newEvent.isActive = true;
    timer.addEvent(newEvent, ASTEROID_SPEED, "asteroid" + i);
}
```

> These method extensions also refer to secondary methods that are used to discern between ship and asteroid contact, a.k.a. collision detection. Hidden/lower level classes, while accessible through these methods, will not formally be explained until Chapter 5.

Menus

As with Paddle Tennis, we will add in the appropriate menu options, but this time we won't include any additional mouse controls (see Examples 3.70–3.73).

Example 3.70. Two-player option.

```
private void TwoPlayer_Click(object sender, System.EventArgs e) {
    gameState.currentMode = GameState.Mode.TwoPlayer;
    Setup();
}
```

Example 3.71. Single-player option.

```
private void SinglePlayer_Click(object sender, System.EventArgs e){
    gameState.currentMode = GameState.Mode.SinglePlayer;
    Setup();
}
```

Chapter 3: Writing Games

Example 3.72. Adding Asteroids.

```
private void UseAsteroids_Click(object sender, System.EventArgs e) {
    this.menuItem5.Checked = !this.menuItem5.Checked;
    useAsteroids = this.menuItem5.Checked;

    for (int i = 0; i < MAX_ASTEROIDS; i++) {
        asteroids[i].isActive = useAsteroids;
        timer.getEvent("asteroid" + i).isActive = useAsteroids;
    }
}
```

Example 3.73. Setup & Initialization

```
// (re) Sets positional data, scores, and other game data
public void Setup() {
    gameState.currentState = GameState.State.Started;
    gameState.currentSpeed = DEFAULT_SPEED;

    player1.imagePosX = SCALE;
    player1.imagePosY = this.ClientSize.Height/2;
    player1.score = 0;
    player1.isActive = true;
    player1.direction = AnimatedImage.EAST;

    player2.imagePosX = this.ClientSize.Width - 2*SCALE;
    player2.imagePosY = this.ClientSize.Height/2;
    player2.score = 0;
    player2.isActive = true;
    player2.direction = AnimatedImage.WEST;

    for (int i = 0; i < MAX_MISSILES; i++) {
        player1Missiles[i].isActive = false;
        player2Missiles[i].isActive = false;
    }

    for (int i = 0; i < MAX_ASTEROIDS; i++) {
        asteroids[i].RescaleImage(2 * SCALE, 2 * SCALE);
    }

    timer.Start();
}
```

Space Fighters: Putting It All Together

Again, a managing subprogram is necessary to weave these components into the game. Here, I've ported the final product to the book's CD-ROM. (Note that Chapter 3 includes four versions of this game, e.g., Forms, GDI+, GDI+ with DirectX, and pure DirectX. See Example 3.74/SpaceFighter on the CD-ROM for details.)

Game 3—Asteroid Miner

We can also construct a third game that relies mainly on what we've already developed. Asteroid Miner includes the goal of destroying asteroids rather than an enemy's vessel. Here we'll also want to review the techniques used to create a rendered version of the game (see Example 3.75).

Brainstorming

Example 3.75. Brainstorming Asteroid Miner.

1. The game should have one player (a spaceship), which starts in the center of the screen.
2. The game starts the moment it's loaded.
3. The player's movement should be two-dimensional in respect to the screen, but it should include diagonal movement.
4. The ship should have a thrust, but not a brake or reverse, allowing momentum to carry it forward.
5. The ship will have weapons, or at least one weapon, namely a missile that can be fired at the asteroids. To keep things simple, the missiles won't be able to injure our player.
6. We'll use a black background with stars randomly placed across it.
7. The ship should make sounds including a thrust, weapon's fire, and an explosion when hit. The Asteroids should also make a sound when they are hit.
8. The ship should not be able to fire when dead, with the asteroids able to pass through the exploding vessel without damage.

Chapter 3: Writing Games

> 9. The player will gain points for destroying the asteroids, losing points when he crashes.
> 10. The player should have the standard three lives, with an automatic game termination.
> 11. We'll include a command that allows the player to revive damaged ships; this control will also double as hyperspace mode.
> The game will keep track of the players score, allowing for a saved high score. (Note: the technique used to save scores will be explained in Chapter 4.)

GDI+ Graphics

For our third game, we'll want to replace our hand-drawn images with some rendered examples. The ship represented in Screen Shot 3.17 can be replaced with a simple GDI+ `DrawPie` command. Here, the changing angle, `player.startAngle ()`, readjusts our ship, and hence only a single reference is required (see Examples 3.76 and 3.77).

Example 3.76. DrawPie display.

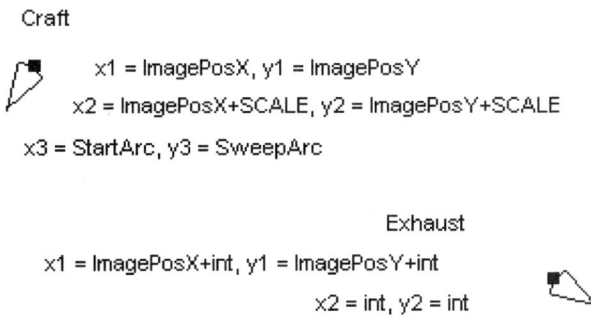

Example 3.77. DrawPie coding.

```
if (player.isActive == true) {
   g.DrawPie(Pens.Blue, player.imagePosX, player.imagePosY,
      SCALE, SCALE, player.startAngle(), 50);
   if (p1Event.isActive) {
      player.Exhuast(g, Brushes.Aqua);
   }
}
```

The Vortex is an alternate version of the sun, e.g.:

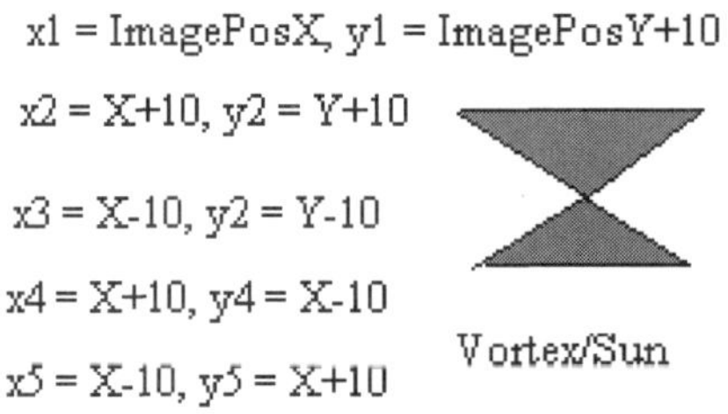

x1 = ImagePosX, y1 = ImagePosY+10

x2 = X+10, y2 = Y+10

x3 = X-10, y2 = Y-10

x4 = X+10, y4 = X-10

x5 = X-10, y5 = X+10

Vortex/Sun

Diagram 3.5. The Vortex/Sun.

Our ship's exhaust is also based on the player's position, but here we'll transfer most of the mathematics to our Exhaust method listed as part of the subprogram Shapes.cs (see Example 3.78).

Example 3.78. Exhaust (Shapes.cs).

```
// game specific - draws an ellipse as connected to a FillPie ship
public int Exhaust(Graphics g, Brush bExhaustColor) {
   switch (this.direction) {
      case 1:
         g.FillEllipse (bExhaustColor, this.imagePosX+21,
           this.imagePosY-1, 5, 5);
         break;
         . . .
```

Given that the asteroids are shared by both Space Fighter and Asteroid Miner, it seems only logical that their polygon constructor would be placed in the class (Shapes.cs) rather then in the actually programs (SpaceFighter.cs and AsteroidMiner.cs). (See Examples 3.79–3.81.)

Example 3.79. Asteroids.

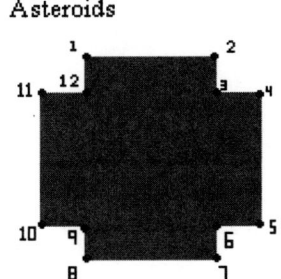

p1 (x-5, y-10)
p2 (x+5, y-10)
p3 (x+5, y-5)
p4 (x+10, y-5)
p5 (x+10, y+5)
p6 (x+5, y+5)
p7 (x+5, y+10)

p8 (x-5, y+10)
p9 (x-5, y+5)
p10 (x-10, y+5)
p11 (x-10, y-5)
p12 (x-5, y-5)

Example 3.80. Do Paint.

```
public void DoPaint(Graphics g) {
     . . .
     // Draw asteroids
     asteroids [0].Asteroid(g, Brushes.Red);
     asteroids [1].Asteroid(g, Brushes.Blue);
     asteroids [2].Asteroid(g, Brushes.Orange);
     asteroids [3].Asteroid(g, Brushes.Yellow);
   }
}
```

Example 3.81. Asteroids (Shapes.cs).

```
// complex shape - reusable as a single item
public void Asteroid(Graphics g, Brush bAsteroidColor) {
    Point[] PolyRoid = {
        new Point(this.imagePosX-this.imageWidth/5,
            this.imagePosY-2*this.imageHeight/5),
        new Point(this.imagePosX+this.imageWidth/5,
            this.imagePosY-2*this.imageHeight/5),
        new Point(this.imagePosX+this.imageWidth/5,
            this.imagePosY-this.imageHeight/5),
        new Point(this.imagePosX+2*this.imageWidth/5,
            this.imagePosY-this.imageHeight/5),
        new Point(this.imagePosX+2*this.imageWidth/5,
            this.imagePosY+this.imageHeight/5),
        new Point(this.imagePosX+this.imageWidth/5,
            this.imagePosY+this.imageHeight/5),
        new Point(this.imagePosX+this.imageWidth/5,
```

C# and Game Programming

```
            this.imagePosY+2*this.imageHeight/5),
        new Point(this.imagePosX-this.imageWidth/5,
            this.imagePosY+2*this.imageHeight/5),
        new Point(this.imagePosX-this.imageWidth/5,
            this.imagePosY+this.imageHeight/5),
        new Point(this.imagePosX-2*this.imageWidth/5,
            this.imagePosY+this.imageHeight/5),
        new Point(this.imagePosX-2*this.imageWidth/5,
            this.imagePosY-this.imageHeight/5),
        new Point(this.imagePosX-this.imageWidth/5,
            this.imagePosY-this.imageHeight/5),};

    g.FillPolygon (bAsteroidColor, PolyRoid);
}
```

The missile by comparison is the simplest of the set with a single call to `FillEllipse`, this coupled with a simple `for` loop allows for multiple images (see Examples 3.81 and 3.82).

Example 3.81. Missiles.

Example 3.82. Missile coding.

```
// Draw missiles
for (int i = 0; i < MAX_MISSILES; i ++) {
    if (playerMissiles [i].isActive)
        g.FillEllipse (Brushes.Blue, playerMissiles [i].imagePosX,
            playerMissiles [i].imagePosY, 5, 5);
}
```

Asteroid Miner: Putting it All Together

Chapter 3 includes four versions of this game (Forms, GDI+, GDI+ with DirectX, and pure DirectX; see AsteroidMiner.cs on the CD-ROM for details).

Chapter 3: Writing Games

Troubleshooting

Here we are again, back in troubleshoot. This time, however, we're more like seasoned veterans, working through the details of games that seemed foreign to us just a few weeks ago. We've built the standard games, we modified them once, twice, a third time maybe, and now we're just trying to figure out the end pieces. Sure, there's obviously something wrong, but try looking at it another way—look how far we've come. Moreover, if it takes a few more days to reach that next level, well then, that's what it takes.

> If however, you happen to be a skimmer, someone who is not already familiar with C#, then I'd recommend that you stop, go back, and do the work that it takes to get here. There's really no point in struggling through the problems of DirectX if you haven't already mastered the safer, yet equally rich, coding presented under GDI+. Remember, much of the gaming structures are identical, so you might as well learn them under the simpler format.

The problems and solutions found in this section are exclusively for DirectX 9.0, listed under the categories of Installing, DirectDraw, DirectInput, and DirectSound. If you have any other compiling or troubleshooting questions, please see the troubleshooting sections in the last two chapters.

When installing DirectX, it's important to remember to uninstall the previous or even the same version of DirectX before installing either a new compiler or a new SDK. Installing the SDK without first removing the old version will result in a bad installation.

DirectDraw's errors seem to center around the bitmap. First, if you attempt to load any file type other than bitmap, you'll have an error. Second, if the program fails to find the designated bitmap, you'll have an error. Third, if the program attempts to display the bitmap anywhere but inside its designated area, you'll have an error. Fourth, if your program attempts to display a bitmap before the last bitmap was drawn, you'll have an error. Of course, the first two errors are physical in nature (a moved file, a mistyped format); it's actually only the second two that can be remedied through code manipulation. Here, we'll have two choices: 1) to include a try-catch block to bypass the exception or 2) to use an ignore exception (see Examples 3.83 and 3.84).

Example 3.83. The try-catch block.

```
try {
    // code
} catch () {
    // some more code
}
```

Example 3.84. The ignore exception.

`Microsoft.DirectX.DirectXException.IgnoreExceptions();`

DirectInput
The most detrimental error caused in DirectInput is a crash when the computer cannot find your joystick. If you've included the `if (joystick == null) {return;}` statement, then this error should have been averted. Therefore, if you're still having trouble, the problem is probably more along the lines of not being able to get our input devices to work. Let's begin with the joystick.

The Joystick
Remember that I cautioned you about the `State` setting, as in `State.X` and `State.Y`. The range here could be off; you should try manipulating the input range itself, perhaps setting it to 0, 1. Here you'd be looking for a response in either direction; again, if you get one response, you'll be able to find the others.

Another possibility is that you've improperly setup your bitmap; does it move with the keyboard? If not, can you set it to move on a for-loop? Check for a changing variable or an invalidating statement. Does the joystick's input include an invalidating statement? Do the pre-assembled programs work with the joystick? How about a third party game? If you're using a special type of joystick, like a steering wheel or multiple joysticks, try replacing them with a simple two-button pad. (For additional possibilities read this section's portion on the keyboard.)

The Keyboard
Here you're far more likely to have forgotten something. A missing command: did you forget to include a `Keyboard.Start ()`? Did you include the timer coding? Remember that the key states began with the lowest setting and worked their way through to the top; did you start the search at a different point? Also, check the obvious; did you forget to include an invalidating reference? (For additional possibilities read this section's portion on the joystick.)

The Mouse

Again, with the mouse you're more than likely to have forgotten something. Forgetting to include the `Mouse.Start ()` and/or `Mouse_Tick` are the most common errors. Another problem with DirectInput's mouse is that it tends to override the other input device, hence, the need for mouse inquiries (see DirectInput: the Mouse for details).

DirectSound

DirectSound cannot play compressed audio data. This is compounded by the fact that DirectSound does not test for faulty audio data. This issue is best solved by testing the wave files used with your game. Replacing a questionable file with a known good file usually helps in identifying the problem. The try-catch block can also be used, but this tends too merely hide the problem. Other problems include corrupt or missing wave files.

Common Errors, Problems, and Pitfalls

1. If the games are compiling, but you get a runtime error and/or you only detect the default sound, your references are probably not to the appropriate directory. For example, if you've copied the games to your D:\\ drive, then the C:\\ listings would all be in error. Make sure all the bitmaps, wav files and classes are not only included as part of your project, but also referenced at the appropriate locations.
2. Check to make sure your files are listed with the appropriate directory. For example, the games listed in the text are clearly marked as coming from the C:\\ drive under the subfolder Games.Net, while the CD-ROM versions are marked as SourceCode\.
3. Are you using Microsoft Visual C# version 7?
   - If your answer is yes, see Question 2.
   - If your answer is no, try looking up any errors or warnings in your compiler's help menu.
4. Can you get any of the animation test programs to work?
   - If your answer is yes, see Question 3.

- If your answer is no, chances are there's a human error. Try beginning with a simple program. Make sure it runs, and then slowly add code.
5. Are you having problems with the linker or the compiler?
    - If you answered linker, your problem lies with either your settings or your subprograms.
    - If you answered compiler, you are more than likely dealing with one of the three basic errors explained in the first two chapters.
6. Did you forget to add a subprogram?
7. Did you open two files and attempt to compile? (Solution: Close everything and start a new workspace with the proper *.CS file.)
8. If all the programs give you the same error, the problem may be in your setup.
9. If you got the Paddle Tennis program to work (project1), but are having trouble with either Space Fighter (project2) or Asteroid Miner (project3), then just try starting again and rebuilding slowly. The only real differences between the two programs are perceptual and will not affect the compiler or computer.
10. If you cannot get the game programs to run on your system, try continuing with the chapters and attempt to recompile these files after you've gained more experience.

Things to Remember

1. Game programming starts with an idea; first you brainstorm and then you refine. Use diagrams and an algorithm as necessary.
2. Always list algorithms in English, not code—you won't always know what language you'll need to use for the program.
3. Use top-down design to simplify your tasks and write your code in modules so that they can be reused.

Chapter 3: Writing Games

> 4. Do not color your characters using the same colors as their backgrounds.
> 5. Make backups of any and all of the games you create. You won't want to lose your hard work.
> 6. Write everything to be reusable; try to limit the number of variables used in the main function.

Questions

1. Using what we've discussed in the last three games, rewrite Paddle Tennis to include three characters on each side. These players should move in unison, i.e., all three characters should play as one. Give this altered game a new file name and title (soccer would be a good choice). You could also limit the scoring area with a goal post, redesign the ball, etc.
2. Using Space Fighter, add a second computer-controlled spaceship that come out only when users choose the deluxe version.
3. Using Asteroid Miner, reinsert the computer as an opponent. Use the data type *bool* to include that choice. Give yourself 25 points each time that ship is destroyed; also, use a time delay to slow the return of that ship.

Arrays, Pointers, and Strings

Chapter Four

*I found Rome a city of bricks and left it
a city of Marble.*
                   –Augustus Caesar

This chapter addresses a concept that lets us combine variables into a collective or aggregated set, provided they share the same base data type and some common purpose. The first portion of this chapter explains this concept—properly referred to as an *array*—from both its singular and multidimensional perspectives. The second portion of this chapter introduces another powerful concept known as the *pointer* and several other keywords and processing commands (including *predefined array/string functions* and *data stream manipulations*). I've also included two gamesthat end this chapter, which allow for the application of these techniques from the perspective of the game programmer. The game will be developed using our basic object-oriented model, including many of the generically written subroutines listed in the previous chapters. There are also several traditional concepts intermixed in this chapter including *bubble sorting*, *array searches*, and calculations of mean, median, mode, and range. (Note: Chapter 5 also offers some intermediate array and string examples that involve an extended knowledge of classes).

Arrays

Arrays are referenced values associated with the collective heap. They are instances of the Base Class Library and thus considered objects, which also makes them subject to the automatic garbage collector. In their simplest form, they can be thought of as a collection of variables used under one data type with similar values and identities. These variables often share the same programming tasks with redundant calculation and similar or redundant concluding data. The information generated is stored collectively, but also with an independent reusability that reduces or prevents the need for repetitive coding.[1] The simplest way to demonstrate the conversion from several variables to an array is to express that process visually, as done in Example 4.1.

Example 4.1. Implementing an array.

```
int number0, number1, number2, number3, number4;
// Is approximately equivalent to
int[] number = new int[5];
// number[0], number[1], number[2], number[3], number[4].
```

As you can see, the first line of code represents the declaration of five variables and the third line represents a value equivalent to five variables. The array's components are broken-down in Example 4.2.

Example 4.2. The components of an array.

```
number[0] // is the first component (or the replacement for number0),
Console.Write(number0); // can be converted to Console.Write(number[0]);

number[1] // is the second component (or the replacement for number1),
Console.Write(number1); // can be converted to Console.Write(number[1]);

number[2] // is the third component (or the replacement for number2),
for (int index = 0; index < number2; index++) // ...
for (int index = 0; index < number[2]; index++)

number[3] // is the fourth component (or the replacement for number3),
if (number3 == 27)   // may be rewritten as if (number[3] == 27)

number[4] // is the fifth component (or the replacement for number4),
while (number4) // ... while (number[4])
```

---

[1] The idea of converting several similarly structured variables to a single or multifunctional array predates the origins of both C++ and C. Arrays could also be thought of as the fathers and grandfathers of structures and classes, respectively.

Component number [5] is not a usable variable and instead holds the null character that terminates the line. Additional indexed variables (for example, number [6], [7]), will also exceed the array's declared space, which may not be flagged as a compilation error.

> In Example 4.2, the first value is zero (not one).[2] In addition, you might conclude that this array should hold six values since number [5] was not used. This conclusion would be in error since C#, like C/C++ before it, withholds that last space as a termination marker. C#, however, does not use the zero-null character namely "\0" to assign that value. Our first chore then will be to convert a simple singular variable program into one that can take advantage of the new array format (the potential of arrays will become obvious very shortly).

Declaring and Referencing Arrays

The declaration of an array doesn't vary greatly from the declaration of either a standard or a constant variable. They are generally written using lowercase lettering, and all of the rules of variable naming still apply. The one significant difference is in the insertion of the square brackets (demonstrated in the last example), which both define an array and allow us to reference its components. The capacity of an array is determined by the size of the value placed inside those initializing brackets. The formal name for this type of value is the *indexed variable*, but it is also known as the *subscripted variable*, or less precisely, as an *element* (i.e., an element of an array). The number of indexed variables (total spaces reserved) is called the *declared size*, or just the size, while the data type used to declare that array is called the *base type* (see Examples 4.3 and 4.4).

Example 4.3. Converting from singular variables to an array—part 1.

```
using System;

namespace Chapter4 {
    class Class1 {
        static void Main() {
            string input;

            char student0, student1, student2, student3, student4;
```

----

[2] In C#, as with C/C++ and assembled languages, the array's numeric notation can be seen as a measure of the distance from one space in the array to another. Since the first space has no space or distance from itself this would in fact be noted as zero. Although it is possible for higher-level languages to alter this value to one, there are still no formal procedures that allow us to convert those values in C#.

```
            Console.WriteLine("Enter student 1's grade :");
            input = Console.ReadLine();
            student0 = char.Parse(input);
            Console.WriteLine("Enter student 2's grade :");
            input = Console.ReadLine();
            student1 = char.Parse(input);

            Console.WriteLine("Enter student 3's grade :");
            input = Console.ReadLine();
            student2 = char.Parse(input);

            Console.WriteLine("Enter student 4's grade :");
            input = Console.ReadLine();
            student3 = char.Parse(input);

            Console.WriteLine("Enter student 5's grade :");
            input = Console.ReadLine();
            student4 = char.Parse(input);

            Console.WriteLine("\nYour input was {0}, {1}, {2}, {3}, {4}",
                student0, student1, student2, student3, student4);
        }
    }
}
```

Example 4.4. Converting from multiple variables to an array—part 2.

```
using System;

namespace Chapter4 {
    class Class1 {
        static void Main() {
            string input;
            char[] student = new char[5];

            for (int index = 0; index < 5; index++) {
                Console.WriteLine("Enter student 1's grade :");
                input = Console.ReadLine();
                student[index] = char.Parse(input) ;
            }
```

Chapter 4: Arrays, Pointers, and Strings

```
            Console.WriteLine ("\nYour input was {0}, {1}, {2}, {3}, {4}",
                student[0], student[1], student[2], student[3],
                student[4]);
        }
    }
}
```

In addition to displaying the values as fragments, we can also display them as a whole (see Example 4.5).

Example 4.5. Converting from multiple variables to an array—part 3.

```
using System;

namespace Chapter4 {
    class Class1 {
        static void Main() {
            string input;
            char[] students_grades = new char[5];

            for (int index = 0; index < 5; index++) {
                Console.WriteLine("Enter student {0}'s grade:",
                    (index+1));
                input = Console.ReadLine();
                students_grades[index] = char.Parse(input);
            }

            Console.Write ("Your input was ");
            for (int index = 0; index < students_grades.Length; index++)
                Console.Write(students_grades[index]);

            Console.WriteLine() ;
        }
    }
}
```

> Using Variable Names as Indexed Variables:
> You can also use variable names when declaring and referencing arrays of undetermined sizes. The one catch here is that those arrays are then limited by that declaration. This holds true even when the variable used to declare that array's range is not a constant (see the section on dynamic arrays). For a simple example of a variable declaration, see Example 4.6.

Example 4.6. Variable declaration for an array.

```
int total_students = 35;
// this is equivalent to students_grades[35]
char[] students_grades = new char[total_students];
```

Assigning Values to Arrays

In addition to declaring arrays, we will need to assign values to them, which can be done either after the array is declared, or as a part of the declaration. There are three standard formats; all include a reference to the data type followed by the array symbol [ ], and the array's definition. In each case, we will include a host of values contained within an opening and closing set of curly braces, as shown in Example 4.7.

Example 4.7. Assigning values to arrays.

```
// all in one
int[] array1 = new int[7] {16, 15, 12, 99, 31, 2, 34};
// split
int[] array1;
array1 = new int[7] {16, 15, 12, 99, 31, 2, 34};
// shorthand
int[] array1 = {16, 15, 12, 99, 31, 2, 34};

// all in one
double[] array2 = new double[4] {16.5, 54.95, 3.14159, 34.0};
// split
double[] array2;
array2 = new double[4] {16.5, 54.95, 3.14159, 34.0};
// shorthand
double[] array2 = {16.5, 54.95, 3.14159, 34.0};

// all in one
char[] array3 = new char[13] {'a', 'b', 'c', 'd', 'e', 'f', 'g',
                              'h', 'i', 'j', 'k', 'l', 'm'};
// split
char[] array3;
array3 = new char[13] {'a', 'b', 'c', 'd', 'e', 'f', 'g',
                       'h', 'i', 'j', 'k', 'l', 'm'};
// shorthand
char[] array3 = new char[13] {'a', 'b', 'c', 'd', 'e', 'f', 'g',
```

Chapter 4: Arrays, Pointers, and Strings

```
                 'h', 'i', 'j', 'k', 'l', 'm'};
// all in one
int[] array4 = new int[] {1, 2, 3};
// split
int[] array4;
array4 = new int[] {1, 2, 3};
// shorthand
int[] array4 = {1, 2, 3};
```

> Here, the brackets are used to indicate that a value is an array. The assignment statement is always enclosed by two braces and again, commas are required to separate those values. Single quotation marks are also used to store single character values and the assignments themselves can be used to replace the formal parameters.

Another useful tool is to include a *string value reference*, replacing the older value type character array with a dynamic value. This new format eliminates the need to make arbitrary guestimations about string size, and thus it will be much less likely that we'll have to tamper with the coding in order to deal with any unusual changes (see Example 4.8).

Example 4.8. String value reference.

```
string String1 = "Damn it boy, its three o'clock in the morning."
string String2 = "What the hell are you doing up so late? \n";
string String3 = "I'm just doing my homework Dad.\n";
string String4 = "Oh, I know what you're doing, turn those games off and
                  go to bed! \n";
string String5 = "That's it! I'm quitting school and joining a software
                  company! \n";
string String6 = "Oh no you're not mister! We didn't raise you to develop
                  software! \n";
```

Passing Arrays to Functions

In addition to using arrays inside of user-defined functions, we can also pass their values either as elements or in their entirety. The techniques for doing so are similar to passing standard arguments, but a few minor changes should be noted. The first type we'll look at are the elements themselves, since they require the least amount of alteration (see Example 4.9).

Example 4.9. Passing the elements of an array.

```
using System;

namespace Chapter4 {
    class Class1 {
        static void Main() {
            string input;
            int[] childrens_ages = new int[20];

            for (int counter = 0; counter < childrens_ages.Length;
                counter++) {
                Console.WriteLine("Enter student {0}'s age:",
                    (counter+1));
                input = Console.ReadLine();
                childrens_ages [counter] = int.Parse(input);
                Ageism(childrens_ages [counter]);
            }
        }

        static void Ageism(int tester) {
            if (tester > 6)
                Console.WriteLine("Your child is to old.\n") ;
        }
    }
}
```

> We can also pass arrays containing literal constants, such as ages [0], ages [1], and ages [2], etc.

We can also reapply this program using a call-by-reference marker as shown in Example 4.10.

Example 4.10. Calls-by-reference in arrays.

```
using System;

namespace Chapter4 {
    class Class1 {
        static void Main() {
            string input;
            int[] childrens_ages = new int[20];

            for (int counter = 0; counter < childrens_ages.Length;
                counter++) {
                Console.WriteLine("Enter student {0}'s age:",
                    (counter + 1));
                input = Console.ReadLine();
                childrens_ages[counter] = int.Parse(input);

                Ageism(ref childrens_ages[counter]);

                if (childrens_ages[counter] > 6)
                    Console.WriteLine("Your child is to old.\n");
            }
        }

        static void Ageism (ref int tester) {
            Console.WriteLine(tester); // we're all too old
            tester += 7;
        }
    }
}
```

The procedure for passing an entire argument differs somewhat from the method used to pass a single element. For example, the initial identifying brackets are not required when sending those values, but they are essential to the receiving statement (see Example 4.11). In C++, it was also important to include a secondary reference that included the array's size; however, this is no longer the case since an array's length can always be found using the *length extension* (included as a method that is accessible by all properly declared arrays).

C# and Game Programming

Example 4.11. Passing an entire array.

```
using System;

namespace Chapter4 {
    class Class1 {
        static void Main() {
            string input;
            const int array_size = 20;
            int[] childrens_ages = new int[array_size];

            for (int counter = 0; counter < array_size; counter++) {
                Console.WriteLine("Enter student {0}'s age:", (counter+1));
                input = Console.ReadLine();
                childrens_ages[counter] = int.Parse(input);
                Ageism(childrens_ages, counter);
            }
        }

        static void Ageism(int[] tester, int index) {
            if (tester[index] > 6)
                Console.WriteLine("Your child is to old.\n");
            else
                Console.WriteLine("Okay.\n") ;
        }
    }
}
```

Of course, we could have rewritten these values as *int* [ ] childrens_ages = new int [20] and Ageism (childrens_ages, 20), but then we'd also have to individually change each value every time the classroom's size changed.

Although unnecessary, it is quite possible to pass an array's declarative size as a call-by-reference variable. This dangerous maneuver may lead to the accidental alteration of that array's size, thus causing a runtime error and possibly a system crash.

The three most effective ways to prevent such an error are:
1) Using the array's length when referring to the array's size;
2) Declaring the array using a constant variable;

> 3) Using call-by-mechanism variables when passing the variable.
>
> These steps may seem a bit redundant, but they almost become mandatory when dealing with multidimensional arrays (see the next section).

Multidimensional Arrays

Multidimensional arrays (also known as *multiple subscript arrays*) are arrays specifically declared to hold more than one set of values. These values are usually linked in a way that makes viewing them simpler than just writing them as independent variables or singular arrays. They are initialized in the same manner as standard arrays, only with the addition of a few more brackets. The practicality of using multidimensional arrays varies from project to project, but in general, they tend to drain the system resources and are usually computed slower than standard arrays; thus, anything over four dimensions should be avoided (see Example 4.12).

Example 4.12. Multidimensional arrays.

```
using System;

namespace Chapter4 {
    class Class1 {
        static void Main() {
            string input;
            char[,] students_grades = new char[5, 5];

            for (int i = 0; i < 5; i++) {
                Console.WriteLine("Enter student {0}'s grades "
                    + "from first to last:", (i+1));
                for (int j = 0; j < 5; j++) {
                    input = Console.ReadLine();
                    students_grades[i, j] = char.Parse(input) ;
                }
            }

            Console.Write ("Your input was");
            for (int i = 0; i < 5; i++) {
                for (int j = 0; j < 5; j++)
                    Console.Write (" {0} ", students_grades[i, j]) ;
            }
```

```
            Console.WriteLine();
        }
    }
}
```

 C# includes a localized reference when dealing with variables declared as part of the *for* loop. Thus any secondary *for* loops using the same variable name would also have to be redeclared. This differs from C++, which only asks for a second declaration if the variable falls out of scope.

You also should have noticed that our first array didn't have any individual values, i.e., the elements of the first dimension were actually only the first element of each of the secondary arrays. This is usually described as an *array of arrays*, but that tends to confuse people. The best way to think about it is as a set of single arrays listed together in a single column as demonstrated in Example 4.13.

> a[0][0] a[0][1] A[0][2] a[0][3] a[0][4]
> a[1][0] a[1][1] A[1][2] a[1][3] a[1][4]
> a[2][0] a[2][1] A[2][2] a[2][3] a[2][4]
> a[3][0] a[3][1] A[3][2] a[3][3] a[3][4]
> a[4][0] a[4][1] A[4][2] a[4][3] a[4][4]
> a[5][0] a[5][1] A[5][2] a[5][3] a[5][4]
> a[6][0] a[6][1] A[6][2] a[6][3] a[6][4]
> a[7][0] a[7][1] A[7][2] a[7][3] a[7][4]
> a[8][0] a[8][1] A[8][2] a[8][3] a[8][4]
> a[9][0] a[9][1] A[9][2] a[9][3] a[9][4]
>
> Where, a[10] [0]–a[10] [4] are Null (\0).

Example 4.13. Array values.

Chapter 4: Arrays, Pointers, and Strings

Just as standard arrays can be initialized, passed, and included as entire arrays inside functions, so can multidimensional arrays. Although slightly different in appearance, they follow the same rules and have the same basic limitations. The next few examples show how this type of coding is implemented (see Example 4.14).

> The program in Example 4.14 accepts a list of six names of five letters each. The values are stored in a multidimensional array (6x5).

Example 4.14. Two-dimensional arrays.

```
using System;

namespace Chapter4 {
    class Class1 {
        static void Main() {
            string[,] names = new string[6, 5];

            for (int i = 0; i < 6; i++) {
                Console.WriteLine("Enter student's name "
                    + "(all names must include 5 letters): ");
                for (int j = 0; j < 5; j++) {
                    names[i, j] = Console.ReadLine();
                }
            }

            file(names);
        }

        static void file(string[,] tester) {
            for (int i = 0; i < 6; i++) {
                for (int j = 0; j < 5; j++)
                    Console.WriteLine(tester[i, j]);
            }
        }
    }
}
```

Three-Dimensional Arrays

Algebra uses Cartesian coordinates to graph dimensions, e.g., x, y, and z. Physics uses the letters i, j, and k, which mean exactly the same thing (see Examples 4.15 and 4.16).

Example 4.15. Graphing coordinates x, y, z.

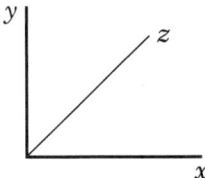

Example 4.16. Graphing coordinates i, j, and k.

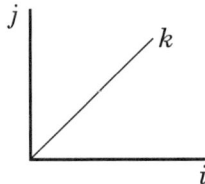

Most programmers use i, j, and k to reference an array's memory locations, as well as to represent nested loops, three-dimensional space, etc. The values for a three-dimensional array are basically the same in coding terms, but the data's reference points are quite different, as shown in Example 4.17.

Example 4.17. Three-dimensional array values.

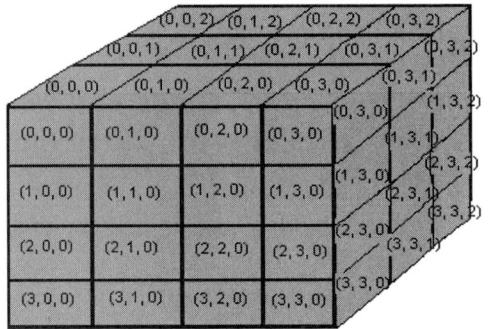

Chapter 4: Arrays, Pointers, and Strings

This cube shows us how the values are laid out from 0, 0, 0 to 3, 3, 2. We can assign reference points such that *i* equals the list of arrays, *j* is the first value of each array, and *k* is the last value stored for each list.

Example 4.18. Declaring, initializing, and passing a three-dimensional array.

```
using System;

namespace Chapter4 {
    class Class1 {
        static void Main() {
            char [, ,] names = new char[7, 5, 6] {
                {
                    {'T', 'h', 'i', 's', ' ', 'i'},
                    {'s', ' ', 'a', ' ', 't', 'e'},
                    {'s', 't', ',', ' ', 't', 'h'},
                    {'i', 's', ' ', 'i', 's', ' '},
                    {'o', 'n', 'l', 'y', ' ', 'a'},
                },
                {
                    {' ', 't', 'e', 's', 't', '.'},
                    {'\n', 'F', 'o', 'r', ' ', 't'},
                    {'h', 'e', ' ', 'n', 'e', 'x'},
                    {'t', ' ', 'm', 'i', 'n', 'u'},
                    {'t', 'e', ' ', 'y', 'o', 'u'},
                },
                {
                    {'r', ' ', 'c', 'o', 'm', 'p'},
                    {'u', 't', 'e', 'r', ' ', 'w'},
                    {'i', 'l', 'l', ' ', 'b', 'e'},
                    {' ', 'c', 'o', 'n', 'd', 'u'},
                    {'c', 't', 'i', 'n', 'g', '\n'},
                },
                {
                    {'a', ' ', 't', 'e', 's', 't'},
                    {' ', 'o', 'f', ' ', 't', 'h'},
                    {'e', ' ', 'm', 'u', 'l', 't'},
                    {'i', 'd', 'i', 'm', 'e', 'n'},
                    {'s', 'i', 'o', 'n', 'a', 'l'},
                },
```

```
            {
                {' ', 'a', 'r', 'r', 'a', 'y'},
                {' ', 's', 'e', 'q', 'u', 'e'},
                {'n', 'c', 'e', '.', '\n', 'T'},
                {'H', 'I', 'S', ' ', 'I', 'S'},
                {' ', 'O', 'N', 'L', 'Y', ' '},
            },
            {
                {'A', ' ', 'T', 'E', 'S', 'T'},
                {'!', '\n', 'A', 'B', 'C', 'D'},
                {'E', 'F', 'G', 'H', 'I', 'J'},
                {'K', 'L', 'M', 'N', 'O', 'P'},
                {'Q', 'R', 'S', 'T', 'U', 'V'},
            },
            {
                {'W', 'X', 'Y', 'Z', 'a', 'b'},
                {'c', 'd', 'e', 'f', 'g', 'h'},
                {'i', 'j', 'k', 'l', 'm', 'n'},
                {'o', 'p', 'q', 'r', 's', 't'},
                {'u', 'v', 'w', 'x', 'y', 'z'},
            }
        };

        Display (names) ;
    }
    static void Display(char[,,] print) {
        const short sets = 7, rows = 5, columns = 6;
        for (int i = 0; i < sets; i++) {
            for (int j = 0; j < rows; j++)
                for (int k = 0; k < columns; k++)
                    Console.Write("{0}\a", print [i, j, k]);
        }
        Console.WriteLine();
    }
  }
}
```

Multidimensional arrays are also considered to be either jagged (without a constant shape) or rectangle/square (to have two or more sides with the same length).

Sorting Arrays

Sorting, as related to an array, is the action of rearranging or reorganizing the order of elements to make a particular task easier to follow. This usually involves some logical reference point such as letters placed in alphabetical order and numbers listed in a numeric order. The principle method used to displace these values involves both the comparison and reassignment of that data. The techniques used to sort these values range from the very simple to the complex, but they all do pretty much the same thing; thus, the need for alternate techniques then has more to do with the speed of the process than the result. The simplest of these is known as the *bubble sort* (also referred to as the *sinking sort*); values are listed in a single array, compared with one another and swapped as needed, until all the values are in the proper order. The word bubble is used to aid in visualizing the smaller (lighter) values rising to the top and the word sinking is used to visualize the larger (heavier) values sinking to the bottom. The coding for this type of sort is also very straight forward—see Example 4.19.

Example 4.19. Bubble sort.

```
using System;

namespace Chapter4 {
    class Class1 {
        static void Main() {
            const short array_size = 12;
            int[] simple_array = new int[array_size] {
                31, 31, 54, 0, 60, 35, 34, 29, 18, 17, 13, 10};

            BubbleSort (simple_array, array_size);
        }

        static void BubbleSort (int[] my_array, short size) {
            int temp = 0;
            Console.WriteLine("\nRandom numbers inputted in this order");

            for (int i = 0; i < size; i++)
                Console.WriteLine("{0}   ", my_array[i]);
            for (int i = 0; i < size; i++)
                for (int j = 0; j < size-1; j++)
                    if (my_array[j] > my_array[j+1]) {
                        temp = my_array[j];
```

```
                    my_array[j] = my_array[j+1];
                    my_array[j+1] = temp ;
                }

            Console.WriteLine("\nsorting...\n" +
                "\nIn ascending order");
            for (int i = 0; i < size; i++)
                Console.WriteLine("   {0}", my_array[i]);

            Console.WriteLine("\nand in descending order");
            for (int i = size-1; i > -1; i--)
                Console.WriteLine("   {0}", my_array[i]) ;
        }
    }
}
```

Searching Arrays

There are two basic types of searches that are useful and relate directly to data stored in an array. The first is the *linear search*, which, as its name implies, is a consecutive comparison that tests each element until the correct information is found. This is a very common and particularly useful search algorithm, especially when dealing with random or unrelated data that cannot be sorted. The second, also considered the more efficient search, is the *binary search*. This search divides and compares two criteria, where the total value is divided into two sets and the irrelevant set is discarded. This process is repeated as many times as possible before reverting back to a basic linear search. Both searches are considered effective, but the binary search is preferred when dealing with longer, sortable data streams that require repeated searches (see Examples 4.20 and 4.21). The binary search also requires that the data be presorted; the presorted data can also be stored as a secondary file, thus, eliminating the need for continuous resorting.

Example 4.20. Linear search(finding a number in an array).

```
using System;

namespace Chapter4 {
    class Class1 {
        static void Main() {
            string input;
            const int array_size = 100;
```

```csharp
            int[] our_array = new int[array_size];
            int number, total;

            CreateArray(our_array, array_size);

            Console.WriteLine("Enter a number between 1-100:");
            input = Console.ReadLine();
            number = int.Parse(input);

            total = Comparison (our_array, number, array_size);
            Console.WriteLine("That number occurred {0} times", total);
        }

        // creates a random array with values between 1 and 100
        static void CreateArray (int[] random_array, int size) {
            Random rnd = new Random();

            for (int index = 0; index < size; index++)
                random_array[index] = (int)Math.Round (rnd.NextDouble () * 100) ;
        }

        // searches that array with a linear search
        static int Comparison (int[] array, int input, int size) {
            int count = 0;
            for (int index = 0; index < size; index++)
                if (array[index] == input) count++;
            return count;
        }
    }
}
```

Example 4.21. Bubble sort and binary search(finding a number in an array).

```csharp
using System;

namespace Chapter4 {
    class Class1 {
        static void Main() {
            string ScreenInput;
            const long array_size = 100;
            long[] our_array = new long[array_size];
            long input;
```

```csharp
        bool found = false;

        CreateArray (our_array);
        BubbleSort (our_array);

        while (true) {
            Console.WriteLine("Enter a number between 1-100:");
            ScreenInput = Console.ReadLine();
            input = long.Parse(ScreenInput);

            BinarySearch(our_array, array_size, input, array_size - 1,
                    0, ref found);

            if (found)
                Console.WriteLine("Value found!");
            else
                Console.WriteLine("Value not found!");

            found = false;
        }
    }

    // This function creates a random array of numbers
    // with values between 1 and 100
    static void CreateArray (long[] random_array) {
        Random rnd = new Random ();

        for (int index = 0; index < random_array.Length; index++)
            random_array[index] = (long)(rnd.NextDouble () * 100+1);
    }

    static void BubbleSort (long[] my_array) {
        long temp = 0;
        Console.WriteLine("\nRandom numbers inputted in this order");

        for (int i = 0; i < my_array.Length; i++) {
            Console.WriteLine(my_array[i]);}
        // sort
        for (int i = 0; i < my_array.Length; i++) {
            for (int j = 0; j < my_array.Length-1; j++) {
                if (my_array[j] > my_array[j+1]) {
                    temp = my_array[j];
                    my_array[j] = my_array[j+1];
                    my_array[j+1] = temp ;
                }
```

```csharp
            }
        }
        Console.WriteLine("\nsorting...\n"
            + "\nIn ascending order");

        for (int index = 0; index < my_array.Length; index++) {
            Console.WriteLine(my_array[index]);
        }

        Console.WriteLine();
    }

    // this function searches and compares
    // data using a binary search pattern.
    static void BinarySearch(long[] array, long size, long input,
        long high, long low, ref bool found) {
        if (input < array[(size / 2) - 1]) {
            if (input == array[high - 1])
                found = true;
            else if (input < array[(high / 2) - 1])
                BinarySearch (array, size, input, high / 2, low,
                    ref found);
            else if (high > low)
                BinarySearch (array, size, input, (high - 1), low,
                    ref found) ;}
        else if (input > array[(size / 2) - 1]) {
            if (low < 0 && input == array[low])
                found = true;
            else if (input > array[((high + low) / 2) - 1] &&
                (high - low) >= 2)
                BinarySearch (array, size, input, high,
                    (high + low) / 2, ref found);
            else if (low < high)
                BinarySearch (array, size, input, high, (low + 1),
                    ref found) ;
        }
    }
}
}
```

Dynamic Arrays in C#

The word dynamic is defined as the ability to adapt or alter an otherwise restricted set of coding. The most prominent example of this is the dynamic variable (what we think of as the standard variable). This variable, unlike a "constant," can be adjusted to virtually any value both at compile time and during execution. While the definition of the C# array is far more dynamic then that of the C++ or C version, it is still a constant parameter that cannot be changed while the program is in motion. We can, however, set up arrays to include dynamically calculated assessments that occur at runtime using a nonconstant integer variable type. Again, this is fairly similar to the method used to create dynamic arrays under Native C++, with the coding actually matching the basic C# references.

The most inconvenient aspect of declaring an array is in its requirement of a constant variable, or literal constant, which always forces the programmer to make a guestimation that can lead to arrays that are either too small (making them incapable of the task) or oversized (unnecessarily tying up much needed system resources). The solution to both of these problems lies in the use of *dynamic arrays*. Dynamic arrays, as the term implies, are arrays that do not require predetermined constants at declaration, but they do require a constant size once that value is assigned, which is almost the same thing, but it does offer up a few new options.

Since C# always uses the new keyword to declare its arrays, we won't actually have to change the way we reference those values to make them dynamic. In addition, since the .Net structure offers a managed heap, we won't need to refer to a deallocating method (as was done with the word delete in C++). We should, however, at least formally define the word new. The keyword new allows us to declare dynamic arrays using standard variables, which are then referenced from inside the heap. The heap is a special area of memory reserved for dynamic arrays, reference variables, etc. To assign an array's parameters, simply follow the format listed in Example 4.22 (char my_array = new char [array_size];).

Example 4.22. Dynamic arrays.
```
using System;

namespace Chapter4 {
    class Class1 {
        static void Main() {
            string input;
            int array_size;

            Console.Write ("How many students in the classroom? ");
            input = Console.ReadLine();
            array_size = int.Parse(input);
```

```
        char[] students_grades = new Char[array_size];

        for (int index = 0; index < students_grades.Length; index++) {
            Console.WriteLine("Enter the {0}'s student's grade:",
                (index + 1));
            input = Console.ReadLine();
            students_grades[index] = char.Parse(input);
        }

        Console.Write("The grades were ;");
        for(int index = 0; index < students_grades.Length; index++)
            Console.Write(" {0} ", students_grades[index]);

        Console.WriteLine();
        }
    }
}
```

The `foreach` loop

The `foreach` loop is a specialized process that is used to skim or scan through an array's elements without the common drudgery usually associated with listing that array's components. It is generally written to include both the keywords `foreach` and `in` and for the most part, it physically resembles the notation used when describing the for-loop process. One key difference, however, is that the indexing or searching value is not allowed to be altered; this would include even subtle manipulation, such as the incrementing or decrementing operators. The `foreach` process (as I'm sure many of you are aware) is actually an add-in from the language Visual Basic, thus there is no equivalent in native C++ (see Example 4.23).

Example 4.23. The `foreach` loop.

```
using System;

namespace Chapter4 {
    class Class1 {
        static void Main(string[] args) {
            char[] integer = {'a', 'g', 'n', 'u'};
```

```
            foreach (char find in integer) {
                if (find == 'u')
                    Console.WriteLine("I found {0}", find);
            }
        }
    }
}
```

Enumerating Constant Integers

Another limited version of a collective set of values is the integer data type known as the `enumerator`. This constant integer type (as in `signed` and `unsigned short`, `integer`, and `long` values) is a basic aggregated type that promotes simple reference manipulations. It also allows for some unique references such as user-defined data structures and lists of assignments to those declarations. Initial structures are declared using the keyword `enum` with instances of those values declared and assigned as if they were class references. If no values are assigned to these references, then the initial point would be zero, and each new component would automatically increment by one. However, we can also short step this process by beginning at some arbitrary point (such as 2000), or we could individually declare each value (see Example 4.24).

Example 4.24. Enumerating integers.

```
using System;

namespace Chapter4 {
    class Class1 {
        public enum Months {
            Jan = 1, Feb, Mar, Apr,
            May, Jun, Jul, Aug, Sep, Oct, Nov, Dec}
        public enum Day {
            AprilFools = 1, Birthday = 16,
            XMas = 25, Feb29 = 29, NYeve = 31}

        public enum Year {Year2 = 2002, Year3, LeapYear}

        static void Main() {
            string input;
            int TheMonth, TheDay, TheYear;
```

```
        while (true) {
           Console.Write("Enter the current Month (Example: \"Jan\" =
                   1): ");
           input = Console.ReadLine();
           TheMonth = int.Parse(input);

           Console.Write("What day of the Month is it? ");
           input = Console.ReadLine();
           TheDay = int.Parse(input);

           Console.Write("What year is it 2002, 2003... ");
           input = Console.ReadLine();
           TheYear = int.Parse(input);

           if (TheMonth == (int)Months.Feb &&
               TheDay == (int)Day.Feb29 &&
               TheYear == (int) Year.LeapYear)
               Console.WriteLine("Happy Leap Year!");

           if (TheMonth == (int)Months.Apr &&
               TheDay == (int)Day.AprilFools)
               Console.WriteLine("April Fool's");

           if (TheMonth == (int)Months.Sep &&
               TheDay == (int)Day.Birthday)
               Console.WriteLine("Happy Birthday!");

           if (TheMonth == (int)Months.Dec) {
              if (TheDay == (int)Day.XMas)
                  Console.WriteLine("Merry Christmas!");
              if (TheDay == (int)Day.NYeve)
                  Console.WriteLine("Happy New Year!");
           }
        }
      }
   }
}
```

Pointers

A *pointer* is a special type of variable used to access the space in memory occupied by traditional variables. They point at the values held inside of those locations, and although they are capable of assessing and even changing that information, they remain

C# and Game Programming

only links to the address. This should remind you of the call-by-reference in Chapter 2. These were, for the most part, limited pointers, which as you'll recall, enabled us to both access and alter the passed variables from inside our subprograms. This gave us the power to use those values as if they were global variables, but with the increased plug-n-play ability of local variables, which makes pointers very useful, but also potentially dangerous. Thus, C# allows pointer manipulations, but only under the newly defined `unsafe` mode.

Enabling `unsafe` Mode

Once a project is loaded into the .Net compiler, it becomes only a simple matter of altering that project's build configuration to enable `unsafe` mode. From the folder labeled "View," select the file titled "Solution Explorer" (see Screen Shot 4.1).

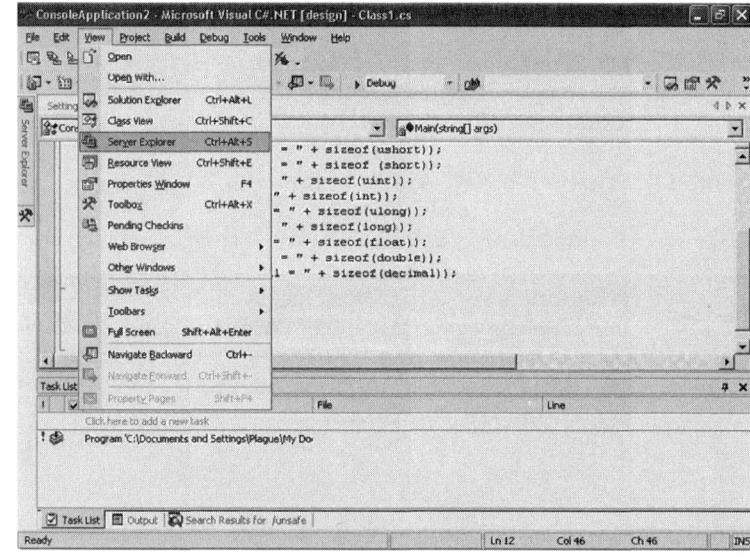

Screen Shot 4.1.

A second side window will open; make sure to highlight the project rather than the file name. Select "Properties," the third icon, depicted in that smaller window (see Screen Shot 4.2).

Chapter 4: Arrays, Pointers, and Strings

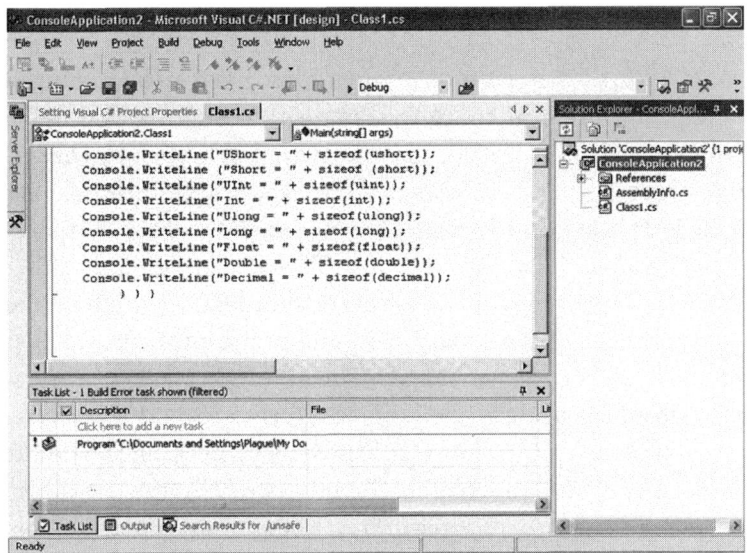

Screen Shot 4.2.

Now go to the listing labeled "Configuration Properties." Select "Build" from that sublist and click on the "False" value under the "Allow unsafe code blocks." From there, an arrow will appear—use it to select the "True" setting and press "Apply" (see Screen Shot 4.3).

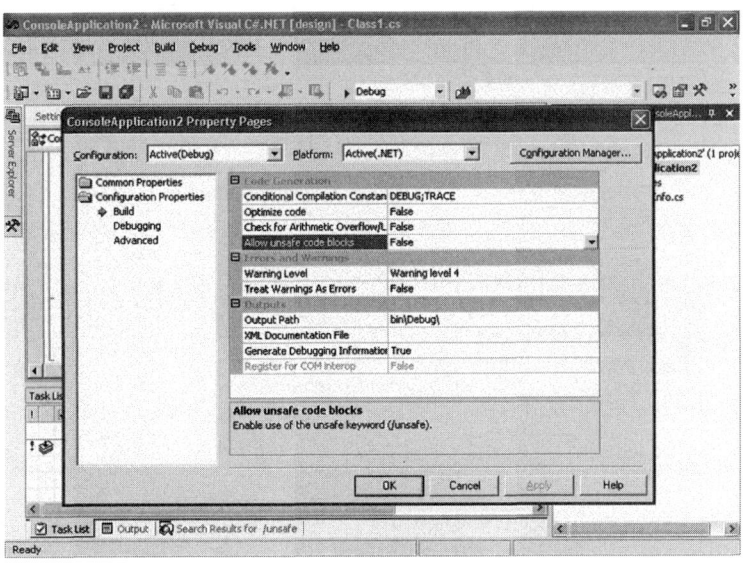

Screen Shot 4.3

Pointer Variables

Pointer variables, like all other types of variables, need to be declared, but because they require a location to point to, they also need to be assigned before they can be referenced. Pointers are also limited, like standard variables, by their data types and rules of naming. Thus, it stands to reason that pointers declared as integers can only point to standard variables that were also declared as integers, doubles with doubles, floats to floats, and characters to characters. The one key visual difference when declaring pointers is the insertion of the asterisk symbol (*), which is placed in front of the data type's reference. This asterisk tells the compiler that this data type is actually intended to declare pointer variables. The asterisk, in this case, is referred to as the *dereferencing operator*, and the variable is referred to as the *dereferenced variable*. The second step is to assign the pointer; this is done by making the pointer equal to the standard variable. An ampersand symbol (&) must precede the standard variable (ampersands are referred to as *address operators*). Remember, a pointer that has not been assigned has nothing to point to, and cannot be used (see Example 4.25). Note: There is also a void data type pointer, which is a generalized pointer that can be linked to any of the other data types. Void pointer data types are discussed later in this chapter.

Example 4.25. Pointers.

```
using System;

namespace Chapter4 {
    class Class1 {
        static unsafe void Main() {
            int* pointer1;
            int variable1 = 1;
            float* pointer2;
            float variable2 = 2.0f;
            double *pointer3;
            double variable3 = 3.01;
            char *pointer4;
            char variable4 = 'A';

            pointer1 = &variable1;
            pointer2 = &variable2;
            pointer3 = &variable3;
            pointer4 = &variable4;
```

Chapter 4: Arrays, Pointers, and Strings

```
            Console.WriteLine ("{0}        {1}", variable1, *pointer1);
            Console.WriteLine ("{0}        {1}", variable2, *pointer2);
            Console.WriteLine ("{0}        {1}", variable3, *pointer3);
            Console.WriteLine ("{0}        {1}", variable4, *pointer4);
        }
    }
}
```

We can also assign numeric values to pointers, but only after they have been assigned memory locations. Again, we'll use the equal sign to assign the values and the asterisk symbol to reference the pointer. You should note that since pointers place their new values in the memory locations used by standard variables, any previous information is overwritten.

"I just got this new pointer VISA—it has my name on it,
but the charges are linked to someone else's account."
"Are you sure that's legal?"
"Well, not always, I have to use it in *unsafe* counties."

Pointers can also assign locations to other pointers—see the code in Example 4.26.

Example 4.26. Assigning values and memory locations to pointers.

```
using System;

namespace Chapter4 {
    class Class1 {
        static unsafe void Main() {
            int* pointer1, pointer2;
            // Warning, pointer3 is not an actual pointer!
            int variable1 = 1, pointer3;

            // Assigning a pointer to a value
            pointer1 = &variable1;
            // Pointer to pointer assignments DO NOT require the asterisk.
            pointer2 = pointer1;
            // Pointers can also pass values to variables.
            pointer3 = *pointer2;
```

C# and Game Programming

```
            Console.WriteLine("{0}      {1}     {2}     {3}",
                variable1, *pointer1, *pointer2, pointer3);

            *pointer1 = 20;  // the value inside that address is now 20.

            Console.WriteLine("{0}      {1}     {2}     {3}",
                variable1, *pointer1, *pointer2, pointer3);
        }
    }
}
```

> **The Keyword null:**
> The keyword null is the only value that can be assigned to an unassigned pointer without causing an error. The null statement is also useful when passing meaningless values to a generalized function as in MyFunction (SomeNumber, null); where a second value is not required when the first value represents a short-circuit event. The *null* value works in basically the same manner as did the NULL value in C++, except now it's actually a keyword.

Call-By-Reference Values with Pointer Arguments

As you'll remember from Chapter 2, we were able to write function calls as both calls-by-value and calls-by-reference, but calls-by-reference also let us change the values of the original variables. You should also recall (from our introduction to pointers) that calls-by-reference are actually limited forms of pointers. This makes it possible to rewrite those programs so that they use actual pointer notation without significantly changing those programs (see Example 4.27)

Example 4.27. Calls-by-reference with pointer arguments.

```
using System;

namespace Chapter4 {
    class Class1 {
        static unsafe void Main() {
            string input;
            char race = 'Y';
```

```csharp
        int winner, number1 = 0, number2 = 0, number3 = 0;

    Console.WriteLine("Let's have a horse race.\n"
        + "To play select one of the horses below");

    while (char.ToUpper (race) != 'N') {
        Console.WriteLine("(1) for Whitefire\n"
            + "(2) for The Train and, \n"
            + "(3) for Noisy Glue");

        input = Console.ReadLine();

        the_race(&number1, &number2, &number3);
        tie_breaker(&number1, &number2);
        tie_breaker(&number2, &number3);
        tie_breaker(&number1, &number3);

        winner = the_winner(&number1, &number2, &number3);
        Console.Write("And the winner is ");

        if (winner == '1')
            Console.WriteLine("Whitefire");
        else if (winner == '2')
            Console.WriteLine("The Train");
        else
            Console.WriteLine("Noisy Glue");

        Console.Write("Would you like to play again (Y/N)?");
        input = Console.ReadLine();
        race = char.Parse(input);
    }
}

static unsafe void the_race(int *number1, int *number2,
    int *number3) {
    Random rnd = new Random();

    *number1 = (int)(rnd.NextDouble() * 100);
    *number2 = (int)(rnd.NextDouble() * 100);
    *number3 = (int)(rnd.NextDouble() * 100);
    Console.Write(".");
}

static unsafe void tie_breaker(int *num1, int *num2) {
    if (*num1 == *num2)
```

```
            *num2 = *num2 - 1;
            Console.Write(".");
        }

        static unsafe char the_winner(int *num1, int *num2, int *num3) {
            char winner;
            if (*num1 > *num2 && *num1 > *num3)
                winner = '1';
            else if (*num2 > *num1 && *num2 > *num3)
                winner = '2';
            else winner = '3';
            Console.Write(".");

            return(winner);
        }
    }
}
```

Pointer Arithmetic

Pointer arithmetic is simply variable arithmetic as applied to pointers (note: asterisks are required). In pointer arithmetic, pointers are used like variables to add, subtract, multiply, divide, and find the remainder of stored values. Pointers can also be used with shorthand notation and the incrementing and decrementing operators (incrementing & decrementing operators also require the insertion of parentheses—see Examples 4.28 and 4.29).

Example 4.28. Arithmetic with pointers.

```
using System;

namespace Chapter4 {
    class Class1 {
        static unsafe void Main() {
            int number1 = 0, number2 = 0;
            int* pointer1 = &number2;

            number1 = number1 + 10;         // Addition
            *pointer1 = *pointer1 + 10;
            Console.WriteLine ("{0}    {1}", number1, number2);

            number1 = number1 - 1;      // Subtraction
```

```
            *pointer1 = *pointer1 - 1;
            Console.WriteLine ("{0}     {1}", number1, number2);

            number1 = number1*2;    // Multiplication
            *pointer1 = *pointer1*2;
            Console.WriteLine ("{0}     {1}", number1, number2);

            number1 = number1/2;    // Division
            *pointer1 = *pointer1/2;
            Console.WriteLine ("{0}     {1}", number1, number2);

            number1 = number1%3;    // Remainders
            *pointer1 = *pointer1%3;
            Console.WriteLine ("{0}     {1}", number1, number2);
        }
    }
}
```

Example 4.29. Shorthand notation and the incrementing and decrementing operators.

```
using System;

namespace Chapter4 {
    class Class1 {
        static unsafe void Main() {
            int number1 = 0, number2 = 0;
            int* pointer1 = &number2;

            for (int index = 0; index < 10; index++) {
                number1 = number1++;
                *pointer1 = (*pointer1) ++ ;
            }
            Console.WriteLine ("{0}     {1}", number1, number2);
            number1 = number1 - 1;
            *pointer1 = (*pointer1)--;
            Console.WriteLine ("{0}     {1}", number1, number2);

            // number1 = number1 + number1
            number1 = number1 += number1;
            // *pointer1 = *pointer1 + *pointer1
            *pointer1 = *pointer1 += *pointer1;
```

```
            Console.WriteLine ("{0}    {1}", number1, number2);
            // number1 = number1 - number1
            number1 = number1 -= number1;
            // *pointer1 = *pointer1 - *pointer1
            *pointer1 = *pointer1 -= *pointer1;
            Console.WriteLine ("{0}    {1}", number1, number2);

            number1 = 5;
            *pointer1 = 5;
            number1 = number1*=2;
            *pointer1 = *pointer1*=2;
            Console.WriteLine ("{0}    {1}", number1, number2);
            number1 = number1/=2;
            *pointer1 = *pointer1/=2;
            Console.WriteLine ("{0}    {1}", number1, number2);
            number1 = number1/=2;
            *pointer1 = *pointer1/=2;
            Console.WriteLine ("{0}    {1}", number1, number2);
            number1 = 5;
            *pointer1 = 5;
            number1 = number1%=2;
            *pointer1 = *pointer1%=2;
            Console.WriteLine ("{0}    {1}", number1, number2);
        }
    }
}
```

String and Address Arithmetic

String arithmetic is also fairly simple, but it doesn't involve changing numeric values. Instead, we'll use arithmetic commands to move an array's index from address to address. This is possible because of the strings sequentially stored memory locations. Since we cannot know the spatial difference between any two strings, this type of memory manipulation must be limited to arrogated variables that are part of the same string (see memory mapping for further details).

Example 4.30. Mapping Memory.

Computers allocate a certain amount of Random Access Memory (RAM) to each variable declared inside of a program. This memory is actually part of a computer's hardware, and is reused and/or overwritten every time we run a new program. The methods used to store variables and the exact locations in memory of those variables are irrelevant to us as programmers, and will be left to books related to computer operating systems and hardware. Our understanding of how and where data is placed will have to be on an abstract scale. This therefore includes an imaginary point of reference that we can build upon to access and alter any arrays or strings of data declared in our programs.

First off, let's assume that we've just declared and initialized a character array or string to the values A, B, C, D, and E. We know that the strings' positions will reflect our points (as in zero equals A, one equals B and two equals C, etc.), but we don't know how this will relate to the computer's placement of that data. If we then reason that the computer places the first component A in some arbitrary location (say memory location 1000), using the basic form of 1 byte per character, we can deduce that the location 1001 would hold the value B, location 1002 would hold C, and so on. From this, we can also graph a map of the locations:

Memory Location		Referencing Array		Value in Memory
[1000]	=	array[0]	=	A
[1001]	=	array[1]	=	B
[1002]	=	array[2]	=	C
[1003]	=	array[3]	=	D
[1004]	=	array[4]	=	E
[1005]	=	array[5]	=	\0

If a character takes up 2 bytes per element, their memory locations would be listed as

Memory Location		Referencing Array		Value in Memory
[1000 – 1001]	=	array[0]	=	1
[1002 – 1003]	=	array[1]	=	2
[1004 – 1005]	=	array[2]	=	3
[1006 – 1007]	=	array[3]	=	4
[1008 – 1009]	=	array[4]	=	5

In addition, if a data type takes up 4 bytes per element, it would produce a larger span or cluster of data.

Memory Location		Referencing Array		Value in Memory
[1000 – 1003]	=	array[0]	=	1
[1004 – 1007]	=	array[1]	=	2
[1008 – 1011]	=	array[2]	=	3
[1012 – 1015]	=	array[3]	=	4
[1016 – 1019]	=	array[4]	=	5

Further, this could continue on and on at least up to 64 bits (the 128-bit machines are not quite ready yet). Data that takes up 8 bytes is equivalent to:

Memory Location		Referencing Array		Value in Memory
[1000 – 1007]	=	array[0]	=	1
[1008 – 1015]	=	array[1]	=	2
[1016 – 1023]	=	array[2]	=	3
[1024 – 1031]	=	array[3]	=	4
[1032 – 1039]	=	array[4]	=	5

Chapter 4: Arrays, Pointers, and Strings

Manipulating strings using arithmetic is fairly straightforward, but we'll still have to make a few tiny adjustments (see Example 4.31).

> You can also subtract one pointer location from another as long as they're referencing the same string. This special situation gives us an integer value equal to the distance between the two.
>
> The program in Example 2.31 converts letters from uppercase to lowercase and back from lowercase to uppercase using string (address) arithmetic rather than the ToUpper and ToLower functions.

Example 4.31. String arithmetic.

```
using System;

namespace Chapter4 {
    class Class1 {
        static void Main() {
            char input;

            do {
                input = char.Parse(Console.ReadLine());
                input = MyToupper(input);
                Console.WriteLine("{0}", input);
                input = MyTolower(input);
                Console.WriteLine(input);
            } while (input != 'z');
        }

        static char MyToupper(char input) {
            string alpha =
                "abcdefghijklmnopqrstuvwxyzABCDEFGHIJKLMNOPQRSTUVWXYZ";

            for (int index = 0; index < 26; index++)
                if (input == (alpha[index]))
                    input = (alpha[index + 26]);
```

```
            return (input);
        }

        static char MyTolower(char input) {
            string alpha =
                "abcdefghijklmnopqrstuvwxyzABCDEFGHIJKLMNOPQRSTUVWXYZ";

            for (int index = 26; index < 52; index++)
                if (input == (alpha[index]))
                    input = (alpha[index - 26]);
            return (input);
        }
    }
}
```

The void Pointer

The `void` data type can be used to declare generalized pointers, that is, pointers that *do not*, as yet, have a set data type. These all-purpose pointers can be reassigned to different data types with each function call or as part of an abstract subroutine. `void` pointers can be converted to any of the other data types and can be used as a sort of template, always changing to fit the needs of a program (see Example 4.31).

Example 4.32. The void pointer.

```
using System;

namespace Chapter4 {
    class Class1 {
        static unsafe void Main() {
            short variable1 = 20;
            int variable2 = 20;
            long variable3 = 100000;
            float variable4 = 6.0F;
            double variable5 = 123.456789;
            decimal variable6 = 321.123456M;

            Console.WriteLine ("{0}\n{1}\n{2}\n{3}\n{4}\n{5}\n",
                variable1, variable2, variable3, variable4, variable5,
                variable6);
```

Chapter 4: Arrays, Pointers, and Strings

```
    MyFunction (&variable1,'s');     // s for short
    MyFunction (&variable2, 'i');    // i for integer
    MyFunction (&variable3, 'l');    // l for long
    MyFunction (&variable4, 'f');    // f for float
    MyFunction (&variable5,'d');     // d for double
    MyFunction (&variable6, 'e');    // e for decimal

    Console.WriteLine ("{0}\n {1}\n {2}\n {3}\n {4}\n {5}\n",
        variable1, variable2, variable3, variable4, variable5,
          variable6);
}

static unsafe void MyFunction (void *values, char data_type) {
    switch (data_type) {
        case 's': {
            *((short *)values) += 1;
            break;
        }

        case 'i': {
            *((int *)values) -= 1;
            break;
        }

        case 'l': {
            *((long *)values) *= 2;
            break;
        }

        case 'f': {
            *((float *)values) /= 2;
            break;
        }

        case 'd': {
            *((double *)values) = *((double *)values) + 2;
            break;
        }

        case 'e': {
            *((double *)values) = *((double *)values) - 2;
            break;
        }
```

```
                default: {
                    Console.WriteLine ("ERROR");
                    break;
                }
            }
        }
    }
}
```

Finding the Mean, Median, Mode, and Range

Another important exercise that we can illustrate with pointers and/or arrays is to use them to find the mean, median, mode, and range of data. These can be very important tasks when the need arises, but for now let's just look at them as exercises we can do to improve our skills. All four tasks will be wrapped into one large program, and the coding will be left for you to go through as needed (see Example 4.33). Note: multiple modes mean that there was a tie when calculating the most frequently referenced variable.

Example 4.33. Mean, median, mode, and range with pointers and arrays.

```
using System;

namespace Chapter4 {
    class Class1 {
        static void Main() {
            Random rnd = new Random();
            const short aSize = 25;
            short[] random_array = new short[aSize];

            for (int i = 0; i < aSize; i++)
                random_array[i] = (short)(rnd.NextDouble() * 100);

            Display(random_array);
            Mean(random_array);
            Median(random_array);
            Mode(random_array);
            Range(random_array);
        }

        // The mean is the average of the sum of the
        // values placed inside the array.
        static void Mean(short[] array) {
```

Chapter 4: Arrays, Pointers, and Strings

```csharp
    short average = 0, array_sum = 0;
    for (int index = 0; index < array.Length; index++)
        array_sum += array[index];

    average = (short)(array_sum/array.Length);
    Console.WriteLine("\nThe mean is " + average);
}

// The median is the number that sits in the middle of the list
// take the middle two numbers, add them and divide by two.
static void Median(short[] array) {
    if (array.Length%2 > 0)
        Console.WriteLine("The median is "
            + array[(array.Length/2)]);
    else
        Console.WriteLine("The median value is "
            + (array[array.Length/2 - 1]
            + array[array.Length/2])/2) ;
}

// The mode is the most frequent number in the list.
// Note: If there's a tie multiple modes will appear
static void Mode(short[] array) {
    short[] counter = new short[25], temp = new short[25];

    for (int index = 0; index < array.Length; index++) {
        for (int index2 = 0; index2 < array.Length; index2++) {
            if (array[index] == array[index2])
                counter[index] += 1;
        }
    }

    for (int index = 0; index < array.Length; index++)
        temp[index] = counter[index];

    Array.Sort(array);

    for (int index = 0; index < array.Length; index++) {
        if (counter[index] == temp[array.Length-1]) {
            if (index != 0 && array[index] != array[index-1])
                Console.WriteLine("The mode is {0}",
                    array[index]);
        }
    }
}
```

```
        // Range- the difference between the
        // highest number and the lowest number.
        static void Range (short[] array) {
            Console.WriteLine("The range spans from {0} to {1}",
                array[0], array[array.Length-1]);
        }

        static void Display (short[] my_array) {
            Console.WriteLine("\nRandom numbers inputted in this "
                + "order\n");
            for (int i = 0; i < my_array.Length; i++)
                Console.WriteLine(my_array[i]);

            Array.Sort(my_array);

            Console.WriteLine("\nsorting...\n"
                + "\nIn ascending order\n");

            for (int i = 0; i < my_array.Length; i++)
                Console.WriteLine("   {0}", my_array[i]);

            Console.WriteLine("\nand in descending order\n");

            Array.Reverse(my_array);

            for (int i = 0; i < my_array.Length; i++)
                Console.WriteLine("   {0}", my_array[i]) ;
        }
    }
}
```

Pointers as Arrays: The Keyword `stackalloc`

We can manipulate pointers to include a basic value type array (this is equivalent to the standard C++ stackable array). To do so, we'll also have to call on the stack allocating command, `stackalloc`. Stack allocated arrays are limited to only one dimension and are generally written with the pointer reference replacing reference of the array's square brackets: for example, `int* our_pointer = stackalloc int [array_size];` (see Example 4.34).

Example 4.34. Pointers as arrays.

```
using System;

namespace Chapter4 {
    class Class1 {
        static unsafe void Main() {
            const int array_size = 5;
            int[] kids = new int[array_size];
            int* our_pointer = stackalloc int[array_size];

            for (int counter = 0; counter < array_size; counter++) {
                Console.WriteLine ("Enter student {0}'s age",
                    (counter+1));
                kids[counter] = int.Parse(Console.ReadLine());
                our_pointer[counter] = kids[counter];
            }

            Ageism (our_pointer, array_size);
        }

        static unsafe void Ageism (int* tester, int size) {
            for (int counter = 0; counter < size; counter++) {
                if ((int)*(tester + counter) > 6)
                    Console.WriteLine("Your child is to old.");
                else
                    Console.WriteLine("{0}'s age is Okay", (counter+1));
            }
        }
    }
}
```

> Pointer Subscript Notation:
> $*(array + n_0) == array[n_0]$ // $*(array + 0) == array[0]$;
> $*(array + n_1) == array[n_1]$ // $*(array + 1) == array[1]$;
> ...   // ...
> $*(array + n_¥) == array[n_¥]$ // $*(array + n) == array[n]$;

Double Asterisk Pointers

In addition to being able to pass pointer values to other pointers, you can also set up special *double asterisk* pointers (pointers to pointers). These secondary pointers are as versatile as regular pointers, except that they require some additional notation (see Examples 4.35 and 4.36).

Example 4.35. Pointers to pointers.

```
using System;

namespace Chapter4 {
    class Class1 {
        static unsafe void Main() {
            int* pointer1, pointer2;
            int** pointer3;
            int variable1 = 1;

            pointer1 = &variable1;   // variable to pointer
            pointer2 = pointer1;     // pointer to pointer
            pointer3 = &pointer1;    // pointer to double-pointer.

            Console.WriteLine ("{0}\n {1}\n {2}\n {3}\n",
                variable1, *pointer1, *pointer2, **pointer3);

            **pointer3 = 20; // the value inside that variable1 is now 20.

            Console.WriteLine ("{0}\n {1}\n {2}\n {3}\n",
                variable1, *pointer1, *pointer2, **pointer3);
        }
    }
}
```

Pointers can normally be assigned to other pointers without this special notation (as in pointer1 = pointer2 ;).

Example 4.36. Passing double asterisk pointers.

```
using System;

namespace Chapter4 {
    class Class1 {
        static unsafe void Main() {
            int variable1 = 1;
            int* pointer1 = &variable1, pointer2 = pointer1;
            int** pointer3 = &pointer1;

            Console.WriteLine ("{0}\n {1}\n {2}\n {3}\n",
                variable1, *pointer1, *pointer2, **pointer3);

            **pointer3 = pointers (**pointer3);

            Console.WriteLine ("{0}\n {1}\n {2}\n {3}\n",
                variable1, *pointer1, *pointer2, **pointer3) ;
        }

        static int pointers (int local_number) {
            return (local_number = local_number + 20);
        }
    }
}
```

Functions Returning Pointers

The standard nonvoid, user-defined function typically returns a value that is a variable of one of the four basic data types. This value is then reassigned to a matching/receiving variable and the program continues. This procedure is only slightly altered when dealing with functions that return pointers. The key changes are based on the returning and receiving values, which are both converted into pointers. We'll also need to alter the notation when declaring those functions, but this is done by simply attaching an asterisk to the function's name. Be careful not to confuse this notation with the one used to declare a pointer function (see Example 4.37).

Example 4.37. Returning functions as pointers.

```
using System;

namespace Chapter4 {
    class Class1 {
        static unsafe void Main() {
            int variable;
            int* pointer = &variable;

            Console.WriteLine("Enter a number: ");
            variable = int.Parse(Console.ReadLine());
            pointer = function1(variable, pointer);

            Console.WriteLine("\n{0}", variable);
            pointer = function2(&variable, *pointer);

            Console.WriteLine("\n {0}", variable);
            Console.WriteLine("\n {0}", function3 (pointer));
        }

        // These first two functions return pointers.
        static unsafe int *function1(int variable, int *pointer) {
            *pointer = variable*(*pointer);
            return (pointer);
        }

        // This function returns a variable.
        static unsafe int *function2(int *pointer, int variable) {
            *pointer = variable/ (*pointer);
            return (pointer);
        }

        static unsafe int function3(int *point) {
            return (*point = 20);
        }
    }
}
```

Storage Class Specifiers: `extern` and `static`

C# offers two storage class specifiers—extern and static. The first storage class specifier, extern, which is short for the word external, is primarily used to transcend the limitations caused by moving between files. This keyword is primarily used to convey global references, and are usually of the object data types (as are structures and classes).

Static variables are specialized local variables that are not physically discarded with their function's termination, but instead are stored and reapplied to those functions if and when they are recalled. There are many practical instances when this added flexibility becomes important, and it helps us to remove any further need for global variables.

String Basics

The principles behind arrays and pointers should reveal that characters can be combined to total much more than the sum of their parts. One simple use of this collection is simply to make a sentence such as:

```
char array[] = {'T', 'h', 'i', 's', ' ', 'i', 's', ' ', 'a', ' ', 's',
                't', 'r', 'i', 'n', 'g', ' ', 'o', 'f', ' ', 'd', 'a',
                't', 'a', ' ', 's', 't', 'o', 'r', 'e', 'd', ' ', 'a',
                's', ' ', 'a', 'n', ' ', 'a', 'r', 'r', 'a', 'y'}
```

Note

A slightly less obvious choice would be to include that string as an array of characters, i.e., "This is a string of data." Of course, we've already seen that either of these cases can be used as output (Console.Write (String1); and Console.Write (Array1 [index]);). However, it might not be as obvious to think of modifying these processes to include the passing of arguments and/or the ability to store data.

A literal collection of characters, or a string, can be passed to a function using the same process as a standard array. This string argument requires a defined parameter (formally referred to as a *string parameter*), which is equivalent to an array's parameter. The string will be listed in quotations, e.g., MyString ("This is a string of data"). The literal string will be stored as a string value: static void MyString (string String1) {/* our string function */}. In addition, since strings handle literal constants differently than arrays, we will not suffer the effects of automatic truncation when attempting to add characters that include whitespaces. This should also remind us of the getline function used in C++, as in cin.getline (array, array_size), wherein we were able to avoid such truncations.

Manipulating String Data

Another significant aspect of manipulating string data comes from the use of the *string extensions*. These are methods included in the Base Class Library that make many of the older string manipulations obsolete. A few of the basic references include commands that test, alter, and apply to both strings and their literal counterparts. The use of these string manipulators has found its way through both C ("string.h") and C++ ("cstring"), with these newly defined methods giving the clearest representation yet (see Table 4.1).

Table 4.1. Manipulating string data in C#, C++, and C.

C#	C++	C/C++
Copies the value of our original string to a new string		
using System; namespace Chapter4 {class Class1 {static void Main() {string S = "This is a string\n", S1, S2; S1 = S; S2 = string.Copy(S); Console.WriteLine("{0}\n{1}", S1, S2); } } }	#include <iostream> #include <string> using namespace std; void main(void) {string S("This is a string\n"), S1, S2; S1 = S; S2.assign(S); std::cout << S1 << std::endl << S2 << std::endl; }	#include <iostream> #include <cstring> using namespace std; void main(void) {char S[ ] = "This is a string\n", *S1; S1 = (char*)malloc(strlen(S)+1); strcpy(S1, S); std::cout << S1; }
Copies a limited portion of a longer string to a shorter string		
using System; namespace Chapter4 {class Class1 {static void Main() {string S = "This is a string\n", S1; S1 = S.Substring(0, 4); Console.WriteLine("{0}", S1); } } }	#include <iostream> #include <string> using namespace std; void main(void) {string S("This is a string\n"), S1; S1.assign(S, 0, 4); std::cout << S1 << std::endl;}	#include <iostream> #include <cstring> using namespace std; void main(void) {char S[ ] = "This is a string of data\n", S1[ ] = " "; strncpy(S1, S, 3); std::cout << S1 << std::endl;}
Appends the original string with the additional string		
using System; namespace Chapter4 {class Class1 {static void Main() {string S = "This is a string\n", Extra = "Good bye"; S = S.Insert(17, Extra); Console.WriteLine("{0}", S); } } }	#include <iostream> #include <string> using namespace std; void main(void) {string S("This is a string\n"), Extra("Good Bye\n"); S.append(Extra);	#include <iostream> #include <cstring> using namespace std; void main(void) {char S[50] = "This is a string of data\n", Extra[] = "Good Bye\n"; strcat(S, Extra);

	std::cout << S << std::endl;}	std::cout <<S; }
Appends the original string with a limited portion of the additional string		
using System; namespace Chapter4 {class Class1 {static void Main() {string S = "This is a string\n", Extra = "Good bye"; S = S.Insert(17, Extra.Substring(0, 4)); Console.WriteLine("{0}", S); } } }	#include <iostream> #include <string> using namespace std; void main(void) {string S("This is a string\n"), Extra("Good Bye\n"); S.append(Extra, 0, 4); std::cout << S << std::endl;} Where 0 is the starting point and 4 is the length of the attachment.	#include <iostream> #include <cstring> using namespace std; void main(void) {char OurArray[50] = "This is a string of data\n", Extra[] = "Good Bye\n This string is too long and would cause an error."; strncat(OurArray, Extra, 10); std::cout << OurArray << std::endl; }
Compares two strings		

using System;
namespace Chapter4
{class Class1
{static void Main()
{string S = "This is a string\n",
Extra = "Good bye";
if(Extra.CompareTo(S) == 0)
Console.WriteLine(
"They match!");
else
Console.WriteLine(
"They don't match!");
if(string.Equals(S, S))
Console.WriteLine("Found!");
if(string.ReferenceEquals(S, S
Console.WriteLine("Found!");
} } }
	#include <iostream>
	#include <string>
	using namespace std;
	void main(void)
	{string S("This is a string\n"),
	S1("This is a string\n"),
	S2("Is this string larger?\n");
	if(S == S1)
	std::cout <<
	"I can't tell them a part \n";
	int test =
	S1.compare(S2);
	if(test == 0) std::cout <<
	"There equal";
	else if(test > 0) std::cout << "S2 is greater";
	else if(test < 0) std::cout << "S1 is greater";
	std::cout << std::endl; }
		#include <iostream>
		#include <cstring>
		using namespace std;
		void main(void)
		{char S[ ] = "This is a string\n",
		S1[ ] = "This is a string\n",
		S2[ ] = "Is this string larger?\n";
		if(!strcmp(S, S1))
		std::cout <<
		"I can't tell them a part \n";
		if(strcmp(S, S2) > 0) // T > S
		std::cout <<
		"I think I was cheated \n"; }

Compares a limited portion of string1 to string2		
using System; namespace Chapter4 {class Class1 {static void Main() {string S = "This is a string\n",	#include <iostream> #include <string> using namespace std; void main(void) {int T;	#include <iostream> #include <cstring> using namespace std; void main(void) {char S[ ] = "This is a string\n",

Extra = "This is good bye";
if(Extra.Substring(0, 4).CompareTo(S.Substring(0, 4)) == 0)
Console.WriteLine("They match!");
else
Console.WriteLine(
"They don't match!"); } } }
	string S("This is a string\n"),
	S1("This is a string\n"),
	S2("Is this string larger?\n");
	T = S1.compare(0, S1.size(), S2, 0, S2.size());
	if(T > 0)
	cout << "S2 is greater" << endl; }
	Where 0 to S1.size() equals the length of S1, and 0 to S2 equals the length of the comparison.
		S1[ ] = "This is a string\n",
		S2[ ] = "This is a string of data\n";
		if(strcmp(S1, S2) < 0)
		std::cout << "Super array is better \n";
		if(strncmp(S1, SuperArray, 4) == 0)
		std::cout << "Are first 4 letter are equal \n"; }

Determines the length of a string		
using System; namespace Chapter4 {class Class1 {static void Main() {string S = "This is a string\n"; int ArrayLength = S.Length; Console.WriteLine(S.Length); } } }	#include \<iostream\> #include \<string\> using namespace std; void main(void) {string String1; std::cout << "Enter a test sentence. \n"; std::getline(cin, String1); int Length =	#include \<iostream\> #include \<cstring\> using namespace std; void main(void) {const int array_size = 100; int length; char Array[array_size]; std::cout << "Enter a test sentence. \n"; std::cin.getline(Array,

> **Note:** There are dozens more, all quickly accessible from the visual compiler's pop-up menu.

Converting and Safeguarding Data

In addition to inputting and manipulating data, we can also convert and safeguard against data input errors. For example, when our users need to input numeric data, we can use the broader string data type and then test and convert that data as necessary. The data comparison functions are quite numerous, as shown in Table 4.2.

Chapter 4: Arrays, Pointers, and Strings

Commands/ Examples:	Description:
char.IsLetterOrDigit	Returns true when an alphanumeric character (A-Z, a-z, or 0-9) is found.
char.IsLetter	Returns true when an alphabetic character (A-Z or a-z) is found.
char.IsSymbol	Returns true when a character is found to be a symbol.
char.IsControl	Returns true when a control character (0x00-0x1F or 0x7F) is found
char.IsSeparator	Returns true when a separator character is found
char.IsSurrogate	Returns true when a surrogate character is found
char.IsDigit, char.IsNumber	Returns a nonzero value when a decimal value (0-9) is found
char.IsLower:	Returns true when a lowercase alphabetical character is found
char.IsPunctuation	Returns true when a punctuation mark is found
char.WhiteSpace	Returns true when a whitespace character is found
char.IsUpper	Returns true when an uppercase alphabetical character is found

Table 4.2. Data comparison functions.

In the ancient times, many of the primitive C programmers fell victim to an unspeakable evil known as the Malloc.

From Strings to Streams: System.IO

In addition to storing and retrieving simple character strings, we can also widen our perspective by beginning to access and write to files via our floppy and hard drives. The use of file manipulations also includes the addition of a second reference, `System.IO`, which enables the use of two key file related methods: `StreamReader` and `StreamWriter`. These methods, as their names imply, allow us to read and write to those files. The files in question need to be opened and closed separately, that is, one reference is used to identify the file as a storage device and one to retrieve that data. As with many of the object-based functions, our data streams also offer a host of member accessible functions that will be explored as we uncover the Base Class Library. The correct procedure for accessing these methods always includes an opening statement, a reading or writing to statement, and the closing method (see Table 4.5). Note that forgetting to close these files will produce a runtime error.

265

C#	C++

using System;
using System.IO;
 	
namespace Chapter4
{class Class1
{static void Main ()
{StreamWriter SaveFile = new StreamWriter(@"C:\MyFile.txt");
SaveFile.WriteLine ("This is a test!");
SaveFile.Close();
 	
StreamReader ReadFile = new StreamReader(@"C:\MyFile.txt");
string MyFile = ReadFile.ReadLine();
Console.WriteLine(MyFile);
ReadFile.Close(); }}}
	#include <fstream.h>
	void main(void)
	{char output[80];
	ofstream save;
	save.open("File.dat");
	save << "This is a test!";
	save.close();
	ifstream read;
	read.open("File.dat");
	if(read.fail( ))
	{cout << "File not found!"
	    << endl;
	return; }
	while(!read.eof())
	{read >> output;
	cout << output << " "; }
	cout << endl;
	read.close(); }

Table 4.3. StreamReader and StreamWriter.

Exampling Object Types

Another important point when working with object types involves the use of extensions, which are methods that allow us to manipulate objects, including `Equals ( )`, `GetHashCode(), GetType()`, and `ToString()`. The use of extensions can determine a host of information and thus simplify our tasks (see Table 4.4).

CTS Type	Description
Boolean bool Object.Equals(object obj)	Determines whether the specified Object is equal to the current Object
Boolean bool Object.GetHashCode (object obj)	Serves as a hash function for a particular type, suitable for use in hashing algorithms and data structures like a hash table
Boolean bool Object.GetType(object obj)	Gets the type of the current instance
Boolean bool Object.ToString(object obj)	Returns a string that represents the current object

Table 4.4. Extensions.

The Keywords checked and unchecked

Another weakness when programming in other computer languages is their inability to protect against *arithmetic overflows*. An arithmetic overflow occurs when a variable of a numeric

Chapter 4: Arrays, Pointers, and Strings

data type exceeds its preset range. Once a value exceeds that range, its variable reference no longer produces the implied response, thus that program is considered corrupt and all its data considered invalid. To protect against such errors, the designers of C# implemented two options: first, we can include coding references such as the keywords checked and unchecked; second, we can include a generalized compiler reference that tests our code for us. To implement these references see Examples 4.38–4.30 and Screen Shot 4.5.

Example 4.38. The keyword `checked`.

```
using System;

namespace Chapter4 {
    class Class1 {
        static void Main() {
            byte Max255 = 255;

            Max255++; // this error will go undetected

            checked { // This error will call an exception at run-time
                Max255++;
            }
        }
    }
}
```

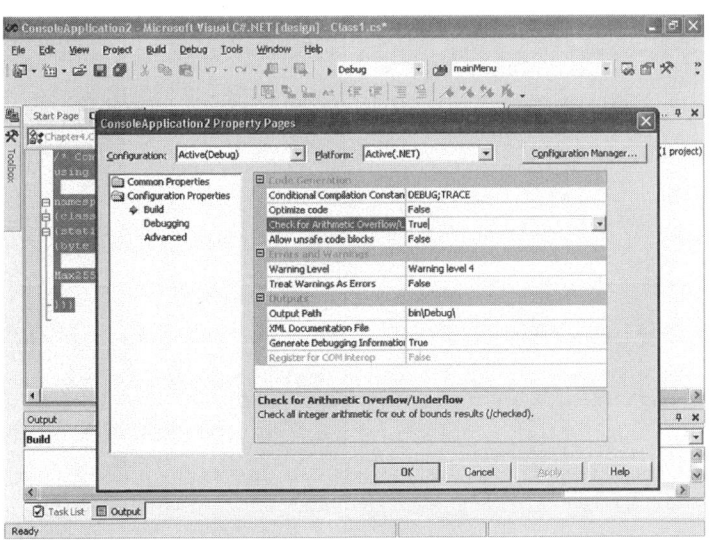

Screen Shot 4.5.

C# and Game Programming

From the "Solution Explorer," modify the program's "Build" properties to include automatic checking and then execute this coding.

Example 4.39. A checked compiler.

```
using System;

namespace Chapter4 {
    class Class1 {
        static void Main() {
            byte Max255 = 255;
            Max255 += 1; // this error will call an exception at run time
        }
    }
}
```

Continuing from the last program, override the system's automatic checking with the keyword *unchecked* encasing the last block (see Example 3.40).

Example 4.40. An unchecked compiler.

```
using System;

namespace Chapter4 {
    class Class1 {
        static void Main() {
            byte Max255 = 255;
            unchecked {
                Max255 += 1; // this error will go undetected
            }
        }
    }
}
```

The goto Statement

The goto statement is probably the most picked-on of all the keywords. Its use is considered a poor programming habit, yet somehow it manages to endure. Its fault lies in its ability to transgress order—the C# help files even mark it as a useful way of getting out of nested statements, but, of course, that would be breaking the rules. Still, there is at least one practical reason for using the `goto` statement in C#, which is to allow for artificial drops when dealing with `switch` statements. Remember, C# no longer allows us to drop between `switch` statements that contain executable statements, so `goto` makes a good fix. C#'s `goto` also has some limitations, including not being able to jump into localized blocks, between classes, and it can't (and shouldn't) be used to alter `try-catch` blocks, as explained in Chapter 5 (see Example 4.41).

Example 4.41. The `goto` statement.

```
using System;

namespace Chapter4 {
    class Class1 {
        static void Main() {
            char Character = '1';

            switch (Character) {
                case '1':
                    Console.WriteLine ("1 and a");
                    goto case2;

                case '2':
                    case2:
                        Console.WriteLine ("2");
                    goto case3;

                case '3':
                    case3:
                        Console.WriteLine ("and a 3");
                    break;
            }

            Console.WriteLine ("Program Terminated") ;
        }
    }
}
```

Game 4—Battle Wave

We will now proceed a bit further into the evolution of a game. Using combined knowledge of arrays and pointers, we are finally free to use both multiples of objects and arrays of information determining those multiples. We are also able to shortcut these procedures simply by using pointer notations for both singular and multidimensional arrays. As always, the steps to create a game remain the same, only this time I'll detail certain areas that were cut short in the previous chapter and shortcut some others that were already discussed in detail.

Brainstorming

In our fourth game, I see a wave of aliens starting at the top of the screen and slowly marching downward. They'll step from side to side, walking from one end of the screen to the next, each time moving one step lower. They'll have the power to destroy our ship with energy blasts just as we'll be able to destroy theirs. Finally, they'll either crush us as their lines reach our ship or we'll destroy them all.

Brainstorming

Example 4.42a. Brainstorming Battle Wave.

1. We'll draw out four distinct aliens in four distinct lines (each alien will have four copies of itself on that same line). And each alien in that line will be a different color.
2. The aliens will walk toward the right of the screen and then when at the end, they'll move down one step and proceed to walk to the left of the screen. Again, once there, they'll move down and proceed to the right...
3. Our player's character will be able to move both left and right, but not up or down.
4. Our character will be able to fire a weapon that will move straight up—this beam will destroy any alien it strikes.
5. The aliens will also fire beams at the character, and if they strike it, the character will be destroyed.
6. The character will be given three chances (lives) before the game ends.
7. Also, the aliens will be attempting to reach the bottom of the screen—if that happens, the game ends no matter how many lives are left.

Chapter 4: Arrays, Pointers, and Strings

> 8. If all aliens are destroyed, a new set of ships will appear at the top.
> 9. The destruction of the aliens' ships will be scored and the scores will be saved to a file that keeps high scores.
> 10. The aliens' point values will be from lower (forward ships) to higher (rear ships).
> 11. The aliens will move faster as their numbers dwindle.
> 12. The aliens will also occasionally fire at random.

Drawing Characters and Defining Motions

Once again, we will create our characters using the graphics portion of the compiler. The alien ships will move in unison, trotting along the x-axis with additional movements along the y-axis when the furthest aliens reach either side. Our player's character, by contrast, will only be able to move along the x-axis using the left and right arrows on the numeric keypad with the spacebar used to enable its weapons (see Example 4.42b).

Example 4.42b. Designing Characters.

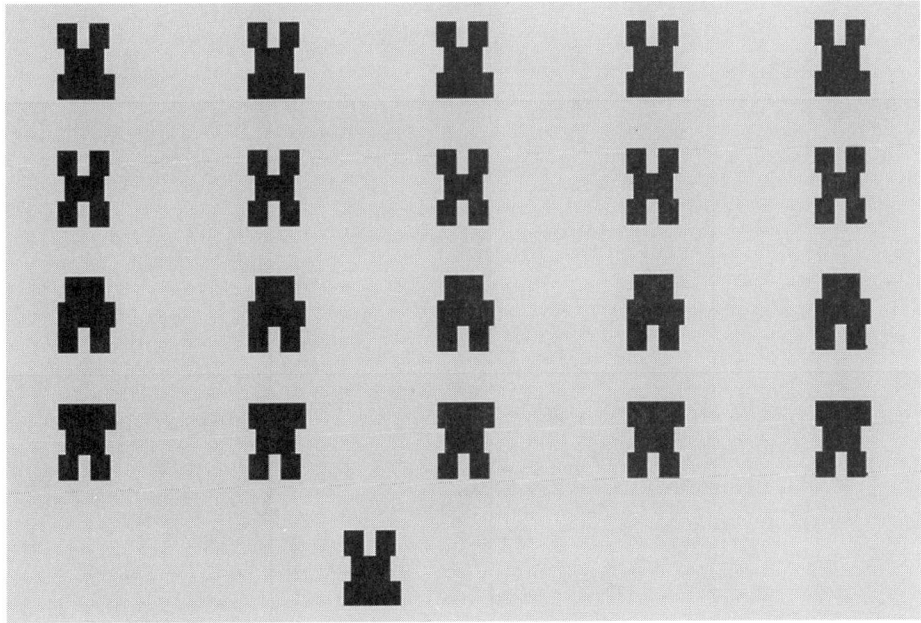

Note: The aliens follow a simple preset pattern of movement, while the player is given use of the keyboard. The controls will be set to values 4 (ß) and 6 (α) with the spacebar set up to release the character's weapons.

Example 4.43. Algorithm for Battle Wave.

BattleWave.cpp:
1. Setup Windows. This includes everything required by our operating system and compiler.
2. Write a set of functions that will animate our characters (including alien/ human ships and weapons fire).
3. Write a function to define screen limitations.
4. Set up a keyboard function to include left and right movements as well as a weapons key.
5. Write a set of functions to control both the players' weapons and an artificially intelligent alien weapons control.
6. Write a function to reset the aliens once the level is complete.
7. Access the two functions used to save and retrieve the players' high scores.

Inside the Gaming Loop:
8. Reset aliens to begin new level(s).
9. Restore/test and display high scores.
10. Display characters.
11. Read keyboard inputs.
12. Track weapons.
13. Test for collisions.
14. Play three sounds while the game is running: Weapon's fire, ship movement, and explosion...
15. Test of limitations (walls).
16. Move characters.
17. Clear screen.

Outer Loop:
18. Repeat the loop until aliens reach our players' y-axis values.
19. Ask player(s) if they want to play again. End or repeat game.

Before going further, make sure everything is set up correctly (creating a new project, a new source file, adding sound files, test compiling, and linking using all of the previous game files—all of which is done as project4).

Drawing Characters

It is important to remember that DirectX requires our graphic files to be stored as bitmaps, and that, while Forms can also use bitmaps, most Windows' Forms programmers prefer to use the lower-resolution graphic file formats such as JPEGs to save resources. It is also important to remember that these distinctions are merely a matter of storage type and that they do not affect the steps used to draw our images. This text's CD-ROM, for example, includes both .JPG and .BMP images, which were created as bitmaps and then resaved under the JPEG format.

Our initial designs included only seven unique drawings, the four target images (each reproduced five times using multiple colors), the target weapons/bombs (also reproduced using multiple colors), and the single human image, as well as his two rockets/missiles. The four alien images include Bulb, Frog, Robot, and Eye, with the Human playfully being referred to as Gus (see Game 4 Designs).

C# and Game Programming

Game 4 Designs

Sketched Design 4.1 Bulb.

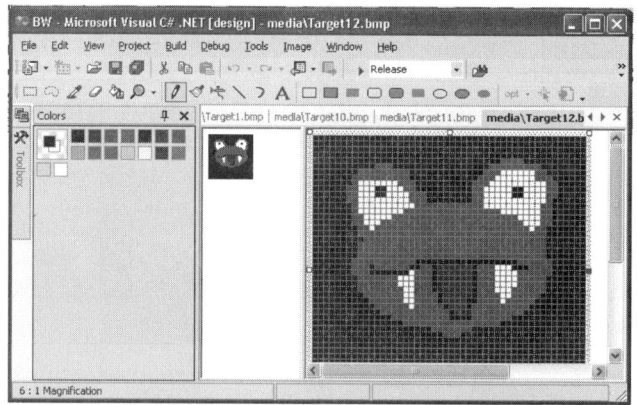

Sketched Design 4.2. Frog.

Chapter 4: Arrays, Pointers, and Strings

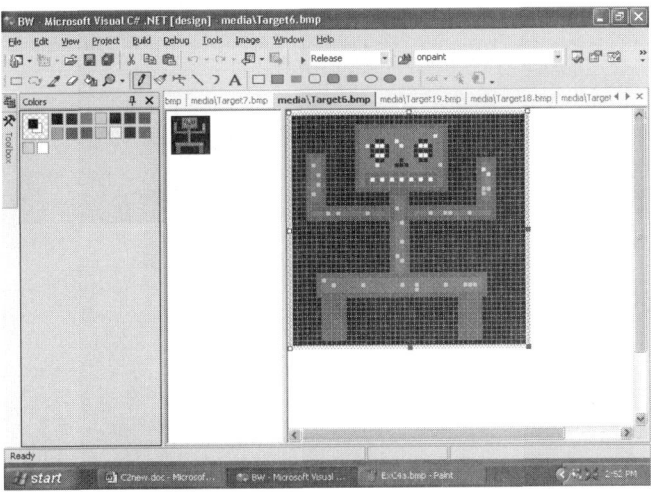

Sketched Design 4.3. Robot.

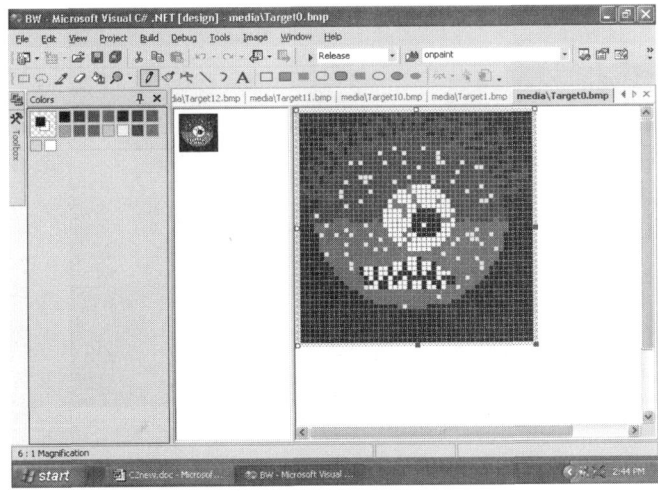

Sketched Design 4.4. Eye.

C# and Game Programming

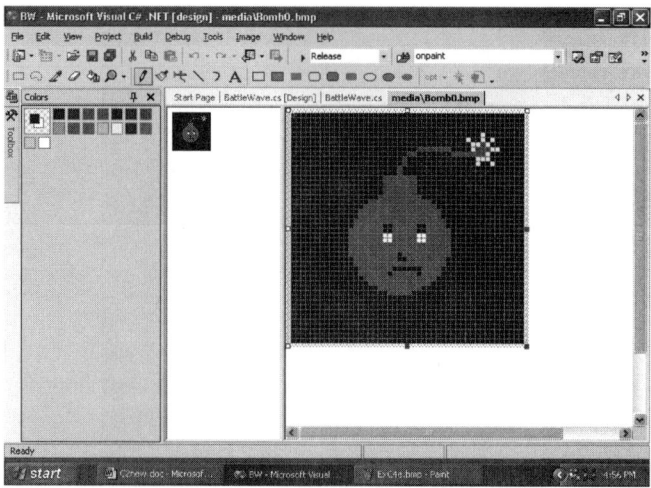

Sketched Design 4.5. Bomb.

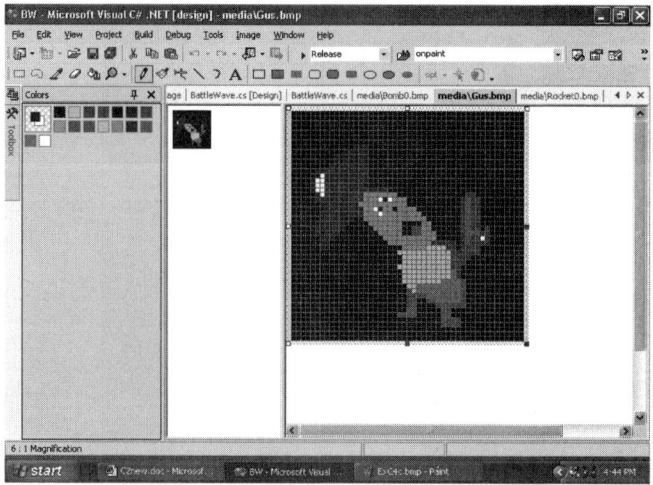

Sketched Design 4.6. Gus (the Hero).

Chapter 4: Arrays, Pointers, and Strings

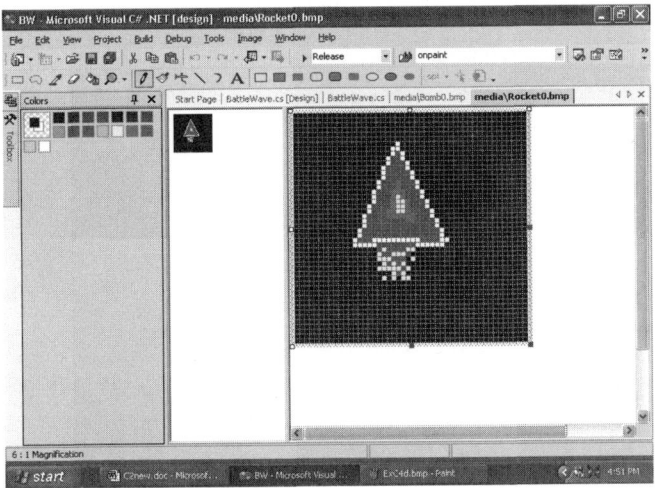

Sketched Design 4.7. Missile.

Alternative Rendered Designs

This set of polygons is used to represent Battle Wave's rendered images. As with the previous drawings, these will be set to a 20x20 Scale with the position ($x =$ imagePosX, $y =$ imagePosY) being the center of the model (see the figures listed below). Note that these polygons will also be incorporated into an inheriting class (see Chapter 5).

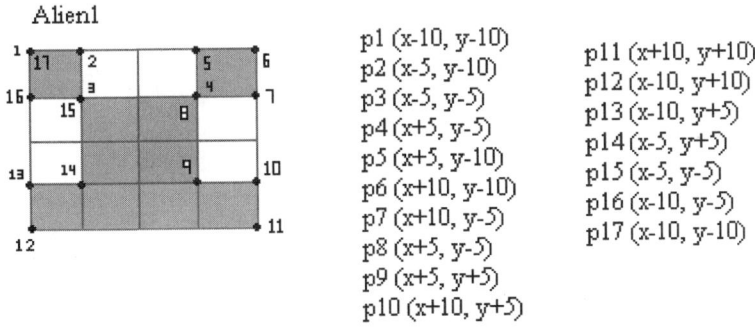

Rendered Design 4.1. Alien1.

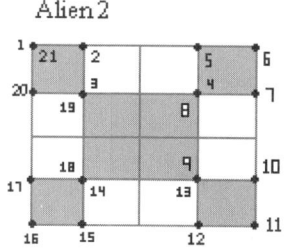

p1 (x-10, y-10)
p2 (x-5, y-10)
p3 (x-5, y-5)
p4 (x+5, y-5)
p5 (x+5, y-10)
p6 (x+10, y-10)
p7 (x+10, y-5)
p8 (x+5, y-5)
p9 (x+5, y+5)
p10 (x+10, y+5)
p11 (x+10, y+10)
p12 (x+5, y+10)
p13 (x+5, y+5)
p14 (x-5, y+5)
p15 (x-5, y+10)
p16 (x-10, y+10)
p17 (x-10, y+5)
p18 (x-5, y+5)
p19 (x-5, y-5)
p20 (x-10, y-5)
p21 (x-10, y-10)

Rendered Design 4.2. Alien2.

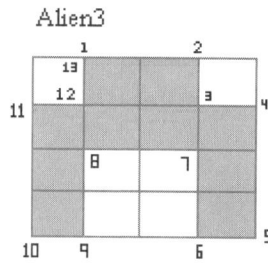

p1 (x-5, y-10)
p2 (x+5, y-10)
p3 (x+5, y-5);
p4 (x+10, y-5)
p5 (x+10, y+10)
p6 (x+5, y+10)
p7 (x+5, y)
p8 (x-5, y)
p9 (x-5, y+10)
p10 (x-10, y-5)
p11 (x-10, y-5)
p12 (x-5, y-5)
p13 (x-5, y-10)

Rendered Design 4.3. Alien3.

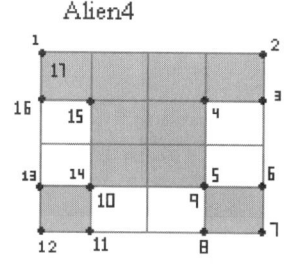

p1 (x-10, y-10)
p2 (x+10, y-10)
p3 (x+10, y-5)
p4 (x+5, y-5)
p5 (x+5, y+5)
p6 (x+10, y+5)
p7 (x+10, y+10)
p8 (x+5, y+10)
p9 (x+5, y+5)
p10 (x-5, y+5)
p11 (x-5, y+10)
p12 (x-10, y+10)
p13 (x-10, y+5)
P14 (x-5, y+5)
p15 (x-5, y-5)
p16 (x-10, y-5)
p17 (x-10, y-10)

Rendered Design 4.4. Alien4.

Chapter 4: Arrays, Pointers, and Strings

Our hero is represented as a simple pie shape, e.g., `g.FillPie (Brushes.Blue, player.imagePosX, player.imagePosY, player.imageWidth, player.imageHeight, 65, 50);`.

Rendered Design 4.5. The Hero.

Animating Characters: Displaying Characters

We'll use a simple `OnPaint` function to draw our characters, which will include the ship, the weapons, and all of the alien crafts. Notice how I've changed the colors on the drawings to give them a distinct look; you should also notice the colorful patterns (see Example 4.44).

Example 4.44. Drawing Battle Wave characters.

```
// Draw the scores
buffer.ColorFill(Color.Black);
buffer.ForeColor = Color.Blue;
if(player.score < HighScore) {
   buffer.DrawText(4 * SCALE, 2*SCALE, HighScore.ToString(), false);
} else {
   buffer.DrawText(4 * SCALE, 2*SCALE, player.score.ToString(), false);
}

buffer.DrawText(16 * SCALE, 2*SCALE, player.score.ToString(), false);


if (player.isActive) {
   try {
      destination = new Rectangle(player.imagePosX, player.imagePosY,
         player.imageWidth, player.imageHeight);
      buffer.Draw(destination, PlayerDraw, DrawFlags.Wait);
       . . .

for (int i = 0; i < NUM_MISSILES; i ++) {
```

```
        if (playerMissiles[i].isActive)
            try {
                destination = new Rectangle(playerMissiles[i].imagePosX,
                    playerMissiles[i].imagePosY, playerMissiles[i].imageWidth,
                    playerMissiles[i].imageHeight);
                buffer.Draw(destination, PlayerMissilesDraw[i],
                    DrawFlags.Wait);
                    . . .
for (int i = 0; i < NUM_TARGETS; i++) {
    if (targets[i].isActive){
        try {
            destination = new Rectangle(targets[i].imagePosX,
                targets[i].imagePosY, targets[i].imageWidth,
                targets[i].imageHeight);
            buffer.Draw(destination, TargetDraw[i], DrawFlags.Wait);
                . . .
    if (targetMissiles[i].isActive) {
        try {
            destination = new Rectangle(targetMissiles[i].imagePosX,
                targetMissiles[i].imagePosY, targetMissiles[i].imageWidth,
targetMissiles[i].imageHeight);
            buffer.Draw(destination, TargetMissilesDraw[i],
DrawFlags.Wait);
                . . .
primary.Flip(buffer, FlipFlags.DoNotWait);
buffer.Dispose();
```

Animating Our Characters: Patterns of Movement

The aliens' animation is based on a pattern of motion determined not by our actions, but by a predetermined set of numbers. This takes us out of the realm of artificial intelligence and redefines their movements as simple motion. For this, the function `Alien_Click` represents a list of simple controls (see Example 4.45).

The function `Alien_Click`, is required to test and compare the positions of the first and last characters of our lines. The `if` and `if-else` statements are used to test the cycles, while the `for` statements are used to facilitate the movements.

Chapter 4: Arrays, Pointers, and Strings

Example 4.45. Patterns of movement for Battle Wave.

```
public void MoveTargets(TimedEvent e, Object obj) {
   . . .
   int newDirection = 0;
   Random rnd = new Random();

   if (targets[0].direction == AnimatedImage.SOUTH) {
      newDirection =
         (targets[0].imagePosX < targets[0].constraintBox.Width / 2) ?
         AnimatedImage.EAST : AnimatedImage.WEST;
   } else {
      for (int i = 0; i < NUM_TARGETS; i++) {
         if (!targets[i].isActive)
            continue;
         if (targets[i].imagePosX <= targets[0].constraintBox.X ||
             targets[i].imagePosX + targets[i].imageWidth >=
             targets[0].constraintBox.X +
             targets[0].constraintBox.Width) {
            newDirection = AnimatedImage.SOUTH;
            break;
            . . .
   for (int i = 0; i < NUM_TARGETS; i++) {
      if (newDirection != 0)
         targets[i].direction = newDirection;

      if (newDirection == AnimatedImage.SOUTH) {
         for (int j = 0; j < 5; j++)
            targets[i].Animate();
         if (targets[i].isActive && targets[i].imagePosY +
             targets[i].imageHeight >= player.imagePosY) {
            EndGame();
         }

      } else {
         targets[i].Animate();
         if (rnd.Next(100) > 85)
            if ((targets[i].direction == AnimatedImage.EAST &&
                 targets[i].imagePosX < player.imagePosX + 50 &&
                 targets[i].imagePosX > player.imagePosX) ||
                (targets[i].direction == AnimatedImage.WEST &&
                 targets[i].imagePosX < player.imagePosX &&
```

```
            targets[i].imagePosX > player.imagePosX - 50)) {
        FireBomb(i);
    . . .
```

Defining Character Limitation

Preventing characters from moving off the screen is just a matter of practicality. Theoretically, the game could be played off the screen, but this would make little sense. Also, since there are limits to the range of our characters' values, it is foreseeable that if a character was left to run amuck, it could exceed those values and cause an error (see Examples 4.46 and 4.47).

Example 4.46. Character limits (from AnimatedImage.cs).

```
// Moves the image to be within the specified boundary.
// Returns whether any position changes were made.
virtual public bool ConstrainToBox() {
    bool retVal = false;

    if (!isActive)
        return false;

    if (imagePosX < constraintBox.X) {
        imagePosX = constraintBox.X;
        retVal = true;
    } else if ((imagePosX + imageWidth) >
            (constraintBox.X + constraintBox.Width)) {
        imagePosX = constraintBox.X +
            constraintBox.Width - imageWidth;
        retVal = true;
    }

    if (imagePosY < constraintBox.Y) {
        imagePosY = constraintBox.Y;
        retVal = true;
    } else if ((imagePosY + imageHeight) >
            (constraintBox.Y + constraintBox.Height)) {
        imagePosY = constraintBox.Y +
            constraintBox.Height - imageHeight;
        retVal = true;
    }
```

```
        return retVal;
}
```

Example 4.47. Character and projectile constraints.

```
// Initialize player's objects
player = new Player(0, 0);
player.constraintBox = new Rectangle(0, 15 * SCALE,
    ClientSize.Width, ClientSize.Height);
player.RescaleImage(SCALE, SCALE);
player.direction = AnimatedImage.EAST;

// Initialize player's missiles
playerMissiles = new AnimatedImage[NUM_MISSILES];
for (int i = 0; i < NUM_MISSILES; i++) {
    playerMissiles[i] = new AnimatedImage(0, 0);
    playerMissiles[i].owner = player;
    playerMissiles[i].constraintBox = ClientRectangle;
    playerMissiles[i].RescaleImage(SCALE / 2, SCALE / 2);
}
```

Keyboard Controls

We'll also want to give our player some simple keyboard controls; these controls should limit our player's movement to only one dimension (see Example 4.48a).

Example 4.48a. Keyboard controls for Battle Wave.

```
private void Keyboard_Tick(object sender, System.EventArgs e) {
   Microsoft.DirectX.DirectXException.IgnoreExceptions();
     . . .
    keyboard = new
       Microsoft.DirectX.DirectInput.Device(SystemGuid.Keyboard);
    keyboard.Properties.BufferSize = 8;
    keyboard.Acquire();

    KeyboardState state = keyboard.GetCurrentKeyboardState();
```

```
for (Key k = Key.Escape; k <= Key.MediaSelect; k++) {
   if (state[k])
      player.isActive = true; // revive player when any key pressed

   if (state[k] && (k == Key.Left || k == Key.LeftArrow)) {
      . . .
```

Force Feedback Controls

The basic joystick controls for Battle Wave are actually much simpler then the code used to control Space Fighter and Asteroid Miner. That's because Battle Wave only requires lateral movement. This, however, affords us the opportunity to test the more advanced features included with Force Feedback. Here we'll imagine that each explosion creates a ripple in space causing a quake-like effect that affects our characters' ability to move. The most important thing to remember about Force Feedback is that it requires exclusive device access (see Example 4.48b).

Example 4.48b. Force Feedback key components.

```
private void Joystick_Tick(object sender, System.EventArgs e) {
   Microsoft.DirectX.DirectXException.IgnoreExceptions();
   if (gameState.currentState == GameState.State.Stopped)
      return;

   foreach (DeviceInstance instance in
       Manager.GetDevices(DeviceClass.GameControl,
       EnumDevicesFlags.AttachedOnly)) {

      joystick = new
         Microsoft.DirectX.DirectInput.Device(instance.InstanceGuid);
      break;
   }

   if (joystick == null) {return;}

   joystick.SetDataFormat(DeviceDataFormat.Joystick);
```

Chapter 4: Arrays, Pointers, and Strings

```
    foreach (DeviceObjectInstance d in joystick.Objects) {
        if ((0 != (d.ObjectId & (int)DeviceObjectTypeFlags.Axis))) {
            joystick.Properties.SetRange(ParameterHow.ById,
                d.ObjectId, new InputRange(-1000, 1000));
        }
    }

    joystick.Acquire();
    joystick.Poll();
    JState = joystick.CurrentJoystickState;

    player.direction = 0;

    bool Joystick = false;

    if (-400 < JState.X) {
        player.direction = AnimatedImage.WEST;
        Joystick = true;
            } else if (-500 > JState.X) {
                player.direction = AnimatedImage.EAST;
                Joystick = true;
    }

    if (Joystick) {
        for(int i = 0; i < 3; i++) {
            player.Animate();
            player.ConstrainToBox();
        }
        Invalidate();
    }

    byte[] buttons = JState.GetButtons();
    foreach (byte b in buttons) {
        if (0 != (b & 0x80)) {
            for (int i = 0; i < NUM_MISSILES; i++) {
                if (playerMissiles[i].isActive == false &&
                    player.isActive) {
                    FireMissile();
                    break;
                } else if (!player.isActive)
                    player.isActive = true;
            }
        }
    }
}
```

Artificial Intelligence

Forced patterns of movement tend to conflict with applicability/necessity of an observant computer controlled-opponent, or what I've defined as artificial intelligence. Yet, because these limitations do not apply to the ability of the alien crafts to engage in weapons fire, we'll still need to program a strategy for our computer to rely upon in battle. It is best if we also tie our computer's weapons fire into a more general weapons control used by both our computer and our players. The three key functions include testing and locating the player's ship, activating our weapons (for both the player and the computer), and detecting any and all collisions from both sides (see Example 4.49).

Example 4.49. Alien weapons fire.

```
private void FireBomb(int index) {
         // don't shoot at a dead player
         if (!targets[index].isActive || !player.isActive)
            return; // Dead guys can't fire

         if (!targetMissiles[index].isActive) {
             targetMissiles[index].isActive = true;
             targetMissiles[index].direction = AnimatedImage.SOUTH;
             targetMissiles[index].imagePosX =
targets[index].imagePosX;
             targetMissiles[index].imagePosY =
targets[index].imagePosY;

             TimedEvent missileEvent =
                 timer.getEvent("targetMissile" + index);
             missileEvent.isActive = true;
              . . .
public void MoveBomb(TimedEvent e, Object obj) {
    if (gameState.currentState == GameState.State.Stopped) {
        e.isActive = false;
        return;
    }

    AnimatedImage bomb = (AnimatedImage) obj;
    if (!bomb.isActive) {
        e.isActive = false;
    }
     . . .
```

Resetting Levels

Once all the aliens are destroyed, rather than ending the game, we can just reset all the aliens and start again. This is essentially a matter of resetting all the variables back to their original positions, but you might also want to either speed up the game or have the aliens start a little lower with each turn. I've left those choices up to you (see Example 4.50).

Example 4.50. Resetting Battle Wave.

```
private void NextLevel() {
    if (gameState.currentState != GameState.State.Started)
        return;

    gameState.currentSpeed++;
    timer.ChangeStep("targets", gameState.currentSpeed < 10 ?
        10 - gameState.currentSpeed : 1);

    for (int i = 0; i < NUM_MISSILES; i++)
        playerMissiles[i].isActive = false;

    for (int i = 0; i < NUM_TARGETS; i++) {
        targets[i].isActive = true;
        targetMissiles[i].isActive = false;

        targets[i].imagePosX = ((i % 5) + 1) * 2 * SCALE;
        targets[i].imagePosY = ((int)(i/5) + 1) * 2 * SCALE + 10;
        . . .
```

Saving and Retrieving Data

As done previously, we're going to give players the challenge of trying to defeat a high score. Again, this can be done through the use of the load and save functions, which were not listed in the previous chapter. Here you'll notice that we used an array to store the name of the file, including its extension (see Examples 4.51 and 4.52). Note that this function requires the included file <fstream.h>; also if no file is available, the high score will read zero. These values are also displayed using a modified version of our basic display function. The key changes here include a string value and a decimal output (see Example 4.51).

Example 4.51. Displaying high scores.

```
public void SaveHighScore(int score) {
    StreamWriter file = null;

    try {
        file = new StreamWriter(@".\HighScore.txt");
        file.WriteLine("Battle Wave High Scores");
        file.WriteLine("----------------------");
        file.WriteLine();
        file.WriteLine(score + "\t" + DateTime.Now);
        file.Flush();
    } catch (Exception e) {Console.WriteLine(e);}
    finally {if (file != null) file.Close();}
}
```

Expanding Our Arsenal

It would also be useful if we included secondary weapons, multicolored of course. These missiles/rockets could be programmed to give off different sounds, run at different speeds, and could have varying striking ability, but those tasks are up to you. However, keep in mind your processor's limitations: Remember, the more objects on the screen, the choppier the game play (see Example 4.52).

Example 4.52. Options for weapons.

```
private void FireMissile() {
    if (!player.isActive)
        return;

    TimedEvent missileEvent;
    // shoot the first missile that's not already out there!
    for (int i = 0; i < NUM_MISSILES; i++) {
        if (!playerMissiles[i].isActive) {
            // set missiles properties so that it will get
            // properly animated
            playerMissiles[i].isActive = true;
            playerMissiles[i].direction = AnimatedImage.NORTH;
```

```
    playerMissiles[i].imagePosX = player.imagePosX;
    playerMissiles[i].imagePosY = player.imagePosY;

    missileEvent = timer.getEvent("playerMissile" + i);
    missileEvent.isActive = true;
    . . .
```

Battle Wave: The Heart of the Game

Once again, we'll need to weave together a managing subprogram that is both subject to our main menu and capable of controlling the plethora of functions listed in the last two chapters. Remember to include all the proper included and subprograms, and to link to the object-oriented model we began to develop in Chapter 3 (you may also use project4 to shortcut these steps—see Example 4.53/BattleWave on the CD-ROM).

Game 5—Battle Tennis

We can also modify the last game to reflect another arcade classic, what we'll call Battle Tennis. This time we'll skip most of the basic steps and include only the essentials. What we'll want is to do is change all of the characters into household breakables like a lamp, window, TV, and potted plant. We'll also want to remove their ability to move and attack, since household items don't really do that. Finally, we'll want to replace our missiles with the tennis ball developed in the first game.

 Brainstorming

> **Example 4.54. Brainstorming Battle Tennis.**
>
> 1. First, we'll want to choose a few household items, for this example I chose a TV set, window, plotted plant, and a lamp.
> 2. Now, we'll want to give them the same rainbow color pattern.
> 3. Next, we'll want to insert these characters into the last game's engine, remembering to delete the AI portion of that game.
> 4. Let's replace the basic missile designs with the motion of the tennis ball found in the first game. Remember, we'll have to

C# and Game Programming

> change the pattern of motion of the tennis ball to work from a vertical reference point.
> 5. Let's include a few sound changes...
> 6. Finally, we'll want to reverse the death cycle, making blocking the ball the right action and avoiding the ball the penalty.

Adding Graphics

By now you should be fairly comfortable using the graphics tools included in the .Net package. Here I might suggest saving and altering the Windows Forms images and coding to include the *.gif, *.jpg, and *.dib formats. The different formats will dictate the size and quality of the images.

Screen Shot 4.6. The window.

```
// from Shapes.cs
public void Window(Graphics g, Brush bWindowColor) {
    Brush GrayBrush = new SolidBrush(Color.Gray);
```

Chapter 4: Arrays, Pointers, and Strings

```
    g.FillRectangle(GrayBrush, this.imagePosX,
        this.imagePosY, 24, 24); // frame
    g.FillRectangle(bWindowColor, this.imagePosX+2,
        this.imagePosY+2, 20, 20); // glass
    g.FillRectangle(GrayBrush, this.imagePosX+11,
        this.imagePosY, 3, 24); // brace
    g.FillRectangle(GrayBrush, this.imagePosX+11,
        this.imagePosY+11, 5, 3); // lock
}
```

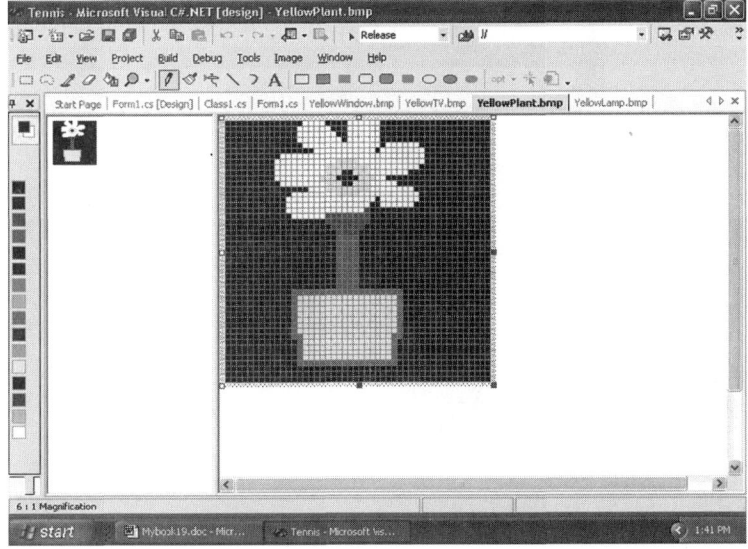

Screen Shot 4.7. The potted plant.

```
// from Shapes.cs
public void Flower(Graphics g, Brush bFlowerColor, Pen pFlowerColor) {
    // pedals
    g.DrawArc(pFlowerColor, this.imagePosX, // down
        this.imagePosY-8, 5, 15, 0, 180);
    g.DrawArc(pFlowerColor, this.imagePosX-10, // left
        this.imagePosY-8, 15, 5, 90, 180);
    g.DrawArc(pFlowerColor, this.imagePosX, // up
        this.imagePosY-17, 5, 15, 180, 180);
    g.DrawArc(pFlowerColor, this.imagePosX+1, // right
        this.imagePosY-8, 15, 5, 270, 180);
    // center
    g.FillEllipse(bFlowerColor, this.imagePosX-2,
        this.imagePosY-10, 10, 10);
```

C# and Game Programming

```
        // base
        Point[] Vase = this.sharpTriangle();
        g.FillPolygon(bFlowerColor, Vase);
    }
```

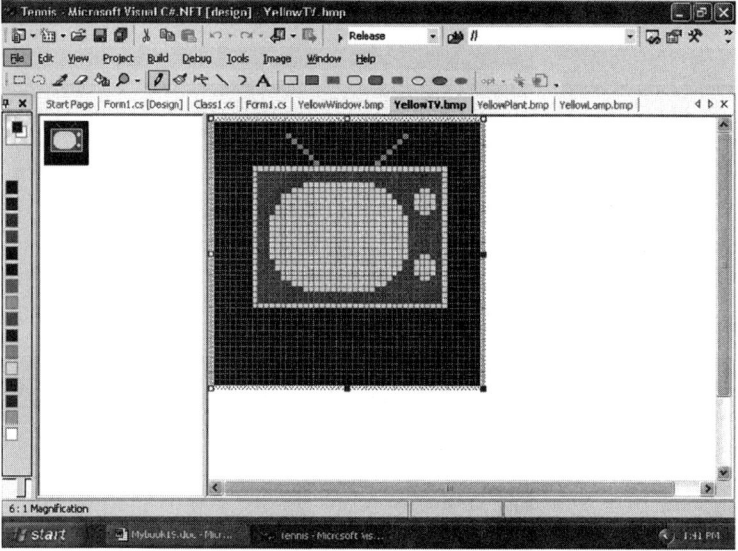

Screen Shot 4.8. The TV set.

```
    public void TV(Graphics g, Brush bTVColor, Pen pTVColor) {
        Brush GrayBrush = new SolidBrush(Color.Gray);

        g.FillRectangle(GrayBrush, this.imagePosX, // console
            this.imagePosY, 25, 15);
        g.FillEllipse(bTVColor, this.imagePosX+1, // tube
            this.imagePosY+1, 15, 13);
        g.FillEllipse(bTVColor, this.imagePosX+18, // 1st dial
            this.imagePosY+2, 5, 5);
        g.FillEllipse(bTVColor, this.imagePosX+18, // 2nd dial
            this.imagePosY+7, 5, 5);
        g.DrawLine(pTVColor, this.imagePosX+12, this.imagePosY, // ant. left
            this.imagePosX+5, this.imagePosY-5);
        g.DrawLine(pTVColor, this.imagePosX+14, this.imagePosY, // ant. right
            this.imagePosX+19, this.imagePosY-5);
    }
```

Chapter 4: Arrays, Pointers, and Strings

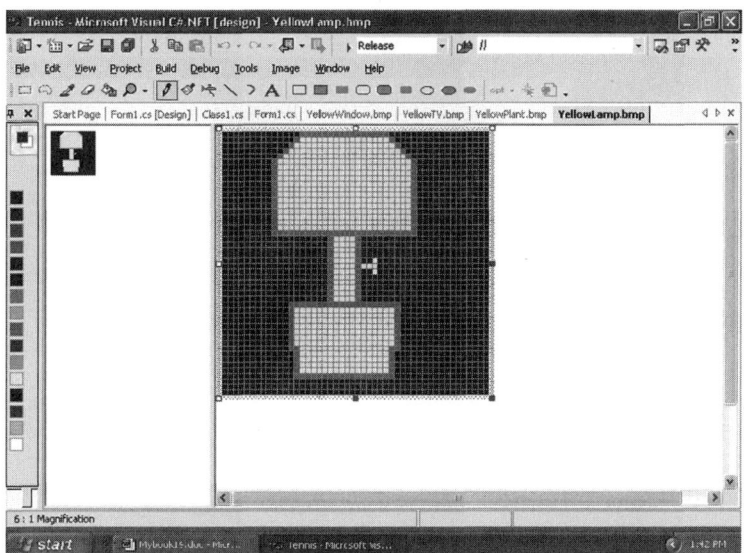

Screen Shot 4.9. The lamp.

```
public void Lamp(Graphics g, Brush LampColor, Brush LampshadeColor) {
    Point[] DrawLamp = this.sharpTriangle();
    Point[] DrawLampshade = this.Trapezoid();
    g.FillPolygon(LampColor, DrawLamp);
    g.FillPolygon(LampshadeColor, DrawLampshade);
}
```

We'll tie these images together in a simple OnPaint function (see Example 4.55).

Example 4.55. OnPaint function for objects of Battle Tennis.

```
protected override void OnPaint(PaintEventArgs e) {
    // Write start-up text if game is stopped
    if (gameState.currentState == GameState.State.Stopped) {
        . . .
        if (!MouseInquire) {
            DialogResult result = MessageBox.Show(this,
                "Do you want to enable the mouse?",
                "Mouse Detected", MessageBoxButtons.YesNo,
                MessageBoxIcon.Question, MessageBoxDefaultButton.Button1,
                MessageBoxOptions.RightAlign);
```

```csharp
                MouseInquire = true;
                if (result == DialogResult.Yes) {
                    MouseOverride = true;
                }
            }

        } else {
            // draw background color
            buffer.ColorFill(Color.Black);
            buffer.ForeColor = Color.Blue;
            // Draw the scores
            if (player.score < HighScore) {
                buffer.DrawText(4*SCALE, 2*SCALE, HighScore.ToString(),
                    false);
            } else {
                buffer.DrawText(4*SCALE, 2*SCALE, player.score.ToString(),
                    false);
            }

            buffer.DrawText(16 * SCALE, 2*SCALE, player.score.ToString(),
                    false);

            // Draw the player
            try {
                destination = new Rectangle(player.imagePosX,
                    player.imagePosY, player.imageWidth, player.imageHeight);
                buffer.Draw(destination, PlayerDraw, DrawFlags.Wait);
                . . .
            // Draw the ball
            if (theBall.isActive) {
                try {
                    destination = new Rectangle(theBall.imagePosX,
                        theBall.imagePosY,
                        theBall.imageWidth, theBall.imageHeight);
                    buffer.Draw(destination, TheBallDraw, DrawFlags.Wait);
                    . . .
            // Draw the targets
            for (int i = 0; i < NUM_TARGETS; i++) {
                if (targets[i].isActive) {
                    try {
                        destination = new Rectangle(targets[i].imagePosX,
                            targets[i].imagePosY, targets[i].imageWidth,
                            targets[i].imageHeight);
```

```
            buffer.Draw(destination, TargetDraw[i],
                DrawFlags.Wait);
            . . .
        primary.Flip(buffer, FlipFlags.DoNotWait);
        buffer.Dispose();
    }
}
```

Input Devices: Keyboard, Joystick, and Mouse

Once again, we'll want to give our players movement. The Keyboard will hold the standard direction, animation, and constraint methods, as will the Joystick. Here, the Mouse is used again as Battle Tennis offers similar tennis-like movement, the main different being the lateral calibrations.

Example 4.56. Keyboard controls for Battle Tennis.

```
private void Keyboard_Tick(object sender, System.EventArgs e) {
   Microsoft.DirectX.DirectXException.IgnoreExceptions();
     . . .
    keyboard = new
       Microsoft.DirectX.DirectInput.Device(SystemGuid.Keyboard);
    keyboard.Properties.BufferSize = 8;
    keyboard.Acquire();

    KeyboardState state = keyboard.GetCurrentKeyboardState();

    for (Key k = Key.Escape; k <= Key.MediaSelect; k++) {
       if (state[k] && k == Key.Left) {
           player.direction = AnimatedImage.WEST;
           player.Animate();
           player.ConstrainToBox();
           if (theBall.isActive == false)
               Invalidate();
           break;
            . . .
```

Example 4.57. Joystick controls for Battle Tennis.

```
private void Joystick_Tick(object sender, System.EventArgs e) {
   Microsoft.DirectX.DirectXException.IgnoreExceptions();
```

```csharp
        if (gameState.currentState == GameState.State.Stopped)
            return;

        foreach (DeviceInstance instance in
           Manager.GetDevices(DeviceClass.GameControl,
           EnumDevicesFlags.AttachedOnly)) {
              joystick = new
                 Microsoft.DirectX.DirectInput.Device(instance.InstanceGuid);
              break;
        }

        if (joystick == null) {return;}

        joystick.SetDataFormat(DeviceDataFormat.Joystick);

        foreach (DeviceObjectInstance d in joystick.Objects) {
            if ((0 != (d.ObjectId & (int)DeviceObjectTypeFlags.Axis))) {
                joystick.Properties.SetRange(ParameterHow.ById,
                    d.ObjectId, new InputRange(-1000, 1000));
            }
        }
        joystick.SetCooperativeLevel(this,
           Microsoft.DirectX.DirectInput.CooperativeLevelFlags.Background |
           Microsoft.DirectX.DirectInput.CooperativeLevelFlags.NonExclusive);
        joystick.Properties.AxisModeAbsolute = true;
        joystick.Acquire();
        joystick.Poll();
        JState = joystick.CurrentJoystickState;

        player.direction = 0;

        if (-400 < JState.X) {
            player.direction = AnimatedImage.WEST;
        } else if(-500 > JState.X) {
            player.direction = AnimatedImage.EAST;
        }
        . . .

        byte[] buttons = JState.GetButtons();
        if (theBall.isActive == false &&
            gameState.currentState != GameState.State.Stopped) {
             foreach (byte b in buttons) {
```

```
        if (0 != (b & 0x80)) {
          FireBall();
        . . .
```

Example 4.58. Mouse controls for Battle Tennis.

```
private void Mouse_Tick(object sender, System.EventArgs e) {
   Microsoft.DirectX.DirectXException.IgnoreExceptions();
   mouse = new Microsoft.DirectX.DirectInput.Device(SystemGuid.Mouse);
   MouseState mouseData = new MouseState();

   mouse.SetDataFormat(DeviceDataFormat.Mouse);
   mouse.Acquire();
   mouse.Poll();

   // Get the current state of the mouse device.
   mouseData = mouse.CurrentMouseState;

   if (MouseOverride) {
      player.imagePosX = Cursor.Position.X;
      player.imagePosY = Cursor.Position.Y;
      player.ConstrainToBox();

      byte[] buttons = mouseData.GetMouseButtons();
      if (0 != buttons[0] && !theBall.isActive) {
         FireBall();
      }
   }
}
```

The Properties of Sound

In Chapter 3 we looked at the fundamentals of DirectSound. There, we studied the basics of creating a sound device and setting its cooperative level, as well as the basics of execution. In this section, we'll study the BufferDescription's properties used to modify our sounds. The BufferDescription method is used to initializes a new instance of an object (see Table 4.5).

Properties:	Description:
`BufferBytes`	A read/write integer property, `BufferBytes` must be set to zero when creating a buffer with `PrimaryBuffer` set to true.
`CanGetCurrentPosition`	A read/write Boolean property, used with emulated sounds.
`Control3D`	A read/write Boolean property, not to be mistaken with `BufferCaps.Control3D`, used to indicate type compatibility for sound production in 3D space. `Control3D` cannot be used with `ControlPan`.
`ControlEffects`	A read/write Boolean property, used to determine if a buffer can use effect processing, conditions include 8/16 bit PCM format and no more than two stereo channels.
`ControlFrequency`	A read/write Boolean property, used to determine if a buffer's frequency could be altered.
`ControlPan`	A read/write Boolean property, used to determine if a buffer could support panning, `ControlPan` cannot be used with `Control3D`.
`ControlPositionNotify`	A read/write Boolean property, used to determine if a buffer would support position notification.
`ControlVolume`	A read/write Boolean property, used to determine if a buffer could support the volume.
`DeferLocation`	A read/write Boolean property, used to determine if a buffer should be assigned to a hardware or software resource at playtime. This flag must be set for buffers that use voice management.
`Flags`	A read/write enumeration property, used to assign Boolean references relating to the other `BufferDescriptions`.
`GlobalFocus`	A read/write Boolean property, used to determine if a buffer is global.
`Guid3DAlgorithm`	A read/write GUID property specifies the algorithm used for 3D virtualization.
`LocateInHardware`	A read/write Boolean property, used to determine if a buffer requires hardware.
`LocateInSoftware`	A read/write Boolean property, used to determine if a buffer requires software (note that this setting ignores any available hardware).

Table 4.5

`Mute3DAtMaxiumDistance`	A read/write Boolean property, used to determine if a sound has exceeded its maximum distance (used with software only).
`PrimaryBuffer`	A read/write Boolean property, used to determine if a buffer is a primary buffer.
`StaticBuffer`	A read/write Boolean property, used to determine hardware availability (if available buffer is placed in hardware, if not the buffer is placed in software). `ControlEffects` must equal false.
`StickyFocus`	A read/write Boolean property, used to determine if a buffer uses sticky focus. `StickyFocus` allows for sound play whenever DirectSound is not engaged.
`WaveFormat`	A read/write `WaveFormat` property specifies the wave format of our stored audio data.

Table 4.5 (continued)

Three-Dimensional Sound

Most people are inherently familiar with monophony or monophonic sound (the reproduction of sound through the use of a single transmission path), as well as stereophony or stereophonic sound (the recording and transmission of sound using multiple channels). Many are also becoming acquainted with three-dimensional sound and surround sound systems. Thus, DirectX or the DirectSound API has been equipped with methods used to simulate three-dimensional space. The two key methods are Buffer3D and Control3D, used to manipulate the source as well as the position and orientation, respectively. It is important to remember that while Buffer3D controls the 3D settings, we'll still be relying on the original buffer to control our play settings (see Table 4.6).

Properties:	Descriptions:
`ConeAngles`	A read/write structured property, used to record and retrieve the internal and external angles of a cone.
`ConeOrientation`	A read/write structured property, used to manipulate a sounds orientation.
`ConeOutsideVolume`	A read/write integer property, used to manipulate the volume of an external cone.
`Deferred`	A read/write Boolean property, used to determine if a property change should be updated immediately (false) or deferred (true). Settings are not applied until the application (true) calls the `Listener3D.CommitDeferredSettings ()`.
`MaxDistance`	A read/write float property, used to determine the maximum distance from the listener.
`MinDistance`	A read/write float property, used to determine the minimum distance from the listener.
`Mode`	A read/write enumeration property, used to determine the 3D mode for sound processing.
`Position`	A read/write structured property, used to determine the sounds current position.
`Velocity`	A read/write structured property, used to determine the sound's velocity (in meters per second).

Table 4.6

Listener3D must be used with a primary buffer; there is only one listener per device (see Table 4.7).

Using Sound Effects

DirectSound's API also comes with several simple sound effects; these can be used in conjunction with the basics sounds (included in Chapter 3) and with the three-dimensional aspects discussed earlier in this chapter. The practically of using sound effects generally relates to the environment that the programmer creates. For example, if we wanted to

Properties:	Description:
`CommitDeferredSettings`	A void property, used to determine if any new settings have been deferred, if they have then those settings are committed.
`DistanceFactor`	A read/write float property, used to manipulate the number of meters in a vector.
`DopplerFactor`	A read/write float property, used to manipulate the multiplier for the Doppler effect.
`Deferred`	A read/write Boolean property, used to determine if a property change should be updated immediately or deferred.
`Orientation`	A read/write structured property, used to manipulate the orientation of the listener.
`RolloffFactor`	A read/write float property, used to determine the rate of attenuation over distance.
`Position`	A read/write structured property, used to determine the current position of the listener.
`Velocity`	A read/write structured property, used to determine the velocity of the listener (in meters per second).

Table 4.7.

create the illusion of a hall or canyon, we could include an echo effect. Other manipulations might include distortion, compressions, or reverberation (see Table 4.8).

Example 4.59. 3D and sound effects.

```
// DirectSound3D
private Microsoft.DirectX.DirectSound.Device sound = null;
private SecondaryBuffer SoundBuffer = null;
private Buffer3D SoundBuffer3D = null;
. . .
sound = new Microsoft.DirectX.DirectSound.Device();
sound.SetCooperativeLevel(this, CooperativeLevel.Priority);

BufferDescription desc = new BufferDescription();
desc.Control3D = true;
desc.GlobalFocus = true;
. . .
SoundBuffer = new SecondaryBuffer(MEDIA_ROOT + "NextLevel.wav", sound);
```

```
SoundBuffer3D = new Buffer3D(SoundBuffer);
SoundBuffer.Play(0, BufferPlayFlags.Default);
SoundBuffer3D.Position = new Vector3(-0.2f, 0.0f, 1.0f);
. . .
SoundBuffer = new SecondaryBuffer(MEDIA_ROOT + "Racket.wav", sound);
EffectDescription[] effects = new EffectDescription[1];
effects[0].GuidEffectClass = DSoundHelper.StandardGargleGuid;
SoundBuffer.SetEffects(effects);
SoundBuffer.Play(0, BufferPlayFlags.Default);
. . .
```

Effect:	Description:
Chorus	A voice-doubling effect, the original sound is repeated after a short delay. The sound is also slightly altered, creating the illusion of multiple voices.
Compression	A reduction in the fluctuation of amplitude as it is measured from the signal's average.
Distortion	An abrupt slicing of the top of a waveform created by adding harmonics to the signal as the level increases.
Echo	Sounds are repeated after a fixed delay, usually at a diminished volume. This process repeats for several cycles.
Environment Reverberation	An implementation of the listener properties; a sound reaching the listener has three temporal components: direct path, early reflections, and late reverberation. The combination of early reflections and late reverberation is also referred to as the room effect.
Flange	Also known as flanger, an echo/sweeping effect, which includes a shorter delay and some variance.
Gargle	An intonation/modulation of a signal's amplitude meant to causes a unique sound.
Parametric Equalizer	Used to amplify or attenuate a signal, allowing for different pitches that can be applied in parallel.
Waves Reverberation	Intended for use with music, the wave's reverberation DirectX Media Object (DMO) is based on the wave's MaxxVerb technology.

Table 4.8

Changing Levels

Another key aspect to creating a multilevel game is to include a level changing or resetting method. In this case, we'll also want to use this method to demonstrate DirectSound's 3D and special effect features explained in the last few sections. The NextLevel method uses a for-loop to reactivate all target creators. The NextLevel method is referenced as part of a time based comparison (see Examples 4.60 and 4.61).

Example 4.60. Next level.

```
private void NextLevel() {
   try {
      // DirectSound3D
      SoundBuffer = new SecondaryBuffer(MEDIA_ROOT + "NextLevel.wav",
          sound);
      SoundBuffer3D = new Buffer3D(SoundBuffer);
      SoundBuffer.Play(0, BufferPlayFlags.Default);
      SoundBuffer3D.Position = new Vector3(-0.2f, 0.0f, 1.0f);
   } catch {
      Utils.PlaySound(MEDIA_ROOT + "NextLevel.WAV");
   }
   for (int i = 0; i < NUM_TARGETS; i++) {
      targets[i].isActive = true;
      . . .
```

Example 4.61. Projectile animation.

```
public void MoveBall(TimedEvent e, Object obj) {
   if (gameState.currentState != GameState.State.Started)
      return;

   if (theBall.isActive) {
      theBall.Animate();

   if (theBall.Intersects(player)) {
      HitTheBall();
      return;
   }

   if (theBall.ConstrainToBox()) {
```

```
        if (theBall.imagePosY + theBall.imageHeight >=
            ClientSize.Height) {
            player.deaths++;
            theBall.isActive = false;

        if (player.deaths >= NUM_LIVES) {
            gameState.currentState = GameState.State.Stopped;
            if (player.score > HighScore)
                SaveHighScore(player.score);
            Cursor.Show();
            Application.Exit();
        }
    }

    theBall.Deflect();
    return;
    . . .
```

Completing the Game

Finally, we'll want to build our managing or main program. Remember to include the DirectX and Game Classes (see Example 4.62/BattleTennis.cs on the CD-ROM).

Troubleshooting

In this troubleshooting section, we'll begin learning how to use our compilers to isolate, identify, and explain our errors. This is done in three steps; first, use the "Task List" as a hyperlink, which can isolate our errors to within a few lines. Second, use the error "Description" to identify the error. Third, use the "Help Menu" to explain the error. Let's test these three aspects by adding a bit of sabotage to our last game, Asteroid Miner. Here I've commented out the Game Classes.

Common Errors, Problems and Pitfalls

1. If the games are compiling, but you get a runtime error and/or you only detect the default sound, this indicates that your references are not to the appropriate director. For example, if you've copied a game to your D:\\ drive, then C:\\ listings

would all be in error. Make sure all the bitmaps, wav files and classes are not only included as part of your project, but also referenced at the appropriate locations.
2. Attempting to access elements that go beyond an array's size will result in a system error.
3. Attempting to alter the size of an array inside of a user-defined function will result in a system error.
4. Attempting to use floating point numbers or integers that are negative as array elements will result in a system error.
5. Attempting to assign pointers to variables and/or pointers to other pointers of different data types will result in a system error.
6. You *cannot* allocate more system memory than available to your system. (Note: If you do not test for successful allocation of that memory, your system may act incorrectly or crash).
7. Attempting to access a pointer that has not been assigned an address, will result in a program error.
8. Attempting to copy a larger array into a smaller one will result in a program error.

Things to Remember

1. An array is an aggregated set of variables that are of the same data type. They are linked by their location in memory and can be accessed either individually (by their subscripts) or as a whole (when a terminating value "\0" is assigned).
2. Array subscripts can be either literal constants or variables declared as constants. Dynamic arrays allow for standard variables, but once declared, the array's size must not be altered.
3. Arrays can be passed as elements (as in array[x]), or as whole arrays (as in array).
4. Multidimensional arrays list their rows first and then their columns.
5. Linear searches compare data in a consecutive order beginning with one element and moving to the next, while binary searches short cut that process by repeatedly dividing the total by two and then searching the final nondivisible portion.

6. Binary searches tend to be faster when working with longer lists of data and they are the preferred method when working with a longer list that requires repeated searches. (Note: Binary searches must be sorted before they can be tested).
7. Pointers are usually assigned to variables, but they can also be assigned to the values zero and null.
8. The ampersand symbol is required when assigning pointers to variables, but it is not required when assigning pointers to pointers or when passing an array.
9. An array is a constant equivalent to a pointer address.

Questions

1. Describe an array.
2. Declare and assign an array of 5 real numbers using the values 3.5, 2.34, 25.4, 2.002, 1.0.
3. Write a program that uses an array to print the word "hello." (Hint: array[4] = "hello.")
4. Revise the last program so that the word "hello" is passed to a secondary function before being displayed.
5. Write a program that displays the values 1, 2, 3, 4, 5, 6, 7, 8, 9.
6. Revise the last program so as to use a multidimensional array.
7. Write a simple bubble sort program using letters rather than numbers.
8. Write a simple linear search program that counts the total number of lower case letters.
9. Write a simple binary search program that attempts to find a number between 1 and 100. Allow the user to enter a searchable number.
10. Write a program to find the mode, mean, median, and range.
11. Declare and assign a dynamic array.
12. Describe a pointer.
13. Declare and assign a pointer variable.

14. Write a program that displays the word "world" using a pointer string.
15. Revise that last program, allowing the pointer to be passed before the word is displayed.
16. Write a program that allows the user to add, subtract, multiply, divide, and find the remainder of two integers.
17. Use pointer arithmetic to move from one point in an array to another.
18. Write a program that begins with a void pointer, but then assigns that pointer to the four basic data types.
19. Write a function that returns a value as a pointer.

Object-Oriented Design

Chapter Five

If I have seen farther than others, it is because I was standing on the shoulders of giants.
— Isaac Newton

This chapter begins with several sections that define and detail the many attributes of the collective data type known as the `structure`. This aggregated data type includes several options that aid in the removal of literal limitations, and thus help us to further our move into object-oriented programming. Once the basics of these simpler concepts are committed to memory, we'll want to progress onto the extended topics using `classes`. Classes, while not meant to totally replace structures, do allow for a greater level of control, which includes the use of reference types. The second portion of this chapter will also offer several new keywords and operators whose potential can only be reached through class manipulations. Finally, we'll conclude with the underlying classes used to power all the games, and I've thrown in two additional games that add a few final touches.

Structures

Structures are user-defined data types that allow for groupings of similar or related data that do not have a single base data type. These groups can include all the basic value data types, as well as a list of methods used to manipulate those values. The data types declared inside a structure are referred to as the structure's *members* (or *fields*), while their declarations are referred to as its *instances*. The correlations between these internal values and

C# and Game Programming

our structures are usually guided by some common theme or purpose. A structure is made up of the keyword `struct`, the structure's tag (or name), a list of the fields (written as declared members), and a list of possible methods used to manipulate that data. Structures are generally contained within a single block placed inside our referencing namespace, but as shown below, they can also be used to invoke our main method (see Example 5.1).

> While the use of a C++ style terminating semicolon is allowed, it is not required when working with C#.

Example 5.1. A simple structure.

```
using System;

namespace Chapter5 {
    struct BankAccount {
        string first_name;
        string last_name;
        long account_number;
        decimal Checking;
        decimal Savings;
        short pin_number;

        static void Main() {
            BankAccount Balance;
            Balance.account_number = 1234;

            Console.WriteLine(Balance.account_number);
        }
    }
}
```

Declaring and Assigning Fields

Fields are not declared and assigned values directly; rather, they are declared as objects through the use of instances and are assigned as a combination of those instances and their referencing points. The combination of terms is marked by a connecting dot as the member selection operator (.), which is necessary because fields are essentially generalized variables that can be used for multiple purposes. Thus, the use of assignment statements is also restricted from within those structures. Once a structure is listed, the proper declaration and assignment includes both a declaring structure's instance and an assignment to that field (see Examples 5.2 and 5.3).

Example 5.2. Declaring and assigning structures.

```
using System;

namespace Chapter5 {
    struct BankAccount {
        public string first_name;
        public string last_name;
        public long account_number;
        public decimal checking;
        public decimal savings;
        public short pin_number;

        public static void Main() {
            BankAccount account;
            Console.Write("Enter your pin number here (2001): ");
            account.pin_number = short.Parse(Console.ReadLine());

            if (account.pin_number == 2001) {
                account.account_number = 43297;
                account.first_name = "John";
                account.last_name = "Doe";
                account.checking = 0;
                account.savings = 112.53M;
                Console.WriteLine("Account Number: {0}",
                    account.account_number);
                Console.WriteLine("Identity: {0} {1}",
                    account.first_name, account.last_name);
                Console.WriteLine("Savings Account Balance: {0}",
                    account.savings);
                Console.WriteLine("Checking Account Balance: {0}",
                    account.checking);
            }
        }
    }
}
```

C# and Game Programming

Screen Shot 5.1.

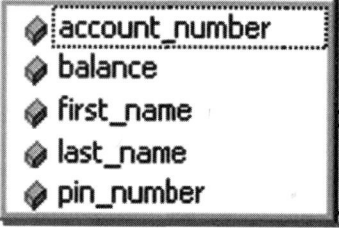

When inserting the dot operator, visual compiler users may encounter a popup window resembling Screen Shot 5.1. This window is generally used as a reminder indicating to the programmer that certain fields are available. If a certain item is not present, this may indicate that it was coded incorrectly or that a certain reference is missing or incomplete. A padlock symbol indicates a protected or private member/field.

Example 5.3. Declaring and assigning multiple instances.

```
using System;

namespace Chapter5 {
    struct BankAccount {
        public string first_name;
        public string last_name;
        public long account_number;
        public decimal checking;
        public decimal savings;
        public short pin_number;
    }

    class Class1 {
        static void Main () {
            BankAccount account1, account2;

            account1.pin_number = 2001;
            account1.account_number = 43297;
            account1.first_name = "John";
            account1.last_name = "Doe";
            account1.savings = 0;
            account1.checking = 112.53M;
```

```
            account2.pin_number = 2002;
            account2.account_number = 78978;
            account2.first_name = "Jane";
            account2.last_name = "Happy";
            account2.savings = 312.43M;
            account2.checking = 2134.65M;

            Console.Write("\nEnter your pin number here: ");
            short input = short.Parse(Console.ReadLine());

            if (input == account1.pin_number) {
               Console.WriteLine("Account Number: {0}",
                  account1.account_number);
               Console.WriteLine("Identity: {0} {1}",
                  account1.first_name, account1.last_name);
               Console.WriteLine("Savings Account Balance: {0}",
                  account1.savings);
               Console.WriteLine("Checking Account Balance: {0}",
                  account1.checking);
            } else if (input == account2.pin_number) {
               Console.WriteLine("Account Number: {0}",
                  account2.account_number);
               Console.WriteLine("Identity: {0} {1}",
                  account2.first_name,
                  account2.last_name);
               Console.WriteLine("Savings Account Balance: {0}",
                  account2.savings);
               Console.WriteLine("Checking Account Balance: {0}",
                  account2.checking);
            }
         }
      }
}
```

Multiple Structures

Another useful technique when dealing with structures is the use of an *array of structures*. This can quickly become a necessity when dealing with large groups of instances that also share a common set of comparisons. Notice how the structure's name is used in place of the basic data type, and how its format emulates that of a basic array style reference. This array is also subject to the limitation of size, but it also inherently takes on some of the capabilities of a multidimensional array (see Examples 5.4). While arrays of structures are allowed, internal structural arrays are not. This is due to the fact that structures by definition are value based, while arrays rely on referenced-based structures (which, in C#, is defined as a class).

> The keyword new is used as both an operator and a modifier. As an operator, it is used to declare instances and to create objects. As a modifier, it is used to hide members inherited from a base class. The new operator cannot be overloaded or used with an override statement.

Example 5.4. Arrays of structures.

```
using System;

namespace Chapter5 {
    struct BankAccount {
        public string first_name;
        public string last_name;
        public long account_number;
        public decimal checking;
        public decimal savings;
        public short pin_number;
    }

    class Class1 {
        public static void Main() {
            BankAccount[] account = new BankAccount[3];

            account[0].pin_number = 2000;
            account[0].account_number = 78434;
            account[0].first_name = "Bad";
            account[0].last_name = "Dog";
            account[0].savings = 1000.15M;
            account[0].checking = 43.12M;
            account[1].pin_number = 2001;
            account[1].account_number = 43297;
            account[1].first_name = "John";
            account[1].last_name = "Doe";
            account[1].savings = 0;
```

```
            account[1].checking = 112.53M;
            account[2].pin_number = 2002;
            account[2].account_number = 78978;
            account[2].first_name = "Jane";
            account[2].last_name = "Happy";
            account[2].savings = 2134.65M;
            account[2].checking = 312.43M;

            while (true) {
               Console.Write("Enter your pin number here: ");
               short input = short.Parse(Console.ReadLine());
               for (int index = 0; index < 3; index++) {
                  if (input == account[index].pin_number) {
                     Console.WriteLine("Account Number: {0}",
                        account[index].account_number);
                     Console.WriteLine("Identity: {0} {1}",
                        account[index].first_name,
                        account[index].last_name);
                     Console.WriteLine("savings Account Balance: {0}",
                        account[index].savings);
                     Console.WriteLine("checking Account Balance: {0}",
                        account[index].checking);
                  }
               }
            }
         }
      }
   }
}
```

Complex Structures

Complex structures are nothing more than structures that contain references to other structures. These secondary structures are accessed in much the same manner as standard structures, with the addition of a secondary dot operator and an additional member's name. The inclusion of one structure inside another is also referred to as *composition* and/or *nesting*. Note that unlike C++, the referencing of an outer structure does not inherently reference the inner values, thus; these two structures must be declared separately (see Example 5.5).

Example 5.5. Nested structures.

```
using System;

namespace Chapter5 {
    struct BankAccount {
        public string first_name;

        public struct NestedStruct {
            public decimal swiss_account;
        }
    }

    class Class1 {
        static void Main() {
            BankAccount Account;
            BankAccount.NestedStruct HiddenAccount;

            Account.first_name = "MR.RICH";
            HiddenAccount.swiss_account = 5000000.00M;
        }
    }
}
```

Structures as Function Arguments: Calls-by-Value

In addition to being able to pass our standard variables as both call-by-value and call-by-reference values, we can also pass fields using either of these techniques. In this section we'll apply the simpler of the two, the call-by-value procedure, for which we've already defined the self-contained nature of those values. Remember, calls-by-value are used to pass data that is mutable from within that referencing method, but which ultimately does not affect the source values (see Example 5.6).

Example 5.6. Calls-by-value with structures.

```
using System;

namespace Chapter5 {
    class Class1 {
        struct BankAccount {
            public string first_name;
```

```
        public string last_name;
        public long account_number;
        public decimal checking;
        public decimal savings;
        public short pin_number;
    }

    static void Main() {
        BankAccount account;

        short input;
        account.pin_number = 2001;
        account.savings = 0M;
        account.checking = 112.53M;

        Console.Write("Enter you pin number now: ");
        input = short.Parse(Console.ReadLine());

        if (account.pin_number == 2001) {
            Console.WriteLine("savings");
            account.savings = function(account.savings);
            Console.WriteLine("checking");
            account.checking = function(account.checking);
            Console.WriteLine("Updating account...");
            Console.WriteLine("savings {0}", account.savings);
            Console.WriteLine("checking {0}", account.checking);
        }
    }

    static decimal function(decimal balance) {
        decimal input;
        Console.WriteLine("Your current balance: {0}", balance);
        Console.Write("\nAmount to deposit: ");
        input = decimal.Parse(Console.ReadLine());
        balance = balance + input;
        return (balance);
    }
}
}
```

Structures as Function Arguments: Calls-by-Reference

Next, we will pass fields using a call-by-reference procedure. Call-by-reference procedures are, simply put, limited pointer values. Any alterations in the passed variable's values now alter the member's stored values. These, like their variable counterparts, are also referenced with the keywords `ref` and `out` as shown below (see Example 5.7).

Example 5.7. Calls-by-reference with structures.

```
using System;

namespace Chapter5 {
    class Class1 {
        struct BankAccount {
            public string first_name;
            public string last_name;
            public long account_number;
            public decimal checking;
            public decimal savings;
            public short pin_number;
        }

        static void Main () {
            BankAccount account;

            account.pin_number = 2001;
            account.savings = 10M;
            account.checking = 112.53M;
            Console.Write("Enter you pin number now: ");
            short input = short.Parse(Console.ReadLine());

            if (account.pin_number == 2001) {
                Console.WriteLine("savings");
                function (ref account.savings);
                Console.WriteLine("checking\n");
                function (ref account.checking);

                Console.WriteLine("Updating account...");
                Console.WriteLine("savings {0}", account.savings);
                Console.WriteLine("checking {0}", account.checking);
            }
        }
```

```
        static void function(ref decimal balance) {
            decimal input;
            Console.WriteLine("Your current balance: {0}", balance);
            Console.WriteLine("Amount to deposit: ");
            input = decimal.Parse(Console.ReadLine());
            balance = balance + input;
        }
    }
}
```

Passing Entire Structures

In addition to being able to pass single structural members, we can also pass an entire structure using a call-by-value or call-by-reference procedure. In both cases, the reasoning for doing so would involve the increased portability and reusability of such generalized user-defined functions (see Examples 5.8 and 5.9).

Example 5.8. Calls-by-value for entire structures.

```
using System;

namespace Chapter5 {
    struct BankAccount {
        public string first_name;
        public string last_name;
        public long account_number;
        public decimal checking;
        public decimal savings;
        public short pin_number;
    }

    class Class1 {
        static void Main() {
            BankAccount account;

            account.pin_number = 2001;
            account.account_number = 43297;
            account.first_name = "John";
            account.last_name = "Doe";
            account.savings = 100.00M;
            account.checking = 112.53M;
            function(account);
            function(account);
        }
```

```csharp
        static void function(BankAccount acc) {
            Console.Write("Enter your pin number here: ");
            short input = short.Parse(Console.ReadLine());

            if (input == acc.pin_number) {
                Console.WriteLine("Account Number: {0}",
                    acc.account_number);
                Console.WriteLine("Identity: {0} {1}",
                    acc.first_name, acc.last_name);
                Console.WriteLine("savings Account Balance: {0}",
                    acc.savings);
                Console.WriteLine("checking Account Balance: {0}",
                    acc.checking);

                Console.Write("Enter a new pin number here: ");
                acc.pin_number = short.Parse(Console.ReadLine());
                Console.WriteLine("Deposit into savings account: ");
                input = short.Parse(Console.ReadLine());
                acc.savings = acc.savings + input;
            }
        }
    }
}
```

Example 5.9. Calls-by-reference for entire structures.

```csharp
using System;

namespace Chapter5 {
    struct BankAccount {
        public string first_name;
        public string last_name;
        public long account_number;
        public decimal Checking;
        public decimal Savings;
        public short pin_number;
    }

    class Class1 {
        static void Main() {
            BankAccount account;

            account.pin_number = 2001;
            account.account_number = 43297;
```

```
            account.first_name = "John";
            account.last_name = "Doe";
            account.Savings = 100M;
            account.Checking = 112.53M;
            function (ref account);
            function (ref account);
        }

        static void function (ref BankAccount acc) {
            Console.WriteLine("Enter your pin number here: ");
            short input = short.Parse(Console.ReadLine());

            if (input == acc.pin_number) {
                Console.WriteLine("Account Number: {0}",
                    acc.account_number);
                Console.WriteLine("Identity: {0} {1}",
                    acc.first_name, acc.last_name);
                Console.WriteLine("Savings Account Balance: {0}",
                    acc.Savings);
                Console.WriteLine("Checking Account Balance: {0}",
                    acc.Checking);

                Console.Write("Enter a new pin number here: ");
                acc.pin_number = short.Parse(Console.ReadLine());
                Console.WriteLine("Deposit into savings account: ");
                input = short.Parse(Console.ReadLine());
                acc.Savings = acc.Savings + input;
            }
        }
    }
}
```

Storing and Retrieving Data

In the last few examples, we altered our user's accounts only to have those alterations lost at the end of the program. This, of course, would be quite impractical, but it was only done to simplify the learning process. The next few examples include coding techniques that link and store our data for further reference after our programs have been terminated. The processes involved in data storage and retrieval are not actually based on the C# language, but instead are linked to the Base Class Library. Here, we'll use the namespace reference System.IO with the instances StreamReader and StreamWriter and a list of

C# and Game Programming

ReadLine and WriteLine references (see Example 5.10). Note that you must create a file before it can be viewed.

Example 5.10. Storing and retrieving data.

```csharp
using System;
using System.IO;

namespace Chapter5 {
    struct BankAccount {
        public string first_name;
        public string last_name;
        public long account_number;
        public decimal checking;
        public decimal savings;
        public short pin_number;
    }

    class Class1 {
        static void Main() {
            BankAccount account1;

            account1.pin_number = 0;
            account1.first_name = "";
            account1.last_name = "";
            account1.account_number = 0;
            account1.checking = 0;
            account1.savings = 0;

            char input;

            while (true) {
                Console.WriteLine("Enter <C> to create new file or <V> " +
                    "to view account");
                input = char.Parse(Console.ReadLine());

                if(Char.ToUpper(input) == 'C') {
                    CreateFile(out account1);
                } else if (Char.ToUpper (input) == 'V') {
                    ReadFile(ref account1);
                } else {
                    break;
                }
```

```csharp
            Console.WriteLine("Pin Number: {0}",
                account1.pin_number);
            Console.WriteLine("Account Number: {0}",
                account1.account_number);
            Console.WriteLine("Name: {0} {1}",
                account1.first_name, account1.last_name);
            Console.WriteLine("savings Balance: {0}",
                account1.savings);
            Console.WriteLine("checking Balance: {0}",
                account1.checking);

            SaveFile(account1, 0, 0);
        }
    }

    static void CreateFile(out BankAccount acc) {
        Console.WriteLine("Enter Your New Pin Number: ");
        acc.pin_number = short.Parse(Console.ReadLine());

        Random rnd = new Random();

        acc.account_number = rnd.Next(1, 100);

        Console.WriteLine("\nYour New Account Number is: {0}",
            acc.account_number);
        Console.Write("\nEnter your first name: ");
        acc.first_name = Console.ReadLine();
        Console.Write("\nEnter your last name: ");
        acc.last_name = Console.ReadLine();
        Console.WriteLine("\nEnter your savings Balance: ");
        acc.savings = decimal.Parse(Console.ReadLine());
        Console.WriteLine("\nEnter your checking Balance: ");
        acc.checking = decimal.Parse(Console.ReadLine());

        SaveFile(acc, 0, 0);
    }

    static void SaveFile(BankAccount acc, short input1,
        short input2) {

        StreamWriter file = new StreamWriter(@"C:\MyFile.txt");
        file.WriteLine(acc.pin_number);
        file.WriteLine(acc.account_number);
        file.WriteLine((acc.savings + input1));
        file.WriteLine((acc.checking + input2));
```

C# and Game Programming

```
        file.WriteLine(acc.first_name);
        file.WriteLine(acc.last_name);
        file.Close();
    }

    static void ReadFile(ref BankAccount acc) {
        StreamReader file = new StreamReader(@"C:\MyFile.txt");
        acc.pin_number = short.Parse(file.ReadLine());
        acc.account_number = long.Parse(file.ReadLine());
        acc.savings = decimal.Parse(file.ReadLine());
        acc.checking = decimal.Parse(file.ReadLine());
        acc.first_name = file.ReadLine();
        acc.last_name = file.ReadLine();
        file.Close();
    }
}
}
```

> In getting back to classes, I should mention that there are many aspects that we'll now cover for classes that are just as viable within the previously discussed structure types. These, of course, include the `private`, `protected`, and `public` references, as well as the basic member and method references.

Introducing Classes

As we've seen through this text, the application of classes is quite vital to the manipulation of the C# language. An immediate comparison between classes and structures can be made, and all of the previous information can be reapplied to class references. Note that classes are both capable of using reference data types as well as single inheritance, but not multiple inheritance as is available with C++. Classes mimic the naming references used with structures, including tags, fields, methods, and data blocks, as well as other key reference points including `public`, `private`, and `protected` access (these concepts will be explained shortly). A basic class reference can also be used to implement a simple do-nothing style program, but this time we'll also need to include a dynamically linked instance (see Example 5.11).

Example 5.11. A simple class.

```
using System;

namespace Chapter5 {
    class BankAccount {
        string first_name;
        string last_name;
        long account_number;
        decimal checking;
        decimal savings;
        short pin_number;

        static void Main() {
            BankAccount Info = new BankAccount();
            Info.account_number = 4353;
            Console.WriteLine(Info.account_number);
        }
    }
}
```

> The keyword `static` is used to modify constructors, fields, methods, operators, and properties. *Static constructors*, for example, are called automatically and are used to initialize the rest of the class before any members are referenced. *Static fields*, then, are not part of a specific instance and instead are referenced as a single memory address.

Replacing Structures with Classes

Since classes are declared and assigned in basically the same manner as structures, and since we haven't as yet defined the other access levels, it only makes sense than that we should begin with a simple public reference. In addition, if just to avoid the monotony of repeating all of the previous examples, I thought that I'd just jump ahead to the final example given on structures and modify it just enough to represent a working model of a class (see Example 5.12). Remember you must first create a file before you can view it.

 As we examine this program, we'll find that the most important modification pertains to the dynamic instance. This change was necessary because classes are, in fact, referencing data types. You should also notice that the key methods, namely `SaveFiles`, `CreateFiles`, and `ReadFiles` did not need to be edited for use with this altered program. This adheres to the principles behind structured programming, wherein our functions are written as generic coding that can be reused by several applications; this is also the underlying principle of object-oriented program, as we will see in the next section.

Example 5.12. Storing and retrieving data with classes.

```
using System;
using System.IO;

namespace Chapter5 {
    class BankAccount {
        public string first_name;
        public string last_name;
        public long account_number;
        public decimal checking;
        public decimal savings;
        public short pin_number;
    }

    class Class1 {
        static void Main() {
            BankAccount account1 = new BankAccount();

            char input;

            while (true) {
                Console.WriteLine("Enter <C> to create new file or " +
                    "<V> to view account");
                input = char.Parse(Console.ReadLine());

                if (Char.ToUpper(input) == 'C') {
                    CreateFile(ref account1);
                } else if (Char.ToUpper(input) == 'V') {
                    ReadFile(ref account1);
                } else {
                    break;
```

```csharp
        }

        Console.WriteLine("Pin Number: {0}",
            account1.pin_number);
        Console.WriteLine("Account Number: {0}",
            account1.account_number);
        Console.WriteLine("Name: {0} {1}",
            account1.first_name, account1.last_name);
        Console.WriteLine("Savings Balance: {0}",
            account1.savings);
        Console.WriteLine("Checking Balance: {0}",
            account1.checking);

        SaveFile(account1, 0, 0);
    }
}

static void CreateFile(ref BankAccount acc) {
    Console.WriteLine("Enter Your New Pin Number: ");
    acc.pin_number = short.Parse(Console.ReadLine());

    Random rnd = new Random();
    acc.account_number = rnd.Next(1, 100);

    Console.WriteLine("\nYour New Account Number is: {0}",
        acc.account_number);
    Console.Write("\nEnter your first name: ");
    acc.first_name = Console.ReadLine();
    Console.Write("\nEnter your last name: ");
    acc.last_name = Console.ReadLine();
    Console.WriteLine("\nEnter Your Savings Balance: ");
    acc.savings = decimal.Parse(Console.ReadLine());
    Console.WriteLine("\nEnter Your Checking Balance: ");
    acc.checking = decimal.Parse(Console.ReadLine());

    SaveFile(acc, 0, 0);
}

static void SaveFile(BankAccount acc, short input1,
    short input2) {
    StreamWriter file = new StreamWriter (@"C:\MyFile.txt");
    file.WriteLine(acc.pin_number);
    file.WriteLine(acc.account_number);
    file.WriteLine((acc.savings + input1));
    file.WriteLine((acc.checking + input2));
```

```
            file.WriteLine(acc.first_name);
            file.WriteLine(acc.last_name);
            file.Close();
        }

        static void ReadFile(ref BankAccount acc) {
            StreamReader file = new StreamReader(@"C:\MyFile.txt");
            acc.pin_number = short.Parse(file.ReadLine());
            acc.account_number = long.Parse(file.ReadLine());
            acc.savings = decimal.Parse(file.ReadLine());
            acc.checking = decimal.Parse(file.ReadLine());
            acc.first_name = file.ReadLine();
            acc.last_name = file.ReadLine();
            file.Close();
        }
    }
}
```

private and *protected* Fields

Another programming technique that can improve program portability is the use of `private` and/or `protected` member fields. These are class or structure members that allow for restricted or limited access based on user-defined methods written specifically for those values. These user-defined methods are declared as part of that class' internal structure with the option of being declared as `public`, `protected`, or `private` member functions.

Methods are user-defined functions that are declared from within classes. These functions are given both standard access to our main program and special access to our now private member variables. Public member functions can be accessed through any user-defined function that is aware of that defined class. The call to that function will need to include a class identifying statement and a dot member selection operator, while these user-defined functions include the class' identity, a type qualifier (the function's name), and a connecting binary scope resolution operator. For obvious reasons, member functions are also referred to as *assessor functions* (see Examples 5.13 and 5.14).

Example 5.13. Private members.

```
using System;
using System.IO;
```

```csharp
namespace Chapter5 {
    class BankAccount {
        private string first_name;
        private string last_name;
        private long account_number;
        private decimal checking;
        private decimal savings;
        private short pin_number;

        public void CreateFile(ref BankAccount acc) {
            Console.WriteLine("Enter Your New Pin Number: ");
            acc.pin_number = short.Parse(Console.ReadLine());

            Random rnd = new Random();
            acc.account_number = rnd.Next(1, 100);

            Console.WriteLine("\nYour New Account Number is: {0}",
                acc.account_number);
            Console.Write("\nEnter your first name: ");
            acc.first_name = Console.ReadLine();
            Console.Write("\nEnter your last name: ");
            acc.last_name = Console.ReadLine();
            Console.WriteLine("\nEnter Your Savings Balance: ");
            acc.savings = decimal.Parse(Console.ReadLine());
            Console.WriteLine("\nEnter Your Checking Balance: ");
            acc.checking = decimal.Parse(Console.ReadLine());

            SaveFile(acc, 0, 0);
        }

        public void SaveFile(BankAccount acc, short input1,
            short input2) {

            StreamWriter file = new StreamWriter(@"C:\MyFile.txt");
            file.WriteLine(acc.pin_number);
            file.WriteLine(acc.account_number);
            file.WriteLine((acc.savings + input1));
            file.WriteLine((acc.checking + input2));
            file.WriteLine(acc.first_name);
            file.WriteLine(acc.last_name);
            file.Close();
        }

        public void ReadFile(ref BankAccount acc) {
            StreamReader file = new StreamReader(@"C:\MyFile.txt");
```

```csharp
            acc.pin_number = short.Parse(file.ReadLine());
            acc.account_number = long.Parse(file.ReadLine());
            acc.savings = decimal.Parse(file.ReadLine());
            acc.checking = decimal.Parse(file.ReadLine());
            acc.first_name = file.ReadLine();
            acc.last_name = file.ReadLine();
            file.Close();
        }

        public void ViewFile(BankAccount acc) {
            Console.WriteLine("Pin Number: {0}", acc.pin_number);
            Console.WriteLine("Account Number: {0}", acc.account_number);
            Console.WriteLine("Name: {0} {1}", acc.first_name,
                acc.last_name);
            Console.WriteLine("Savings Balance: {0}", acc.savings);
            Console.WriteLine("Checking Balance: {0}", acc.checking);
        }
    }

    class Class1 {
        static void Main() {
            BankAccount account = new BankAccount ();

            char input;
            while (true) {
                Console.WriteLine("Enter <C> to create new file or " +
                    "<V> to view account");
                input = char.Parse(Console.ReadLine());

                if (Char.ToUpper(input) == 'C') {
                    account.CreateFile (ref account);
                } else if (Char.ToUpper (input) == 'V') {
                    account.ReadFile (ref account);
                } else {
                    break;
                }

                account.ViewFile(account);
                account.SaveFile(account, 0, 0);
            }
        }
    }
}
```

>
> While private is the default setting, many programmers choose to explicitly restate that command to remove any ambiguity.
>
> The programs in Examples 5.13 and 5.14 are especially important when dealing with the migration of thinking from the standard structured programming model to our modern day object-oriented programming principles. Notice how the previous sections user-defined functions have been modified to serve as public methods.

Example 5.14. Protected members.

```
using System;
using System.IO;

namespace Chapter5 {
    class BankAccount {
        protected string first_name;
        protected string last_name;
        protected long account_number;
        protected decimal checking;
        protected decimal savings;
        protected short pin_number;

        public void CreateFile(ref BankAccount acc) {
            Console.WriteLine("Enter Your New Pin Number: ");
            acc.pin_number = short.Parse(Console.ReadLine());

            Random rnd = new Random();
            acc.account_number = rnd.Next(1, 100);

            Console.WriteLine("\nYour New Account Number is: {0}",
                acc.account_number);
            Console.Write("\nEnter your first name: ");
            acc.first_name = Console.ReadLine();
            Console.Write("\nEnter your last name: ");
            acc.last_name = Console.ReadLine();
            Console.WriteLine("\nEnter Your Savings Balance: ");
            acc.savings = decimal.Parse(Console.ReadLine());
            Console.WriteLine("\nEnter Your Checking Balance: ");
            acc.checking = decimal.Parse(Console.ReadLine());
```

```csharp
            SaveFile(acc, 0, 0);
        }

    public void SaveFile(BankAccount acc, short input1,
            short input2) {

            StreamWriter file = new StreamWriter(@"C:\MyFile.txt");
            file.WriteLine(acc.pin_number);
            file.WriteLine(acc.account_number);
            file.WriteLine((acc.savings + input1));
            file.WriteLine((acc.checking + input2));
            file.WriteLine(acc.first_name);
            file.WriteLine(acc.last_name);
            file.Close();
        }

    public void ReadFile(ref BankAccount acc) {
            StreamReader file = new StreamReader(@"C:\MyFile.txt");
            acc.pin_number = short.Parse(file.ReadLine());
            acc.account_number = long.Parse(file.ReadLine());
            acc.savings = decimal.Parse(file.ReadLine());
            acc.checking = decimal.Parse(file.ReadLine());
            acc.first_name = file.ReadLine();
            acc.last_name = file.ReadLine();
            file.Close();
        }

    public void ViewFile(BankAccount acc) {
            Console.WriteLine("Pin Number: {0}", acc.pin_number);
            Console.WriteLine("Account Number: {0}", acc.account_number);
            Console.WriteLine("Name: {0} {1}", acc.first_name,
                acc.last_name);
            Console.WriteLine("Savings Balance: {0}", acc.savings);
            Console.WriteLine("Checking Balance: {0}", acc.checking);
        }
}

class Class1 {
    static void Main() {
        BankAccount account = new BankAccount ();

        char input;
        while (true) {
            Console.WriteLine("Enter <C> to create new file or " +
```

```
                "<V> to view account");
            input = char.Parse(Console.ReadLine());

            if(Char.ToUpper(input) == 'C') {
                account.CreateFile(ref account);
            } else if (Char.ToUpper (input) == 'V') {
                account.ReadFile(ref account);
            } else {
                break;
            }

            account.ViewFile(account);
            account.SaveFile(account, 0, 0);
        }
    }
  }
}
```

The Internal Access Modifier

An *internal access modifier* is a type member used to access class components. The advantage of the internal modifier is that it allows for limited access from within a single assembly. A key disadvantage is that it is only accessible from within that assembly. In addition to the basic internal modifier, we can also use the keyword *internal* in combination with *protected* to create a *internal protected modifier* (see Example 5.15).

Example 5.15. Internals.

```
using System;
using System.IO;

namespace Chapter5 {
    internal class BankAccount {
        internal protected string first_name;
        internal protected string last_name;
        internal protected long account_number;
        internal protected decimal Checking;
        internal protected decimal Savings;
        internal protected short pin_number;

        internal void ReadFiles (ref BankAccount acc) {
            StreamReader ReadFile = new StreamReader(@"C:\MyFile.txt");
```

```csharp
            acc.pin_number = short.Parse(ReadFile.ReadLine());
            acc.account_number = long.Parse(ReadFile.ReadLine());
            acc.Savings = decimal.Parse(ReadFile.ReadLine());
            acc.Checking = decimal.Parse(ReadFile.ReadLine());
            acc.first_name = ReadFile.ReadLine();
            acc.last_name = ReadFile.ReadLine();
            ReadFile.Close();
        }

        internal void CreateFiles (ref BankAccount acc) {
            Console.WriteLine("Enter Your New Pin Number: ");
            acc.pin_number = short.Parse(Console.ReadLine());
            Random rnd = new Random();
            acc.account_number = (long)Math.Round(rnd.NextDouble() *
                100) + 1;
            Console.WriteLine("\nYour New Account Number is: {0}",
                acc.account_number);
            Console.Write("\nEnter your first name: ");
            acc.first_name = Console.ReadLine();
            Console.Write("\nEnter your last name: ");
            acc.last_name = Console.ReadLine();
            Console.WriteLine("\nEnter Your Savings Balance: ");
            acc.Savings = decimal.Parse(Console.ReadLine());
            Console.WriteLine("\nEnter Your Checking Balance: ");
            acc.Checking = decimal.Parse(Console.ReadLine());
            SaveFiles(acc, 0, 0);
        }

        internal void SaveFiles (BankAccount acc, short input1,
             short input2) {
            StreamWriter SaveFile = new StreamWriter(@"C:\MyFile.txt");
            SaveFile.WriteLine(acc.pin_number);
            SaveFile.WriteLine(acc.account_number);
            SaveFile.WriteLine((acc.Savings+input1));
            SaveFile.WriteLine((acc.Checking+input2));
            SaveFile.WriteLine(acc.first_name);
            SaveFile.WriteLine(acc.last_name);
            SaveFile.Close();
        }

        internal void ViewFiles(BankAccount acc) {
            Console.WriteLine("Pin Number: {0}",
                acc.pin_number);
            Console.WriteLine("Account Number: {0}",
                acc.account_number);
```

```
            Console.WriteLine("Name: {0} {1}",
                acc.first_name, acc.last_name);
            Console.WriteLine("Savings Balance: {0}",
                acc.Savings);
            Console.WriteLine("Checking Balance: {0}",
                acc.Checking);
        }
    }

    class Class1 {
        static void Main() {
            BankAccount account = new BankAccount();

            char input;
            while (true) {
                Console.WriteLine("Enter <C> to create new file or " +
                    "<V> to view account");
                input = char.Parse(Console.ReadLine());

                if(Char.ToUpper(input) == 'C') {
                    account.CreateFiles(ref account);
                } else if (Char.ToUpper(input) == 'V') {
                    account.ReadFiles(ref account);
                } else
                    break;

                account.ViewFiles(account);
                account.SaveFiles(account, 0, 0);
            }
        }
    }
}
```

Arrays as Member Fields

Another key component to implement when dealing with a list of classes is the *array reference type*. This powerful, yet somewhat supplemental, string type is still a very useful data block, especially when dealing with the integral data types. Here, we'll want to examine the proper forms when working with arrays both as part of the class and as a component of its methods. Note also that while the array in our example was declared as a private value, its length is still left as a public reference, and thus will not cause an error (see Example 5.16).

Example 5.16. Arrays as member fields.

```
using System;

namespace Chapter5 {
    class DynamicVariables {
        private short[] array = new short[10];

        public DynamicVariables (int n) {
            array = new short[n];
        }

        public void SetElement(short i) {
            array[i] = i;
        }

        public short ReadElement(short i) {
            return(array[i]);
        }

        static void Main() {
            DynamicVariables instance = new DynamicVariables(10);
            for (short i = 0; i < instance.array.Length; i++) {
                instance.SetElement(i);
                Console.Write("{0} ", instance.ReadElement(i)); }
            Console.WriteLine();
        }
    }
}
```

Overloading Member Functions

Overloading occurs whenever two or more user-defined functions are referenced using a single definition. To avoid conflicts, however, definitions must differ by at least one passing argument. Logically, if two functions were similar enough to warrant the same name, and if their arguments were identical, then efforts should be taken to unify those functions. Here I've listed two examples, one to demonstrate how to implement two similar, but overloaded functions, and the other to demonstrate how to avoid unnecessary overloads (see Examples 5.17 and 5.18).

Example 5.17 Combining two similar overloaded functions.

```
/* This function just saves the account. */
public void SaveFiles(BankAccount acc) {
   StreamWriter SaveFile = new StreamWriter(@"C:\MyFile.txt");
   SaveFile.WriteLine(acc.pin_number);
   SaveFile.WriteLine(acc.account_number);
   SaveFile.WriteLine((acc.Savings));
   SaveFile.WriteLine((acc.Checking));
   SaveFile.WriteLine(acc.first_name);
   SaveFile.WriteLine(acc.last_name);
    SaveFile.Close();
}

// This function alters our account balances and then saves those
// values to a designated file
public void SaveFiles(BankAccount acc, short input1, short input2) {
   StreamWriter SaveFile = new StreamWriter(@"C:\MyFile.txt");
   SaveFile.WriteLine(acc.pin_number);
   SaveFile.WriteLine(acc.account_number);
   SaveFile.WriteLine((acc.Savings + input1));
   SaveFile.WriteLine((acc.Checking + input2));
   SaveFile.WriteLine(acc.first_name);
   SaveFile.WriteLine(acc.last_name);
    SaveFile.Close();
}
```

Example 5.18. Avoiding overloads.

```
public void SaveFiles(BankAccount acc, short input1, short input2) {
   StreamWriter SaveFile = new StreamWriter(@"C:\MyFile.txt");
   SaveFile.WriteLine(acc.pin_number);
   SaveFile.WriteLine(acc.account_number);
   SaveFile.WriteLine((acc.Savings + input1));
   SaveFile.WriteLine((acc.Checking + input2));
   SaveFile.WriteLine(acc.first_name);
   SaveFile.WriteLine(acc.last_name);
    SaveFile.Close();
}
```

As you can see, the function in Example 5.18 could have been separated to include two overloading functions, but with a simple adjustment using the zero input, our two functions become one.

private and *protected* Member Functions

Private and protected member functions (also known as *predicate* or *utility* functions) are specialized member functions used only for that class' internal reference. These functions can be used to read or display data, and are generally used to support the operations of that class' public member function. Private/protected member functions are not intended for use by outside references, but are generally written without any specific notation. To convert our previous program into one that uses private member functions, we simply need to revise our class' internal definition (see Examples 5.19 and 5.20).

Example 5.19. Private member functions (methods).

```
using System;
using System.IO;

namespace Chapter5 {
    class BankAccount {
        protected string first_name;
        protected string last_name;
        protected long account_number;
        protected decimal checking;
        protected decimal savings;
        protected short pin_number;

        private void ReadFile(ref BankAccount acc) {
            StreamReader file = new StreamReader(@"C:\MyFile.txt");
            acc.pin_number = short.Parse(file.ReadLine());
            acc.account_number = long.Parse(file.ReadLine());
            acc.savings = decimal.Parse(file.ReadLine());
            acc.checking = decimal.Parse(file.ReadLine());
            acc.first_name = file.ReadLine();
            acc.last_name = file.ReadLine();
            file.Close();
        }

        private void SaveFile(BankAccount acc, short input1,
            short input2) {

            StreamWriter file = new StreamWriter(@"C:\MyFile.txt");
            file.WriteLine(acc.pin_number);
            file.WriteLine(acc.account_number);
            file.WriteLine((acc.savings + input1));
```

```csharp
            file.WriteLine((acc.checking + input2));
            file.WriteLine(acc.first_name);
            file.WriteLine(acc.last_name);
            file.Close();
        }

        public void CreateFile(ref BankAccount acc) {
            Console.WriteLine("Enter Your New Pin Number: ");
            acc.pin_number = short.Parse(Console.ReadLine());

            Random rnd = new Random ();
            acc.account_number = rnd.Next(1, 100);

            Console.WriteLine("\nYour New Account Number is: {0}",
                acc.account_number);
            Console.Write("\nEnter your first name: ");
            acc.first_name = Console.ReadLine();
            Console.Write("\nEnter your last name: ");
            acc.last_name = Console.ReadLine();
            Console.WriteLine("\nEnter Your Savings Balance: ");
            acc.savings = decimal.Parse(Console.ReadLine());
            Console.WriteLine("\nEnter Your Checking Balance: ");
            acc.checking = decimal.Parse(Console.ReadLine());

            SaveFile(acc, 0, 0);
        }

        public void ViewFile(BankAccount acc) {
            Console.WriteLine("Pin Number: {0}", acc.pin_number);
            Console.WriteLine("Account Number: {0}", acc.account_number);
            Console.WriteLine("Name: {0} {1}", acc.first_name,
                acc.last_name);
            Console.WriteLine("Savings Balance: {0}", acc.savings);
            Console.WriteLine("Checking Balance: {0}", acc.checking);
        }
    }

    class Class1 {
        static void Main() {
            BankAccount account = new BankAccount();

            char input;
            while (true) {
                Console.WriteLine("Enter <C> to create new file or " +
                    "<V> to view account");
```

```
            input = char.Parse(Console.ReadLine());

            if(Char.ToUpper(input) == 'C') {
               account.CreateFile(ref account);
            } else if (Char.ToUpper(input) == 'V') {
               account.ViewFile(account);
            } else {
               break;
            }

            account.ViewFile(account);
         }
      }
   }
}
```

Example 5.20. Protected member functions (methods).

```
protected void ReadFiles(ref BankAccount acc) {
   StreamReader ReadFile = new StreamReader(@"C:\MyFile.txt");
   acc.pin_number = short.Parse(ReadFile.ReadLine());
   acc.account_number = long.Parse(ReadFile.ReadLine());
   acc.Savings = decimal.Parse(ReadFile.ReadLine());
   acc.Checking = decimal.Parse(ReadFile.ReadLine());
   acc.first_name = ReadFile.ReadLine();
   acc.last_name = ReadFile.ReadLine();
   ReadFile.Close();
}

protected void SaveFiles(BankAccount acc, short input1, short input2) {
   StreamWriter SaveFile = new StreamWriter (@"C:\MyFile.txt");
   SaveFile.WriteLine(acc.pin_number);
   SaveFile.WriteLine(acc.account_number);
   SaveFile.WriteLine((acc.Savings + input1));
   SaveFile.WriteLine((acc.Checking + input2));
   SaveFile.WriteLine(acc.first_name);
   SaveFile.WriteLine(acc.last_name);
   SaveFile.Close();
}
```

Constructors

Constructors are member functions that are automatically implemented with the declaration of that class' instance. Each new instance triggers this execution, and generally,

Chapter 5: Object-Oriented Design

those values are made specific to that instance's reference. Constructors, like standard member functions, are declared from within those classes, but constructors do not require a base data type. Constructors are defined using the same definition as their declaring class, while their actual functions are expressed as a combination of both definitions and a connecting binary scope resolution operator. Since constructors **do not** declare a data type, they are also incapable of returning values (see Example 5.21).

> Each declared instance is allocated a portion of system memory (commonly referred to as the heap). In native C++ it is also important to define the restoration of that memory (normally referenced by that classes destructor—see this chapter's section on destructors).[1]

Example 5.21. Constructors.

```
using System;
using System.IO;

namespace Chapter5 {
    class BankAccount {
        public decimal InterestRate;
        public decimal LoanRate;

        // Default Constructor
        public BankAccount() {
            InterestRate = .03M; LoanRate = .13M;
        }
    }

    class Class1 {
        static void Main() {
            BankAccount account = new BankAccount();
        }
    }
}
```

---

[1] While destructors are an important part of native C++, their importance is minimized in C#, where the process of destructing an object has become the primary concern of the compiler, normally occurring when the object is no longer referenced.

341

Overloading Constructors

Constructors can be overloaded in numerous ways. Again, these functions will be automatically referenced when the appropriate instances are declared, and again, their arguments will determine the accessible function. One such class revision might include a secondary constructor that gives a special rate to some depositors and a third that determines an alternate rate for both their savings and loans (see Example 5.22).

Example 5.22. Overloading constructors.

```
using System;
using System.IO;

namespace Chapter5 {
    class BankAccount {
        public decimal InterestRate;
        public decimal LoanRate;

        // Default Constructor
        public BankAccount() {
            InterestRate = .03M; LoanRate = .13M;
        }

        // Overloaded Constructor
        public BankAccount(decimal IRate) {
            InterestRate = .03M;
            LoanRate = .13M;
        }

        // Overloaded Constructor
        public BankAccount(decimal IRate, decimal LoanRate) {
            InterestRate = .03M;
            LoanRate = .13M;
        }
    }

    class Class1 {
        static void Main() {
            BankAccount account = new BankAccount();
        }
    }
}
```

Assigning Instances

Once two or more instances are declared by the same class, the values of those instances can be passed using the assignment statement; for example, account1 = account2; // *where BankAccount account1, account2;*. In Example 5.23, the values from account2 are passed to account1 (this process is commonly referred to as a *memberwise copy*). It is worth noting that restrictions in systems implementations can potentially cause errors when dealing with dynamically allocated storage.

Example 5.23. Memberwise copy—assigning instances.

```
using System;
using System.IO;

namespace Chapter5 {
    class BankAccount {
        public decimal InterestRate;
        public decimal LoanRate;

        public BankAccount() {
            InterestRate = .03M;
            LoanRate = .13M;
        }

        public BankAccount(decimal IRate) {
            InterestRate = .03M;
            LoanRate = .13M;
        }

        public BankAccount(decimal IRate, decimal LoanRate) {
            InterestRate = .03M;
            LoanRate = .13M;
        }
    }

    class Class1 {
        static void Main() {
            BankAccount account = new BankAccount();
            BankAccount account1 = new BankAccount();
            BankAccount account2 = new BankAccount(23);
```

```
            account = account1;
            account = account2;
        }
    }
}
```

Reading and Writing to Private Members

Encapsulation is a key point when working with private members, but for varying reasons we often find that we need to gain at least limited access in order to implement changes within our programs. These changes can be facilitated with the use of specialized member functions. Practically, these functions are usually broken up into two forms: the first to read (compare, get) those values, and the second to set (put, write) or alter those values. Typically, the setting functions are void, while the reading functions are meant to return the implied value. Both are usually only used to access one class member, but several equivalent member functions may be written to include as many members as required (see Example 5.24).

Example 5.24. Reading and writing to private members.

```
public decimal ReadInterestRate() {
    return(InterestRate);
}
public void SetInterestRate(decimal IRate) {
    InterestRate = IRate;
}
```

The Keyword *this*

The keyword `this` is a specialized reference signature used to indicate the referencing object of a passing class, therefore, `this` is a longhand version for the otherwise abbreviated member. While the `this` reference is implied, its definitions can become ambiguous and should be included to prevent this error (see Examples 5.25 and 5.26).

Chapter 5: Object-Oriented Design

> Unlike C++, C#'s single dot reference can be used for both reference and nonreference. The proper notation for a this pointer depends upon the purpose of its referencing class, e.g., the this->variable versus the (*this).variable.

Example 5.25. The this reference.

```
/* Written with the this reference. */
using System;
using System.IO;

namespace Chapter5 {
    class BankAccount {
        protected string first_name;
        protected string last_name;
        protected long account_number;
        protected decimal checking;
        protected decimal savings;
        protected short pin_number;

        private void ReadFile() {
            StreamReader file = new StreamReader(@"C:\MyFile.txt");
            this.pin_number = short.Parse(file.ReadLine());
            this.account_number = long.Parse(file.ReadLine());
            this.savings = decimal.Parse(file.ReadLine());
            this.checking = decimal.Parse(file.ReadLine());
            this.first_name = file.ReadLine();
            this.last_name = file.ReadLine();
            file.Close ();
        }

        public void CreateFile() {
            Console.WriteLine("Enter Your New Pin Number: ");
            this.pin_number = short.Parse(Console.ReadLine());

            Random rnd = new Random();
            this.account_number = rnd.Next(1, 100);
            Console.WriteLine("\nYour New Account Number is: {0}",
                this.account_number);
            Console.Write("\nEnter your first name: ");
            this.first_name = Console.ReadLine();
            Console.Write("\nEnter your last name: ");
            this.last_name = Console.ReadLine();
```

345

```csharp
            Console.WriteLine("\nEnter Your Savings Balance: ");
            this.savings = decimal.Parse(Console.ReadLine());
            Console.WriteLine("\nEnter Your Checking Balance: ");
            this.checking = decimal.Parse(Console.ReadLine());
            this.SaveFile(0, 0);
        }

        private void SaveFile(short input1, short input2) {
            StreamWriter file = new StreamWriter(@"C:\MyFile.txt");
            file.WriteLine(this.pin_number);
            file.WriteLine(this.account_number);
            file.WriteLine((this.savings + input1));
            file.WriteLine((this.checking + input2));
            file.WriteLine(this.first_name);
            file.WriteLine(this.last_name);
            file.Close ();
        }

        public void ViewFile() {
            this.ReadFile();
            Console.WriteLine("Pin Number: {0}",
                this.pin_number);
            Console.WriteLine("Account Number: {0}",
                this.account_number);
            Console.WriteLine("Name: {0} {1}",
                this.first_name, this.last_name);
            Console.WriteLine("Savings Balance: {0}",
                this.savings);
            Console.WriteLine("Checking Balance: {0}",
                this.checking);
        }
    }

    class Class1 {
        static void Main() {
            BankAccount account = new BankAccount();

            char input;
            while (true) {
                Console.WriteLine("Enter <C> to create new file or " +
                    "<V> to view account");
                input = char.Parse(Console.ReadLine());

                if(Char.ToUpper(input) == 'C') {
                    account.CreateFile();
```

```
            } else if (Char.ToUpper(input) == 'V') {
               account.ViewFile();
            } else {
               break;
            }

            account.ViewFile();
         }
      }
   }
}
```

Example 5.26. This as an implied keyword.

```
/* "this" as an implied keyword. */
using System;
using System.IO;

namespace Chapter5 {
    class BankAccount {
        protected string first_name;
        protected string last_name;
        protected long account_number;
        protected decimal checking;
        protected decimal savings;
        protected short pin_number;

        private void ReadFile() {
           StreamReader file = new StreamReader(@"C:\MyFile.txt");
           pin_number = short.Parse(file.ReadLine());
           account_number = long.Parse(file.ReadLine());
           savings = decimal.Parse(file.ReadLine());
           checking = decimal.Parse(file.ReadLine());
           first_name = file.ReadLine();
           last_name = file.ReadLine();
           file.Close();
        }

        public void CreateFile() {
           Console.WriteLine("Enter Your New Pin Number: ");
           pin_number = short.Parse(Console.ReadLine());
           Random rnd = new Random();
           account_number = rnd.Next(1, 100);
```

```csharp
            Console.WriteLine("\nYour New Account Number is: {0}",
                account_number);
            Console.Write("\nEnter your first name: ");
            first_name = Console.ReadLine();
            Console.Write("\nEnter your last name: ");
            last_name = Console.ReadLine();
            Console.WriteLine("\nEnter Your Savings Balance: ");
            savings = decimal.Parse(Console.ReadLine());
            Console.WriteLine("\nEnter Your Checking Balance: ");
            checking = decimal.Parse(Console.ReadLine());
            SaveFile(0, 0);
        }

        private void SaveFile(short input1, short input2) {
            StreamWriter file = new StreamWriter(@"C:\MyFile.txt");
            file.WriteLine(pin_number);
            file.WriteLine(account_number);
            file.WriteLine((savings + input1));
            file.WriteLine((checking + input2));
            file.WriteLine(first_name);
            file.WriteLine(last_name);
            file.Close();
        }

        public void ViewFile() {
            ReadFile();
            Console.WriteLine("Pin Number: {0}",
                pin_number);
            Console.WriteLine("Account Number: {0}",
                account_number);
            Console.WriteLine("Name: {0} {1}",
                first_name, last_name);
            Console.WriteLine("Savings Balance: {0}",
                savings);
            Console.WriteLine("Checking Balance: {0}",
                checking);
        }
    }

    class Class1 {
        static void Main() {
            BankAccount account = new BankAccount ();
```

```
            char input;
            while (true) {
                Console.WriteLine("Enter <C> to create new file or " +
                    "<V> to view account");
                input = char.Parse(Console.ReadLine());

                if(Char.ToUpper(input) == 'C') {
                    account.CreateFile();
                } else if (Char.ToUpper (input) == 'V') {
                    account.ViewFile();
                } else {
                    break;
                }

                account.ViewFile();
            }
        }
    }
}
```

Destructors

In addition to constructors, we can also use *destructors* to return the allocated portions of an object's memory back to the heap. This destruction, or *deallocation*, of system resources is an extremely important systems saving technique, especially when dealing with thousands of class objects that continue to exist even after they are no longer referenced. Again, while Managed C++ and C# do handle these instances automatically, it is still important to understand the concept of creating a destructor. Destructors are also automatically referenced at the termination of a set of coding, but the exact internal structure will depend on the constructor's applications and thus is user-defined. The correct way to define a destructor is to reproduce the class' definition (as done for the constructor), but with the addition of the tilde operator (~). Destructors contain no arguments and do not require a data type. Classes should be written to include only one destructor. Destructors do not return values, nor can they be overloaded (see Example 5.27).

Example 5.27. Overloaded constructors and a destructor.

```
using System;
using System.IO;
```

```
namespace Chapter5 {
    class BankAccount {
        public decimal InterestRate;
        public decimal LoanRate;

        // Default Constructor
        public BankAccount() {
            InterestRate = .03M;
            LoanRate = .13M;
        }

        // Overloaded Constructor
        public BankAccount(decimal IRate) {
            InterestRate = .03M;
            LoanRate = .13M;
        }

        // Overloaded Constructor
        public BankAccount(decimal IRate, decimal LoanRate) {
            IntercstRate = .03M;
            LoanRate = .13M;
        }

        // Destructor
        ~BankAccount(){}
    }

    class Class1 {
        static void Main() {
            BankAccount account = new BankAccount();
        }
    }
}
```

Introducing Operator Overloading

Another feature available to us through the use of class manipulations is the ability to overload operators. *Operator overloading* is the reapplication of operators to include class manipulations. The standard class operator overloads include *object-to-object* and *object-to-numeric* values (including variables). Traditionally, C++ overloaded operators included *stream-insertion* (<<), *stream-extraction* (>>), and *array notation* ([ ]), but C# has limited the number of operaters that can be overloaded (see Table 5.1). The most important point when dealing with operator overloading is understanding that all abbreviated forms should be made implicit, that is, anyone who references it should inherently know any action implied by an overloaded operator. To accomplish this we need only to take note of the implied meaning before the operator is expanded. For example when working with simple addition, we might conclude that the equation $x = 4 + 2$ returns the value 6. This observation would be based on the implied understanding of the "+" symbol. If we were to abuse the overloading process to include $x = 4/2$ (equaling 6) this would not be inherently implied, thus it could potentially confuse the programmer.

To understand the reasoning behind the application of overloaded operators, simply redefine the task to meet the need. For example, by converting the first value, 4, into a public class member, (Class.number = 4; and X = Class.number + 2;), the numeric calculations would not be altered and operator overloading would not be necessary. In addition, by converting that value into a private class member using a get or read function to retrieve that value (short Class.ReadValue() {return(this.number); } "X = Class.ReadValue() + 2;"), overloading would remain unnecessary. Further, if we express the object Class to imply Class.number, but replace the cumbersome operation of relaying that value through a get or read function with that of a nested class component, the same implicit reasoning still applies ("X = Class.ComponentNumber + 2;"). However, while this is mathematically sound, it is not inherently understood by the computer. Thus, in order to define the action of adding an implied class member to that of a numeric value, it is necessary to build a secondary application for the "+" operator, which, of course, is an overloaded version of that operator, hence the term operator overloading.

+	-	*	/	%	^
>	<	>=	<=	==	!=
>>	<<	!	++	—	~
true	false	|	&		

Table 5.1. C# overload operators.

Again, while C# doesn't formally allow for the overloading of the assignment operator (=), classes can be copied using the built-in function. It should also be noted that whenever any of the mathematical operators (+, -, *, /) are overloaded, the companion shortcuts are implied (+=, -=, *=, /=); see Example 5.28.

Example 5.28. Introducing operator overloading.

```
using System;

namespace ConsoleApplication1 {
    public class Objects {
        int Number;

        public Objects(int value) {
            this.Number = value;
        }

        public static Objects operator +(Objects Ob, int value) {
            Ob.Number += value;
            return(Ob);
        }

        public static Objects operator +(Objects Ob, Objects Ob2) {
            Ob.Number += Ob2.Number;
            return(Ob);
        }

        public static Objects operator -(Objects Ob, int value) {
            Ob.Number -= value;
            return(Ob);
        }

        public static Objects operator -(Objects Ob, Objects Ob2) {
            Ob.Number -= Ob2.Number;
            return(Ob);
        }

        public static Objects operator *(Objects Ob, int value) {
            Ob.Number *= value;
            return(Ob);
        }
```

```csharp
    public static Objects operator *(Objects Ob, Objects Ob2) {
        Ob.Number *= Ob2.Number;
        return(Ob);
    }

    public static Objects operator /(Objects Ob, int value) {
        Ob.Number /= value;
        return(Ob);
    }

    public static Objects operator /(Objects Ob, Objects Ob2) {
        Ob.Number /= Ob2.Number;
        return(Ob);
    }

    static void Main() {
        Objects Class1 = new Objects(4);
        Objects Class2 = new Objects(2);
        // Standard arithmetic
        Class1.Number += 2;
        Console.WriteLine(Class1.Number);

        Class1.Number -= 2;
        Console.WriteLine(Class1.Number);

        Class1.Number *= 2;
        Console.WriteLine(Class1.Number);

        Class1.Number /= 2;
        Console.WriteLine(Class1.Number);

        // Object-to-numeric value (or variable)
        Class1 += 2;
        Console.WriteLine(Class1.Number);

        Class1 -= 2;
        Console.WriteLine(Class1.Number);

        Class1 *= 2;
        Console.WriteLine(Class1.Number);

        Class1 /= 2;
        Console.WriteLine(Class1.Number);
```

```
            // Object-to-Object
            Class1 += Class2;
            Console.WriteLine(Class1.Number);

            Class1 -= Class2;
            Console.WriteLine(Class1.Number);

            Class1 *= Class2;
            Console.WriteLine(Class1.Number);

            Class1 /= Class2;
            Console.WriteLine(Class1.Number);
        }
    }
}
```

Overloading Comparison Operators

Another important type of overloading involves the use of the comparison operators. Here, we'll want to use the Boolean data type with our choice of constants, variables, and object references. We'll also need to include matching comparisons, like greater than and less than symbols, for each overload (see Example 5.29).

Example 5.29. Overloading comparison operators.

```
using System;

namespace Chapter5 {
    class Objects {
        int Number;

        // Constructor
        public Objects(int Value) {
            this.Number = Value;
        }

        public static bool operator>(Objects One, Objects Two) {
            return(One.Number > Two.Number);
        }

        public static bool operator<(Objects One, Objects Two) {
            return(One.Number < Two.Number);
        }
```

```csharp
    public static bool operator<(Objects One, int Value) {
        return(One.Number < Value);
    }

    public static bool operator>(Objects One, int Value) {
        return(One.Number > Value);
    }

    public static bool operator<=(Objects One, Objects Two) {
        return(One.Number <= Two.Number);
    }

    public static bool operator>=(Objects One, Objects Two) {
        return(One.Number >= Two.Number);
    }

    public static bool operator<=(Objects One, int Value) {
        return(One.Number <= Value);
    }

    public static bool operator>=(Objects One, int Value) {
        return(One.Number >= Value);
    }

    static void Main() {
        Objects Class1 = new Objects(4);
        Objects Class2 = new Objects(2);

        // Object-to-numeric value (or variable)
        if (Class1 > 2)
            Console.WriteLine(true);
        if (Class1 < 2)
            Console.WriteLine(true);   // false
        if (Class1 >= 2)
            Console.WriteLine(true);

        // Object-to-Object
        if (Class1 > Class2)
            Console.WriteLine(true);
        if (Class1 < Class2)
            Console.WriteLine(true); // false
        if (Class1 >= Class2)
            Console.WriteLine(true);
    }
  }
}
```

Nesting Overloaded Operators

Another interesting feature that we will want to exploit is the ability to include overloaded operators as part of a subclass or nested class. This allows for several distinct manipulations, which include the ability to reference specific functions and/or specific object references from within our main class. For example, if we were to write the program in Example 5.30 to include two independent classes, we would not be able to reference both classes' sets of objects interdependently, which would force us to do most of our calculation externally. This would also require us to revise the nested class' private members to be included as public references, which would work against our ultimate goal of complete encapsulation (see Example 5.30).

Example 5.30. Nesting overloaded operators.

```
using System;

namespace Chapter5 {
    public class PeriodicTable {
        public class Atoms {
            public string Symbol;
            public int Number;
            public decimal Weight;

            public Atoms() {}

            public Atoms(string Symbol, int Number, decimal Weight) {
                this.Symbol = Symbol;
                this.Number = Number;
                this.Weight = Weight;
            }

            public static bool operator == (PeriodicTable.Atoms NE,
                Atoms At) {
                return (NE.Weight == At.Weight);
            }

            public static bool operator != (PeriodicTable.Atoms NE,
                Atoms At) {
                return (NE.Weight != At.Weight);
            }
```

```csharp
        public override int GetHashCode(){
            return this.GetHashCode();
        }

        public override bool Equals(object Ob) {
            return(this.Equals(Ob));
        }
    }

    public PeriodicTable.Atoms Hydrogen =
        new PeriodicTable.Atoms("H", 1, 1.0079M);
    public PeriodicTable.Atoms Helium =
        new PeriodicTable.Atoms("He", 2, 4.00260M);
    public PeriodicTable.Atoms Lithium =
        new PeriodicTable.Atoms("Li", 3, 6.941M);
    public PeriodicTable.Atoms Beryllium =
        new PeriodicTable.Atoms("Be", 4, 9.01218M);
    public PeriodicTable.Atoms Boron =
        new PeriodicTable.Atoms("B", 5, 10.81M);
    // ...
    public PeriodicTable.Atoms Unnilhexium =
        new PeriodicTable.Atoms("Unh", 106, 263M);

    static void Main() {
        PeriodicTable AllElements = new PeriodicTable();
        PeriodicTable.Atoms NewElement =
            new PeriodicTable.Atoms("XXX", 10, 1.0079M);

        if (NewElement.Weight == AllElements.Hydrogen.Weight)
            Console.WriteLine("Hydrogen Match!");
        else if (NewElement.Weight == AllElements.Helium.Weight)
            Console.WriteLine("Helium Match!");
        else if (NewElement.Weight == AllElements.Unnilhexium.Weight)
            Console.WriteLine("Unnilhexium Match!");
         else
            Console.WriteLine("You've discovered a new element! \n");
    }
  }
}
```

Overloading Unary Operators

There are several rather practical manipulations that involve overloading *unary operators*. One such example would include the use of the `not` operator. This unary operator could be used to simultaneously access a Boolean component while inverting its stored value. Other useful modifiers are the *incrementing* and *decrementing* operators, and the negative notation; inserted in front of a class component's value, they are often used to indicate a reverse in direction and/or an implied mathematical reference (Example 5.31 explores the implementation of these concepts).

Example 5.31. Overloading unary operators.

```
using System;

namespace Chapter5 {
    public class Television {
        public bool Power;
        public short Channel;

        public Television() {
            this.Channel = 2;
            this.Power = false;
        }

        public static bool operator !(Television TV) {
            return(!TV.Power);
        }

        public static Television operator ++(Television TV) {
            TV.Channel++;
            return(TV);
        }

        public static Television operator --(Television TV) {
            TV.Channel--;
            return(TV);
        }

        static void Main() {
            Television TV = new Television();
            if (!TV)
                Console.Write("The TV is not turned on. \n");
```

```
            TV++;
            TV--;
        }
    }
}
```

Introducing Inheritance

It is through the use of *inherited classes*, their virtual functions, and the methods and fields used to construct those classes that transforms this definition from abstraction to a tangible coding methodology. The theory behind object-oriented programming embraces three key principles: encapsulation, inheritance, and polymorphism. It is natural, then, to include in those principles, a generic reusability and a hierarchical structure.

Inheritance is the ability of a specialized, or *derived*, class to appropriate the coding included in an abstract or base class. This appropriation allows for the readministration of the base class' attributes without the cost of redevelopment and testing usually found when attempting to expand upon a previously developed component. Hence, a derived class is a combination of its unique coding and that of the linked coding. Once a derived class is established, it too becomes subject to other derived classes, or what can be thought of as a string of inherited classes. This should not be confused with the term *multiple inheritance*, which signifies the conjoining of two or more distinctly different classes to create an all-purpose class. With single inheritance, each level takes on the attributes of all of the previous levels, creating a hierarchical structure that is based on abstraction rather than distinction, and is therefore the preferred method. Inherited classes are also subject to the three levels of access: `public`, `protected`, and `private`. Our first two examples define a simple, publicly inherited class as it relates to a set of public and protected accessible member variables and functions (see Examples 5.32 and 5.33).

> While C++ is still backward compatible with multiply-inherited structures, C# is not, thus such techniques will not be discussed.

Example 5.32. Public inheritance with public members.

```
using System;

namespace Chapter5 {
    public class BaseClass {
```

```
            public short Width, Length;

            public BaseClass() {}
            public BaseClass(short w, short l) {
                Width = w;
                Length = l;
            }

            public static void ReadWidth(BaseClass X) {
                Console.WriteLine(X.Width);
            }

            public static void ReadLength(BaseClass X) {
                Console.WriteLine(X.Length);
            }
        }

        public class DerivedClass : BaseClass {
            DerivedClass(short w, short l) {
                Width = w;
                Length = l;
            }

            public static void DisplayArea(DerivedClass Y) {
                Console.WriteLine("Area = " + Y.Width*Y.Length);
            }

            static void Main() {
                DerivedClass Instance = new DerivedClass(5, 6);
                ReadWidth(Instance);
                ReadLength(Instance);
                DisplayArea(Instance);
            }
        }
    }
```

Example 5.33. Public inheritance with protected members.

```
using System;

namespace Chapter5 {
    public class BaseClass {
        protected short Width, Length;

        public BaseClass() {}
        public BaseClass(short w, short l) {
            Width = w;
```

```
            Length = l;
        }

        public static void ReadWidth(BaseClass X) {
            Console.WriteLine(X.Width);
        }

        public static void ReadLength(BaseClass X) {
            Console.WriteLine(X.Length);
        }
    }
    public class DerivedClass : BaseClass {
        DerivedClass(short w, short l) {
            Width = w;
            Length = l;
        }

        public static void DisplayArea(DerivedClass Y) {
            Console.WriteLine("Area = " + Y.Width * Y.Length);
        }

        static void Main() {
            DerivedClass Instance = new DerivedClass(5, 6);
            ReadWidth(Instance);
            ReadLength(Instance);
            DisplayArea(Instance);
        }
    }
}
```

Inheritance versus Composition

Inheritance and composition describe two similar but distinct types of references. Composition is formed under a "has a" standard. In other words, a shared class "has a" relationship with a linking class. In contrast, the base component of an inherited class doesn't just "have a" relationship with its derived class, but instead, rather, the derived class "is an" object of the base class. This relationship transcends the objects in question and speaks to the very nature of the components. For example, if we were to say that we had a horse and carriage, it would imply that the horse was needed to pull that carriage. The carriage, then, "has a" relationship connecting its use with the horse. Yet, if we were to say that the carriage was made out of wood, it would be understood that the wood "is a" part of the carriage, just as the base class becomes a part of the inherited class.

Inheriting Constructors and Destructors

As explained in earlier sections, an I is a member function often used to initialize objects as pertaining to the values presented in their declarations, or thereby calculated as part of that class. The initialization is done automatically (at the moment of declaration), with reference to one of possibly several overloading constructor references. Once an inherited class is introduced, this initialization is compounded with the need for both a base class initialization and an inherited class initialization. Base class constructors, however, are not inherited by derived classes, and thus do not need to be overloaded or overridden. The order of derivation with regards to a constructor of an inherited class is always linked from the base class to the derived class, with the reverse order for the destructor (from the derived class to the base class).

`private` versus `protected` Inheritance

Earlier in this chapter `private` and `protected` members seemed almost interchangeable. That is, each protected against unauthorized referencing, granting access to only the properly labeled member functions; they allowed for predicate/utility member functions; and they both seemed to work well with the nested and inherited classes. The uniqueness of the protected class became evident when attempting to access a private member variable from inside an inherited class (review Examples 5.33 and 5.34). In these differing cases, we found that the protected modifier acted much more like the public modifier than its private counterpart, in that it enabled public access to the inherited class while still enforcing its rule of privacy on the accompanying program. To the same extent, the protected inherent classes allow for the sharing of data base and derived classes, but private fields and methods do not, thus they require methods to retrieve that data (see Examples 5.34 and 5.35).

Example 5.34. Public inheritance with protected methods and fields.

```
using System;

namespace Chapter5 {
    public class BaseClass {
        protected short Width, Length;

        protected BaseClass() {}
        protected BaseClass(short w, short l) {
```

Chapter 5: Object-Oriented Design

```
            Width = w;
            Length = l;
        }

        protected static short ReadWidth(BaseClass X) {
            return(X.Width);
        }

        protected static short ReadLength(BaseClass X) {
            return(X.Length);
        }
    }

    public class DerivedClass : BaseClass {
        DerivedClass(short w, short l) {
            Width = w; Length = l;
        }

        protected static void DisplayArea(DerivedClass Y) {
            Console.WriteLine("Area = " + Y.Width * Y.Length);
        }

        static void Main() {
            DerivedClass Instance = new DerivedClass(5, 6);
            Console.WriteLine(ReadWidth(Instance));
            Console.WriteLine(ReadLength(Instance));
            DisplayArea(Instance);
        }
    }
}
```

Example 5.35. Public inheritance with private methods and fields.

```
using System;

namespace Chapter5 {
    public class BaseClass {
        private short Width;
        private short Length;

        protected BaseClass() {}
        protected BaseClass(short w, short l) {
            Width = w;
            Length = l;
        }
```

```csharp
        protected static short ReadWidth(BaseClass X) {
            return(X.Width);
        }

        public static void SetWidth(BaseClass X, short w) {
            X.Width = w;
        }

        protected static short ReadLength(BaseClass X) {
            return(X.Length);
        }

        public static void SetLength(BaseClass X, short l) {
            X.Length = l;
        }
    }

    public class DerivedClass : BaseClass {
        DerivedClass(short w, short l) {
            SetWidth(this, w);
            SetLength(this, l);
        }

        protected static void DisplayArea(DerivedClass Y) {
            Console.WriteLine("Area = " + ReadWidth(Y) * ReadLength(Y));
        }

        static void Main() {
            DerivedClass Instance = new DerivedClass(5, 6);
            Console.WriteLine(ReadWidth(Instance));
            Console.WriteLine(ReadLength(Instance));
            DisplayArea(Instance);
        }
    }
}
```

Using Multiply Linked Single-Inheritance

Once an inherited class is developed, it is subject to any renderings of the prior inherited class. The combined attributes become part of the third object, with the exception of the constructor functions and the assignment statements, since neither of these are passed to an inheriting class. Again, the level of access granted to the inheriting class is primarily based on the security established by the specified members. Once a secondary inherited class is established, it too, becomes subject to other potentially inherited classes, and again, all security levels are enforced (see Example 5.36).

Example 5.36. Linking classes.

```
using System;

namespace Chapter5 {
    public class BaseClass {
        protected short Width, Length;

        protected BaseClass() {}
        protected BaseClass(short w, short l) {
            Width = w;
            Length = l;
        }

        protected static short ReadWidth(BaseClass X) {
            return (X.Width);
        }

        protected static short ReadLength(BaseClass X) {
            return(X.Length);
        }
    }

    public class DerivedClass : BaseClass {
        protected DerivedClass() {}
        protected DerivedClass(short w, short l) {
            Width = w;
            Length = l;
        }

        protected static void DisplayArea(DerivedClass Y) {
            Console.WriteLine("Area = " + Y.Width*Y.Length);
        }
    }

    public class DerivedX : DerivedClass {
        protected DerivedX(short w, short l) {
            Width = w;
```

```
            Length = 1;
        }

        protected static void DisplayArea(DerivedX Z) {
            Console.WriteLine("Area = " + Z.Width * Z.Length);
        }

        protected static void Triangle(DerivedX Z) {
            Console.WriteLine("The Area of the Triangle is " + .5 *
                Z.Width * Z.Length);
        }

        static void Main() {
            DerivedX Instance = new DerivedX(5, 6);
            Console.WriteLine(ReadWidth(Instance));
            Console.WriteLine(ReadLength(Instance));
            DisplayArea(Instance);
            Triangle(Instance);
        }
    }
}
```

Overriding and Virtual Methods

In addition to overloading a function (i.e., changing the signature or parameters of that function), we can also `override` a function so as to force the compiler to accept a secondary version of that function. As its name implies, the keyword `override` is used to override members inherited from a base class. These inherited methods must have matching signatures and be either virtual, abstract, or previously overridden. Overriding also allows us to manipulate a program's data so as to give it the illusion of consistency or to save the trouble of revising a previous class. The secondary version of the function is the obvious choice, as our instance was declared as part of that inherited class. On a cautionary note, it should also be mentioned that if any overriding functions also reference their base version (as is commonly done with privately inherited classes), that function's reference will be diverted back to the inherited function (we can also return access to the original method via the *base* command).

Following this same line of reasoning, we might mistakenly conclude that privately passed inherited classes are only accessible through internal use as with predicate and/or other unity type functions. However, this is not the case, since all the techniques used to access a standard yet privately controlled class are also available from within the derived class. Once a need for a privately inherited class is established, the correct approach is to create a set of member functions that relies on indirect access, thus creating a relay from the inherited to base functions, hence the Set methods.

The keyword `virtual` is a modifier that sets a method of a base class so that it can be overridden in a derived class. When a `virtual` function is referenced it searches for an overriding method. Overriding, as explained above, forces the compiler to accept a secondary version of that function as related to a secondary/inherited class. The polymorphic effect is accomplished at runtime (known as late binding) rather then at compilation (known as early binding), as was the case with operator and member style overloading. `virtual` functions are declared using the standard member's declaration preceded by the keyword `virtual`. Neither constructors or friend functions can be accessed using this method, but `virtual` destructors are allowed (see Example 5.37). In contrast to the definition of an overloading function, a function that is overridden must include an identical list of parameters.

> Inherited classes that do not include properly overwritten virtual functions are then subject to the default virtual functions included in their base classes. If a multilevel inherited class cannot find a properly declared virtual function, it may mistakenly revert through each inherited class until an appropriate function is found.

Example 5.37. Linking classes with keywords override and virtual.

```
using System;

namespace Chapter5 {
    public class Area {
        public short Base, Height;
        public double Radius;
        public short Base2;
```

```csharp
        public Area() {}
        public Area(short w, short h) {
            Base = w;
            Height = h;
        }

        public Area(double r) {
            Radius = r;
        }

        public Area(short a, short b, short h) {
            Base = a;
            Base2 = b;
            Height = h;
        }

        public static short ReadBase(Area X) {
            return(X.Base);
        }

        public static void SetBase(Area X, short a) {
            X.Base = a;
        }

        public static void SetBase2(Area X, short b) {
            X.Base2 = b;
        }

        public static short ReadHeight(Area X) {
            return(X.Height);
        }

        public static void SetHeight(Area X, short h) {
            X.Height = h;
        }

        public static double ReadRadius(Area X) {
            return(X.Radius);
        }

        public static void SetRadius(Area X, double r) {
            X.Radius = r;
        }
```

```csharp
    public static double SumOfBases(Area X) {
        return(X.Base+X.Base2);
    }

    public virtual void CalculateArea() {
        Console.WriteLine("No Shape Found\n");
    }
}

public class Parallelogram: Area {
    public Parallelogram(short w, short l) {
        SetBase(this, w);
        SetHeight(this, l);
    }

    override public void CalculateArea() {
        Console.WriteLine("Area  = " + ReadBase(this) *
            ReadHeight(this));
    }
}

public class Triangle : Area {
    public Triangle(short w, short l) {
        SetBase(this, w); SetHeight(this, l);}
    override public void CalculateArea() {
        Console.WriteLine("\n Area = " + (ReadBase(this) *
            ReadHeight(this)) / 2);}
}

public class Circle : Area {
    public double PI = 3.1415926535897932384626433832795;
    public Circle(double r) {
        SetRadius(this, r);
    }

    override public void CalculateArea() {
        Console.WriteLine("\n Area = " + (PI * ReadRadius(this) *
            ReadRadius(this)));
    }
}

public class Trapezoid : Area {
    public Trapezoid(short a, short b, short h) {
        SetBase(this, a);
```

```csharp
        SetBase2(this, b);
        SetHeight(this, h);
    }

    override public void CalculateArea() {
        Console.WriteLine("\n Area = " + ReadHeight(this) *
            (SumOfBases(this)) / 2);
    }

    public static void CalculateArea(Area Relay) {
        Relay.CalculateArea();
    }

    static void Main() {
        Area Shape = new Area();

        Parallelogram Shape1 = new Parallelogram(5, 5);
        CalculateArea(Shape1);

        Parallelogram Shape2 = new Parallelogram(5, 6);
        CalculateArea(Shape2);

        Triangle Shape3 = new Triangle(5, 6);
        CalculateArea(Shape3);

        Circle Shape4 = new Circle(3);
        CalculateArea(Shape4);

        Trapezoid Shape5 = new Trapezoid(4, 5, 6);
        CalculateArea(Shape5);
    }
}
}
```

Inherited `virtual` functions are considered virtual by default, thus the use of the keyword `virtual` is considered optional and is generally only restated for program clarity. Therefore, application of a `virtual` function should include some type of generalized retrieving notation.

> As stated and restated throughout this chapter, our primary goal is to develop abstract objected-oriented classes to be used as both a foundation and a reusable base that will move us into the higher levels of programming. Therefore, our development of classes must include completely abstracted versions of both member functions and their variables, so that base classes are capable of adapting to a host of scenarios such as calculating either whole or floating-point values, defining Boolean types, and referencing characters without the need to revise our coding. This should be a sustained goal as both a student of C# and throughout your future as a programmer.

Abstract

Another useful feature when dealing with inheritance is the ability to declare a class using an *abstract modifier*, which is a modifier that alters the application of a class by allowing it to be used as a reference only by other inheriting classes. The practical application of abstract modifiers becomes obvious as we restric base references in order to produce a large base of generic classes. Abstract classes cannot be instantiated, nor can they be modified with a sealed modifier (sealed modifiers are defined later in this chapter). Only abstract classes may use abstract methods and abstract accessors, but all nonabstract classes derived from such classes must include implementations of the abstract references to guarantee that those methods will be referenced from the derived class. Abstract methods are also implicitly virtual, thus, that distinction need not be declared. Inheriting classes wishing to duplicate static methods referenced from within an abstract base must also include an *overriding modifier*.

> Individual properties declared with an abstract modifier reference cannot also contain a static modifier (see Example 5.38).

Example 5.38. Abstract base class.

```csharp
using System;

namespace Chapter5 {
    public abstract class Area {
        public short Base, Height;
        public double Radius;
        public short Base2;

        public Area() {}

        public Area(short w, short h) {
            Base = w;
            Height = h;
        }

        public Area(double r) {
            Radius = r;
        }

        public Area(short a, short b, short h) {
            Base = a;
            Base2 = b;
            Height = h;
        }

        public static short ReadBase(Area X) {
            return(X.Base);
        }

        public static void SetBase(Area X, short a) {
            X.Base = a;
        }

        public static void SetBase2(Area X, short b) {
            X.Base2 = b;
        }

        public static short ReadHeight(Area X) {
            return(X.Height);
        }

        public static void SetHeight(Area X, short h) {
            X.Height = h;
```

```csharp
    }

    public static double ReadRadius(Area X) {
        return(X.Radius);
    }

    public static void SetRadius(Area X, double r) {
        X.Radius = r;
    }

    public static double SumOfBases(Area X) {
        return(X.Base + X.Base2);
    }

    public virtual void CalculateArea() {
        Console.WriteLine("No Shape Found\n");
    }

    public static void CalculateArea(Area Relay) {
        Relay.CalculateArea();
    }

    static void Main() {
        Parallelogram Shape1 = new Parallelogram(5, 5);
        CalculateArea(Shape1);

        Parallelogram Shape2 = new Parallelogram(5, 6);
        CalculateArea(Shape2);

        Triangle Shape3 = new Triangle(5, 6);
        CalculateArea(Shape3);

        Circle Shape4 = new Circle(3);
        CalculateArea(Shape4);

        Trapezoid Shape5 = new Trapezoid(4, 5, 6);
        CalculateArea(Shape5);
    }
}

public class Parallelogram : Area {
    public Parallelogram(short w, short l) {
        SetBase(this, w);
        SetHeight(this, l);
    }
```

```csharp
            override public void CalculateArea() {
                Console.WriteLine("Area  = " + ReadBase(this) *
                    ReadHeight(this));
            }
        }

        public class Triangle : Area {
            public Triangle(short w, short l) {
                SetBase(this, w);
                SetHeight(this, l);
            }

            override public void CalculateArea() {
                Console.WriteLine("\n Area = " + (ReadBase(this) *
                    ReadHeight(this)) / 2);
            }
        }

        public class Circle : Area {
            public double PI = 3.1415926535897932384626433832795;
            public Circle(double r) {
                SetRadius(this, r);
            }

            override public void CalculateArea() {
                Console.WriteLine("\n Area = " + (PI * ReadRadius(this) *
                    ReadRadius(this)));
            }
        }

        public class Trapezoid : Area {
            public Trapezoid(short a, short b, short h) {
                SetBase(this, a);
                SetBase2(this, b);
                SetHeight(this, h);
            }

            override public void CalculateArea() {
                Console.WriteLine("\n Area = " + ReadHeight(this) *
                    (SumOfBases(this)) / 2);
            }
        }
    }
}
```

The Keyword *base*

As we continue to work with inherited classes, we find ourselves running into the problem of redundant member references or repeated name use. This wouldn't normally create a problem, unless we also ran into the special circumstance of needing to reference the original base member from within an inherited class. The solution is fairly simple, achieved by applying a *base reference indicator*, or delineated member identifier, as shown in Example 5.39.

> Base references can be used with all aspects of an inheriting class, but their referencing methods cannot include a static modifier.

Example 5.39. The keyword base.

```
using System;

namespace Chapter5 {
    public class BaseClass {
        protected short Width, Length;

        public BaseClass() {}

        public BaseClass(short w, short l) {
            Width = w;
            Length = l;
        }

        public static void ReadWidth(BaseClass X) {
            Console.WriteLine(X.Width);
        }
        public static void ReadLength(BaseClass X) {
            Console.WriteLine(X.Length);
        }
```

```
        public virtual void DisplayArea(DerivedClass Y) {
            Console.WriteLine("Area = " + Y.Width * Y.Length);
        }
    }

    public class DerivedClass : BaseClass {
        DerivedClass(short w, short l) {
            Width = w;
            Length = l;
        }

        public override void DisplayArea(DerivedClass Y) {
            base.DisplayArea(Y);
        }

        static void Main() {
            DerivedClass Instance = new DerivedClass(5, 6);
            ReadWidth(Instance);
            ReadLength(Instance);
            Instance.DisplayArea(Instance);
        }
    }
}
```

Exception Handling

Another feature that adds sophistication to our programs is the ability to catch *exception errors*. Exception errors are errors thrown by a program/Windows during execution, and can range from simple input errors to problems such as missing files, division by zero, etc. All questionable coding is placed inside of what is known as a *try block*, which is a block of coding that may or may not succeed. If this coding does fail, the program immediately turns to a *catch block* (or an assortment of *catch* blocks), which can be either general or specific. Upon completion of either the *try* or the *catch* block, a tertiary block is executed, known as the *final* or *finally block*, which is always executed upon the termination of *try* and *catch* blocks (see Examples 5.40 and 5.41).

Example 5.40. General catch.

```csharp
using System;

namespace Chapter5 {
    public class Errors {
        static void Main() {
            int eight = 8, zero = 0;

            try {
                Console.WriteLine(eight / zero);
            } catch {
                Console.WriteLine("Error Detected");
            } finally {
                Console.WriteLine("Program Complete!");
            }
        }
    }
}
```

Example 5.41. Specific catch.

```csharp
using System;

namespace Chapter5 {
    public class Errors {
        static void Main() {
            int eight = 8, zero = 0;

            try {
                Console.WriteLine(eight / zero);
            } catch (DivideByZeroException) {
                Console.WriteLine("Error: Attempting to Divide by Zero");
            } catch {
                Console.WriteLine("Error Detected");
            } finally {
                Console.WriteLine("Program Complete!");
            }
        }
    }
}
```

Nested *try* Blocks

`Try` block structures can be nested to protect against a host of errors and/or deliberately flawed user inputs (see Example 5.42).

> The *null* reference refers to an object that has not yet been assigned; it basically serves as a blank or nonvalue that can be substituted for later. It is also the default value to any nonassigned reference types, and it can be used to mark a position where no actual reference is needed.

Example 5.42. Nested try blocks.

```
/* Nested try-blocks */
using System;

namespace Chapter5 {
   public class Errors {
      static void Main() {
         int X, Y;

         Console.WriteLine("Let's divide some numbers...");

         while(true) {
            Console.Write("Enter your numerator now: ");
            X = int.Parse(Console.ReadLine());
            Console.Write("Enter your denominator now: ");
            Y = int.Parse(Console.ReadLine());

            try {
               Console.WriteLine(X / Y);
            } catch (DivideByZeroException) {
               Console.WriteLine("Division by Zero Attempted!\n");
               Console.Write("Please enter a new denominator now: ");
               Y = int.Parse(Console.ReadLine());
               try {
                  Console.WriteLine(X / Y);
               } catch {
                  Console.WriteLine("Error!");
                  break;
```

```
            }
        } catch {
            Console.WriteLine("Error Detected");
        }
    }
  }
 }
}
```

The Keyword `throw`

In addition to being able to `try-catch` both generalized and specific exceptions, we can also learn to `throw`, and, subsequently, `recatch` those exceptions. These new exceptions can then be used to readdress our initial responses with specific error correction techniques and/or allow for additional exceptions to be caught. However, if no associated catches are found, the line of processing is sent back to the .Net framework, which ultimately halts the program.

A specific response requires a static method from within the main class, or a nonstatic method as part of a secondary class. The new exception will then be recaptured by the secondary catch clause. Notice that the second clause is specifically set up to repeat whatever quote is included with that method's exception; if needed, we could include a host of exception classes, all using the same type of message reflecting (see Example 5.43).

Example 5.43. Clarifying exceptions—the keyword `throw`.

```
using System;

namespace Chapter5 {
    public class Errors {
        static void Main() {
            string Input;
            int X, Y;

            Console.WriteLine("Let's divide some numbers...");

            while(true) {
                Console.Write("Enter your numerator now: ");
                Input = Console.ReadLine();

                if (char.IsNumber(Input, 0)) {
                    X = int.Parse(Input);
```

```
            } else {
               throw new DivideByZeroException("\nProgram Error!");
            }

            Console.Write("Enter your denominator now: ");
            Input = Console.ReadLine();

            if (char.IsNumber(Input, 0)) {
               Y = int.Parse(Input);
            } else {
               throw new DivideByZeroException("\nProgram Error!");
            }

            try {Console.WriteLine(X / Y);
            } catch(DivideByZeroException) {
               Console.WriteLine("Division by Zero attempted!\n");
               Console.Write("Please enter a new denominator now: ");
               Y = char.Parse(Console.ReadLine());
                try {
                   Console.WriteLine(X / Y);
                } catch {Console.WriteLine("Error!");
                   break;
                }
            } catch {
               Console.WriteLine("Error Detected");
            }
         }
      }
   }
}
```

User-Defined Exception Classes

Occasionally, we'll want to define our own exception classes. These are special case exceptions that may require additional information and/or input. An exception class is an inherited class that is derived (either directly or indirectly) from a key base class (namely System.ApplicationException). In all other respects, an exception class mimics the rules of a standard inherited class (see Example 5.44).

Example 5.44. User-defined exceptions.

```csharp
using System;

namespace Chapter5 {
    public class MyException : System.ApplicationException {
        public MyException(string Comment) : base(Comment) {}
    }

    public class Errors {
        static void Main() {
            Errors Er = new Errors();
            Er.TryMethod();
        }

        public void TryMethod() {
            string Input;
            int X, Y;

            Console.WriteLine("Let's divide some numbers...");

            while(true) {
                Console.Write("Enter your numerator now: ");
                Input = Console.ReadLine();

                if(char.IsNumber(Input, 0)) {
                    X = int.Parse(Input);
                } else {
                    throw new IndexOutOfRangeException("\nCharacter " +
                        "Detected where Integer Value was Excepted!");
                }

                Console.Write("Enter your denominator now: ");
                Input = Console.ReadLine();

                if (char.IsNumber(Input, 0)) {
                    Y = int.Parse(Input);
                } else {
                    throw new IndexOutOfRangeException("\nCharacter " +
                        "Detected where Integer Value was Excepted!");}

                try {
                    Console.WriteLine(X / Y);
                } catch (DivideByZeroException) {
                    Console.WriteLine("Division by Zero attempted!\n");
```

```
                Console.Write("Please enter a new denominator now: ");
                Y = char.Parse(Console.ReadLine());

                try {
                    Console.WriteLine(X / Y);
                } catch {
                    Console.WriteLine("Error!");
                    break;
                }
            } catch {
                Console.WriteLine("Error Detected");
            }
        }
      }
    }
}
```

Nested Exceptions

In addition to creating simple `try` block structures, `catches`, and class based exceptions, we can nest those exceptions to provide an even greater level of protection. Placing a second `try-catch` block inside of a secondary catch exception allows us to add a third *catchall block*, which will execute if the error was still not contained (see Examples 5.44a and 5.45b)

Example 5.45a. Nested exceptions.

```
namespace Chapter5 {
    class Mathematics {
        public static void Division(ref int X, ref int Y) {
            if (X == 0 && Y == 0) {
                X = Y = 1;
                throw new Exception("ZeroByZeroException");
            } else
                Console.WriteLine(X/Y);
        }

        public static void Main() {
            string Input;
            int X, Y;

            Console.WriteLine("Let's divide some numbers...");
```

```csharp
            while (true) {
                Console.Write("Enter your numerator now: ");
                Input = Console.ReadLine();
                X = int.Parse(Input) ;

                Console.Write("Enter your denominator now: ");
                Input = Console.ReadLine();
                Y = int.Parse(Input);

                try {
                    Division(ref X, ref Y);
                } catch (DivideByZeroException) {
                    Console.WriteLine("Attempting to divide by zero!");
                } catch (System.Exception e) {
                    Console.WriteLine(e.Message);
                     try {
                         Division(ref X, ref Y);
                     } catch {
                         Console.WriteLine("Error Detected");
                     }
                }
            }
        }
    }
}
```

Example 5.45b. Applied exceptions.

```csharp
namespace Chapter5 {
    class Mathematics {
        public static void Division(ref int X, ref int Y) {
            if (X == 0 && Y == 0) {
                X = Y = 1;
                throw new Exception("ZeroByZeroException");
            } else
                Console.WriteLine(X/Y);
        }

        public static void Main() {
            string Input;
            int X, Y;

            Console.WriteLine("Let's divide some numbers...");

            while (true) {
```

```
            Console.Wrtie("Enter your numerator now: ");
            Input = Console.ReadLine();

            try {
                X = int.Parse(Input);
            } catch (System.FormatException) {
               Console.WrtieLine("\nInvalid Input Detected!");
                continue;
            }

            Console.WriteLine("Enter your denominator now: ");
            Input = Console.ReadLine();

            try {
               Y = int.Parse(Input);
            } catch (System.FormatException) {
               Console.WriteLine("Invalid Input Detected - " +
                   "Calculation Terminated!\n");
               continue;
            }

            try {
               Division(ref X, ref Y);
            } catch (DivideByZeroException) {
               Console.WriteLine("Attempting to divide by zero!");
            } catch (System.Exception e) {
               Console.WriteLine(e.Message);
                try {
                   Division(ref X, ref Y);
                } catch {
                   Console.WrtieLine("Unrecoverable Error Detected");
                }
            }
         }
      }
   }
}
```

The Binary Operator as

The binary operator as allows for conversion of an expression to a data type. This operator is considered a more elegant data type, since its expressions can return null data and do not call exceptions. *As* expressions also require reference types and are used to express a reference type or *object* such as the formula "*expression* is *type*," which is also equivalent to a single call to "expression is type? (type) expression: (type) null" (see Example 5.46).

> The *null* reference refers to an object that has not yet been assigned; it basically serves as a blank or nonvalue, which can be substituted for later. It is also the default value to any nonassigned reference types, and can be used to mark a position where no actual reference is needed.

Example 5.46. The binary operator `as`.

```
using System;

namespace Chapter5 {
    public class TestAS {
        public static void Main() {
            object MyString = new object();
            MyString = 123;

            string s = MyString as string;

            if (s != null)
                Console.WriteLine(MyString);
            else
                Console.WriteLine("Test Failed!");
        }
    }
}
```

Delegates

Delegates are objects used as references to encapsulate specific methods, which include signatures and formal return types. The delegate, while similar to the C++ function pointer, is actually type safe and considered OOP (Object-Oriented Programming) compliant. Delegates also allow for six key modifiers: `new`, `public`, `protected`, `internal`, `private`, and `unsafe` (`unsafe` is only used when dealing with parameters that are also pointers). Delegates are most frequently used to pass methods as parameters. Type safety is based on the matching of signatures as part of their declaration—delegates need to be declared before they are called (see Example 5.47).

Example 5.47. A simple delegate.

```
using System;

namespace Chapter5 {
    // Prototype
    public delegate void TryDelegate();

    public class Delegates {
        static void Main() {
            TryDelegate();
        }

        public static void TryDelegate() {
            Console.WriteLine("Hello World!");
        }
    }
}
```

Events

Events are used to pass information between delegates; they are null before they are referenced, and their properties must include both an add and a remove accessor. Events are used to specify delegates and are referenced at runtime; they can include multiple methods, and are applicable to other programs. When defining events, we must make sure to include a delegate. If the event is redefined, then we'll only need to reference that delegate (see Example 5.48).

Example 5.48. Events.

```
using System.Collections;

namespace Chapter5 {
    public delegate void TryDelegate(int i);

    public class EventSetup {
        private Hashtable Test = new Hashtable();

        public event TryDelegate Event {
            add {
                Test["Event"] = (TryDelegate)Test["Event"] + value;
            }
```

```
            remove {
                Test["Event"] = (TryDelegate)Test["Event"] - value;
            }
        }
    }

    public class Events {
        public static void Main() {
        }
    }
}
```

Preprocessor Directives

Preprocessor directives redirect and/or skip different portions of coding. This becomes necessary for a number of complex reasons, but the actual application of these directives are rather simple. For example, we can define an area of coding, insert clauses for execution, and include error warnings and/or data filters allowing us to test specific aspects and/or troubleshoot otherwise untestable clauses. The most commonly used preprocessor directives are the #region and #endregion markers, which are a special set of directives that can hide previously tested or otherwise cumbersome coding to allow the programmer a more comfortable view of the applications at hand. For a complete list of preprocessor definitions, see Table 5.2 (also see Example 5.49).

Example 5.49. Implementing preprocessor directives.

```
#define DebugTest
#define ReleaseTest

#if DebugTest
#undef DebugTest
#elif ReleaseTest
#warning "This is a warning!"
#else
#error "Error Detected"
#endif

using System;
namespace Chapter5 {
    class Class1 {
        static void Main() {}
    }
}
```

#define and #undef	The defined value is used like a variable and can be tested and even undefined.
#error and #warning	Error and warning work in basically the same way; both allow for a statement always placed in quotes.
#if, #elif, #else, and #endif	#if works in basically the same manner as the if statement, including the else-if (#elif) and I (#else) statement. The only addition would be the #endif which works like the standard Iblock.
#line	The line directive is used to alter output that is caught by warning and error messages. You'll need to include the line number and file name as in #line 12 "chapter5.cs."
#region and #endregion	The region and end region markers are used to mark a certain block of coding. That block can then be collapsed and even given a name.

Table 5.2. Definitions of preprocessor directives.

The external Modifier

The *external modifier* (`extern`), as its name implies, indicates that the method will be implemented externally, such as with the DllImport attribute. The external method will contain all appropriate declarations, but because it is executed outside of our programs, its declaration does not require a function body. External references do require a terminating semicolon, and they cannot be used to modify abstract classes. We can also declare our methods using external modifiers, but these methods will not include implementation, thus, their definitions will contain no bodies (these methods will also require a terminating semicolon). C++ users will find this version of *extern* a bit more constrictive (see Example 5.50).

Example 5.50. The extern modifier.

```
using System;
using System.Runtime.InteropServices;
namespace Chapter5 {
```

```csharp
public class Class1 {
    [DllImport("winmm.dll")]
    public static extern long PlaySound(String lpszName, long hModule,
        long dwFlags);

    static void Main() {
        PlaySound(@"media\Mouse.wav", 0, 0);
    }
}
}
```

The `explicit` Operator

The keyword `explicit` is used to define an explicit type conversion, which is a conversion that would not normally be allowed by basic implicit reasoning. The standard implicit types convert only from lower to higher accuracy, which prevents data loss. Occasionally, however, the programmer will want to reverse that process and formally reduce the accuracy of the data type, anticipating no relevant loss in computations. In such cases, an explicit modifier can be applied (they are used with a standard class in Example 5.51).

Example 5.51. The explicit operator.

```csharp
using System;

namespace Chapter5 {
    class IsByte {
        byte value;

        public IsByte(int value) {
            if (value < 0 || value > 255)
                throw new ArgumentException();
            this.value = (byte)value;
        }

        public static explicit operator IsByte(byte Byte) {
            return new IsByte(Byte);
        }

        public static void Main() {
            int Integer = 3;
            IsByte Byte = (IsByte)Integer;
        }
    }
}
```

The `implicit` Operator

The keyword `implicit` is used when declaring a user-defined conversion operator. Implicit conversions are called implicitly, thus they do not need to be referenced using explicit casts, increasing source code readability as well as safety. However, since implicit conversion can occur without the programmer's knowledge, care must be taken: Implicit conversions should never be allowed to throw exceptions, nor should they be allowed to truncate relevant data. Implicit classes can be defined using static modifiers and are referenced using instances (see Example 5.52).

Example 5.52. The `implicit` operator.

```
using System;

namespace Chapter5 {
    class IsByte {
        byte value;

        public IsByte(byte value) {
            this.value = value;
        }

        public static implicit operator byte(IsByte Byte) {
            return Byte.value;
        }

        public static void Main() {
            IsByte Byte = new IsByte(3);

            byte Byte2 = Byte;
        }
    }
}
```

Fixed Pointers

The keyword `fixed`, used only in unsafe mode, is a modifier that sets unmanaged pointers to managed variable locations. These positions are then fixed, which means that they won't be subject to automatic garbage collection (or random relocation): the term *pinned* is also commonly associated with this process. Pointers initialized in fixed statements cannot be modified; however, once the statement is executed, the variables are no longer pinned, hence any references to those variables should be done in the appropriate fixed reference (see Example 5.53).

Example 5.53. Fixed pointers.

```
using System;

namespace Chapter5 {
    class ClassFixed {
        public int variable;
    }

    class Class1 {
        static unsafe void Main () {
            ClassFixed TestFixed = new ClassFixed();

            Console.Write("Enter a number: ");
            TestFixed.variable = int.Parse(Console.ReadLine());

            fixed (int* pointer = &TestFixed.variable) {
                Console.WriteLine("\n{0}", TestFixed.variable);
                Console.WriteLine("\n{0}", *pointer);
            }
        }
    }
}
```

The `get` and `set` Accessors

The `get` and `set` accessors aren't officially keywords, rather, they are parameterless methods named to match certain fields, and are used in classes and interfaces that hold a body of executable data pertaining to the storage and retrieval of those fields. Their executable statements may include calculations, conversions, and a large host of other tasks, but their underlying purpose must include reading or recording those properties. The body of an accessor is considered equivalent to a method, although they do not include identity signatures. The `get` accessor returns a value and may be set to throw a value when needed; in contrast, the `set` accessor is always set to void. The keyword `value` is also used as an implicit parameter when setting our fields. Thus, `value` takes on the value of any passed variables. The `get` and the `set` accessors always share the same user-defined name, thus they cannot exist in the same base class. It is therefore considered natural to place the `set` accessor in the base class, and the `get` accessor in the nested derived class. It is also important to remember that the value retrieved by the `get` property is for reference only, while the value recorded in the `set` property is write only (see Example 5.54).

Example 5.54. The `get` and `set` accessors—linking classes.

```
using System;

namespace Chapter5 {
    public class BaseClass {
        public short width, length;

        protected BaseClass() {}

        protected BaseClass(short w, short l) {
            Width = w;
            Length = l;
        }

        public short Width {
            set {
                width = value;
            }
        }

        public short Length {
            set {
                length = value;
            }
        }
    }

    public class DerivedClass : BaseClass {
        protected DerivedClass() {}

        protected DerivedClass(short w, short l) {
            width = w;
            length = l;
        }

        public new short Width {
            get {
                return(width);
            }
```

```
        }

        public new short Length {
            get {
                return(length);
            }
        }

        protected static void DisplayArea(DerivedClass Y) {
            Console.WriteLine("Area = " + Y.Width * Y.Length);
        }
    }

    public class DerivedX : DerivedClass {
        protected DerivedX(short w, short l) {
            width = w;
            length = l;
        }

        protected static void DisplayArea(DerivedX Z) {
            Console.WriteLine("Area = " + Z.Width * Z.Length);
        }

        protected static void Triangle(DerivedX Z) {
            Console.WriteLine("The Area of the Triangle is " + .5 *
                Z.Width * Z.Length);
        }

        static void Main() {
            DerivedX Instance = new DerivedX(5, 6);
            Console.WriteLine(Instance.Width);
            Console.WriteLine(Instance.Length);
            DisplayArea(Instance);
            Triangle(Instance);
        }
    }
}
```

Linking Interfaces

An *interface* is a structured set of coding used to guarantee a basic level of execution. An interface's definition includes an attribute, an access modifier, the keyword *interface*, its identifying value, and a base list. All five of the class modifiers are also compatible with interfaces, including the protected internal modifier. Interfaces also follow the same rules of naming used by classes, methods, and simple variables. Once an interface is in place it can also be inherited, including multiple inheritances, which is not formally allowed with C# classes.

> An interface-class reference also requires that the base class be referenced first (see Example 5.55).

Example 5.55. Introducing interfaces.

```
using System;

namespace Chapter5 {
    interface BaseInterface {
        short Width {get; set;}
        short Length {get; set;}
    }

    public class BaseClass : BaseInterface {
        private short BIWidth;
        private short BILength;

        protected BaseClass() {}

        protected BaseClass(short Width, short y) {
            BIWidth = Width;
            BILength = y;
        }

        public short Width {
            get {return(BIWidth);}
            set {BIWidth = value;}
        }

        public short Length {
            get {return(BILength);}
            set {BILength = value;}
        }

        protected static short ReadWidth(BaseClass X) {
            return (X.Width);
```

```
        }

        protected static short ReadLength(BaseClass X) {
            return(X.Length);
        }
    }

    public class DerivedClass : BaseClass {
        protected DerivedClass() {}

        protected DerivedClass(short w, short l) {
            Width = w;
            Length = l;
        }

        protected static void DisplayArea(DerivedClass Y) {
            Console.WriteLine("Area = " + Y.Width * Y.Length);
        }
    }

    public class DerivedX : DerivedClass {
        protected DerivedX(short w, short l) {
            Width = w;
            Length = l;
        }

        protected static void DisplayArea(DerivedX Z) {
            Console.WriteLine("Area = " + Z.Width * Z.Length);
        }

        protected static void Triangle(DerivedX Z) {
            Console.WriteLine("The Area of the Triangle is " + .5 *
                Z.Width * Z.Length);
        }

        public static void Main() {
            DerivedX Instance = new DerivedX(5, 6);
            Console.WriteLine(ReadWidth(Instance));
            Console.WriteLine(ReadLength(Instance));
            DisplayArea(Instance);
            Triangle(Instance);
        }
    }
}
```

The `is` Operator

As we move into the use of interfaces, we'll need to test objects for compatibility errors. These tests can be done most efficiently with the `is` operator. The keyword `is`, then, is a practical expression used to determine if an object included at runtime is compatible with a given type. The `is` operator will then evaluate to true if both of the following conditions are met: The expression must not return a null value, and the expression can be cast to type (meaning that the expression will not throw an exception).

> A compile-time warning will also be issued if the expression is always shown to be either true or false, and the `is` operator cannot be overloaded (see Example 5.56).

Example 5.56. The `is` operator.

```
using System;

namespace Chapter5 {
    class TestClass {
        /* Empty */
    }

    public class Class1 {
        public static void Test(object ob) {
            TestClass test;

            if (ob is TestClass) {
                test = (TestClass)ob;
                Console.WriteLine("True");}
            else {
                Console.WriteLine("false");}
        }

        public static void Main() {
            TestClass TC = new TestClass();
            Test(TC);
        }
    }
}
```

The Keyword `lock`

A `lock` is a temporary, mutual exclusion used to ensure that multiple threads do not inadvertently access the same section of coding. The specified object, must, of course, be a reference type. If the object is a static variable, or if the critical section occurs in a static method, then the given class' expression will usually relate to a protected instance of a variable or type of class. Expressions are written as: `lock (expression), executable block`, with the expression representing the reference type, and the statement block representing the critical section to be protected (see Example 5.57)

Example 5.57. The keyword *lock*.

```
using System;
using System.Threading;

namespace Chapter5 {
    class MyName {
        private string name;
        protected MyName(string fn) {this.name = fn;}
        protected string TestName(string fn) {
            if (fn == "Sal") {
                throw new Exception("Welcome Home!");
            }

            lock (this) {
                if (fn != null) {
                    return ("nice to meet you" + this.name);
                }
            }
            return "The End";
        }

        protected void YourName() {
            Console.WriteLine("What is your name?");
            string input = Console.ReadLine();
            TestName(input);
        }

        static protected Thread[] test = new Thread[2];

        public static void Main() {
            MyName FirstName = new MyName("Salvatore");
```

```
            MyName LastName = new MyName("Buono");
            Thread first = new Thread(new
ThreadStart(FirstName.YourName));
            test[0] = first;
            test[0].Start();

            Thread last = new Thread(new ThreadStart(LastName.YourName));
            test[1] = last;
            test[1].Start();
        }
    }
}
```

The Keyword params

The keyword params, which is short for parameters, is a useful way to pass an array of any object type without the inherent requirement of explicitly declaring that the data type be declared as an array. No additional parameters may follow the definition, and only one object may be passed as a params per declaration. This method is useful when declaring an argument where the number of arguments is unknown. It is also important to remember to include read and/or out commands to avoid losing data changes (see Example 5.58).

Example 5.58. The keyword params.

```
using System;

namespace Chapter5 {
    public class Class1 {
        public static void Params(params string[] list) {
            foreach(string i in list)
                Console.Write("{0}", i);
        }

        public static void Main() {
            Params("Salvatore ", "A. ", "Buono\n");
        }
    }
}
```

The Keyword `sealed`

Occasionally, we'll want to prevent other programmers from overriding our mission critical methods. This can be done through the use of the `sealed` modifier. Once a class is sealed it can no longer be inherited, hence it cannot be overridden or altered in any other way; for this reason, we cannot use `sealed` with the abstract modifier. Refer back to the structures we learned about at the start of this chapter and note that they were also implicitly sealed, thus they cannot be inherited (see Example 5.59).

Example 5.59. The keyword `sealed`.

```
using System;
using System.IO;

namespace Chapter5 {
    sealed class BankAccount {
        public decimal InterestRate;
        public decimal LoanRate;

        // Default Constructor
        public BankAccount() {
            InterestRate = .03M;
            LoanRate = .13M;
        }

        // Overloaded Constructor
        public BankAccount(decimal IRate, decimal LoanRate) {
            InterestRate = .03M;
            LoanRate = .13M;
        }
    }

    class Class1 {
        static void Main() {
            BankAccount account = new BankAccount ();
        }
    }
}
```

The Keyword `stackalloc`

The keyword `stackalloc`, which is short for *stack allocating*, is used to allocate blocks of memory referenced from a stack (this should not be confused with the heap as explained previously). The addresses of these blocks are fixed/pinned, so they are not subject to random garbage collection, their termination linked only to the completion of those methods. A stack allocating reference is written to include three key terms: *unmanaged type*, the *pointer name*, and the *integral expression* (see Example 5.60).

Example 5.60. The keyword `stackalloc`.

```
using System;

namespace Chapter5 {
    class Class1 {
        public static unsafe void Main() {
            int* pointer1 = stackalloc int[3];
            pointer1[0] = 1;
            pointer1[1] = 2;
            pointer1[2] = 3;

            for (int i = 0; i < 3; i++)
                Console.WriteLine(pointer1[i]);
        }
    }
}
```

Metafiles Defined

Metafiles are defined as a collection of graphic functions written in the form of a binary record. Graphic functions include lines, curves, and areas, as well as text. Metafiles include specifications for coordinates, brushes, pens, and embedded bitmaps. Metafiles have the advantage of scalability without degradation, require less memory, and have a greater degree of device independence. Metafiles can also be converted into bitmaps, which can greatly reduce rendering time, though this will cause a loss in resolution. Files saved as metafiles are called *DrawStrings* and are referenced with the file extensions .emf (Enhanced Metafiles) and .wmf (Windows Metafiles). Metafiles are accessed using the standard format, e.g., Image PlayerL = Image.FromFile ("..\\..\\Player1.emf"); and Image PlayerR = Image.FromFile ("..\\..\\Player2.wmf");.

Building Game Classes

As with previous games, our next two also rely on a set of classes, their instances, and a host of methods that manipulate data to produce what we see as our cyber creations. These instances and their components were constructed using the knowledge base gathered in this chapter, it is therefore prudent to discuss these techniques here. The first class that we'll discuss is a key component in all the games; it was used to create the characters, their weapons, and nearly all of the objects that appeared on the screen.

Game Classes—AnimatedImage.cs

The class named `AnimatedImage` will be used to control our characters, including their appearance, movements, and limitations. Preceding this class we'll include a set of System references; these are required by several of the methods included in the next few sections. It is always necessary to wrap our classes inside of a clearly marked namespace, in this case the namespace Games. Then, we'll declare some fields and create our constructors (notice how essential constructor overloading becomes with regard to multiple setups—see `AnimatedImage.cs` in the Game Classes folder on the CD-ROM).

Example 5.61. AnimatedImage.cs

```
/* AnimatedImage.cs: Contains the AnimatedImage class, which is a
 * generic class capable of holding and doing animation logic for
 * an image. You can sub-class this object to customize its behavior.
 */

using System;
using System.Drawing;

namespace GameClasses {
    public class AnimatedImage {
        // Constants
        public const int DEFAULTSTEP = 3;
        public const int SOUTHWEST = 1;
        public const int SOUTH = 2;
        public const int SOUTHEAST = 3;
        public const int EAST = 4;
        public const int NORTHEAST = 5;
        public const int NORTH = 6;
```

```
            public const int NORTHWEST = 7;
            public const int WEST = 8;

            // Member data
            public int imageWidth;   // Width of the image
            public int imageHeight;  // Height of the image
            public int imagePosX;    // X Position in containing object
            public int imagePosY;    // Y Position in containing object
            public Image imageData;  // The image itself

            public int imageOffsetX; // facilitates "relative" positioning
            public int imageOffsetY; // by placing image at a specified
                                     // offset to PosX, PosY.

            public int animationStep; // How much the image should move/step

            public Rectangle constraintBox; // Our sandbox to play in
            public int direction; // current direction the image is heading
            public bool isActive; // whether the image should be animated
            public AnimatedImage owner; // if it's controlled by another image

        #region Constructors
            public AnimatedImage() : this(0,0) {} // default constructor

            public AnimatedImage(int posX, int posY) {
                imagePosX = posX;
                imagePosY = posY;
                isActive = false;
                animationStep = DEFAULTSTEP;
            }
        #endregion
            . . .
```

Remember, C# class references aren't part of the main program, so they do not require a main method. Also, it's important to note that the class is left open-ended, so as to include our methods, which are discussed over the next few sections.

Animation

Animation is the illusion of movement based on a number of elements, which include a change in background, a change in character appearance, and the actual physical displacement of an object. This section, thus, is intended to review animation not just from the standpoint of Cartesian coordinates, but also from the viewpoint of the generic method. The method `Animate ()` will be included as part of the AnimatedImage class. As a generic class/method, AnimatedImage and its component `Animate` will be/have been retrievable by all our games. The expression using GameClasses is what makes these components useable.

`Animate` is a virtual public method that does not return a type. The method includes a `switch` statement using `North, South, East,` and `West` to indicate Up, Down, Left, and Right. `Southeast, Southwest, Northeast,` and `Northwest` allow for diagonal movements.

Example 5.62. Animate objects

Here, we'll want to create our first method-notice how the name `Animate ()` conveys its meaning. Of course, it's really just a simple set of value manipulations controlled by a switch statement, but by placing it inside a class, we dramatically increase its potential.

```
// Animate() performs all position movements on the object.
virtual public void Animate() {
    switch(direction) {
       case SOUTHWEST:
           this.imagePosX -= animationStep;
           this.imagePosY += animationStep;
            break;
       case SOUTH:
           this.imagePosY += animationStep;
            break;
       case SOUTHEAST:
           this.imagePosX += animationStep;
           this.imagePosY += animationStep;
            break;
```

```
        case WEST:
            this.imagePosX -= animationStep;
            break;
        case EAST:
            this.imagePosX += animationStep;
            break;
        case NORTHWEST:
            this.imagePosX -= animationStep;
            this.imagePosY -= animationStep;
            break;
        case NORTH:
            this.imagePosY -= animationStep;
            break;
        case NORTHEAST:
            this.imagePosX += animationStep;
            this.imagePosY -= animationStep;
            break;
    }
}
```

Displaying

The standard image display is simple, having just three steps: 1) a Graphics declaration, for which we'll use the letter g; 2) the method DrawImage, which is included in the drawing Class accessed through g, as in g.DrawImage; and 3) the signatures for the DrawImage reference, e.g., the character's actual image, an *x*-coordinate, a *y*-coordinate, its width, and its height. Note that the variables listed are actually the fields declared at the top part of the class (see AnimatedImage.cs on the CD-ROM and Example 3.46 in Chapter 3).

Rescaling Images

As seen in the last section, the heights and the widths of our images play an important role in their display. The height and width, then, can be reset, increased, or decreased as needed using the method Rescale also located in the file AnimatedImage.cs (see AnimatedImage.cs on the CD-ROM and Example 3.47 in Chapter 3).

Chapter 5: Object-Oriented Design

Adding Substance to Characters

For the most part, characters are just illusions—their images don't have any real substance. Therefore, natural limitations, deflections, and even collisions will all go unnoticed by the computer, unless, of course, we write a host of methods that define those responses. All of these are relatively simple and usually only involve recording a few key points and reversing or disabling the character when he stumbles onto those points (see Examples 5.65–5.68).

Example 5.63. ContainsPoint.

```
// Determines if the point is within the confines of this image
virtual public bool ContainsPoint(int x, int y) {
    return (x >= imagePosX && x <= imagePosX + imageWidth &&
        y >= imagePosY && y <= imagePosY + imageHeight);
}
```

Here we'll need to determine if the rectangle (or wall) intersects with our character. This is done through careful comparisons of each coordinate including the image's height and width. It should be noted that this method is overloaded with one comparison made using actual points and another using the image.

Example 5.64. Intersects.

Collision detection is another key point so common to games, thus it's only logical to place it inside our class.

```
// Determines if the given rectangle intersects this image
virtual public bool Intersects(int x, int y,
    int width, int height) {
    // simple variable renaming
    int x2 = x + width, y2 = y + height, _x = imagePosX;
    int _y = imagePosY, _x2 = imagePosX + imageWidth;
    int _y2 = imagePosY + imageHeight;

    return ((x >= _x && x <= _x2) || (x2 >= _x && x2 <= _x2) ||
```

C# and Game Programming

```
                (_x >= x && _x <= x2) || (_x2 >= x && _x2 <= x2)) &&
                ((y >= _y && y <= _y2) || (y2 >= _y && y2 <= _y2) ||
                (_y >= y && _y <= y2) || (_y2 >= y && _y2 <= y2));
}

virtual public bool Intersects(AnimatedImage img) {
    return Intersects(img.imagePosX, img.imagePosY,
        img.imageWidth, img.imageHeight);
}
```

> Now that we have a handle on the universe, we'll want to focus our attention on the motions used by missiles and/or the ball. Here we'll need to divide the methods up between the potential games. Remember that we don't necessarily know how our methods will be used and/or what new games might be created after this text is published. The objects' movements break down into two possible types: standard weapons fire and the bouncing effect of the ball.

The command `ConstrainToBox` keeps the image inside the screen—the `Box` being the window and the image being our animated character. If a character attempts to move beyond the limit, the X and Y coordinates are adjusted to move him or her back.

Example 5.65. ConstrainToBox.

```
// Moves the image to be within the specified boundary.
// Returns whether any position changes were made.
virtual public bool ConstrainToBox() {
    bool retVal = false;

    if (!isActive)
        return false;

    if (imagePosX < constraintBox.X) {
        imagePosX = constraintBox.X;
        retVal = true;
    } else if ((imagePosX + imageWidth) >
        (constraintBox.X + constraintBox.Width)) {
```

```
        imagePosX = constraintBox.X +
            constraintBox.Width - imageWidth;
        retVal = true;
    }

    if (imagePosY < constraintBox.Y) {
        imagePosY = constraintBox.Y;
        retVal = true;
    } else if ((imagePosY + imageHeight) >
        (constraintBox.Y + constraintBox.Height)) {
        imagePosY = constraintBox.Y +
            constraintBox.Height - imageHeight;
        retVal = true;
    }

    return retVal;
}
```

As with `ConstrainToBox`, `Deflect` limits our character's movement. In this case, however, the character's direction is reversed, forcing our player to move in the opposite direction. The player feels bumped back as he continues to manipulate the controls in the direction he desires.

Example 5.66. Deflect.

```
// Basic deflection
// Returns whether any position changes were made.
virtual public bool Deflect(int x, int y, int width, int height) {
    if (!isActive)
        return false;

    switch(direction) {
        case SOUTHWEST:
            if (imagePosX <= x) {
                direction = SOUTHEAST;
            } else {
                direction = NORTHWEST;
            }
            break;
        case SOUTH:
            direction = NORTH;
            break;
```

```
            case SOUTHEAST:
                if ((imagePosX + imageWidth) >= (x + width)) {
                    direction = SOUTHWEST;
                } else {
                    direction = NORTHEAST;
                }
                break;
            case WEST:
                direction = EAST;
                break;
            case EAST:
                direction = WEST;
                break;
            case NORTHWEST:
                if (imagePosY <= y) {
                    direction = SOUTHWEST;
                } else {
                    direction = NORTHEAST;
                }
                break;
            case NORTH:
                direction = SOUTH;
                break;
            case NORTHEAST:
                if (imagePosY <= y) {
                    direction = SOUTHEAST;
                } else {
                    direction = NORTHWEST;
                }
                break;
        }
        return true;
    }

    // Deflect override -- deflects off of a given AnimatedImage
    virtual public bool Deflect(AnimatedImage img) {
        return Deflect(img.imagePosX, img.imagePosY,
            img.imageWidth, img.imageHeight);
    }

    // Deflect override -- deflects off of default constraint box
    virtual public bool Deflect() {
        return Deflect(constraintBox.X, constraintBox.Y,
            constraintBox.Width, constraintBox.Height);
    }
```

Creating Infinite Space

Another visual illusion or type of motion that will be handled by the AnimatedImage class can be thought of as repeating or infinite space. With the method `WrapInBox`, we can tell the computer to teleport our character from one end of the screen to the next. Since the character is not deflected, a sense of continuous movement is created. `WrapInBox` will still rely on the parameters included with `constraintBox.X` and `constraintBox.Y`. The character's height and width are also important to these calculations as a final position of our character is based on the `constraintBox` position, the `constraintBox` measure, and the image's size (see Example 3.52 in Chapter 3).

Other Types of Deflection

In addition to barriers and limitations, we can also create methods that simply change the direction of our characters. The method `ReverseDirection` does just what its name implies, changing north to south, etc. (see Example 5.67). `RotateDirection` (listed in Chapter 3) allows us to read the current direction of the character and adjusts it using a numbering system from one through eight. The numbers one through eight reflect the basic north, northeast, east, southeast, etc. directions found in the other methods.

Example 5.67. ReverseDirection.

```
// Take whatever direction you are going and go the
// opposite direction
virtual public void ReverseDirection() {
    switch (direction) {
        case SOUTHWEST:
            direction = NORTHEAST;
            break;
        case SOUTH:
            direction = NORTH;
            break;
        case SOUTHEAST:
            direction = NORTHWEST;
            break;
```

C# and Game Programming

```
        case WEST:
            direction = EAST;
            break;
        case EAST:
            direction = WEST;
            break;
        case NORTHWEST:
            direction = SOUTHEAST;
            break;
        case NORTH:
            direction = SOUTH;
            break;
        case NORTHEAST:
            direction = SOUTHWEST;
            break;
    }
}
```

> For the next few sections, we'll be building on our list of subclasses, each controlling one option per method. We'll use descriptive names to save time on definitions; for example, the instance score refers to the character's score, etc. While not every method will apply to every game, the overall potential of these subclasses should become obvious.

Inheriting from AnimatedImage.cs—Player.cs

Now that we've defined the characters, it's time to start thinking about the uniqueness of the player. The player, for example, will require a life and death reference. There is the option of a superego transformation, and each player should have a score to represent his or her work throughout the game (see Example 5.68 and Player.cs on the CD-ROM).

Example 5.68. Player.cs

```
/* Player.cs: Sub-class of AnimatedImage. Responsible for managing all
 * things player-related.
 */
using System;

namespace GameClasses {
    public class Player : AnimatedImage {

        public int score;
        public int deaths;

        public Player() : base() {}
        public Player(int posX, int posY) : base(posX, posY) {
        }
    }
}
```

Inheriting from Player.cs—PlayerImageArray.cs

Remember that while C# does not allow for multiple inheritances, it does allow for single inheritance in a chain of subclasses. Thus, PlayerImageArray.cs can inherit from Player.cs both the properties of Player.cs and AnimatedImage.cs. PlayerImageArray was designed for use with an array of images. A method to load the images is required, as well as notation to indicate the position of the image (see Example 5.69 and PlayerImageArray.cs on the CD-ROM).

Example 5.69. PlayerImageArray.cs

```
using System;
using System.Drawing;

namespace GameClasses {
    public class PlayerImageArray : Player {
        protected Image[] aImages;

        public PlayerImageArray(int nImages) : base(0,0) {
```

```
        aImages = new Image[nImages];
    }

    public void LoadImage(string fileName, int position) {
        if (position >= 0 && aImages.GetLength(0) < position)
            return;

        aImages[position] = Utils.LoadImage(fileName);
    }

    // Loads a series of consecutively named images into the array.
    // Use "%%" to specify where the index in the filename is.
    public void LoadImages(string filePattern, int lowerBound,
        int upperBound) {
        if (lowerBound >=0 && lowerBound < upperBound &&
            aImages.GetLength(0) < (upperBound - lowerBound))
            return;

        for (int i = lowerBound; i <= upperBound; i++)
            aImages[i] = Utils.LoadImage
                (filePattern.Replace("%%", i.ToString()));
    }
```

Again, we'll want to include a few new bitmaps, but as usual, we'll want to keep our coding as generic as possible; thus, we'll reference those images using a few standardized methods. The distinction here is that our methods are split between a preset image and one that is constantly being updated; if you remember, our very first game included only a stagnant player, creating the need for both sets of coding.

```
        // overridden member which displays the image with an index ==
        // to the heading associated with the image.
        override public void Display(Graphics g) {
            if (direction >= 0 && direction <= aImages.GetLength(0))
                g.DrawImage(aImages[direction], imagePosX, imagePosY,
                    imageWidth, imageHeight);
        }
    }
}
```

Chapter 5: Object-Oriented Design

Inheriting from PlayerImageArray.cs—MultiImagePlayer.cs

MultiImagePlayer.cs is the first of two classes that inherit from PlayerImageArray; the second, Shapes.cs, will be defined in the next section. Here, we're essentially redefining the PlayerImageArray. An unique aspect to this class is that it is not part of the Game Class set—instead it is included with the Rat Racer program (Rat Racer is the last game listed in this chapter). (See Example 5.70.)

Example 5.70. MultiImagePlayer.cs

```
// Inherits from PlayerImageArray because that has most of
// the functionality we need. We need to override its
// Display() method so we can implement the chomping action.
using System;
using System.Drawing;

using GameClasses;

namespace Games {
    public class MultiImagePlayer : PlayerImageArray {
        public bool isChomping;

        public MultiImagePlayer(int nImages) : base(nImages) {
            isChomping = false;
        }

        new public void Display(Graphics g) {
            int index;

            switch (direction) {
                case AnimatedImage.NORTH:
                    index = isChomping ? 7 : 6;
                    break;
                case AnimatedImage.SOUTH:
                    index = isChomping ? 1 : 0;
                    break;
                    . . .
            if (index >= 0 && index < aImages.GetLength(0))
                g.DrawImage(aImages[index], imagePosX, imagePosY,
```

```
                    imageWidth, imageHeight);
    }

    public int Display() {
        int index;

        switch (direction) {
            case AnimatedImage.NORTH:
                index = isChomping ? 7 : 6;
                break;
            case AnimatedImage.SOUTH:
                index = isChomping ? 1 : 0;
                break;
                . . .
```

Inheriting from PlayerImageArray.cs—Shapes.cs

An option that we've been playing with since the beginning was the idea of rendered graphics. Here, we used the GDI+ tools to create alternate versions of our characters. In addition, while it was possible to build these characters from our base coding, we opted to develop an inheriting class to allow for reuse. The coding listed in this class is actually discussed in both Chapters 3 and 4; the remainder is listed below (see Example 5.71 and Shapes.cs on the CD-ROM).

Example 5.71. PlayerImageArray.

```
using System;
using System.Drawing;
using System.Drawing.Drawing2D;

namespace GameClasses {
    public class Shapes : PlayerImageArray {
        public Shapes(int n) : base(0) {}

        public Shapes(int posX, int posY) : base(0) {
            imagePosX = posX;
            imagePosY = posY;
            isActive = false;
            animationStep = DEFAULTSTEP;
        }
...
```

The starting Angle defines the position of our spacecraft used in Chapter 3. In Chapter 4 we use a constant angle.

```
// defines the starting angle of a Pie for any given vector
public int startAngle() {
    switch(this.direction) {
        case 1: return(290); // southwest
        case 2: return(250); // south
        case 3: return(200); // southeast
        case 4: return(155); // east
        case 5: return(105); // northeast
        case 6: return(65);  // north
        case 7: return(25);  // northwest
        case 8: return(-25); // west
    }
    return(0); // default northwest
}
```

The aliens here are represented in Chapter 4's Battle Wave, as well as in Ground Assault, which is listed later in this chapter.

```
// complex shape - reusable as a single item
public void Alien0(Graphics g, Brush bAlienColor) {
    Point[] Alien = {
        new Point(this.imagePosX-10, this.imagePosY-10),
        new Point(this.imagePosX-5, this.imagePosY-10),
        new Point(this.imagePosX-5, this.imagePosY-5),
        new Point(this.imagePosX+5, this.imagePosY-5),
        new Point(this.imagePosX+5, this.imagePosY-10),
        new Point(this.imagePosX+10, this.imagePosY-10),
        new Point(this.imagePosX+10, this.imagePosY-5),
        new Point(this.imagePosX+5, this.imagePosY-5),
        new Point(this.imagePosX+5, this.imagePosY+5),
        new Point(this.imagePosX+10, this.imagePosY+5),
        new Point(this.imagePosX+10, this.imagePosY+10),
        new Point(this.imagePosX-10, this.imagePosY+10),
        new Point(this.imagePosX-10, this.imagePosY+5),
        new Point(this.imagePosX-5, this.imagePosY+5),
        new Point(this.imagePosX-5, this.imagePosY-5),
        new Point(this.imagePosX-10, this.imagePosY-5),
        new Point(this.imagePosX-10, this.imagePosY-10)};

    g.FillPolygon(bAlienColor, Alien);
}
```

```csharp
// complex shape - reusable as a single item
public void Alien1(Graphics g, Brush bAlienColor) {
    Point[] Alien = {
        new Point(this.imagePosX-10, this.imagePosY-10),
        new Point(this.imagePosX-5, this.imagePosY-10),
        new Point(this.imagePosX-5, this.imagePosY-5),
        new Point(this.imagePosX+5, this.imagePosY-5),
        new Point(this.imagePosX+5, this.imagePosY-10),
        new Point(this.imagePosX+10, this.imagePosY-10),
        new Point(this.imagePosX+10, this.imagePosY-5),
        new Point(this.imagePosX+5, this.imagePosY-5),
        new Point(this.imagePosX+5, this.imagePosY+5),
        new Point(this.imagePosX+10, this.imagePosY+5),
        new Point(this.imagePosX+10, this.imagePosY+10),
        new Point(this.imagePosX+5, this.imagePosY+10),
        new Point(this.imagePosX+5, this.imagePosY+5),
        new Point(this.imagePosX-5, this.imagePosY+5),
        new Point(this.imagePosX-5, this.imagePosY+10),
        new Point(this.imagePosX-10, this.imagePosY+10),
        new Point(this.imagePosX-10, this.imagePosY+5),
        new Point(this.imagePosX-5, this.imagePosY+5),
        new Point(this.imagePosX-5, this.imagePosY-5),
        new Point(this.imagePosX-10, this.imagePosY-5),
        new Point(this.imagePosX-10, this.imagePosY-10)};

    g.FillPolygon(bAlienColor, Alien);
}

// complex shape - reusable as a single item
public void Alien2(Graphics g, Brush bAlienColor) {
    Point[] Alien = {
        new Point(this.imagePosX-5, this.imagePosY-10),
        new Point(this.imagePosX+5, this.imagePosY-10),
        new Point(this.imagePosX+5, this.imagePosY-5),
        new Point(this.imagePosX+10, this.imagePosY-5),
        new Point(this.imagePosX+10, this.imagePosY+10),
        new Point(this.imagePosX+5, this.imagePosY+10),
        new Point(this.imagePosX+5, this.imagePosY),
        new Point(this.imagePosX-5, this.imagePosY),
        new Point(this.imagePosX-5, this.imagePosY+10),
        new Point(this.imagePosX-10, this.imagePosY+10),
        new Point(this.imagePosX-10, this.imagePosY-5),
        new Point(this.imagePosX-5, this.imagePosY-5),
        new Point(this.imagePosX-5, this.imagePosY-10)};
```

```
        g.FillPolygon(bAlienColor, Alien);
    }

    // complex shape - reusable as a single item
    public void Alien3(Graphics g, Brush bAlienColor) {
        Point[] Alien = {
            new Point(this.imagePosX-10, this.imagePosY-10),
            new Point(this.imagePosX+10, this.imagePosY-10),
            new Point(this.imagePosX+10, this.imagePosY-5),
            new Point(this.imagePosX+5, this.imagePosY-5),
            new Point(this.imagePosX+5, this.imagePosY+5),
            new Point(this.imagePosX+10, this.imagePosY+5),
            new Point(this.imagePosX+10, this.imagePosY+10),
            new Point(this.imagePosX+5, this.imagePosY+10),
            new Point(this.imagePosX+5, this.imagePosY+5),
            new Point(this.imagePosX-5, this.imagePosY+5),
            new Point(this.imagePosX-5, this.imagePosY+10),
            new Point(this.imagePosX-10, this.imagePosY+10),
            new Point(this.imagePosX-10, this.imagePosY+5),
            new Point(this.imagePosX-5, this.imagePosY+5),
            new Point(this.imagePosX-5, this.imagePosY-5),
            new Point(this.imagePosX-10, this.imagePosY-5),
            new Point(this.imagePosX-10, this.imagePosY-10)};

        g.FillPolygon(bAlienColor, Alien);
    }

    // complex shape - reusable as a single item
    public void Tank(Graphics g, Brush bTankColor, Brush bCannonColor) {
        Point[] tank = {
            new Point(this.imagePosX-10, this.imagePosY-10),
            new Point(this.imagePosX+10, this.imagePosY-10),
            new Point(this.imagePosX+10, this.imagePosY-5),
            new Point(this.imagePosX+5, this.imagePosY-5),
            new Point(this.imagePosX+5, this.imagePosY+5),
            new Point(this.imagePosX+10, this.imagePosY+5),
            new Point(this.imagePosX+10, this.imagePosY+10),
            new Point(this.imagePosX-10, this.imagePosY+10),
            new Point(this.imagePosX-10, this.imagePosY+5),
            new Point(this.imagePosX-5, this.imagePosY+5),
            new Point(this.imagePosX-5, this.imagePosY-5),
            new Point(this.imagePosX-10, this.imagePosY-5),
            new Point(this.imagePosX-10, this.imagePosY-10)};
```

```
        g.FillPolygon(bTankColor, tank);
        g.FillPie(bCannonColor, this.imagePosX-12,
            this.imagePosY-12, this.imageWidth, this.imageHeight,
            this.imagePosX, this.imageHeight);
}
```

The trapezoid referred to in Chapter 4 is used to create a number of objects including the potted plant (Battle Tennis).

```
// basic shape - reusable in many formats
public Point[] Trapezoid() {
    Point[] Trapezoid = {
        new Point(this.imagePosX-5, this.imagePosY-10),
        new Point(this.imagePosX+5, this.imagePosY-10),
        new Point(this.imagePosX+10, this.imagePosY),
        new Point(this.imagePosX-10, this.imagePosY)};
    return(Trapezoid);
}
```

The Sharp Triangle is also used to represent a number of objects including Chapter 4's fan (Battle Tennis).

```
// basic shape  - reusable in many formats
public Point[] sharpTriangle() {
    Point[] sharpTriangle = {
        new Point(this.imagePosX, this.imagePosY-5),
        new Point(this.imagePosX+3, this.imagePosY+10),
        new Point(this.imagePosX-3, this.imagePosY+10)};
    return(sharpTriangle);
}
```

Inheriting from Shapes.cs—Patterns.cs

Another class developed specifically for the games listed in Chapter 4 is the inheriting class Patterns. We're building quite a large chain, e.g., AnimatedImage.cs to Player.cs to PlayerImageArray.cs to Shapes.cs to Patterns.cs. The goal of this class is to construct a set of images that move in unison. The patterns are numbered, but there could also be a naming scheme as new patterns are added to the class. Methods such as Flower, TV, etc.

are referenced from the inherited classes, as the original fields are used to coordinate those points (see Example 5.72 and CR-ROM Example Patterns.cs).

Example 5.72. Patterns.cs

```
using System;
using System.Drawing;
using System.Drawing.Drawing2D;

namespace GameClasses {
    public class Patterns : Shapes {
        public Patterns(int n) : base(0) {}

        public Patterns(int posX, int posY) : base(0) {
            imagePosX = posX;
            imagePosY = posY;
            isActive = false;
            animationStep = DEFAULTSTEP;
        }

        public void ItemPattern28(Graphics g, Brush bItemColor,
            Pen pItemColor, int current) {
            if(current >= 0 && current <= 6) {
                this.Window(g, bItemColor);}
            else if(current >= 7 && current <= 13) {
                this.Flower(g, bItemColor, pItemColor);}
            else if(current >= 14 && current <= 20) {
                this.TV(g, bItemColor, pItemColor);}
            else if(current >= 21 && current <= 28) {
                this.Lamp(g, bItemColor, bItemColor);
            }
        }

        public void AlienPattern20(Graphics g, Brush bAlienColor,
            int current) {
            if(current >= 0 && current <= 4) {
                this.Alien0(g, bAlienColor);}
            else if(current >= 5 && current <= 9) {
                this.Alien1(g, bAlienColor);}
            else if(current >= 10 && current <= 14) {
                this.Alien2(g, bAlienColor);}
            else if(current >= 15 && current <= 19) {
                this.Alien3(g, bAlienColor);
```

```
            }
        }

        public void ItemPattern1(Graphics g, Brush bAlienColor,
            int current) {
            if(current >= 0 && current <= 4) {
                this.Alien0(g, bAlienColor);}
            else if(current >= 5 && current <= 9) {
                this.Alien1(g, bAlienColor);}
            else if(current >= 10 && current <= 14) {
                this.Alien2(g, bAlienColor);}
            else if(current >= 15 && current <= 19) {
                this.Alien3(g, bAlienColor);
            }
        }
    }
}
```

GameState.cs

GameState.cs contains the GameState class that is responsible for maintaining simple state information about a game such as the speed, state (started, stopped, etc), and mode (demo, single player, etc.). The GameState class is an independent class, but it is a vital component of all the games constructed in this text (see Example 5.73 and GameState.cs on the CD-ROM).

Example 5.73. GameState.cs

```
using System;

namespace GameClasses {
    public class GameState {
        // Different speeds the game can be run in.
        public const int SPEED_MINIMUM = 1;
        public const int SPEED_DEFAULT = 3;
        public const int SPEED_MAXIMUM = 10;
```

Chapter 5: Object-Oriented Design

```
        // Different "states" the game can be in.
        public enum State : int {
            Unknown = 0,
            Started = 1,
            Stopped = 2,
        }

        // Different "modes" the game can be run in.
        [Flags]
            public enum Mode : int {
            Normal = 0,
            SinglePlayer = 0,
            TwoPlayer = 1,
            Demo = 2,
        }

        // Member variables
        public int currentSpeed;
        public State currentState;
        public Mode currentMode;

        // Constructors
        public GameState() {
            currentSpeed = SPEED_DEFAULT;
            currentState = State.Stopped;
            currentMode = Mode.Normal;
        }

        public GameState(int initialSpeed, State gameState) {
            currentSpeed = initialSpeed;
            currentState = gameState;
            currentMode = Mode.Normal;
        }

        public GameState(int initialSpeed, State gameState,
            Mode gameMode) {
            currentSpeed = initialSpeed;
            currentState = gameState;
            currentMode = gameMode;
        }
    }
}
```

C# and Game Programming

GameTimer.cs

The GameTimer Class serves as a gauge for the game's events; for example, an event can be added, timed, or removed—addEvent, TimedEvent, and removeEvent. The game relies on the timed events to allow for actions not controlled by the player (see Example 5.74 and GameTimer.cs on the CD-ROM).

Example 5.74. GameTimer.cs

```
using System;
using System.Windows.Forms;
using System.Collections;

namespace GameClasses {
    public class GameTimer {
        // Member fields
        Timer gameTimer;   // main timer object
        int baseInterval;  // base interval in ms
        Hashtable events;  // list of TimedEvent objects

        // Default constructor
        public GameTimer(int interval) {
            events = new Hashtable();
            gameTimer = new Timer();
            gameTimer.Interval = interval;
            gameTimer.Tick += new EventHandler(Tick);
            baseInterval = interval;
        }

        // Simple start and stop functionality.
        public void Start() {gameTimer.Start();}
        public void Stop() {gameTimer.Stop();}

        // Add an event to our game timer. Use stepFactor to control the
        // frequency the given TimedEvent's Tick() will be called.
        // Use the given "key" for future reference to this TimedEvent.
        public void addEvent(TimedEvent timedEvent, int stepFactor,
            string key) {
            TimedEventNode node = new TimedEventNode();
            node.data = timedEvent;
            node.timeStep = stepFactor;
```

```csharp
            node.stepCount = 0;
            events.Add(key, node);
        }

        // Returns the event marked with the given key
        public TimedEvent getEvent(string key) {
            return ((TimedEventNode) events[key]).data;
        }

        // Removes an event from the list
        public void removeEvent(string key) {
            events.Remove(key);
        }

        // Changes the step associated with the event indexed by key
        public void ChangeStep(string key, int stepFactor) {
            ((TimedEventNode) events[key]).timeStep = stepFactor;
        }

        // Tick() -- passes on tick event to proper TimedEvent objects
        public void Tick(object sender, EventArgs e) {
            IDictionaryEnumerator itemEnumerator = events.GetEnumerator();
            TimedEventNode node;

            while (itemEnumerator.MoveNext()) {
                node = (TimedEventNode) itemEnumerator.Value;
                if (node.stepCount >= node.timeStep) {
                    node.stepCount = 0;
                    node.data.Tick();
                } else {
                    node.stepCount++;
                }
            }
        }

        // Helper class to hold a extra information relevant to
        // timer event processing.
        class TimedEventNode {
            public int timeStep;   // how many baseInterval ticks to wait
            public int stepCount;  // counter to compare with timeStep
            public TimedEvent data; // the TimedEvent object
        }
    }
}
```

TimedEvent.cs

TimedEvent.cs is a class representing a timer; it is used to monitor events based on a set number of processing cycles. It can monitor that an event happens a set number of times, etc. Deriving from this class and overriding the `Tick ()` method can allow for custom behavior (see Example 5.75).

Example 5.75. TimedEvent.cs

```
using System;

namespace GameClasses {
    public delegate void TickHandler(TimedEvent e, Object payload);

    public class TimedEvent {
        // Member fields
        public int ticks;
        public int tickCounter;
        public bool isCountdown;
        public bool isActive;
        public TickHandler remoteHandler;
        public object payload;

        public TimedEvent() {
            ticks = 0;
            isCountdown = false;
            SetTickHandler(new TickHandler(DoNothing));
        }

        public TimedEvent(TickHandler handler) {
            SetTickHandler(handler);
        }

        public TimedEvent(int numTicks, TickHandler handler) {
            SetCountdown(numTicks);
            SetTickHandler(handler);
        }

        public void SetTickHandler(TickHandler handler) {
            remoteHandler = handler;
        }
```

```
    public void SetCountdown(int numTicks) {
        isCountdown = numTicks > 0;
        ticks = numTicks;
        tickCounter = ticks;
    }

    public void Tick() {
        if (!isActive)
            return;

        // Call any custom function
        remoteHandler(this, payload);

        // decrement the counter
        if (isCountdown)
            if (tickCounter > 0)
                tickCounter--;
            else
                isActive = false;
    }

    public void Reset() {
        tickCounter = ticks;
        isActive = true;
    }

    // Dummy for default tick-handler
    public void DoNothing(TimedEvent e, Object o) {}
    }
}
```

Utils.cs

The file Utils class is a combination of basic utilities with a focus on sound production using Window's Multimedia. It is intended to simplify sound references throughout our Windows Forms and GDI+ games and act as a backup/alternative for DirectSound (see Example 5.76).

Example 5.76. Utils.cs

```csharp
using System;
using System.Drawing;
using System.IO;
using System.Windows.Forms;
using System.Runtime.InteropServices;
using System.Threading;

namespace GameClasses {
    public class Utils {
        // External function to play sounds
        [DllImport("winmm.dll")]
        public static extern long PlaySound(String lpszName, long hModule,
            long dwFlags);

        // Static Variable .config file's contents
        public static System.Collections.Specialized.NameValueCollection
            Config =
System.Configuration.ConfigurationSettings.AppSettings;

        // Error-handling LoadImage function
        public static Image LoadImage(String strFileName) {
            Image imgLoad = null;
            try {
                imgLoad = Image.FromFile(strFileName);
            } catch (FileNotFoundException ex) {
                MessageBox.Show("Please check that the following file " +
                    "exists:\n\n" + ex.Message + "\n\nCorrect the file " +
                    "referenced in the config file.", "File Not Found!");
                Application.Exit();
            }

            return imgLoad;
        }

        // PlaySound simple pass-through function. Removes dependency for
        // other classes to reference winmm.DLL.
        public static void PlaySound(String strFileName) {
            ThreadedSound snd = new ThreadedSound(strFileName);
            Thread worker = new Thread(new ThreadStart(snd.Play));
            worker.Start();
        }
```

```
    class ThreadedSound {
        public string strFileName;

        public ThreadedSound(string file) {
            strFileName = file;
        }

        public void Play() {
            //Console.WriteLine("Playing: " + strFileName);
            PlaySound(strFileName, 0, 0);
        }
    }
  }
}
```

Wall.cs

Wall is a basic concept used to limit the paths of our characters, both friend and foe. The construction of a wall is based on its width, length, and thickness. The wall is positioned using standard Cartesian coordinates. The brushes are used to draw GDI+ models, while DirectX merely retrieves the coordinates and handles the drawing from inside the game (see Examples 5.77–5.79).

Example 5.77. Wall.cs

```
using System;
using System.Drawing;

namespace GameClasses {
    public class Wall {
        public const int HORIZONTAL = 1;
        public const int VERTICAL = 2;
        public const int DEF_THICKNESS = 8;

        public int orientation;
        public Point start;
        public int length;
        public int thickness;
```

```csharp
        private Brush brush;
        private Color color;
        private Rectangle rect;

    public Wall(int orientation, Point start, int length,
        Color color) :
        this(orientation, start, length, DEF_THICKNESS, color) {}

    public Wall(int orientation, Point start, int length,
        int thickness, Color color) {
        this.orientation = orientation;
        this.start = start;
        this.length = length;
        this.thickness = thickness;
        this.color = color;

        rect = new Rectangle(start, (orientation == HORIZONTAL) ?
            new Size(length, thickness) : new Size(thickness,
                length));
        this.brush = new SolidBrush(this.color);
    }
```

Example 5.78. Intersects.

```csharp
    public bool Intersects(AnimatedImage obj) {
        int x = obj.imagePosX, y = obj.imagePosY;
        int x2 = obj.imagePosX + obj.imageWidth;
        int y2 = obj.imagePosY + obj.imageHeight;
        int _x = rect.X, _y = rect.Y;
        int _x2 = rect.X + rect.Width, _y2 = rect.Y + rect.Height;

        return ((x >= _x && x <= _x2) || (x2 >= _x && x2 <= _x2) ||
            (_x >= x && _x <= x2) || (_x2 >= x && _x2 <= x2)) &&
            ((y >= _y && y <= _y2) || (y2 >= _y && y2 <= _y2) ||
            (_y >= y && _y <= y2) || (_y2 >= y && _y2 <= y2));
    }
```

Example 5.79. Display & Rectangle

```csharp
    public void Display(Graphics g) {
        g.FillRectangle(brush, rect);
    }
```

```
    public Rectangle getRectangle() {
        return(rect);
    }
  }
}
```

Introducing Direct3D

Managed Direct3D is a low-level graphics application/programming interface used to render two- and three-dimensional images for static and animated projects relating to both basic and graphically intense programs. Managed Direct3D takes advantage of hardware acceleration to produce high-quality real time graphics, while requiring only a minimal amount of down time relating to the learning curve as compared to the pervious versions of DirectX. The Managed Direct3D's namespace includes nearly 300 classes, structures, enumerations, and delegates, each of which includes a large set of members, properties, and fields. Fortunately, most applications require only a few common references, usually beginning with the device class (see Direct3D's Device Class for details).

Direct3D's Device Class

The device class includes three constructors, of which only one is used in Managed DirectX: `public Device(int adapter, DeviceType deviceType, Control renderWindow, CreateFlags behaviorFlags, PresentParameters []presentationParameters)`;. The first parameter, *adapter*, refers to the physical device referenced by the computer with a *unique adapter identifier* (note that zero indicates the default). The *deviceTypes* include *Hardware, Reference*, and *Software. Hardware* refers to direct access, while *Reference* refers to emulation. (Emulation is required when the hardware does not support the requested feature.) The *Reference* rasterizer is much slower and requires that all users have the SDK installed; hence, it should only be used for debugging. There is also a custom *Software* rasterizer, which has limited availability. The *behaviorFlags* (`behaviorFlags.SoftwareVertexProcessing`) control the device's behavior, specifying our processing unit, e.g., the CPU and GPU. (The GPU offers the best performance; again, this depends on hardware availability). The constructor *presentationParameters* is used to control presentation, which includes two key members: *Windowed* and *SwapEffect*. The Windowed member (a Boolean type) is used to determine the window's status (true for

Windowed mode, false for full screen mode), while SwapEffect is used to control buffer behavior. `SwapEffect.Copy`, `SwapEffect.Discard`, and `SwapEffect.Flip` are used to copy, discard, and flip, respectively. `Flip` creates an extra backbuffer, while `Copy` requires that we set our back buffers to one; `Discard` simply discards the buffer's content.

Device also includes the methods `Clear` and `Present`. `Present` is the simpler of the two, with no arguments, and is used to present our graphics to the screen. `Clear` includes a minimum of four parameters: `ClearFlags`, `Color`, `float zdepth`, and `int stencil`. For the time being we'll limit these setting to their most basic levels: (`ClearFlags.Target`, `Color.Empty`, `0.0f`, `0`). We'll also need to build a Windows application, adding the references DirectX, DirectX.Direct3D, and Direct3DX. (Note that we do not include the phrase `using Microsoft.DirectX.Direct3DX`; see Example 5.80 on the CD-ROM.)

Displaying 2D Images using Direct3D

As with DirectDraw, Direct3D uses a simple Draw command to display its images, however, the Direct3D's version of the Draw command requires seven arguments namely the spriteTexture, sprite, textureSize, scaling, rotation, transition, and color. The first three arguments pertain to the body of the bitmap, with spriteTexture referencing the actual loaded image or bitmap file (*.bmp), sprite is used to link our bitmap to the Device class, and textureSize is used to set the size of that texture. Scaling then dictates the size of the rendered image, with rotationCenter, rotation, and translation relating to the characters position (translation places the image using Cartesian coordinates), color, quite obviously, dictates the images color.

Here we'll also want to introduce the methods used to contain our drawing function, appropriately termed `BeginScene ( ); EndScene ( );`. These can be built into a user-defined graphics call or as part of the OnPaint reference (see Example 5.81 on the CD-ROM).

Direct3D's 2D Animation—Basics

Image position is controlled by the translation coordinates x, y, and potentially z. Adding or subtracting from these values, in essence, creates movement. This movement, however, should not be considered true animation, but rather only a simple form of displacement. To

Chapter 5: Object-Oriented Design

create the effect of true animation, the programmer would have to include some visual changes, a turn to the left, a step to the right, etc. To do this, we'll need to include several alternative images; these will be stored to the `spriteTexture`, which will now be referenced as an array. Here, I've also include a simple try-catch block to monitor the new images. Note that, with Direct3D, a missing file does not halt compilation (see Example 5.82 on the CD-ROM).

Game 6—Ground Assault

Ground Assault is a combination of all the previous games, as well as several of the classes we just discussed. Once again, we need to lay out a simple plan, develop some characters, weapons, and include a line of movement—this time, I think we'll even develop a few walls.

Brainstorming

Since the premise of Ground Assault is that the aliens from the last game actually landed, we should start there. First, we'll redesign the aliens to include whole bodies (the better for attacking on foot, my dear). Second, we'll want to redesign our hero so that he's not always looking up. As I stated just a moment ago, we'll also develop some walls, which will be used to stop the missiles and force our characters to work a little for their kills.

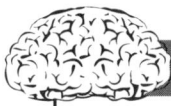 Brainstorming

Example 5.83. Brainstorming Ground Assault

1. Redesign characters to include bodies, also, use only one character from each color group.
2. Redesign the hero so that he's not looking up, and give him the ability to turn in all four directions.
3. Redesign the missiles to include all eight directions.
4. Add four walls that are repositioned after each new level (set up the first pattern to repeat after you complete the fourth).
5. Give the walls a distinct color.
6. Give the hero three lives.
7. Have him score a set number of points for killing each alien.

Graphics

We'll also need to think up some colorful designs. In this case, I used extended versions of our alien attacker. We'll once again want to use a smooth change of colors. The coding is also very similar to that in the last game, it uses a simple overriding OnPaint method (as shown in GrandAssault.cs on the CD-ROM).

Game 7—Rat Racer

For our seventh game, we'll build a simple maze with some obstacles and a goal. The steps are fairly routine: brainstorming, drawing out the characters, and applying the key functions. Here's a mini-version of those steps.

Example. 5.84. Brainstorming Rat Racer.

1. Two mice are racing to see who can eat the most cheese.
2. There's a maze that they must traverse.
3. There will be four cats sitting at each corner of the maze.
4. If you move too close to any of those cats, you'll get eaten.
5. If one player dies, the other still must eat all the cheese.
6. Walking into the walls will kill the mice.
7. The cheese will be placed randomly across the board.
8. If all the cheese is eaten the cheese will reset.

Adding Animation

The mice will have faces and bodies that change slightly as they walk around the board. They will open and close their mouths, curl and uncurl their tails, and rotate their arms. In addition, they should be able to move up, down, left, and right (see Example 5.85)

Chapter 5: Object-Oriented Design

Example 5.85. Animations of characters in Rat Race: a) cats; b) mice; c) cheese

a) Cats.

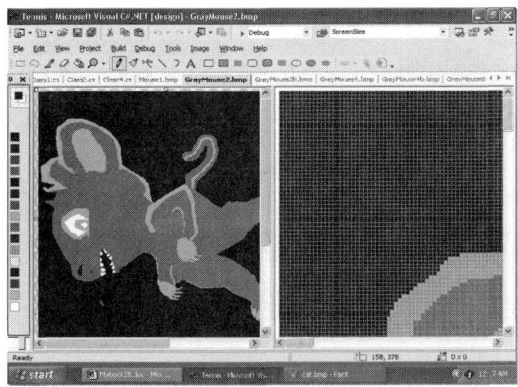
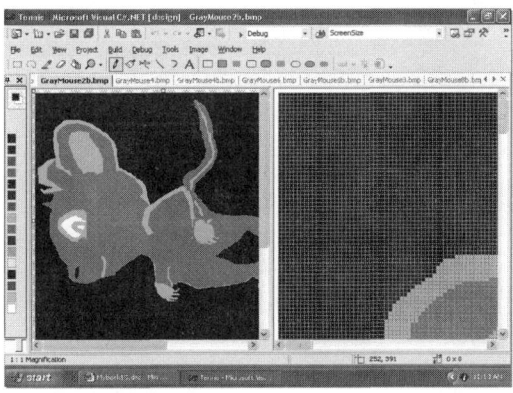
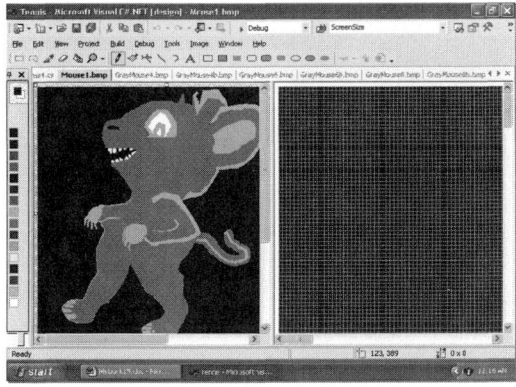
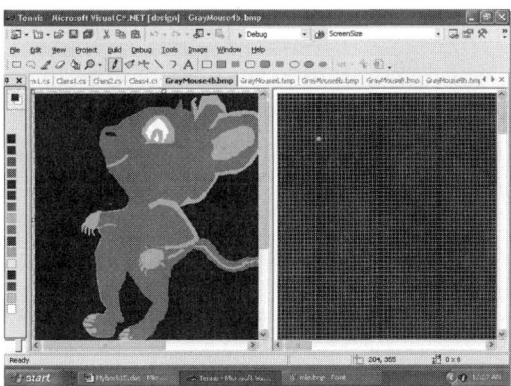

b) mice

433

C# and Game Programming

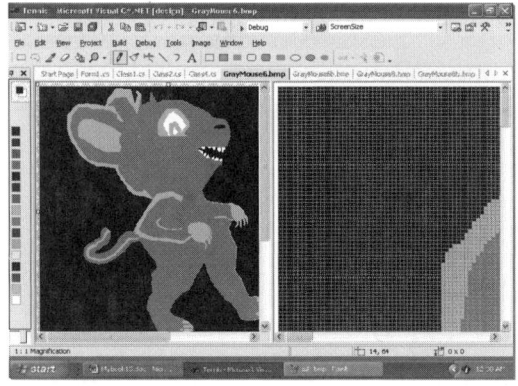 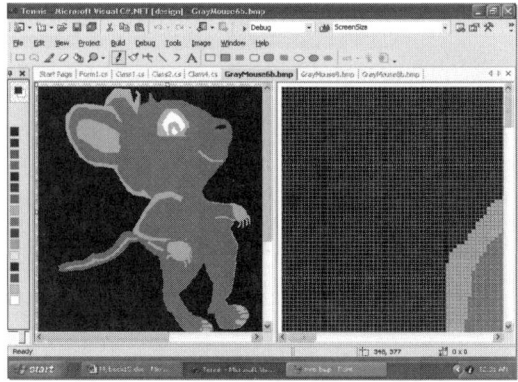

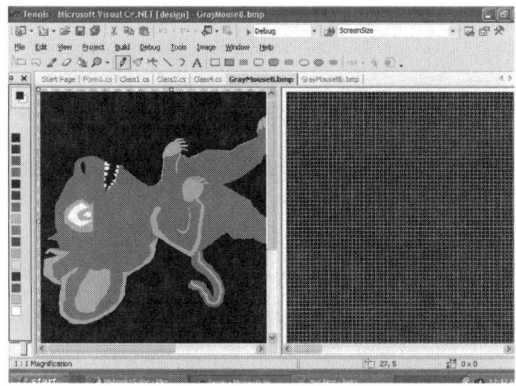 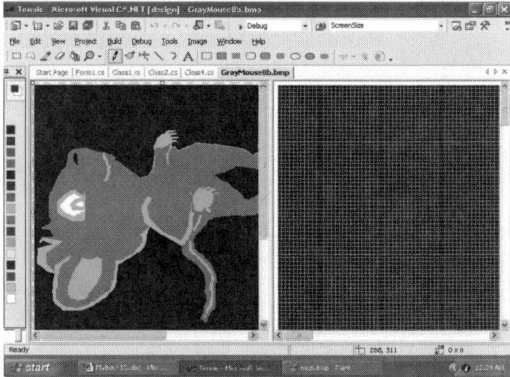

c) cheese

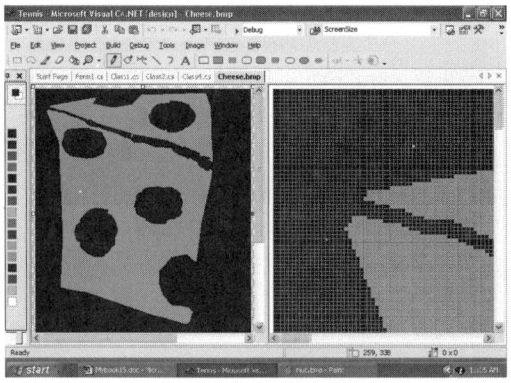

Troubleshooting

If you've gotten the previous programs to run, but are having trouble with these new ones, then the problem must be in the setup. Try going back over the steps and repeating steps from the earlier games. You might also want to try including all the classes as part of the same file. If the combined file runs correctly then there must be something wrong with the way you're setting up the secondary files.

Questions

1. Build a simple structure and reference it from the main method. Then, using public fields, rebuild that structure as a class.
2. From Question 2, convert that class' public fields into protected fields (build as many secondary methods as you need to get the job done).
3. From Question 3, convert those fields into private members. (Hint: You may need to add additional methods.)
4. Write a class that allows for both overloaded arithmetic and comparison operators.
5. Write a simple public, nested class, and then replace that nested class with an inherited class.

Assignments

Now that you have a working knowledge of the C# language and a basic grasp of game programming, it's time that you attempt to develop your own games. First, try developing an eighth game that ties into the classes already developed (Note: No new classes should be added). Next, try developing your own set of classes, possibly with two new games, and then one more game where you are again not allowed to alter those classes (in the second test, however, you may opt to build additional inherited classes).

Conclusion

So, you've mastered the games, and in doing so, have mastered both C# and the concept of object-oriented programming. You might now be wondering, "What is next—where do I go from here?" Or more importantly, "How can I turn these new found skills into a paying profession?" The answer to these questions is, "Through continued study." You'll want to take a good, hard look at the specialties involved with business and game programming, as well as mathematics, electronics, and engineering. For some, a college degree will be the next step; for others, the MCAD/MCSD will seem like the best road. Ultimately, these choices are left to you.

The book's CDROM includes a special selection of text references that my aid you in this journey. I've also included playable and project versions of all the games, as well as the original art, sound clips, and source code to make it possible for you to develop new and/or extended versions. To access the catalog and/or the alternative files, simply search through the CDRom using your Windows' explorer and access the appropriate files.

The release versions of the games are also listed in accordance with their chapters (Chapter\Game Title\Bin\Release\Game Title.exe), and can also be accessed through Windows' explorer; however, for best game play, it is recommended that these games be stored on the hard drive.

If you are using an older version of Windows and would like to access these games without purchasing a .Net compiler, you can do so by downloading the .Net framework which is currently located at http://msdn.microsoft.com/netframework/downloads/default.asp.

Thank you and good luck.

Appendix A: Keywords/Reserved Identifiers

abstract	decimal	float	namespace	return	try
as	default	for	new	sbyte	typeof
base	delegate	foreach	null	sealed	uint
bool	do	goto	object	short	ulong
break	double	if	operator	sizeof	unchecked
byte	else	implicit	out	stackalloc	unsafe
case	enum	in	override	static	ushort
catch	event	int	params	string	using
char	explicit	interface	private	struct	virtual
checked	extern	internal	protected	switch	void
class	false	is	public	this	volatile
const	finally	lock	readonly	throw	while
continue	fixed	long	ref	true	

> It is important not to intermix reserved identifiers with programmer-generated references. However, if a situation arises where such a naming conflict cannot be avoided, it is possible to disassociate that identifier from the compiler using the @ symbol (see Example A.1).

Example A.1.

```
using System;
namespace Appendix_A {
    class Class1 {
        [STAThread]
        static void Main(string[] args) {
            int @true = 325;
            string @while = "Salvatore A. Buono";
            Console.WriteLine(@true);
            Console.WriteLine(@while);
        }
    }
}
```

Appendix B: Reserved Identifiers Defined

abstract

`Abstract` is a modifier used to declare a generic class. Abstract classes cannot be instantiated, nor can they be modified with a sealed or static modifier. Only abstract classes may use abstract methods and accessors, but all nonabstract classes derived from those classes must include implementations of those references. Abstract methods are also implicitly virtual and their inheriting properties may be overridden (see Example B.1).

Example B.1.

```
public abstract class Area {}
class Appendix_B {
    static void Main() {}
}
```

as

`As` is a binary operator that allows for a conversion from an expression to a data type. It is also a useful tool when attempting to avoid exceptions, since it will return a null if the conversion fails (see Example B.2).

Example B.2.

```
public class Appendix_B {
    public static void Main() {
        object MyString = new object();
        string s = MyString as string;
    }
}
```

base

`Base` is the keyword used to access members of a base class from within an inheriting class reference. It is delineated using the keyword `base` followed by that particular member's definition. A base class can be accessed as a constructor, instance, and/or with an overriding modifier, but they cannot be used with the static modifier (see Example B.3).

Example B.3.

```
namespace Appendix_B {
    public class BaseClass {
        public BaseClass() {}
        public virtual void DisplayArea() {}
    }
    public class DerivedClass : BaseClass {
        DerivedClass() {}
        public override void DisplayArea() {
            base.DisplayArea();
        }
        static void Main() {}
    }
}
```

bool

Boolean expressions are mathematical representations for the concepts of both true and false. That is, while their actual evaluations are based on mathematical data, their outcomes are determined by a conceptual understanding. This type of determination is represented in the C# languages as the data type `bool`, with its variables assigned to the Boolean constants *true* or *false* (see Example B.4)

Example B.4.

```
class Appendix_B {
    static void Main() {
        bool Variable1 = true;
    }
}
```

break

Break, as its name implies, terminates any enclosed loop or conditional statement (see Example B.5).

Example B.5.

```
class Appendix_B {
    static void Main() {
        while(true) {
            break;
        }
    }
}
```

byte

`Byte` is an unsigned 8-bit integral date type that stores whole numbers with a range from 0 to 255 (see Example B.6).

Example B.6.

```
class Appendix_B {
    static void Main() {
        byte Number = 100;
    }
}
```

case

The keyword `case` is written and used multiple times from within the *switch* statement. Each *case* statement holds a numeric or character value for comparison. If the value held by a *case* statement matches the value read by the *switch* statement, then everything following that case statement will be executed (see Example B.7).

Example B.7.

```
class Appendix_B {
    static void Main() {
        char test = 'A';
        switch (test) {
            case 'A':
                break;
        }
    }
}
```

catch

The `catch` statement is part of the `try` block, and is used to literally catch and then possibly repair a program when an exception is thrown. Its clauses can include system exceptions, user-defined material, and/or a blank or generalized catch. Note that a *try* block normally includes multiple catch statements, with the most specific statements listed first and the blank or general statement placed in the furthest position. Failure to list catches in that order may result in a less specific catch being executed. It is also possible to rethrow an exception from within the `catch` statement (see Example B.8).

Example B.8.

```
public class Appendix_B {
    static void Main() {
        try {}
        catch {}
    }
}
```

char

The character reference (`char`), is used to declare 16-bit unicode characters that have ranges from U+0000 to U+ffff. Unicode characters are 16-bit characters used to represent nearly all of the known languages as well as most, if not all, of the traditional mathematical and literary symbols. `Char` is also used to represent combined values such as hexadecimal codes and escape sequences (see Example B.9).

Example B.9.

```
class Appendix_B {
    static void Main() {
        char Symbol = 'A';
    }
}
```

checked

Checked is used to monitor both operators and statements for numeric overflow errors as they occur in integral-type arithmetic operations and conversions (see Example B.10).

Example B.10.

```
class Appendix_B {
    static void Main() {
        byte Max255 = 254;
        checked{Max255++;}
    }
}
```

class

Classes are an advanced data type, a few levels beyond a simple byte, but not too dissimilar. They are similar to arrays, yet they're capable of holding tasks and multiple data types (more formally known as tags, fields, methods, etc.). They are called as instances (which also can be thought of as variables) that hold multiple bits of information. Classes are limited and/or enhanced by modifiers, and can be inherited (see Example B.11).

Example B.11.

```
class Appendix_B {
    static void Main() {}
}
```

const

The keyword *constant* (`const`) notifies the compiler of its unchanging nature and allows it to optimize that appropriate values (see Example B.12).

Example B.12.

```
class Appendix_B {
    static void Main() {
        const int OurVariable = 1;
    }
}
```

continue

`Continue`, like `break`, shortcuts its iterations, but rather than ending the loop, it merrily brings the loop back to the top. The loop continues on with a new iteration and everything else continues accordingly (see Example B.13).

Example B.13.

```
class Appendix_B {
    static void Main() {
        while (true) {
            continue;
        }
    }
}
```

decimal

`Decimal` is a 128-bit date type that stores rational and irrational numbers with a range listed from 1.0×10^{-28} to 7.9×10^{28}. Its precision level is between 28–29 significant digits, which makes it suitable for nearly all monetary calculations (see Example B.14).

Example B.14.

```
class Appendix_B {
    static void Main() {
        decimal Number1, Number2;
        Number1 = 1.0M;
        Number2 = 1.1m;
    }
}
```

default

`Default` is usually placed at the end of a `switch` statement, thus allowing the execution of selected statements based on the fact that they do not match any of the previous values (see Example B.15).

Example B.15.

```
using System;
class Appendix_B {
    static void Main() {
        int byNumber = Console.Read();
        switch (byNumber) {
            default:
                break;
        }
    }
}
```

delegate

A delegate's definition includes a public access reference, the keyword `delegate`, the delegate's identity (also following the standard rules of naming), a data type reference, and its set of parameters. Delegates are most commonly used to handle events (See Example B.16).

Example B.16.

```
public delegate void TryDelegate();
public class Appendix_B {
    static void Main() {
        TryDelegate();
    }
    public static void TryDelegate() {}
}
```

do

Do, as part of the do-while combination, allows for the execution of a set of statements, or block. This block will execute indefinitely, terminating only when a false expression is found. Do-while loops begin by executing their blocks, then they test and repeat, guaranteeing at least one execution before the process is terminated (see Example B.17).

Example B.17.

```
class Appendix_B {
    static void Main() {
        do {}
        while (true);
    }
}
```

double

Double is a 64-bit data type used to store floating point values ranging from $\pm 5.0 \times 10^{-324}$ to $\pm 1.7 \times 10^{308}$; its precision level is 15–16 digits (see Example B.18).

Example B.18.

```
class Appendix_B {
    static void Main() {
        double Number1, Number2;
        Number1 = 1.0;
        Number2 = 1.1;
    }
}
```

else

`Else` is the first logical extension to the questioning `if` statement: It adds an additional line of reasoning and an additional path for programs to follow. `Else` cannot be used independently, yet it links easily to the tail end of the `if` statement (see Example B.19).

Example B.19.

```
using System;
class Appendix_B {
    static void Main() {
        double Answer = double.Parse(Console.ReadLine());
        if (Answer == 5)
            Console.WriteLine ("\n That is correct!\n");
        else
            Console.WriteLine("\n Wrong!!!\n");
    }
}
```

enum

The *enumerator* (enum) is a basic aggregated type that promotes simple reference manipulations. It also allows for some unique references such as user-defined data structures and lists of assignments to those declarations. Initial structures are declared using the keyword enum, with instances of those values declared and assigned as if they were class references. If no values are assigned to these references, then the initial point would be zero and each new component would automatically increment by one. However, we can also short step this process by beginning at some arbitrary point, or individually declaring each value (see Example B.20).

Example B.20.

```
class Appendix_B {
    public enum Months {Jan = 1, Feb, Mar, Apr,
        May, Jun, Jul, Aug, Sep, Oct, Nov, Dec}
    public enum Day {AprilFools = 1, Birthday = 16,
        XMas = 25, Feb29 = 29, NYeve = 31}
    public enum Year {Year2 = 2002, Year3, LeapYear}
    static void Main() {}
}
```

event

`Event`s are used to specify delegates that are referenced at runtime; they can include multiple methods, and their coding is applicable to other programs. These events are also then dependent on the program including a delegate to reference. Events are also used with accessor functions add and remove, which need to be declared collectively (see Example B.21).

Example B.21.

```
using System.Collections;
namespace Appendix_B {
    public delegate void Del();
    public class EventSetup {
        private Hashtable Test = new Hashtable();
        public event Del Event {
            add {Test["Event"] = (Del)Test["Event"] + value;
        }
            remove {Test["Event"] = (Del)Test["Event"] - value;
    }
    public class Events {
        public static void Main() {}
    }
}
```

explicit

An `explicit` declaration is a declaration used to express a conversion from a larger to smaller value. Express permission is required because of the potential for lost data. The programmer using this declaration must also safeguard against errors manually (see Example B.22).

Example B.22.

```
namespace Appendix_B {
    class IsByte {
        byte value;
        public IsByte(int value) {this.value = (byte)value;}
        public static explicit operator IsByte(byte Byte) {
            return new IsByte(Byte);
        }
        public static void Main() {}
    }
}
```

extern

The `extern` modifier, as its name implies, indicates that the method will be implemented externally, such as with the DllImport attribute. The external method will contain all appropriate declarations; it does not require a function body, but it does require a terminating semicolon (see Example B.23).

Example B.23.

```
using System;
using System.Windows.Forms;
using System.Runtime.InteropServices;
namespace Appendix_B {
   public class Form1 : System.Windows.Forms.Form {
      [DllImport("winmm.dll")]
      public static extern long PlaySound(String lpszName,
         long hModule, long dwFlags);
      public Form1() {
         PlaySound(@"C:\SourceCode\Mouse.wav", 0, 0);
      }
      static void Main() {
         Application.Run(new Form1());
      }
   }
}
```

false

`False` is a user-defined Boolean type operator that returns a value false (see Example B.24).

Example B.24.

```
class Appendix_B {
   static void Main() {
      bool Variable1 = false;
   }
}
```

finally

The `finally` block is the last block listed in a `try-catch-finally` set; its statements are always executed with the completion of that set (see Example B.25).

Example B.25.

```
public class Appendix_B {
    static void Main() {
        try {}
        finally {}
    }
}
```

fixed

The keyword fixed, used only in unsafe mode, is a modifier that sets unmanaged pointers to managed variable locations. These positions are then fixed to prevent their automatic deletion, as is normally done with C# garbage collection (see Example B.26).

Example B.26.

```
namespace Appendix_B {
    class ClassFixed {
        public int variable;
    }
    class Class1 {
        static unsafe void Main() {
            ClassFixed TestFixed = new ClassFixed();
            TestFixed.variable = 7;
            fixed (int* pointer = &TestFixed.variable) {}
        }
    }
}
```

float

Float is a 32-bit data type used to store floating point values ranging from $\pm 1.5 \times 10^{-45}$ to $\pm 3.4 \times 10^{38}$, with a precision level of 7 digits. Note that since doubles are the default, it is also important to include a suffix when attempting to assign an irrational numeric; failure to do so will result in a compilation error (see Example B.27).

Example B.27.

```
namespace Appendix_B {
    class Class1 {
        static void Main() {
            float Number1, Number2;
```

C# and Game Programming

```
            Number1 = 1.0f;
            Number2 = 1.1f;
        }
    }
}
```

for

The `for` loop, also known as the `for` statement, is a repetitive process that is set up under certain conditions to run a particular number of times. This terminating factor helps to separate it from the other two looping processes because it's not dependent on an unknown variable. The `for` loop thus predefines its variable as part of its initial statement. The comparison operators are still used to determine whether to continue or terminate, but this will always happen at a predetermined point in the loop, when our variable equals 10, 100, or X number of cycles. The `for` statement is constructed much like the `while`-loop, but with its initializing variable and its incrementing operator both becoming one with its declaration (see Example B.28).

Example B.28.

```
class Appendix_B {
    static void Main() {
        for (int i = 0; i < 5; i++) {/* */}
    }
}
```

foreach

The `foreach` loop is a specialized process that is used to skim or scan through an array of elements without the common drudgery usually associated with listing that array's components. It is generally written to include both the keywords `foreach` and `in`, and for the most part, it physically resembles the notation used when describing the `for` loop process. One key difference, however, is that the indexing or searching value is not allowed to be altered; this would include even subtle manipulation, such as the incrementing or decrementing operators (see Example B.29).

Example B.29.

```
class Appendix_B {
    static void Main() {
```

```
        char[] integer = {'a', 'g', 'n', 'u'};
        foreach (char find in integer){/* */}
    }
}
```

goto

The goto statement is probably the most picked-on of all the keywords. Its use is consider poor programming habit, yet somehow it manages to endure. Its fault lies in its ability to transgress order; the C# help files even mark it as useful way of getting out of nested statements, but, of course, that would be breaking the rules. Still, there is at least one practical reason for using the goto statement in C#, which is to allow for artificial drops when dealing with switch statements. Remember C# no longer allows us to drop between switch statements that contain executable statements, so *goto* makes a good fix. C#'s goto also has some limitations, including not being able to jump into localized block or between classes, nor should it be used to alter our try-catch blocks (see Example B.30).

Example B.30.

```
class Appendix_B {
    static void Main() {
        char Character = '1';
        switch (Character) {
            case '1':
                goto case2;
                break;
            case '2':
                case2:
                goto case3;
                break;
            case '3':
                case3:
                break;
        }
    }
}
```

if

The if statement is a conditional statement that tests an expression or set of expressions and executes a statement or block of statements when that expression is found to be true (see Example B.31).

Example B.31.

```
class Appendix_4 {
    static void Main() {
        int Number = 7;
        if (Number == 7)
            Number++;
    }
}
```

`implicit`

The keyword `implicit` is used when attempting to declare a user-defined conversion operator. Implicit conversions can improve source code readability and safety, and generally occur without the programmer's awareness. (Note: Implicit operators should not throw exceptions—see Example B.32).

Example B.32.

```
namespace Appendix_B {
    class IsByte {
        byte value;
        public IsByte(byte value) {this.value = value;}
        public static implicit operator byte(IsByte Byte) {
            return Byte.value;
        }
        public static void Main() {}
    }
}
```

`in`

The keyword `in` is used with the `In` statement when reading the contents of an array (see Example B.33).

Example B.33.

```
using System;
class Appendix_B {
    static void Main() {
        char[] integer = {'a', 'g', 'n', 'u'};
        foreach (char find in integer){/* */}
    }
}
```

int

Integer (int) is a 32-bit integral data type used to store values ranging from -2,147,483,648 to 2,147,483,647 (see Example B.34).

Example B.34.

```
class Appendix_1 {
    static void Main() {
        int OurVariable = 1;
    }
}
```

interface

To create an interface is to declare a reference type that is noted for having only abstract members. Once created, it can exist either as an independent body or as part of a class reference. Interfaces are also capable of inheriting from other interfaces, including multiple inheritances (not allowed with C# classes). Note: When creating an inherited class with a combined interface, remember to include the base class first (see Example B.35).

Example B.35

```
using System;
namespace Appendix_B {
    interface BaseInterface {
        short Width {get; set;}
        short Length {get; set;}
    }
    public class BaseClass : BaseInterface {
        private short BIWidth;
        private short BILength;
        protected BaseClass() {}
        protected BaseClass(short Width, short y) {
            BIWidth = Width;
            BILength = y;
        }
        public short Width {
            get{return(BIWidth);}
            set{BIWidth = value;}
        }
```

```
        public short Length {
            get{return(BILength);}
            set{BILength = value;}
        }
        public static void Main() {}
    }
}
```

internal

An `internal` access modifier is a type member used to access class components. The advantage of the `internal` modifier is that it allows for limited access from within a single assembly. A key disadvantage then is that it is only accessible from within that assembly. In addition to the basic internal modifier, we can also use the keyword `internal` in combination with `protected` to create a `internal protected` modifier (see Example B.36).

Example B.36.

```
namespace Appendix_B {
    internal class BankAccount {
        internal protected string first_name;
        internal void ViewFiles(BankAccount acc) {}
    }
    class Class1 {
        static void Main() {}
    }
}
```

is

The `is` operator is used as part of a Boolean expression to test the compatibility of a specific object type. For example, if an object is an `is` expression, then it will evaluate to true if the expression is not null and the expression can be cast without throwing an exception (see Example B.37).

Example B.37.

```
using System;
namespace Appendix_B {
    class TestClass {}
    public class Class1 {
```

```
        public static void Test(object ob) {
            TestClass test;
            if (ob is TestClass) {
                test = (TestClass)ob;
            }
        }
        public static void Main() {}
    }
}
```

lock

A lock is a temporary, mutual exclusion used to ensure that multiple threads do not inadvertently access the same section of coding. locks are used with the this statement and the typeof command, and are written as: lock (expression) executable block. Note: lock statements also require that their expressions be referenced types (see Example B.38).

Example B.38.

```
namespace Appendix_B {
    class MyName {
        private string name;
        protected MyName(string fn) {this.name = fn;}
        protected string TestName(string fn) {
            lock (this) {
                if (fn != null) {
                    return (this.name);
                }
            }
            return(null);
        }
        public static void Main() {}
    }
}
```

long

Long is a 64-bit data type used to store values ranging from −9,223,372,036,854,775,808 to 9,223,372,036,854,775,807 (see Example B.39).

Example B.39.

```
class Appendix_B {
    static void Main() {
        long Number;
    }
}
```

namespace

When we encompass our coding inside a `namespace`, we are actually declaring a scope or globally unique partition. The types contained in that namespace are accessible through direct access (from within that body), and through the using-namespace-directive, which allows us to use its values without qualification (see Example B.40)

Example B.40.

```
namespace Appendix_B {
    class Class1 {
        static void Main() {}
    }
}
```

new

The keyword new is used as both an operator and a modifier. As an operator, it is used to declare instances and to create objects. As a modifier, it is used to hide members inherited from a base class. Note that the new operator cannot be overloaded, nor can it be used with the `override` statement (see Example B.41).

Example B.41.

```
namespace Appendix_B {
    public class BaseClass {
        public short x;
        protected BaseClass() {}
        public short X {set{x = value;}}
    }

    public class DerivedClass : BaseClass {
        protected DerivedClass() {}
```

```
        public new short X {get{return(x);}}
        static void Main(){}
    }
}
```

null

The `null` reference refers to an object that has not yet been assigned. It basically serves as a blank or nonvalue, which can be substituted for later (see Example B.42).

Example B.42.

```
namespace Appendix_B {
    public class TestAS {
        public static void Main() {
            object MyString = new object();
            MyString = 123;
            string s = MyString as string;
            if (s != null)
                MyString = "X";
        }
    }
}
```

object

The keyword `object` is used to assign values to objects. We can apply these techniques to include both value-to-reference and reference-to-value conversions. This process is most commonly referred to as *boxing*, with the term *unboxing* denoting the returning of those values to their original state. The process follows the same steps used with basic type casting, but with an added note of caution when attempting to return or unbox values, since they can return to new variables, but those variables must be of the originally boxed data type. The conversions are done using the keyword object as is shown below.

Example B.43.

```
public class Appendix_B {
    public static void Main() {
        object MyString = new object();
    }
}
```

operator

Operator overloading is the reapplication of operators to include class manipulations. The standard class `operator` overloads include object-to-object and object-to-numeric values (including variables). The most important point when dealing with operator overloading is the understanding that all abbreviated forms should be made implicit.

Example B.44.

```
namespace Appendix_B {
    public class Objects {
        int Number;
        public Objects(int Value) {this.Number = Value;}
        public static Objects operator +(Objects Ob, int Value) {
            Ob.Number += Value; return(Ob);
        }
        static void Main() {}
    }
}
```

out

The keyword `out` is a special exception marker that notifies the compiler so that the variable under scrutiny does not need to be assigned before it can be passed as a referenced variable. This is usually the case when dealing with values that wouldn't otherwise have a meaningful value before the appropriate functions can be executed. Since an `out` value is also a referenced value, this keyword negates the need for the second *reference* (`ref`) (see Example B.45).

Example B.45.

```
using System;
class Appendix_B {
    static void Main() {
        int iNumber1;
        TheRace (out iNumber1);
    }

    static void TheRace(out int Num) {
        Num = 1;
    }
}
```

override

In addition to being able to overload a function (for example, to chang the signature or parameters of that function), we can also `override` a function so as to force the compiler to accept a secondary version of that function. As its name implies, the keyword `override` is used to override members inherited from a base class. These inherited methods must have matching signatures and be either virtual, abstract, or previously overridden. This technique also allows us to manipulate that program's data so as to give it the illusion of consistency, or to save us the trouble of revising our previous class. The secondary version, then, becomes the obvious choice, as our instance was declared as part of that inherited class (see Example B.46). On a cautionary note, it should also be mentioned that if an overriding function had also referenced its base version (as is commonly done with privately inherited classes), that function's reference would then be diverted back to the inherited function. Note that we can also return access to the original method via the `base` command.

Example B.46.

```
namespace Appendix_B {
    public class Area {
        public Area() {}
        public virtual void CalculateArea() {}
    }
    public class Parallelogram: Area {
        override public void CalculateArea() {}
        static void Main() {}
    }
}
```

params

The keyword `params` is used to pass an array of any object type without explicitly declaring that data as an array. Only one object may be passed as a `params` per declaration, and any other declaration must precede that statement (see Example B.47).

Example B.47.

```
public class Appendix_B {
    public static void Params(params string[] list) {
    }
    public static void Main() {
    }
}
```

private, protected, and public

Private, protected, and public are class or structure members that allow for restricted or limited access based on user-defined methods written specifically for those values. These user-defined methods are declared as part of that class' internal structure (see Examples B.48–B.50).

Example B.48.

```
namespace Appendix_B {
    class BankAccount {
        private string first_name;
        private void ReadFiles(ref BankAccount acc) {}
        static void Main() {}
    }
}
```

Note: While private is the default setting, many programmers choose to explicitly restate that command to remove any ambiguity.

Example B.49.

```
namespace Appendix_B {
    class BankAccount {
        protected string first_name;
        protected void ReadFiles(ref BankAccount acc) {}
        static void Main() {}
    }
}
```

Example B.50.

```
namespace Appendix_B {
    class BankAccount {
        public string first_name;
        public void ReadFiles(ref BankAccount acc) {}
        static void Main() {}
    }
}
```

readonly

Readonly is a constant data type used as part of a class reference declared as a field. It is assignable at only one point in the program and then acts as a constant (see Example B.51).

Example B.51.

```
class Appendix_B {
    public readonly double variable2 = 3.14159;
    static void Main() {}
}
```

ref

The keyword ref is used to reflect a variable's control back to the original parameters, thereby allowing the method's, or function's, alterations to be known by the main or calling body (see Example B.52).

Example B.52.

```
class Appendix_B {
    static void Main() {
        int iNumber1 = 0;
        TheRace(ref iNumber1);
    }

    static void TheRace(ref int Num) {}
}
```

return

The keyword `return` is used to pass back a single value to that of the calling function. The value in question must be the qualified type, and in cases where the returning type is void, it can be omitted. Return statements are required with all nonvoid user-defined functions and methods (see Example B.53).

Example B.53.

```
using System;
class Appendix_B {
    static void Main() {
        RandomNumber();
    }

    static int RandomNumber() {
        return(0);
    }
}
```

sbyte

The keyword `sbyte` is an 8-bit integer used to store values ranging from -128 to 127 (see Example B.54).

Example B.54.

```
class Appendix_B {
    static void Main() {
        sbyte Number1 = 1;
    }
}
```

sealed

Once a class is `sealed`, it can no longer be inherited, hence it cannot be overridden or altered in any other way. For the same reason, we cannot use `sealed` with the `abstract` modifier (see Example B.55).

Example B.55.

```
sealed class Appendix_B {
    static void Main() {}
}
```

short

The keyword `short` is a 16-bit integer data type used to store values ranging from -32,768 to 32,767 (see Example B.56).

Example B.56.

```
class Appendix_B {
    static void Main() {
        short Number1 = 1;
    }
}
```

sizeof

The `sizeof` keyword is used to gather information pertaining to the size of our data types. Unfortunately, this also requires the use of a secondary command, `unsafe`, which is used to mark the unsafe nature of that code (see Example B.57).

Example B.57.

```
using System;
class Appendix_B {
    static unsafe void Main() {
        Console.WriteLine ("Byte = " + sizeof(byte));
    }
}
```

stackalloc

The keyword `stackalloc` (stack allocating), is used to allocate blocks of memory referenced from a stack. The addresses of these blocks are stored as pointers and they are protected from garbage collection, thus they do not have to be fixed/pinned. Note: All blocks are lost when their methods are terminated (see Example B.58).

Example B.58.

```
class Appendix_B {
    public static unsafe void Main() {
        int* pointer1 = stackalloc int[3];
        pointer1[0] = 1;
    }
}
```

static

The keyword static is used to modify constructors, fields, methods, operators, and properties. Static constructors, for example, are called automatically, and are used to initialize the rest of the class before any members are referenced. Static fields, then, are not part of a specific instance, and instead are referenced as a single memory address.

Example B.59.

```
class Appendix_B {
    static void Main() {}
}
```

string

A string is a reference data type that encompasses the more recently developed unicode characters. These characters can be transferred to string references using simple quotation marks, these expressions can also be made literal by first noting them with the @ symbol (see Example B.60).

Example B.60.

```
class Appendix_B {
    static void Main() {
        string MyDog = "Brownie";
    }
}
```

struct

Structures (struct) are user-defined data types that allow for groupings of similar or related data that do not have a single base data type. These groups can include all the basic value data-types as well as a list of methods used to manipulate those values. The data types declared inside a structure are referred to as the structure's *members* (or *fields*), while their declarations are referred to as its *instances*. The correlations between these internal values and structures are usually guided by some common theme or purpose. A structure is made up of the keyword struct, the structure's tag (or name); a list of the fields (written as declared members); and a list of possible methods used to manipulate that data. Structures are generally contained within a single block placed inside our referencing namespace, but as shown in Example B.61, they can also be used to invoke the main method.

Note that while the use of a C++ style terminating semicolon is allowed, it is not required when working with C#.

Example B.61.

```
struct Appendix_B {
    static void Main() {}
}
```

switch

The `switch` statement, like the `if` and `else-if` statements, is used to execute a statement or set of statements that equal the variable's value. However, unlike the `if` and `else-if` statements, the `switch` statement doesn't use comparison operators; instead, it simply reads the value of the variable and attempts to direct the program to the proper channel. A second keyword, `case`, is also used in this process. The keyword `case` is written and used multiple times from within the `switch` statement. Each `case` statement holds a numeric or character value for comparison. If the value held by a `case` statement matches the value read by the `switch` statement, then everything following that `case` statement will be executed.

Example B.62.

```
class Appendix_B {
    static void Main() {
        int Grades = 1;
        switch (Grades) {
            case 1:
                break;
            default:
                break;
        }
    }
}
```

this

The keyword `this` is a specialized reference signature used to indicate the referencing object of a passing class; in other words, it is a longhand version for the otherwise abbreviated member. While the `this` reference is implied, its definitions can become ambiguous and should be included to prevent this error (see Example B.63).

Example B.63.

```
class Appendix_B {
    protected short pin_number;
    private void ReadFiles() {
        this.pin_number = 1;
    }
    static void Main() {}
}
```

throw

In addition to being able to catch both generalized and specific exceptions, we can also learn to throw a few of our own. This is not usually necessary for the context of this book, but the technique can serve to clarify the definitions of some otherwise confusing errors (see Example B.64).

Example B.64.

```
using System;
public class Appendix_B {
    static void Main() {
        int Y = 0;
        if (Y == 0) {
            throw new DivideByZeroException("\nProgram Error!");
        }
    }
}
```

true

A user-defined Boolean type operator that returns the value true (see Example B.65).

Example B.65.

```
class Appendix_B {
    static void Main() {
        bool Variable1 = true;
    }
}
```

try

When it comes to user input, we can never guarantee the results, therefore, we need to think ahead and plan for possible errors. The try block scenario is a test application that is used in conjunction with several `catch` responses. The information in question is placed between the `try` block's parameters and is given only one chance to succeed (see Example B.66).

Example B.66.

```
public class Appendix_B {
    static void Main() {
        try{}
        catch{}
        finally{}
    }
}
```

typeof

The `typeof` operator is used to determine an object's type, fields, methods, properties (see Example B.67)

Example B.67.

```
using System;
namespace Appendix_B {
    public class Class1 {
        public static void Main() {
            Type Ob = typeof(Class1);
            Console.WriteLine(Ob.GetFields());
            Console.WriteLine(Ob.GetMethods());
        }
    }
}
```

uint

The keyword `uint` is a unsigned 32-bit integral type used to store values ranging from 0 to 4,294,967,295 (see Example B.68).

Example B.68.

```
class Appendix_B {
    static void Main() {
        uint Number1 = 1;
    }
}
```

ulong

The keyword `ulong` denotes a unsigned 64-bit integral type used to store values ranging from 0 to 18,446,744,073,709,551,615 (see Example B.69).

Example B.69.

```
class Appendix_B {
    static void Main() {
        ulong Number1 = 1;
    }
}
```

unchecked

The keyword `unchecked` is used to block the Solution Explorer\Configuration Properties\ Build \ Check for an arithmetic overflow/underflow true statement. This statement is false by default, but if we were to change this default and then attempt to break the barriers of our designated type, we could block the error with the `unchecked` statement (see Example B.70).

Example B.70.

```
class Appendix_B {
    static void Main () {
        byte Max255 = 255;
        unchecked {Max255 += 1 ;}
    }
}
```

unsafe

The keyword `unsafe` denotes a change in settings to unsafe mode. The `unsafe` feature was developed to aid in bridging the gap between C++ and C# programming, allowing us to use time tested techniques that are not officially permitted under C#'s `safe` mode (see Example B.72). In addition to including the keyword `unsafe` to our coding, we must also change the compiler's settings in Configuration Manager (see Chapter 1—Sizeof and Unsafe Coding for details).

Example B.71.

```
class Class1 {
    static unsafe void Main() {}
}
```

ushort

The keyword ushort denotes a 16-bit integral data type used to store values ranging from 0 to 65,535 (see Example B.72).

Example B.72

```
class Appendix_B {
    static void Main() {
        ushort Number1 = 1;
    }
}
```

using

The using directive allows us to include a host of system and user-defined namespaces including a namespace is not equivalent to including a file, as was done in C++). Here, we'll only be notifying the compiler of where to find the references written in shorthand. User-defined namespaces are accessed in exactly the same manner as the system type (see Example B.73).

Example B.73.

```
using System;
class Appendix_B {
    static void Main() {}
}
```

virtual

The keyword virtual denotes a modifier that sets a method of a base class so that it can be overridden in a derived class. When a virtual function is referenced, it searches for an overriding method.

Example B.74.

```
namespace Appendix_B {
    public class Area {
        public Area() {}
        public virtual void CalculateArea() {}
    }
    public class Parallelogram : Area {
        public Parallelogram() {}
        override public void CalculateArea() {}
        static void Main() {}
    }
}
```

void

`Void` is a data type that holds no data, thus, serves the purpose of telling the compiler that no data will be required by this variable or returning function. This is logical, since the ending of the main function is also the ending of the program and there would be no program to which information could be sent. `Void` is also most commonly associated with user-defined functions that use reference-variables (explained in Chapter 2) and generalized pointers-variables (explained in Chapter 4). Unlike the other data types, `Void` does not take a position in memory, therefore, we won't need to measure its size in bytes.

Example B.75.

```
class Appendix_B {
    static void Main(){}
}
```

volatile

The keyword `volatile` is used to denote a variable that cannot be optimized, which is usually due to some unpredictable change or reference made to it, frequently from an outside source such as the operating system or hardware device (see Example B.76).

Example B.76.

```
class Appendix_B {
  public volatile char variable3 = 'A';
  static void Main(){}
}
```

while

The `while` loop can be set up to repeat and/or terminate in several different ways. The most common include using a predetermined count (as in to repeat an iteration five times then end) according to the user's input (end by request), and a termination command (a command that shortsteps or breaks the loop—see Example B.77).

Example B.77.

```
class Appendix_B {
  static void Main() {
    while(true){}
  }
}
```

Appendix C: Accessors

`get` & `set`

The `get` and `set` accessors aren't officially keywords, rather, they are parameterless methods named to match certain fields and used in classes and interfaces that hold a body of executable data pertaining to the storage and retrieval of those fields. Their executable statements may include calculations, conversions, and a large host of other tasks, but their underlying purpose must include reading or recording to those properties. The body of an accessor is considered equivalent to a method although they do not include identity signatures. The `get` accessor returns a value and may be set to throw a value when needed; in contrast, the `set` accessor is always set to *void*. The keyword `value` is also used as an implicit parameter with setting fields, thus it takes on the value of any passed variables. The `get` and the `set` accessors always share the same user-defined name, thus they cannot exist in the same base class. It is then considered natural to place the `set` accessor in the base class with the `get` accessor listed in the `nest` derived class. It is also important to remember that the value retrieved by the `get` property is for reference only, while the value recorded in the `set` property is write only (see Example C.1).

Example C.1.

```
namespace Appendix_C {
    public class BaseClass {
        public short width;
        protected BaseClass() {}
        public short Width {set{width = value;}}
    }
    public class DerivedClass : BaseClass {
        protected DerivedClass() {}
        public new short Width {get{return(width);}}
        static void Main() {}
    }
}
```

`value`

`value` types are implicit fields declared as part of a methods signature, and are referenced as if they were actual fields. They have the same limitations and abilities associated with a field of their declared type and should be treated as such (see Example C.2).

Example C.2.

```
namespace Appendix_C {
  public class Objects {
    int Number;
    public Objects(int value) {
      this.Number = value;
    }
    static void Main(){}
  }
}
```

Appendix D: Order of Precedence

Symbol(s)	Description
.	Dot operator
[ ]	Array indexing
( )	Function call
++	Postfix increment operator (placed after the variable)
−−	Postfix decrement operator (placed after the variable)
new, typeof	
checked, unchecked	
++	Prefix increment operator (placed before the variable)
−−	Prefix decrement operator (placed before the variable)
!	Not
-	Unary minus
+	Unary Plus
~	Unary
(T)x	
*	Multiply
/	Divide
%	Remainder
+	Addition
-	Subtraction
<<	Shift
>>	Shift
<	Less than
>	Greater than
<=	Less than or equal to
>=	Greater than or equal to
as, is	
==	Equal to
!=	Not equal to
&	Logical AND
^	Logical XOR
|	Logical OR
&&	And
||	Or
?:	IF
= += -= *= /= %= <<= >>= |= &= ^=	Assignment, add, subtract, multiply, divide, remainder...

Appendix E: Displaying Message Boxes

Message boxes are predefined dialog boxes that are used to send and receive simple data streams between the user and the program. These messages may include titles, comments, and buttons that allow for a short list of responses, such as yes, no, ok, and cancel (see Examples E.1–E.17).

Example E.1. The message box.

```
using System;
using System.Drawing;
using System.Collections;
using System.ComponentModel;
using System.Windows.Forms;
using System.Data;
using System.IO;
using System.Runtime.InteropServices;

namespace Appendix_E {
    public class Form1 : System.Windows.Forms.Form {
        [DllImport("winmm.dll")]
        public static extern long PlaySound(String lpszName,
            long hModule, long dwFlags);

        public Form1() {
            MessageBox.Show("Place message here");
        }

        [STAThread]
        static void Main() {
            Application.Run(new Form1());
        }

        private void Form1_Load(object sender, System.EventArgs e){}
    }
}
```

> **Note:** We can also reuse this program to test the rest of the message box references—please insert those changes as necessary.

Example E.2.

```
MessageBox.Show("Place message Here", "Place caption here");
```

Example E.3.

```
MessageBox.Show("Place message Here", "Place caption here",
    MessageBoxButtons.OK);
```

Example E.4.

```
MessageBox.Show("Place message here", "Place caption here",
    MessageBoxButtons.AbortRetryIgnore);
```

Example E.5.

```
MessageBox.Show("Place message here", "Place caption here",
    MessageBoxButtons.OKCancel);
```

Example E.6.

```
MessageBox.Show("Place message here", "Place caption here",
    MessageBoxButtons.RetryCancel);
```

Example E.7.

```
MessageBox.Show("Place message here", "Place caption here",
    MessageBoxButtons.YesNo);
```

Example E.8.

```
MessageBox.Show("Place message here", "Place Caption here",
    MessageBoxButtons.YesNoCancel);
```

Example E.9.

```
MessageBox.Show("Place message here", "Place caption here",
    MessageBoxButtons.OK, MessageBoxIcon.Asterisk);
```

Example E.10.

```
MessageBox.Show("Place message here", "Place caption here",
    MessageBoxButtons.OK, MessageBoxIcon.Error);
```

Example E.11.

```
MessageBox.Show("Place message here", "Place caption here",
    MessageBoxButtons.OK, MessageBoxIcon.Exclamation);
```

Example E.12.

```
MessageBox.Show("Place message here", "Place caption here",
    MessageBoxButtons.OK, MessageBoxIcon.Hand);
```

Example E.13.

```
MessageBox.Show("Place message here", "Place caption here",
    MessageBoxButtons.OK, MessageBoxIcon.Information);
```

Example E.14.

```
MessageBox.Show("Place message here", "Place caption here",
    MessageBoxButtons.OK, MessageBoxIcon.None);
```

Example E.15.

```
MessageBox.Show("Place message here", "Place caption here",
    MessageBoxButtons.OK, MessageBoxIcon.Question);
```

Example E.16.

```
MessageBox.Show("Place message here", "place caption here",
    MessageBoxButtons.OK, MessageBoxIcon.Stop);
```

Example E.17.

```
MessageBox.Show("Place message here", "Place caption here",
    MessageBoxButtons.OK, MessageBoxIcon.Warning);
```

We can also test and build new actions based on the responses received by message boxes (see Examples E.18–E.26).

Example E.18.

```
DialogResult result = MessageBox.Show("Place message here",
    "Place caption here", MessageBoxButtons.OK);

if (result == DialogResult.OK) {
    PlaySound(@"C:\SourceCode\Fire.wav", 0, 0);
}
```

Example E.19.

```
DialogResult result = MessageBox.Show("Place message here",
    "Place caption here", MessageBoxButtons.OKCancel);

if (result == DialogResult.Cancel) {
    PlaySound(@"C:\SourceCode\Fire.wav", 0, 0);
}
```

Example E.20.

```
DialogResult result = MessageBox.Show("Place message here",
    "Place caption here", MessageBoxButtons.YesNo);

if (result == DialogResult.Yes) {
    PlaySound(@"C:\SourceCode\Fire.wav", 0, 0);
}
```

Example E.21.

```
DialogResult result = MessageBox.Show("Place message Here",
    "Place caption here", MessageBoxButtons.YesNo);

if (result == DialogResult.No) {
    PlaySound(@"C:\SourceCode\Fire.wav", 0, 0);
}
```

Example E.22.

```
DialogResult result = MessageBox.Show("Place message here",
    "Place caption here", MessageBoxButtons.YesNoCancel);

if (result == DialogResult.Cancel) {
    PlaySound(@"C:\SourceCode\Fire.wav", 0, 0);
}
```

Example E.23.

```
DialogResult result = MessageBox.Show("Place message here",
    "Place caption here", MessageBoxButtons.AbortRetryIgnore);

if (result == DialogResult.Abort) {
    PlaySound(@"C:\SourceCode\Fire.wav", 0, 0);
}
```

Example E.24.

```
DialogResult result = MessageBox.Show("Place message here",
    "Place caption here", MessageBoxButtons.AbortRetryIgnore);
if (result == DialogResult.Retry) {
    PlaySound(@"C:\SourceCode\Fire.wav", 0, 0);
}
```

Example E.25.

```
DialogResult result = MessageBox.Show("Place message here",
    "Place caption here", MessageBoxButtons.AbortRetryIgnore);

if (result == DialogResult.Ignore) {
    PlaySound(@"C:\SourceCode\Fire.wav", 0, 0);
}
```

Example E.26.

```
DialogResult result = MessageBox.Show(this, "Place message here",
    "Place title here", MessageBoxButtons.YesNoCancel);

if (result != DialogResult.None) {
    PlaySound(@"C:\SourceCode\Fire.wav", 0, 0);
}
```

> We could have also inserted the MessageBoxIcon feature into any of these examples.

We'll also want to take advantage of two of the useful MessageBoxOptions, RightAlign and RtlReading. These are essentially message alignment tools with RightAlign moving the

C# and Game Programming

message text to the far right (user's perspective), and RtlReading moving the message to the left (placing the icon on the right). We'll can also set a default, or preselected button; this will not affect the user's ability to choose, but it generally serves as the recommended option (see Examples E.27–E.29).

Example E.27.

```
DialogResult result = MessageBox.Show(this, "Place message here",
    "Place caption here", MessageBoxButtons.YesNoCancel,
    MessageBoxIcon.Question, MessageBoxDefaultButton.Button1,
    MessageBoxOptions.RightAlign);

if (result == DialogResult.Yes) {
    PlaySound(@"C:\SourceCode\Fire.wav", 0, 0);
}
```

Example E.28.

```
DialogResult result = MessageBox.Show(this, "Place message here",
    "Place caption here", MessageBoxButtons.YesNoCancel,
    MessageBoxIcon.Question, MessageBoxDefaultButton.Button2,
    MessageBoxOptions.RtlReading);

if (result == DialogResult.No) {
    PlaySound(@"C:\SourceCode\Fire.wav", 0, 0);
}
```

Example E.29.

```
DialogResult result = MessageBox.Show(this, "Place message here",
    "Place caption here", MessageBoxButtons.YesNoCancel,
    MessageBoxIcon.Question, MessageBoxDefaultButton.Button3,
    MessageBoxOptions.RtlReading);

if (result == DialogResultCancel) {
    PlaySound(@"C:\SourceCode\Fire.wav", 0, 0);
}
```

> It is also important to remember not to place message boxes such as these inside of OnPaint or other graphics handling methods, the result is a potential invalidating loop.

Appendix F: Graphics

Windows Forms has provided us with several methods used to produce everything from the basic shapes to some intricate designs. Here, I'll introduce some of the alternative drawing tools and many of the techniques associated with the color references.

Points & Size

The first aspect to drawing is the `point` reference, which describes the locations that delineate shapes. A point is declared using the Cartesian coordinate system (the x, y coordinate system), where x is the horizontal position and y is the vertical position as in Point(int x, int y). Once our points are defined, we'll then need to include a `size` reference, which also relies on an x, y scheme—Size(int x, int y). Both `point` and `Size` can be referenced as individual objects or as part of a specific shape (see Example F.1).

Example F.1.

```
using System;
using System.Drawing;
using System.Windows.Forms;
namespace Appendix_F {
    public class Form1 : System.Windows.Forms.Form {
        public Form1() {}
        protected override void OnPaint(PaintEventArgs e) {
            Point point = new Point(10, 15);
            Size size = new Size(15, 200);
            Brush GreenBrush = new SolidBrush (Color.Green);
            Graphics MyText = e.Graphics;
            Font Normal = new Font("Times New Roman", 14, FontStyle.Bold);
            MyText.DrawString("TEST", Normal, GreenBrush,
                new Rectangle(point, size));
            MyText.DrawString("TEST", Normal, GreenBrush,
                new Rectangle(new Point(50, 15), new Size(15, 200)));
        }
        static void Main() {
          Application.Run(new Form1());
        }
    }
}
```

> PointF and SizeF are used to indicate floating point values, which are necessary when drawing with pixels.

Brushes & Pens

We can also use what are known as *brushes* and *pens* to enhance graphics and text-supported displays. Brushes and pens are declared and accessed in basically the same manner, with brushes being used for text and to fill, rather than to draw shapes. Brushes are also abstract by definition and hence cannot be instantiated. There are, however, five derived classes used to create different types of brushes: HatchBrush, LinearGradientBrush, PathGradientBrush, SolidBrush, and TextureBrush. Pen is also derived from the abstract brush class; it can be written to take advantage of all five of the derived classes, but it has a constant color rather than a gradient. For our purposes, we'll want to look at how to declare and reference both the basic SolidBrush and the pen (see Example F.2).

Example F.2.

```
using System;
using System.Drawing;
using System.Windows.Forms;
namespace Appendix_F {
    public class Form1 : System.Windows.Forms.Form {
        public Form1() {}
        protected override void OnPaint(PaintEventArgs e) {
            Graphics Figures = this.CreateGraphics();
            Brush RedBrush = new SolidBrush(Color.Red);
            Pen BluePen = new Pen(Color.Blue, 3);
            Figures.FillRectangle(RedBrush, 10, 10, 25, 25);
            Figures.DrawRectangle(BluePen, 20, 20, 25, 25);
        }
        static void Main() {
            Application.Run(new Form1());
        }
    }
}
```

> The second value associated with the pen statement, Pen(Color, *int*), is used to reference its width.

Lines

Now that we have some basic points to reference and our pen in hand, the next logical step is to learn how to link those points to create lines and, of course, curves. Lines are straightforward enough, with four basic references: DrawLine(Color, Point1, Point2), DrawLine(Color, int x, int y, int x_2, int y_2), DrawLine(Color, PointF1, PointF2), and DrawLine(Color, float x, float y, float x_2, float y_2)—see Example F.3.

Example F.3.

```
using System;
using System.Drawing;
using System.Windows.Forms;
namespace Appendix_F {
    public class Form1 : System.Windows.Forms.Form {
    public Form1() {}
    protected override void OnPaint(PaintEventArgs e) {
        Point point1 = new Point(10, 10);
        Point point2 = new Point(250, 250);
        PointF pointf1 = new PointF(125F, 10F);
        PointF pointf2 = new PointF(125F, 250F);

        Graphics Figures = this.CreateGraphics();
        Pen RedPen = new Pen(Color.Red);
        Pen GreenPen = new Pen(Color.Green);
        Pen BluePen = new Pen(Color.Blue);
        Pen YellowPen = new Pen(Color.Yellow);

        Figures.DrawLine(RedPen, point1, point2);
        Figures.DrawLine(GreenPen, 250, 10, 10, 250);
        Figures.DrawLine(BluePen, pointf1, pointf2);
        Figures.DrawLine(YellowPen, 10F, 125F, 250F, 125F);}
        static void Main() {
            Application.Run(new Form1());
        }
    }
}
```

Curves

Curves are a bit more complex with seven, potential references: DrawCurve(Color, ArrayOfPoints, Offset, Segment, Tension); DrawCurve(Color, ArrayOfPoints, Tension);

DrawCurve(Color, ArrayOfPoints); DrawCurve(Color, ArrayOfPoints, Offset, Segment, Tension); DrawCurve(Color, ArrayOfPoints, Offset, Segment); DrawCurve(Color, ArrayOfPoints, Tension); and DrawCurve(Color, ArrayOfPoints)—see Example F.4.

Example F.4.

```
using System;
using System.Drawing;
using System.Windows.Forms;
namespace Appendix_F {
    public class Form1 : System.Windows.Forms.Form {
        public Form1() {}
        protected override void OnPaint(PaintEventArgs e) {
            PointF pointf1 = new PointF(125F, 10F);
            PointF pointf2 = new PointF(125F, 125F);
            PointF pointf3 = new PointF(250F, 250F);
            PointF pointf4 = new PointF(250.0F, 150.0F);
            PointF pointf5 = new PointF(150F, 100F);
            PointF pointf6 = new PointF(250F, 200F);
            PointF pointf7 = new PointF(125F, 125F);

            PointF[] ArrayOfPoints = {pointf1, pointf2, pointf3, pointf4,
                pointf5, pointf6, pointf7};

            Graphics Figures = this.CreateGraphics();
            Pen RedPen = new Pen(Color.Red);

            Figures.DrawCurve(RedPen, ArrayOfPoints, 2, 4, 1.0F);
            Figures.DrawCurve(RedPen, ArrayOfPoints, 0);
            Figures.DrawCurve(RedPen, ArrayOfPoints);
        }
        static void Main() {
            Application.Run(new Form1());
        }
    }
}
```

Drawing Shapes

We'll definitely want to take advantage of all the potential shapes stored in the Windows Forms. We'll look at the basic ellipse, polygon, and rectangle. We'll also want to have a look at the FillPolygon and FillPie (see Example F.5).

Example F.5.

```
using System;
using System.Drawing;
using System.Windows.Forms;
namespace Appendix_F {
    public class Form1 : System.Windows.Forms.Form {
        public Form1() {}
        protected override void OnPaint(PaintEventArgs e) {
            Point point1 = new Point(10, 10);
            Point point2 = new Point(250, 250);
            PointF pointf1 = new PointF(125F, 10F);
            PointF pointf2 = new PointF(125F, 125F);
            PointF pointf3 = new PointF(250F, 250F);
            PointF pointf4 = new PointF(250.0F, 150.0F);
            PointF pointf5 = new PointF(150F, 100F);
            PointF pointf6 = new PointF(250F, 200F);
            PointF pointf7 = new PointF(125F, 125F);
            PointF[] ArrayOfPoints = {pointf1, pointf2, pointf3, pointf4,
                pointf5, pointf6, pointf7};
            Graphics Figures = this.CreateGraphics();
            Pen RedPen = new Pen(Color.Red);
            Pen GreenPen = new Pen(Color.Green);
            Pen BluePen = new Pen(Color.Blue);
            Brush YellowBrush = Brushes.Yellow;
            Brush OrangeBrush = Brushes.Orange;
            Figures.DrawRectangle(RedPen, 10, 10, 100, 100);
            Figures.DrawEllipse(GreenPen, 25, 25, 50, 50);
            Figures.DrawPolygon(BluePen, ArrayOfPoints);
            Figures.FillPolygon(YellowBrush, ArrayOfPoints);
            Figures.FillPie(OrangeBrush, 40, 150, 70, 70, 40, 50);
        }
        static void Main() {
            Application.Run(new Form1());
        }
    }
}
```

Diagonal lines can also be created using DrawLine, but if the line is asymmetrical it will appear coarse or jagged. In GDI+, a solution known as anti-aliasing is used. Anti-aliasing is a smoothing technique, based on shading, which is used to reduce sharpness. To the artist this would mean including a softer shade of the line's color that surrounds the line; thus, to the programmer this will mean adding additional lines.

Once we have the basic shapes, creating complex designs becomes nothing more than a question of ingenuity. Here, we'll combine a triangle, three rectangles, and a few area fills to create a small house and a garden (see Example F.6).

Example F.6.

```
using System;
using System.Drawing;
using System.Windows.Forms;
namespace Chapter3 {
    public class Form1 : System.Windows.Forms.Form {
    public Form1() {}
        protected override void OnPaint(PaintEventArgs e) {
            //Triangle
            PointF pointf1 = new PointF(125F, 50F);
            PointF pointf2 = new PointF(50F, 110F);
            PointF pointf3 = new PointF(200F, 110F);
            PointF[] ArrayOfPoints = {pointf1, pointf2, pointf3};

            Graphics Figures = this.CreateGraphics();
            Brush GreenBrush = Brushes.Green;
            Brush BlueBrush = Brushes.Aqua;
            Brush BrownBrush = Brushes.Brown;
            Brush BurlyWoodBrush = Brushes.BurlyWood;
            Figures.FillRectangle(BlueBrush, 0, 0, 300, 175);
            Figures.FillRectangle(BurlyWoodBrush, 75, 90, 100, 85);
            Figures.FillRectangle(BrownBrush, 90, 140, 20, 35);
            Figures.FillRectangle(BrownBrush, 130, 130, 30, 30);
            Figures.FillRectangle(GreenBrush, 0, 175, 300, 175);
            Figures.FillPolygon(BrownBrush, ArrayOfPoints);
        }
        static void Main() {
            Application.Run (new Form1 ());
        }
    }
}
```

Appendix G: Colors

The Windows Forms colors are based on the Alpha-Blending Red Green Blue (ARGB) model. There are 140 predefined colors and one user-defined color. To use a color it must first be defined as an instance, and then assigned to as specific brush/pen (see Example G.1). For a complete list of colors, see Table G.1.

Example G.1.

```
using System;
using System.Drawing;
using System.Windows.Forms;
namespace Appendix_G {
    public class Form1 : System.Windows.Forms.Form {
        public Form1() {InitializeComponent();}
        private void InitializeComponent() {}
        protected override void OnPaint(PaintEventArgs e) {
            Graphics test = e.Graphics;
            Font AlgerianFont = new Font("Algerian", 10);
            SolidBrush MyBrush = new SolidBrush(Color.Red);
            test.DrawString("Salvatore A. Buono", AlgerianFont,
                MyBrush, 60, 25);
        }
        static void Main() {
            Application.Run(new Form1());
        }
    }
}
```

We can also define our own colors using the static methods Color Color.FromArgb(*int* ARGB); Color.FromArgb(int alpha, Color color); Color.FromArgb(int red, int green, int blue); and Color.FromArgb(int alpha, int red, int green, int blue) (see Example G.2).

Example G.2.

```
using System;
using System.Drawing;
using System.Windows.Forms;
namespace Appendix_F {
    public class Form1 : System.Windows.Forms.Form {
        public Form1() {InitializeComponent();}
        private void InitializeComponent() {}
        protected override void OnPaint(PaintEventArgs e) {
            Graphics test = e.Graphics;
```

```csharp
            Font AlgerianFont = new Font("Algerian", 10);
            SolidBrush MyBrush = new SolidBrush(Color.FromArgb(255, 0,
                 0));
            test.DrawString("Salvatore A. Buono",
                AlgerianFont, MyBrush, 60, 25);
        }
        static void Main() {
            Application.Run(new Form1());
        }
    }
}
```

AliceBlue	DarkOliveGreen	Indigo	MediumPurple	Purple
AntiqueWhite	DarkOrange	Ivory	MediumSeaGreen	Red
Aqua	DarkOrchid	Khaki	MediumSlateBlue	RosyBrown
Aquamarine	DarkRed	Lavender	MediumSpringGreen	RoyalBlue
Azure	DarkSalmon	LavenderBlush	MediumTurquoise	SaddleBrown
Beige	DarkSeaGreen	LawnGreen	MediumVioletRed	Salmon
Bisque	DarkSlateBlue	LemonChiffon	MediumBlue	SandyBrown
Black	DarkSlateGray	LightBlue	MintCream	SeaGreen
BlanchedAlmond	DarkTurquoise	LightCoral	MistyRose	SeaShell
Blue	DarkViolet	LightCyan	Moccasin	Sienna
BlueViolet	DeepPink	LightYellow	NavajoWhite	Silver
Brown	DeepSkyBlue	LightGray	Navy	SkyBlue
BurlyWood	DimGray	LightGreen	OldLace	SlateBlue
CadetBlue	DodgerBlue	LightPink	Olive	SlateGray
Chartreuse	Firebrick	LightSalmon	OliveDrab	Snow
Chocolate	FloralWhite	LightSeaGreen	Orange	SpringGreen
Coral	ForestGreen	LightSkyBlue	OrangeRed	SteelBlue
CornflowerBlue	Fuchsia	LightSlateGray	Orchid	Tan
Cornsilk	Gainsboro	LightSteelBlue	PaleGoldenrod	Teal
Crimson	GhostWhite	LightYellow	PaleGreen	Thistle
Cyan	Gold	Lime	PaleTurquoise	Tomato
DarkBlue	Goldenrod	LimeGreen	PaleVioletRed	Turquoise
DarkCyan	Gray	Linen	PapayaWhip	Violet
DarkGoldenrod	Green	Magenta	Peachpuff	Wheat
DarkGray	GreenYellow	Maroon	Peru	White
DarkGreen	Honeydew	Med Aquamarine	Pink	WhiteSmoke
DarkKhaki	HotPink	MediumBlue	Plum	Yellow
DarkMagenta	IndianRed	MediumOrchid	PowderBlue	YellowGreen

Table G.1. Complete list of ARBG colors.

Appendix H: Algorithms

I'd like to take a moment to demonstrate a more explicit version of an algorithm. Here, every detail must be documented and made as vivid as possible, with no assumptions placed on the part of the programmer(s). Reasonable timelines should be developed with additional exit strategies placed on optional material and research. A text outline, drawings, and even some suggestive coding could be included with this model, but it should remain only a model.

Introduction

Pawns is a game I developed back in the late 1980s as an alternative to a traditional Chess game. It resembles Chess down to its very last detail, but there's one key difference: In my version, the players are no longer considered to be the Kings and instead are forced to choose alternative persona. They can select their own Queen, a Rook, Bishop, Knight, or any of their pawns, but if their player is captured, they're captured, meaning that the game is over and the other player wins. Thus, the true purpose of the game is not to capture the King, but instead to attempt to capture the other player's piece. Both sides should try their best to avoid revealing their identities, but at the same time they must defend the King and play the traditional game.

Basic Rules

The game is played on an eight by eight checkered board with all sixty-four squares open for play (see Figure H.1). Two players, one lighter and the other darker, rotate between moves with the lighter player beginning the game.

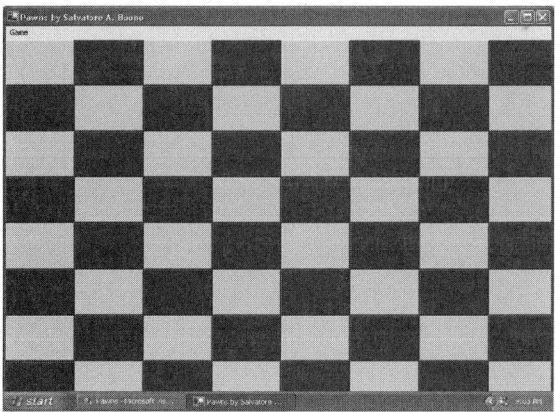

Figure H.1.

Each player begins with sixteen characters: one King, one Queen, two Rooks, two Bishops, two Knights and eight Pawns. The players are lined up on opposite sides of the board with the lighter side placing its right-hand, or King-side Rook, on a lighter square. The arrangement of the key pieces is from left to right and is listed as follows: Queen-side Rook, Queen-side Knight, Queen-side Bishop, The Queen, The King, King-side Bishop, King-side Knight, and King-side Rook. The Pawns are then placed in the squares directly in front of them with their positions defining their identities, i.e., Queen-Rook's Pawn, Queen-Knight's Pawn, Queen-Bishop's Pawn, Queen's Pawn, King's Pawn, King-Bishop's Pawn, King-Knight Pawn, King-Rook's Pawn. The darker side mirrors these positions (see Figure H.2). Note: The Queen's of each side should be lined up vertically with the lighter Queen placed on a lighter square and the darker Queen placed on a darker square.

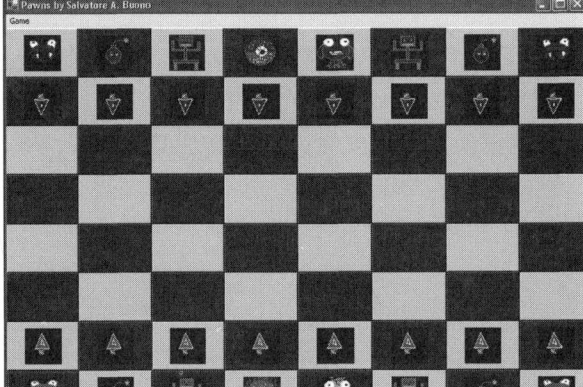

Figure H.2.

Each player is only allowed one move per turn; no two pieces may occupy the same square at any one time; and a player can only capture pieces form the opponent's side. Once a piece is captured, the attacking piece takes that square and the turn is complete. At the beginning of the game, each player is instructed to secretly choose a piece from their own set of characters which will represent them. The King is not considered a valid choice, nor are any of the opponent's pieces; if a player fails to select a valid character, he automatically forfeits the game.

Once the game is in play, it can only be terminated by one of six situations: 1) A player's chosen piece is captured, which immediately ends the game giving the win to the player that captured the piece; 2) A King is placed in checkmate, which also immediately terminates the game, but this time it is considered to be a draw; 3) A player cannot

Appendix H: Algorithms

move any piece without placing his king in check, which would count as a draw; 4) A player resigns, forfeiting the game, with the win going to the remaining player. 5) Both players agree to withdraw (in this case, the player who was ahead wins the game). 6) All players on either side have been captured except for King and the player's choice—the game is then considered a victory for the player with the fewest pieces.

The King

Each piece has its own set of movements. Beginning with the King, we find that he is subject to several limitations and one key exception: The King is only able to step a distance of one space, but he can move in any direction (see Figure H.3). He is not able to step onto a square controlled by his enemy, nor can he remain on a square that his enemy has taken control over; this second situation is known as checking the King.

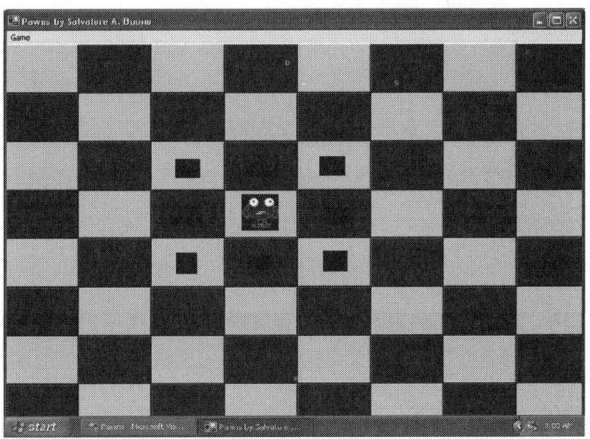

Figure H.3.

If the King is placed in check, there are three potential solutions: 1) He can move to an alternative space, assuming there is one that is available that doesn't break the rules listed above; 2) He or another same-side piece can capture the opposing piece, assuming this move can be done without leaving the King in any additional checks; and 3) It may be possible to block the opposing player's line of attack, by placing a lesser piece between the King and his opponent. It is against the rules to cause a check by moving one's own pieces if they inadvertently reveal a check. However, if an opponent can open a path by removing one of his own obstacles, it would be considered legal, or what is called a revealed check. If two or more piece are threatening the King (a double check) this second choice will be negated. Also, if the King is unable to relieve any and/or all checks he is considered to be checkmated and the game is terminated.

A key exception to the King's one-step rule is when he exercises his right to *castle*. Castling is a special maneuver wherein two pieces are actually displaced. First, the King is allowed to jump two spaces to either side, and the appropriate Rook is placed on the other side of him. This means that the rook will literally jump over the King (see Figures H.4 and H.5). There are several restrictions that may inhibit the maneuver: 1) This must be the King's first move; 2) All spaces between the Rook and the King must be free of any pieces; and 3) The King must not be in check, and he must not pass or move onto a square that is controlled by the opponent's side.

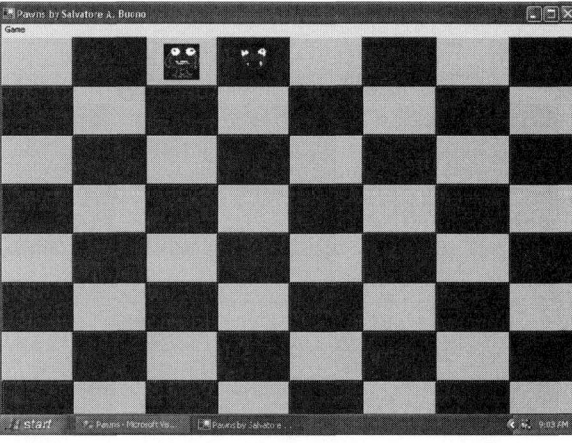

Figure H.4.

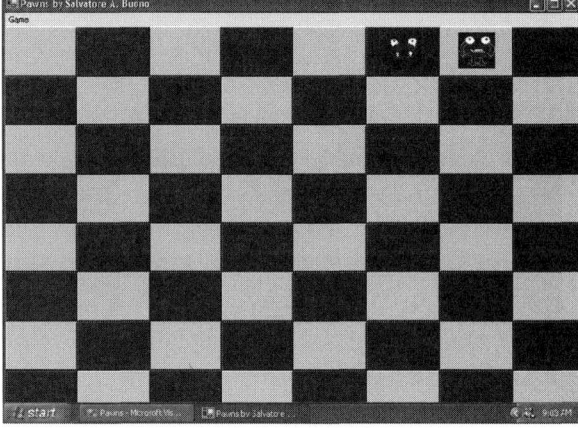

Figure H.5.

Appendix H: Algorithms

The Queen

The Queen is considered to be the strongest piece on the board because of her wide range of motion. She is capable of traveling across the entire board in one step, and can move vertically, horizontally, and diagonally (limited to only one direction per move). The Queen's only obstacles are the other pieces, since she cannot leap or skip over occupied squares (see Figure H.6).

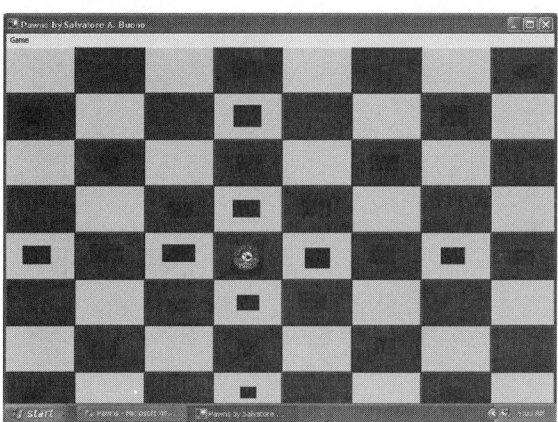

Figure H.6.

The Rook

The Rook is the next strongest piece after the Queen. It is capable of traveling across the entire board in one step, and is capable of both vertical and horizontal movements (limited to only one direction per move). The Rook cannot leap or skip over occupied squares (see Figure H.7).

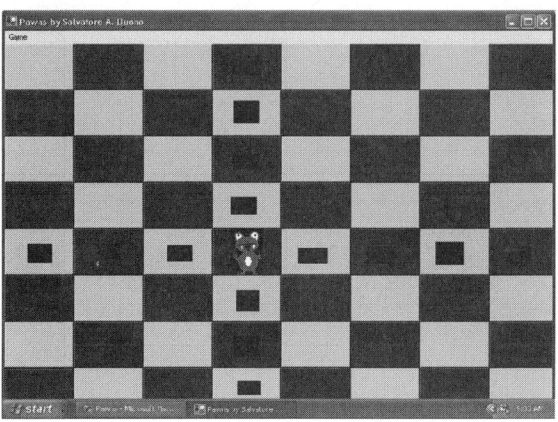

Figure H.7.

495

The Bishop

The Bishop is capable of traveling across the entire board in one step, but is only capable of diagonal movement (limited to only one direction per move). The Bishop cannot leap or skip over occupied squares (see Figure H.8).

Figure H.8.

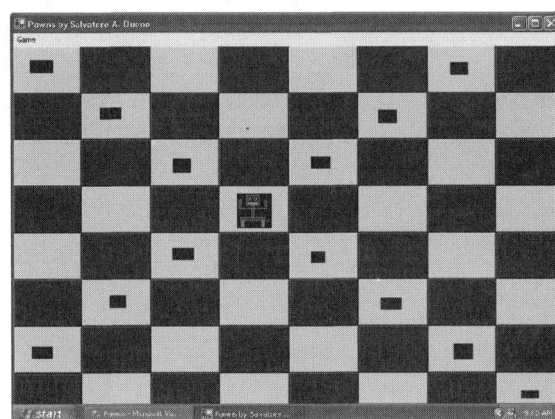

The Knight

The Knight is considered equivalent in strength to the Bishop. It is, however, the only piece that can both change directions while in play and jump over the other characters. It moves in what can be described as an "L" shaped pattern, i.e., one to two squares in any direction followed by one to two squares on a left or right angle (for a total of three squares—see Figure H.9).

Figure H.9.

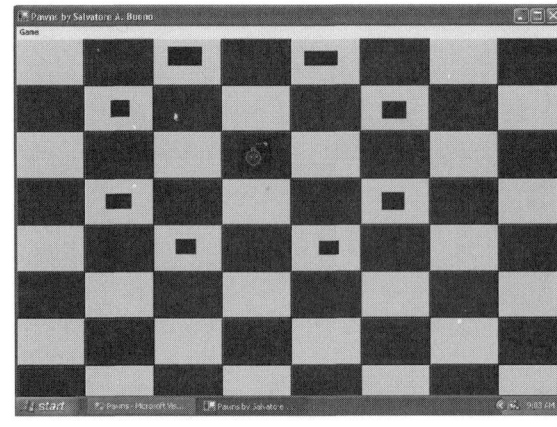

Appendix H: Algorithms

The Pawn

The Pawn can only move forward, straight, and diagonally to capture an opponent's piece. The Pawn is only allowed one step per move, except on his first move, when he has the option of moving up to two steps (see Figures H.10 and H.11).

Figure H.10.

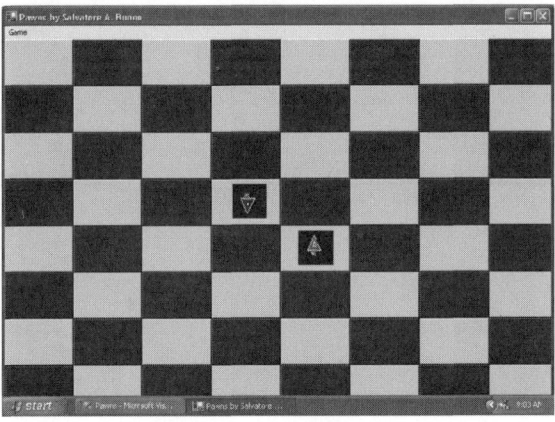

Figure H.11.

Pawns also hold a special right to capture other Pawns. This special case is known as the "en Passant," but two conditions must be upheld: 1) The capturing Pawn must be on the fifth rank (ranks counted from their players side); and 2) The opponents Pawn must exercise his initial two-step option. The adjacent Pawn can then step diagonally onto the unoccupied square and take the opponent's Pawn. This special right can only be executed immediately after the two-step advance. Also, if a Pawn reaches the other end of the board,

C# and Game Programming

he is then promoted; this can be to any one of the other ranking players—a **Queen**, **Rook**, **Bishop**, or **Knight** (see Figures H.12 and H.13).

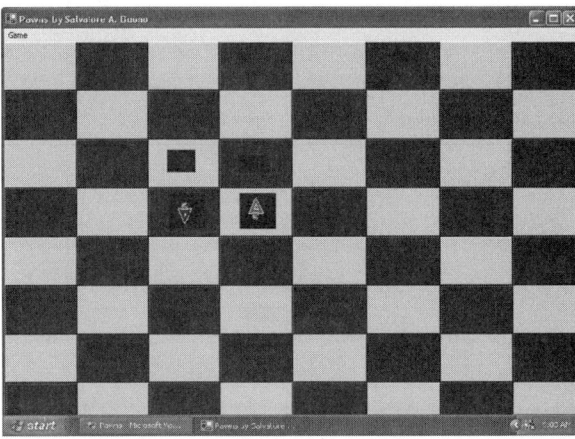

Figure H.12.

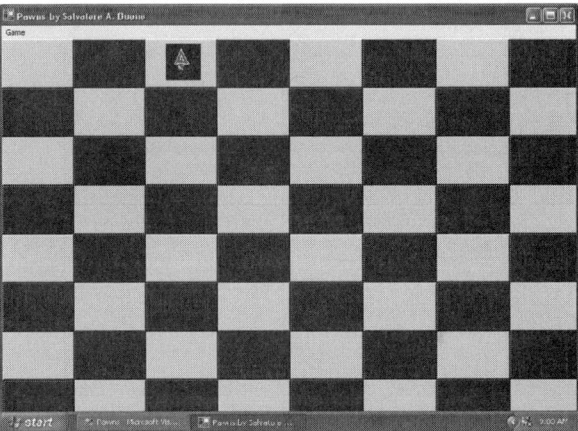

Figure H.13.

Appendix I: Adding DirectX References to Windows Applications

Step 1. From the Window's fold-down menu, first select "Project," and then "Add Reference" (see Screen Shot I.1).

Screen Shot I.1

Step 2. As the "Add Reference" popup window appears, simply scroll down, noting the listings"Microsoft.DirectX,""Microsoft.DirectX.DirectDraw," "Microsoft.DirectX.DreictInput," and Microsoft.DirectX.DirectSound." Double click on all four of these entries and then press "OK" (see Screen Shot I.2).

C# and Game Programming

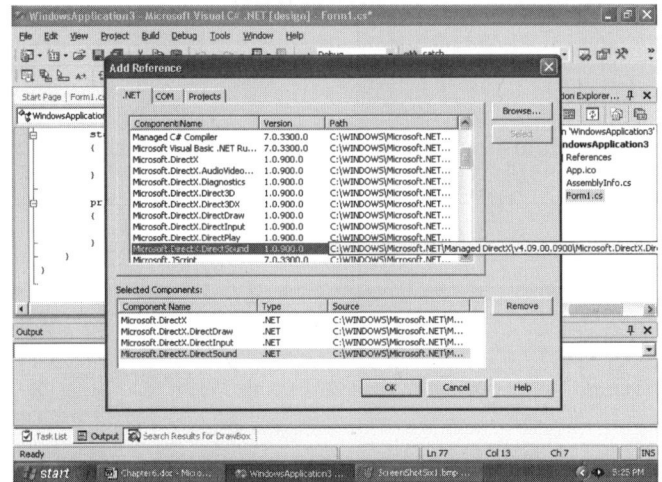

Screen Shot I.2

Step 3. Now, in order to use these links, you'll have to include a set of "using" statements, as in "using Microsoft.DirectX," "using Microsoft.DirectX.DirectDraw," "using Microsoft.DirectX.DirectSound," "using Buffer=Microsoft.DirectX.DirectSound.SecondaryBuffer," and "using Microsoft.DirectX.DirectInput."

Index

Symbols

.net design xviii
.net framework 5

A

abstract 25, 371–374, 399, 437, 439
access modifier 46–48, 333–335, 393–395, 454
addition 38
Algol 60 4
algorithm xxi, 7–8, 139–142, 183, 491
AMD xviii, xxiii
American National Standards Institute (ANSI) 4
and 68–69
animation 403–404
Apple-Macintosh xviii
arithmetic 38–43, 71–73
array 216, 217–237
    assigning values 220–221
    call-by-reference 222–225
    declaring and referencing 217–220
    dynamic 235–237
    multidimensional 225–227, 228–232
    passing 222, 223–225
    searching 232–235
artificial intelligence xix, 96, 176–178, 196–199, 280, 286
as 25, 384–386, 437, 439, 475
Assembly Language 9
Asteroid Miner 204–205, 208
    brainstorming 204–205
    GDI+ graphics 205
AT&T Bell Laboratories 4

B

base 25, 375–376, 386, 437, 439
BASIC 3, 8
Battle Bit 77–80
Battle Tennis 289–304
    adding graphics 290–295
    brainstorming 289–290
    changing levels 303–304
    input devices 295–297
Battle Wave 269–289
    algorithm for 272–273
    animation 280–282
    artificial intelligence 286
    brainstorming 270
    character limits 282–283
    characters and motions 271
    drawing characters 273–274
    joystick 284–285
    keyboard 283–284
    rendered designs 277
    saving and retrieving data 287–288
    setting levels 287
    weapons 288–289
binary scope resolution operator 328–333
bool 25, 90–91, 437, 440
boxing 100–101, 457
break 25, 76–77, 86–88, 437, 440
byte 25, 28, 437, 441

C

C/C++ history 4
Caesar, Augustus 215
call-by-mechanism 224, 319–321
call-by-reference 103, 112–114, 240, 244–246, 316–321
call-by-value 103, 108–110, 112–114
Camel notation 102
case 25, 85–88, 437, 441
catch 25, 376–377, 437, 441–442
CD-ROM xix, xxiii, 307
char 25, 31–32, 94–98, 437, 442
checked 25, 266–268, 437, 442, 475
cin 88–90, 261
class 25, 437, 443

classes 324-344, 352-354
  arrays 335-336
  assigning instances 343-344
  constructors 340
  destructors 349-350
  internal access modifier 333-335
  overloading 336-337
  overloading constructors 342
  private 324
  private and protected 328-333, 338-340
  protected 324
  public 324, 325-328
collision detection 405-408
colors 160, 489
comments 15-16
Common Language Runtime 5
compound if 66-67
conditional operator 92-93
cons 46-48
Console.Write 16
Console.Writeline 20
const 25, 437, 443
continue 25, 77, 437, 443
cout 88-90
Cyrix xviii

D

decimal 25, 30, 437, 444
declaring variables 26-28, 50
decrementing operators 48-49, 75, 149, 247-248
default 25, 85-88, 437, 444
delegate 25, 385-387, 437, 444-445
Delphi 5
Direct3D 429-431
DirectDraw 144-145, 194, 430, 499
DirectInput 149-150, 169-171
  joystick 169-171, 210
  keyboard 188-189, 210
DirectSound 162-164, 211, 297, 299-304
division 40-41
do 25, 81-83, 437, 445
double 25, 28-30, 437, 445
Dr. Dobb's Journal 5

E

Einstein, Albert 3
else 25, 63-64, 437, 446
else-if 64-65
enum 25, 238-239, 437, 446
European Computer Manufacturers' Association xvii, 4
event 25, 386-387, 437, 447
exception handling 376-377
exceptions
  classes 380-384
explicit 25, 389, 437, 447
explicit conversions 99-100
Extended Markup Language (XML) 16
extern 25, 260-261, 388-389, 437, 448

F

false 25, 91, 437, 448
fields
  private 328-333
  protected 328-333
finally 25, 376-377, 437, 448-449
fixed 25, 390-391, 437, 449
float 25, 28-30, 437, 449-450
for 25, 83-85, 437, 450
force feedback 284-285
foreach 25, 237-238, 242, 437, 450-451
formatting strings 37-38
FORTRAN 3

G

garbage collection 5, 390, 400, 463
get 391-393, 473
goto 25, 268-269, 437, 451-452
Ground Assault 431
  brainstorming 431
  graphics 432

H

heap 112, 215, 236, 341, 353, 400
Hejlsberg, Anders 4
Hewlett-Packard 4
Hungarian notation 24-25, 52, 102

I

if 25, 59-67, 437, 451-452
if-else 63-64
implicit 25, 390, 437, 452
implicit conversion 36
in 25, 437, 452
incrementing operator 48-49
Indenting 23
inheritance 324, 359-366
inline functions 119
int 25, 26-28, 437, 453
Intel xxiii
interface 25, 393-395, 437, 453-454
internal 25, 333-335, 454
Interntional Standards Organization (ISO) 4
intersects 405
is 25, 396, 437, 454-455, 475

J

Java 5
JIT 5, 9

K

Keller, Helen 59
keyword defaults 50-51

L

Lee, Meng 4
Linux xviii
Lisp 3
lock 25, 397-398, 437, 455
Logo 3

long 25, 28, 437, 455-456
loops
   nested 87-88

M

Machine Language 8
Malloc 265
Managed C++ 4, 353
mean 254-256
median 254-256
member selection operator 310-313, 328
memberwise copy 343-344
menus 171-176
metafiles 400
methods 328
metonym data types 50-51
Michelangelo 129
Microsoft's Intermediate Language (MSIL) 5
mode 254-256
Modula-2 3
momentum 180, 183, 184, 200
multiplication 40

N

namespace 25, 51-52, 437, 456
naming variables 23-26
Native C++ 6, 14, 143, 237, 242
native C++ 341
nested 70
   class 351, 356, 392-393, 435
   classes 362
   exceptions 382-384
   loops 82-83, 228, 269

   statements 70
   structures 316
   try blocks 378-379
new 25, 236, 437, 456-457, 475
new, 475
newline 18-20
not 68-69
null 25, 244, 437, 457

O

object 25, 437, 457
object-oriented programming xxi, xxii, 146, 324, 359, 385, 435
operators 25, 354-355, 437, 458
   nesting 356-357
   overloading 350-355
   unary 358-359
or 68-69
order of precedence 475
out 25, 114-115, 437, 458
overloading 115-117
   comparison operators 354-355
   constructors 342
   member function 336-337
override 25, 366-371, 437, 459

P

Paddle Tennis 132-179
   adding files 146-148
   algorithm 139-142
   artificial intelligence 176-178
   brainstorming 132-133

collision detection 151–152, 152–154, 154–155
colors 160
details 156–159
DirectDraw 144–145
drawing characters 133–138
game controls 157–159
joystick 169–171
keyboard 149–150
menus 171–176
mouse 164–167, 168–169
multimedia 161–162
plotting motions 138–139
residual images 150–151
sound 161–162, 162–164
params 25, 398, 437, 459–460, 460
Pascal 3, 5
Pascal notation 24, 52
passing variables 103, 108, 112–114
pointer 239–240, 240–241, 242–244, 244–246, 246–248, 248–252, 252–254, 254–256, 256–257, 258–259, 259–260
pointer arithmetic 246–248
polymorphism 59, 115–117, 359
predefined functions 93–98
preprocessor directives 22, 387–388
printf 88–90
private 25, 437, 460, 460–461
members 338–340
private and protected 338–340
reading and writing 344
protected 25, 437, 460–461
members 338–340
public 25, 325–328, 437, 460–461

Q

questions 57–58, 123–124, 213, 306–307, 435

R

range 254–256
Rat Racer 432, 432–433
adding animation 432–433
brainstorming 432
readonly 25, 437, 461
recursion 118
ref 25, 112–114, 437, 461
reserved indentifiers 437, 439
return 25, 105–108, 437, 462

S

sbyte 25, 28, 437, 462
scanf 88–90, 148
sealed 25, 399, 437, 462
semicolon 22, 26, 120, 310, 388, 465
set 391–393, 473
short 25, 28, 437, 463
short circuit evaluation 91–92
Simula67 4
sizeof 25, 33, 437, 463
Software Development Kit (SDK) 130, 209, 429
sorting 231–232
sound 161–162, 299–300
properties of 297
three-dimensional 299–300
sound effects 300–302
Space Fighters 181–204
algorithm 183–185
artificial intelligence 196–199
brainstorming 180–181
characters and motion 181–183
compiler 185
DirectDraw 194
hyperspace 190–191
limits 191–193
menus 202–203
momentum 200
obstacles 199–200, 201–202
OnPaint 189–190
stackalloc 25, 256–257, 400, 437, 463
Standard Template Libary 4
static 25, 260–261, 325, 437, 464
Stepanov, Alexander 4
storage class specifiers 260–261
string 25, 31–32, 437, 464
Stroustrup, Bjarne 4

struct 25, 310, 437, 464-465
structures
    arrays of 309-324
    complex 315-316
    fields 310-313
    instances of 309--313
    mechanism with 316-317
    methods 328
    passing 319-321
    private 328
    protected 328
    public 325, 328
    reference 318-319
    reference mechanism with 319-321
    storing and retrieving 321-324
    tag 310
subtraction 39
switch 25, 85-88, 437, 465
system requirements xxiii
system.IO 265-266

T

this 25, 344-349, 437, 465-466
throw 25, 379-380, 437, 466
troubleshooting 53-56, 119-121, 209-212, 304-305, 435
true 25, 91, 437, 466
try 25, 378-379, 437, 466-467
Turbo Pascal 5
type
    casting 99-100, 457
    compatibility 298
    computability 36-37
    safety 9, 49, 385
typedef 50-51
typeof 25, 437, 467, 475

U

uint 28, 437, 467
ulong 25, 28, 437, 468
unboxing 100-101, 457
unchecked 25, 266-268, 437, 468-469, 475
unit 25
UNIX xviii
unsafe 25, 33, 240-241, 437, 468-469

user-defined functions 101
ushort 25, 28, 437, 469
using 25, 51-52, 437, 469-470
utils.cs 425-427

V

value 473
variable scope 103-105
virtual 25, 366-371, 437, 469-470
Visual Basic 237
void 25, 35, 437, 470
void pointer 242, 252-254
volatile 25, 46-48, 437, 470

W

while 25, 73-77, 437, 471
Windows API 5, 33
WriteLine 20-22

X

XML 16

Z

zero-impact installation 5